Foreign Policy of Hadrat Muhammad (saw)

FOREIGN POLICY
OF
HADRAT
MUHAMMAD
(SAW)

PROF. MUHAMMAD SIDDIQUE QURESHI

KITAB BHAVAN
New Delhi-110002

KITAB BHAVAN
Publishers, Distributors, Exporters & Importers
1784, Kalan Mahal, Darya Ganj,
New Delhi - 1100 02 (India)

Phones : (91-11) 23277392/93, 23274686, 32906494
Fax : (91-11) 23263383
Website : www.nusratalinasri.com
: www.kitabbhavan.com
Email : nasri@vsnl.com
: nusrat@bol.net.in

2nd Edition : 2011

ISBN : 81-7151-140-6

Book Code No. : F00093

Printed & Published in India by :
Nusrat Ali Nasri for **KITAB BHAVAN**
1784, Kalan Mahal, Darya Ganj,
New Delhi - 1100 02 [India]

CONTENTS

****

بسم الله الرحمن الرحيم

Preamble

At the advent of Islam world had deteriorated spiritually and morally. Human grandeur was being burnt in the Persian "Fire." But the world got emanicipation from the clutches of ignorant prejudices and curses of territorial, linguistic and cultural ethnocentrisms. Humanity reached its zenith and the darkness of the universe was changed into the holy brightness which spread over from the mosques to markets, schools to courts, residences to the battlefields. The merits of wit,sympathy, mutual understanding and justice were created among the Arabs. Thus not only Arabia but the whole world was united in one whole—the name of this peace and equality is Islam.

Historians, chroniclers and biographers have written excellent books on Seerah. Yet there are certain angles of the life of this unlettered prophet which need attention. Out of these various ramifications of his life, one corner is his Foreign Policy which needs further research. An independent enquirer may honestly erase apparent contradictions.

In the contemporary world, international rivalries are on the increase. Cultural tensions are splitting human society. Change, constant change, like sheer speed, in every sphere of world is an abiding element. Man has achieved "abundant" but he is ashamed because social injustice has torn his soul. His very existence is threatened by the forces of his own creation. Therefore if he wishes to play his role as vanguard for humanity in the march of its destiny, the Muslims will have to study the example of Muhammad (P.B.U.H.) as we have been commended to follow the guidance of the prophets.[1] But interests are dearer to the people instead of principles in the present world thus there remains no discrimination between good and evil. It is confronted with innumerable problems that stagger its soaring ingenuity to find solution. If we abide by the fundamental international principles of Muhammad (P.B.U.H.), the distressed improverished world can again get mental ascendency.[2] Therein lies a political and administrative sagacity of the first magnitude and fit to be accepted by the modern world. His consummate skill as statesman, administrator, policy-maker and legislator still remains ideal[3] for all the Muslims who are ruling in more than 44 countries with an ever-increasing might in all fields of international relations. Islam, after fourteen hundred years, is still alive and expanding as it was from its very beginning potentially a universal religion. Its followers dwell the burning sands of Africa, in the snows of Siberia, the coral reefs of the Malays, and a barren valley of Arabia. It is good that they should keep in mind that 'civilizations do not perish in storms, conquests or earthquakes. They succumb slowly to the cancer of injustice, tyranny and arrogancy which spreads and corrodes its inside before it starts gnawing at its texture.'

For an extensive and novel subject like that of this book I have tried to consult ancient sources and modern scholarly discussions. I found them all helpful in different ways and I cherish earnestly that nothing of importance has been omitted. I have tried my utmost to glean and rearrange the possible available data which I could get. And I have gathered scattered facts into one focus. The readers, particularly the non-Muslims, will come to know that Muhammad (P.B.U.H.) was not a sinister politician or a grasping despot as many orientalists have made fumbling attempts to project his distorted picture. And this is the raison d'etre of my monograph. But this is just a modest beginning. Our young generation has further avenues of research and exploration before it.

I owe to my friend Professor Muhammad Nawaz for a careful revision of my manuscript, and for several valuable suggestions. Several other friends were also kind and helpful to me. They placed me for ever in their debt by their welcoming and generous acceptance. They have been patient and encouraging above and beyond the call of duty. And thanks, as always, to Safia, my consort, for constant encouragement and provocative criticism.

Muhammad Siddique Qureshi,
Naya Mohalla Road, Jhelum.

1

Foreign Policy.

States maintain relations among themselves just as the individuals are bound to have various relations with other fellowbeings. A state consists of individuals and the relations among states are relations among individuals. Only the nature of these relations is different and a bit complicated. They are known as international affairs and sometimes identified with foreign affairs. There are relations between nations which are international in the strict sense of the word ––– for instance, international football matches or the Olympic games. So:

> "International affairs are the relations between groups, between groups and individuals and between individuals, which essentially affect international society as such." Whereas "international relations are the relations among powers."

These relations are determined by foreign policy. What is meant by foreign policy? What are the objects which are sought for by the nations in these relations? How the means of policy and agencies are identified? Are these elements essential in playing an ideal character in the formation of foreign policy of a particular nation? Is it necessary that the objects of a foreign policy may be comparing? Can the policies of different nations be determined towards the principle of art and conducts which shall end the war as the sole means of policy? The nature of foreign policy, procedure of its formation and the analysis of the methods of its fulfilment give extraordinary challenges to the students of international affairs in relation to establishing inter-relations among states as the basic element with a very few problems.

Foreign policy is an important key to understand the explanation of the international conduct. We have to seek support of international co-operation in order to solve the intermingled problems among states, which will help in attaining peace.

The recorded history of Man is seven thousand years old. From that time the nation states have participated in the wide sphere of relations which can be discussed under the various subjects such as formal or informal, official or unofficial, organized or unorganized and directed or undirected. These relations depict every field of national life. Every state appoints its ambassadors and consuls in other states and receives their representatives at home. It discusses treaties and expresses mutual will to impose levies. It gives and takes the territories. It extends and accepts loans. It exchanges students, teachers, experts and minority population. It trades in grain, wheat, farm machinery, films and air planes. It participates in world conferences. It serves as a host to religious congresses or Olympic games and sends its spies across the borders of unfriendly states. International society is woven with these strings and uncounted complicated political, social, economic and cultural contacts.

First of all it is necessary to distinguish the foreign policy from that great heap of various contacts which the individuals, groups and government of a state keep with their agents in other states. It is a standard by which common international contacts can be separated from those which are particularly connected with foreign policy. Only those matters in the wide sphere of international relations are considered with foreign policy which are created by the government of a state, or enjoy the co-operation of government openly or secretly. In this sense policy is official in contrast with the contacts of individuals or groups which are accidental, unauthorized and unofficial. Foreign policy is formulated by that government which works as an instrument or agency of a state.

Second observation is that one side of procedure of formulating policy is often ousted in the presence of other factors. Therefore, policy is the name of those objectives, to one school of thought, which the people of a state seek in the international community. To others the plans, chalked out to achieve those objectives are supreme. Still another school thinks that the real procedure of such plans formulates the real matter of the policy. The reality is that all these three factors are present. So :–

> Foreign policy covers the fomulation and execution of groups of principles which are adopted by a state in its ideal attitude when it negotiates with other states to develop or safeguard its interests.

Foreign policies are the courses of action adopted by a state in the interests of the welfare of its subjects. It is formulated to maintain its integrity. It elevates national prestige, develops interests of economy and prepares means for defence if need arises. It consists not only of what a nation does, but also of what it seeks and hopes for in world affairs. Following elements cannot be ignored while formulating the foreign policy of a state.

The politico-military involvements of the situation and the physical environment of a state are two important restrictions on the foreign policy. Area, topography and climate are important and ideal standards for the first part.

1. Adequate area to create a balance between population and its resources. The state may maintain enough forces for its defence having a reasonable standard of living for its subjects.
2. Uniform climate which is helpful for physical vigour. A moderate or warm climate is quite suitable.
3. Topography providing good frontiers for natural defence such as mountains, forests, gauge, rivers, deserts and seas.
4. Continuous and contiguous area - - - geographically united area so that the defence may be easy in traditional warfare.

The importance of geographical elements created the science of geopolitics although Ibn Khaldun had already discussed it deliberately in the fourteenth century. Karl E. Nikolas Haushofar (1869-1946), an adviser of Hitler, was its great exponent in the present era. He advocated the theory of lebensraum, i.e. the area should also be enlarged alongwith the expansion of population. This theory was ardently supported by Herbert Mackinder after the World War I. He pleaded that the State should formulate its foreign policy keeping in view its geographical environments. Same is the case with Rudolf Kjellen (1864-1922) who is called the father of modern géopolitics.

The above-mentioned factors exert their influence on a state even today but the concept of air defence has been particularly changed since October 4, 1957 when the USSR launched Sputnik into the space.

These days the international relations are also affected more or less by the economic factors. A state with a large population shall, naturally, desire to have a good supply. The present world is divided into Dollar and Sterling areas. The weaker states want to link themselves up with economically strong states. The industrially advanced states try their utmost to find out new markets where they can sell their manufactured goods in abundance. At the same time, they are anxious to get raw material. Certain spheres of influence crop up in less advanced areas which can create conflicts in international affairs. Among the economic factors the distribution and exploitation of natural resources such as coal, oil, iron, etc. can be enlisted. Competition and rivalry to occupy these resources are the results.

The number, character and distribution of population of a nation are prominent in the political, economic and military aspects of its foreign policy. The problems like immigration and imperialism are the results of rehabilitation of surplus population in any other area. Similarly the racial discriminations play an important role in the international affairs. It is also impossible to ignore the language, customs, manners, racial standards and similar other cultural factors. The relations among nations are also deeply affected by the nature of their ancestoral relations. A state may have strained relations with another state because they had not cordial relations in the past. So is the case with that state which helped another state at a certain juncture of history.

Obviously it will be accommodating and courteous to her in its dealings.

The sentimental feelings based on arrogance, selfishness and aspirations, also, deeply affect the international relations. Education and propaganda can create extremity in them. The importance of nationality, also, cannot be overlooked. The concept of nationality was born before the advent of a nation state. It is characterized by patriotism, and by faith in political and cultural values of a nation and its destiny.

In dimmest antiquity, states were either city-states like Athens, Sparta, Macedonia, ancient Rome or vast states like Persia. The racial cultural differences were even known to the nations at that time. Every nation thought itself supreme under the feelings of indomitable pride. The Greeks coined the term "barbarian" for the non-Greeks and Aristotle asserted that "nature intended barbarians to be slaves"[1] of the Greeks. Plato, although he advised his countrymen to be more lenient in their mutual treatment, never entertained the idea that non-Greeks deserved any share in the milder treatment he proposed.[2] On the other hand, the Jews considered themselves a chosen nation. But these racial feelings were unlike the modern spirit of nationality which has got a new sphere of adopting a new form of political organization of nation state, because this element took the form of rebellions for the national liberty.

Scientific inventions, too, have left their far-reaching effects on international relations. It is due to these inventions that the world has been shrunk to one point. Power has created power politics. The extent to which a state can exert its influence upon the other state depends upon the number of its forces. This is the goal for the achievement of which there is a race of armaments among the states. This is the element which instigated the sentiments of doubts, jealousy and rivalry and often this has had been the root-cause of world collision. So power in politics is like energy in physics. It is the driving force that penetrates the whole body politic. Both politics and power are manifestations of the state.

As things stand, contemporary world politics is divided into two gigantic power blocs. One camp is the champion of democratic theory of life while the other claims communism. The future of the world depends upon the peaceful co-existence between these two camps. 'A world arrangement, whatever its form, will be possible only on the basis of some sort of reconciliation between the two contending ideologies, or by building a half-way house for mutual co-operation.'

There were four aspects for the establishment and application of foreign policies, namely :

(a) the fixing of objectives to be sought;
(b) the formulation of means, methods, principles, or policies by which the objectives are to be attained;
(c) the execution of giving effect to politics; and
(d) the review or reconsideration of policies.

Islam establishes a universal and ideological state which is based on only principle instead of colour, race, language or geographical attachments. It is not a state intended to maintain discipline within and defence without. Rather it is an aimful state which is based on peaceableness and international justice. This is the role of religion in the formulation of foreign policy.

Before Islam there was no central authority in Arabia. It was ushered in strife and disorder. It offered a wretched spectacle of assassination, dissoluteness, and brutality. *Bellum omnium contra omnes* has so often been pictured as the normal condition of Arabia before Islam. Tribal and family feuds filled the land, as Zuhayr says, with evil fumes. "What the Arab lacked was the consciousness of national unity. For him there existed only the tribe and family, but no Arab nation. What he further lacked was a sense of subordination."[3] Revenge and vendetta were the sacred obligations. Few would suffer to remain under the domination of another man, no matter whether he was his own father, brother or a tribal chief; and they had many chiefs.[4] The country was divided among warrior tribes. Devotion to the clan was the strongest tie the Arab possessed. 'The whole clan acted as one being and one injury done to one member was revenged by all.' 'Be loyal to the tribe,' wrote a poet, 'its claim upon its members is strong enough to make a husband give up his wife.' The history of the early Arabs is full of traditions of slight quarrels and their horrible results - - - secret assassinations and the long-lasting blood-feuds. The Arabs were extremely ignorant of Truth. Their darkest tragedy, deeper than their tribal feuding and their disunity, was their multiplicity of deities, for the achievement of their multifarious desires; thus their number touching the figure 360 - - - a figure characteristic of an astral cult (one for every day in the year). Human sacrifice on their altars was a common spectacle to appease an angry god. This practice was common among the other branches of the Semitic races, the Phoenicians, the Moabites, the Carthagians, etc. The whole of Arabia was engrossed in such vices. Besides the tribal gods, individual households had their special Penates. A portion of the Quraish worshipped the three moon goddesses - - - al-Lat, the bright moon, al-Manat, the dark, and al-Uzza, the union of the two, - - - who were regarded as the daughters of the high god *(Banat-Ullah).*[5] Entire Arabia was divided between Lat and Manat. Al-Uzza was worshipped under the form of a tree, al-Manat of a large stone, Yaghuth of a lion, Sawa of a woman, Ya'uq of a horse, Nasr of an eagle. Hubal, the figure of a man carved in red agate and holding seven wingless arrows in his hands. It was installed on the front wall of the Ka'ba. The Arabs worshipped the sun, moon and innumerable stars. The tribe Hunain used to worship the sun, the Kinanah the moon, and the Qais the stars. Mecca was the centre of a far-reaching idolatry, ramifications of which extended throughout the tribes of the peninsula.[6] They boasted of fornication. Wine drinking, licentiousness, gambling and chessplaying were their second nature. 'The passion for gambling was so reckless that a man would often stake all his possessions; and after losing them at a throw, would next stake his freedom, and, losing that also, become a slave. Female infanticide was common because they thought that 'the best son-in-law is the grave.'

Idolatry bred superstition among the Arabs. They

also believed in numerous animist spirits. Relic and saint worship had become universal. They consulted their seers *kahins* on such matters as omens, the interpretation of dreams and forecasts of the future. Divination by arrows was a favourite method of finding out the will of God. When killing any animal for food, they used to consecrate it by invoking the names of their gods and goddesses. In one of his expeditions Mundhir III of Hirah in 6th century captured a son of Kinda, and "immediately sacrificed him to Aphrodite", i.e. to the Arabian goddess al-Uzza. On another occasion he sacrificed four hundred Christian nuns to the same goddess. It was admirable for them to usurp the belongings of the orphans. There was not the least idea of chastity and honour. Women were regarded as chattles and they were marketable and heritable. A widow (other than the mother) was considered to be an integral part of the inheritance of the son. It was branded under the name of *Nikah ul-Mekt* ("shameful or odious marriage"). Polygamy was universal and quite unrestricted; equally so was divorce, at least as far as the man was concerned. The Bedouin view of life was thoroughly hedonistic. Love, wine, gambling, hunting, the pleasures of song and romance, the brief, pointed and elegant expression of wit and wisdom - - - these things he knew to be good.[8]

On the whole innumerable social diseases had rotten the human society. To the Byzantines and the Persians, the Arabs were a barbarous nation. The Roman historians called them *natio perniciosa.* The Arabs were neither dependable friends nor dependable enemies. But despite this the Romans and the Persians did not invade Arabia because they hoped nothing to get from there. Because it was dwelt-in by "a people whom the great empires of the ancient world in vain essayed to conquer, against whom the power of Persia, Egypt, Rome, Byzantium was proven impotence, and at whose hands even the superb Alexander, had he lived to test his dream, might for once have learnt the lesson of defeat."[9] It is a river-less land. 'There are barren mountains, dry gravelly plains and the rare green valleys.'

At the advent of Islam, Yemen was one of the most

ancient neighbouring states of Arabia. It had an advanced culture and glorious past. It was the most fertile part owing to the plentiful rains. Maa'rib, in the extreme south of the Arabian peninsula, used to be its capital in the olden times but after a ruinous flood San'a was built. 'The twenty-storey high castle of Ghomdam in San'a; the temple of Ma'rib, whose walls, ellipse-like enriched a natural elevation and reached a height of 9½ metres; again the immerse dam of Ma'rib.[10] Abraha al-Ashram, the Abyssinian viceroy of Yemen, built a magnificent church *(al-Qalis)* at San'a. The like of which was not to be seen at that time in the whole world. He wrote to Najashi that he would not be content until he had diverted thither every pilgrim in Arabia.[11] Consequently he made an abortive attempt to conquer Hijaz. The kings of Yemen were known as *Tubba'* since centuries. It is an African word which means "powerful". For some fifty years from about 525 A.C. the region was under the Abyssinians. They were succeeded by the Persians, and these retained the nominal sovereignty until the various districts were incorporated into the Islamic state.

Persian frontiers were guarded by the Arab levies of Hirah (Kufa) and Ghassan. The long, narrow strip of land facing the Persian Empire was called the kingdom of Hirah. It has been painted by poetry and fiction in rich colours. Doubtless it was a home of culture - - - but hardly Arabian culture - - - rather a culture representing in all essentials, Persian culture.[12] Hirah, a subordinate kingship of Yemen, was situated in the north-east. It occupied a favourable and healthy situation a few miles to the south of Kufa. The name was applied to the originally mobile camp of the Persian Arabs and retained as the designation of the garrison town. Several of the kings of Hirah are said to have been Christian. They were collateral and belonged to the same race of San'a. At different times they rendered allegiance to Persia. The inhabitants of Hirah during the reign of Ardashir Babkan, the first Sassanian king of Persia (226-241 A.C.) consisted of three classes, viz:[13]

(a) The *Tanukh,* who dwelt west of the Euphrates between Hirah and Anbaar in tents of camel's hair.

(b) The *'Ibad*, who lived in houses in Hira.

(c) The *Ahlaf* (clients), who did not belong to either of the above mentioned classes, but attached themselves to the people of Hirah and lived among them blood-guilty fugitives–pursued by the vengeance of their own king, or needy seeking to mend their fourtunes.

Ghassan was the third kingdom situated in the north-west corner. This five or six hundred years ancient state paid pseudo allegiance to its strong neighbours. It was an Arab-Christian state. It had no prominent capital, but a permanent camp, which was its centre of activity. It was generally to be found in the Gaulonitis (al-Jawlan), south of Damascus. Its chiefs were called *Phylarks* by the Byzantines, and kings by the Arabs. The Ghassanids were descended from 'Amr al-Muzaygiya, and had migrated from Yemen to Syria towards the end of the third century. His son Jafna is generally regarded as the founder of the dynasty. It is true that Yemen had subjugated a vast area and its suzerainty was acknowledged in one form or the other but Arabia still remained the nucleus of tribes of different races. These Arabs had no aptitude towards architecture, fine arts and agriculture but their ideal was unmanageable and unwieldy like desert. Anyhow the Ghassanids had developed a superior civilization under Hellenistic culture. The Ghassanid Arabs lived a simple and bedouin life. Five tribes were prominent despite their sub-tribal division. In the middle of the Arabian Peninsula there was race of Rabia which claimed its kingship with Yemen. The Quraish were the occupants of Mecca and had settled in the west. They were the acknowledged hereditary guardians of the Ka'ba which had become a great national rendezvous. It elevated their position over other Arab clans. The city-state of Mecca, "the merchant republic" had its relations with the Byzantines. These relations had been developed by Abde Manaf, Qusaiy's son. The Quresh extended their commerce to Syria, Hirah and South Arabia. Their contacts certainly brought intellectual awakening and fresh aspirations to them.

In the north were the Qais, Tamim and Hawazin. During the reign of Abd al-Muttalib, international situation became critical; the Kindite dynasty of Yemen disappeared and the Abyssinians began to replace them.

A new sun arose on Monday 22nd April, 571, A.C. from the ignorant chest of Hijaz whose rays illuminated the world within no time. He was Muhammad (p.b.u.h.). He changed the destiny of the human beings for all the times to come.

At the time of Muhammad's (p.b.u.h.). advent international obligations were unknown. He launched his campaign of reforming the ever-warring humanity at the very door steps of the Quraish and their allies who were occupants of the northern part of the western coast. First of all, he united the jeering elements of Arabia. Afterwards he invited the innumerable tribes of the Central Arabia to Islam and in the last the Yemeni rulers of San'a, Hira and Ghassan were the focus of his preachings.

At that time the Roman Empire was deteriorating in its eastern and western hemispheres. It was plagued by various kinds of cancer. The Romans never realized the duties of international morality or of humanity although they took thirteen centuries to evolve a system of laws. "The sacredness of treaties were unknown; pacts were made and broken, just as convenience dictated." On the contrary, the Byzantine artisans had constructed strong godowns accumulated with ammunitions. There was no scarcity of ships, catapults and strong forts. There were modern military academies, according to the needs of the time, where advance training in strategy was given. But there was lack of individuals who could use these arms effectively - - - such individuals who could become practical embodiment of the theories of war.

The rulers are the fathers of the nation. If they are morally upright and sympathetic towards the nation then it hastily makes progress in different walks of life. With the accession of Justinian on the throne of the Caesar through an intrigue with a prostitute, Asia and Eurpoe burnt into flames of tremendous revolts. The king was openly disobeyed. His statues were smashed. In utter disgust soldiers humiliated their generals. The images of Jesus Christ, hanging on the Cross, were stoned at. This tragic chapter was closed with the suicide of Emperor Maurice alongwith his sons. Their dead bodies were thrown into the sea where they served as a food for the fish. People reproached their mutilated heads and rejoiced over it. Phocas ruled for few years over the Eastern Empire. This dwarfish king was not acquainted even with law, art, science or strategy of war. His reign was voluptuous but he had, also, to see his doomsday. In rags he was shackled. He was stripped naked and brought in the presence of zealous men and women who held him in derision. He was beheaded with a single blow of sword. Such a tragic was the end of this furious king. His headless body was thrown into a huge bonfire. Now Hercules ascended the throne. The Roman sun was about to set but there were glimpses of its light yet. The strong empire of Justinian had been shattered. The Lombards occupied the major portion of the Italian dominions. On the other hand, the floods of Auvras and the Slavs swept the territory up to Adriatic which is the passage of the Danube.

In the east of the Arabian Peninsula was the grand empire of Persia where Khusro II had got great achievements like his grandfather, Khusro I. He had heavy forces and strong forts for the defence of his empire. His forces had recently occupied Chaledon and were now waiting for his signal to subjugate Damascus and Jerusalem. Certainly the Persian forces succeeded there and there was every possibility of their march towards Yathrib, Mecca and Sina. The Emperors of Persia called themselves Chosroes implying that divine blood flowed in their veins. There Mazdukia had socialized woman, wealth and land.

Under these international circumstances Muhammad (P.B.U.H.) purified the religious horizon. Peoples, at that time, were suffering from incurable diseases. Judaism had several aspects of attraction in it. Muhammad (P.B.U.H.) could adopt the efforts and zeal for monotheism of Moses and Abraham but Judaism was the name of Jewish arrogance in practice. It was out-dated and a bit harsh too. The Jews had evolved a peculiar culture of their own under Moses and the Divine Pentateuch. They were sworn enemies of some foreign nations and could not even imagine to have peaceful relations with them. Moreover, they were directed to kill not only the enemy on the battlefields, but also the aged, the women, and the children in the houses.[14]

From some aspects two less important religions were Zoroastrianism and Manichaeism. The Zoroastrians do not worship the idols. Ormazd and Ahriman or Afrasiab are their only two gods. Former is the symbol of rightness and generosity while the latter is the god of darkness and evil. The Zoroastrians worship fire. The teachings of Zoroaster were not explicit so it came soon under the sway of the soothsayers. 'Among them the marriage with sister, mother and daughter was considered more meritorious and charitable than with strangers.' Their book was Avesta which had disappeared at the time of Muhammad (P.B.U.H.). In short, a corrupt Zoroastrianism. . . had stifled the voice of humanity, and converted some of the happiest portions of the globe into a veritable Aceldama.[15] Its fire burnt in temples only but not in the hearts of the people. On the contrary, Mani or Manes was himself an astronomer, a physicist, a musician and an artist of eminence. He divided his disciples into two classes; one, the "elect" or "perfect", and the other, the "hearers" or "auditors." It is strange that Mani himself opined that he had nothing to say new. Moreover, his teachings were beyond common sense therefore this religion did not suit the simple-hearted people of Arabia

The Romans considered themselves civilized. They took thirteen centuries to evolve a system of laws but they could never realize the duties of international morality. They, in reality, had developed a private international law yet the laws of war were in the main based on the discretion of individual commanders. They waged war only to quench their thirst of subjugating others. They turned their empire into a slaughter-house for the non-Romans. Actually they were "civilized" barbarians.

So far as the Christianity is concerned, its message was enough to create confidence among the depressed. Its teachings were less ambiguous. It propagated virtue and fraternity. It soon became popular among the people who liked monotheism but the piety of Christ could not weld together the heterogeneous and conflicting elements. Soon the Christians instituted trinity, Jesus was declared to be God. Pork and wine were allowed. Sabbath and circumcision were abolished. Later on, the Church was divided into numerous sects and love with Christ was massacre, slavery of the innocent and committing inhuman acts. Every act of violation was sanctified by the Church which had substituted the "purities of superstition for the pure and expansive faith of early ages." It was itself decrepit and corrupt.[16] Those who accepted the teachings of Christ otherwise and propagated them were recognized as the saints of the Church. Relic and saint worship became universal and thus Christianity reverted to heathenism. 'It had become a thing of the head instead of the heart, and the refinements of monophysite and monothelite doctrines gained no hold upon the Arab mind.'

Now there remain Hinduism, Buddhism and Sabeanism. Rama was the advocate of Hinduism. Veda, Mahabharata and Geeta are the sacred books of the Hindus. They believe that there are 400 millions of gods (the cow is most prominent of them) besides God. These gods consist of the manifestations of God, be that His creatures or His attributes. One must be born in a Hindu family to be a Hindu. Another main characteristic is metempsychosis (Avagavan). Buddhism was a protest against the teachings of Hinduism. Buddha Shakyamuni, its founder, was a prince of Kapila-Vastu - -an ancient city beneath the shadow of giant mountains of Nepal. He preached charity, renunciation of the world and idolatry. But gradually the Buddhists made the statues and images of Buddha and began their worship. Last of all, comes Sabeanism. Its followers worshipped stars and believed in their influence.

Plato and Aristotle both discussed human nature in the light of the Greek city-states as being political animal. They advocated that Man participates in the political organizations simply to avoid anarchy. Both John Locke (1632-1704 A.C.) and Jean Jacquius Rousseau (1712-1778 A.C.) believed in the goodness of human nature. John Locke was in favour of possibilities of a society in wider perspectives. Rousseau thought that interdependence created doubts and inefficiency. Thomas Hobbes (1588-1679 A.C.) believed that Man was primarily an evil-doer and thirsty for the blood of others. Same was the case with Jane Paul (1763-1825) who considered that people co-operated with one another because it was necessary to live. So the theory of social contract should be enforced coercively and this is the function of the state.

Muhammad (P.B.U.H.) preached Islam convincingly so it attracted masses. It provided an economic, social, and political system, the *Pax Islamica.* Before migrating to Yathrib he got the consensus of the people inhabiting that city through Pledges of Aqba. On the contrary, the British people came to the Indo-Pak sub-continent under the disguise of the merchants and then flag followed the trade. On reaching Yathrib Muhammad (P.B.U.H.) concluded a treaty with the tribes known as the Treaty of Medina. This was the first written constitution of the world which illuminated the truthfulness of Islam. This was concluded with those who were steadfast in cruelty and sin. It compiled principles for guidance for the succeeding generations of Muslim rulers down the ages.

The foreign policy of the Holy Prophet was not based upon the principle of geo-politics, rather it was universal in nature. Had Islam accepted this principle it would have been restricted within the Arabian desert. Individuals from every corner of the globe can accept these principles. The message of Jesus Christ was for the lost sheep of the Israelites[17] while Muhammad's(P.B.U.H.) teachings were meant for the whole of mankind.

Before Islam the world was divided into three spheres of race, language and colour. "It was an attack upon that web of priestcraft which Brahmanism had woven round the whole frame-work of Indian society."[18] Islam negated the specific rights which the Brahmans (priests) had got over the Kshatriyas (the military-men), Veshas (farmers and merchants), Shudras (labourers) and Chandals (untouchables). Islam, also, ruled out the claim that the Bani Lawi from amongst the Israelites had only right to rule. It eliminated, too, the racial supremacy of the Quraish which they enjoyed over other tribes.

Sanskrit got paramount importance over Prakrit and Tamil; Hebrew over other dictionaries; Italian over other languages of Europe; English over local languages of the British dominations; Persian over that time of India, Kabul, Khurasan and Turkistan; and Arabic over all the languages of the known world and the Arabs regarded others as dumb. Islam deleted this linguistic paramountcy.

Third division was that of colour---red, yellow, brown, white or black. The distinctions underlying human rights and ranks and the part played by every sovereign while uplifting the principle of the racial discrimination are the darkest chapters of human history.

At the advent of Muhammad (P.B.U.H.) there were "great civilized" empires of Persia and Byzantine. In the world of architecture Man had constructed Pyramids, Allora, Ajanta and Hagia Sophia. Great shrines, temples, stupas, churches and synagogues had been founded. Several religions had tried to put the Man on the right path. "The harshness of Torah and mildness of Bible had come."[19] Similarly great books like Politics, Vedas, Mahabharta and Artha Shastra had been written before the advent of Islam. Kinship was dear to people and Confucius had advised his followers to remember the relations at least for one hundred ancestral stages.

Notwithstanding these "achievements" there was no respect for humanity. Human veneration was burning at the Persian fire temple where Fire had itself become the Divinity. Woman was a creature of misery to the Greeks. 'In India it was the era of Pranas and Bam Margi were dominant. They were diverting the mankind towards their nasty practices and used to display nude images in the temples and worshipped them." She was sacrificed at the holy altar of deities in India. "Women," says Manu, "have impure appetites; they show weak flexibility and bad conduct. Day and night must they be kept in subjection." Similarly in Persia woman enjoyed no respect. A *shaktak* (sacred) priest could, of right, command the company of others' wives for his pleasure. 'Man had been accustomed to associate nobility with those who claimed themselves to be the progeny of gods and demi-gods. The Arabs were proud of their linguistic richness so they regarded the Persians as dumbs. The Persians were white and were so much colour-conscious that they regarded the Negroes and the Indians as crows. The Indian society was divided into four castes and the untouchables could not imagine equality. They could not worship in temples standing by the side of the sons of a superior caste. If a Shudra tried to touch Vedas or only over-heard a Brahman reciting it, molten lead was poured in his ears. This system of caste and untouchability was so strictly followed that the touch of the Shudra was pollution. All the religious rites, peculiar to the three higher castes, were strictly forbidden to the Shudras.

But Islam declared:[20] "And the variations in your languages and your colours: verily in that are Signs for those who know". In view of this Divine injunction there remained no difference between Bilal, a negro and the first Muezzin of Islam, and Suhaib. Muhammad (P.B.U.H.) uttered in the plenitude of his power, of the head of a sufficiently strong and well-organized state, on the occasion of Hajjat-ul-Wada'a (Pilgrimage of Farewell, 632 A.C.): "People! All mankind is the progeny of Adam and he was fashioned out of clay. Neither the Arabs have superiority over the Persians nor the Persians over the Arabs. Same is the case with the white and the black. Piety and obedience to God are the criteria of a good citizen."[21] Thus honours do not go to nobility of birth but of conduct. Therefore neither the Turks lynched the negroes nor the Arabs felt any difficulty to lead a peace-ful life with the Chinese. The Holy Prophet had told the people that the Mankind is the family of Allah; therefore, all differences, all distinctions and all limitations collapsed all of a sudden.

Islam negated racial discriminations and said:

a) "He Who has made everything which He has created most Good: He began the creation of man with (nothing more than) clay, and made his progeny from a quin-tessence of the nature of a fluid despised."[22]

b) "The Believers are but a single brotherhood: so make peace and reconciliation between your two (contending) brothers; and fear God, that ye may receive Mercy."[23]

c) "Verily the most honoured of you in the sight of God is (he who is) the most righteous of you."[24]

The Holy Prophet raised human beings from the abyss of degradation and purified them from abominations. 'He sought to establish a community based on egalitarian principles incomprehensible to a mind brought up in tribal tradition! He preached explicitly, "No more pride in ancestry." On an occasion he said, "Muslims are brethren unto one another."[25] Today the battle for rights is being fought. The workers are at daggers drawn with the capitalists. Both distrust one another. The world is divided into class groups. It is remarkable that the slogans of freedom, fraternity and equality were echoed for the first time in the European history during the French Revolution (1789). These three principles have been originally derived from the Islamic teachings because the Holy Quran had been translated into all the major European languages uptil 1000 A.C. and before this the echo of these slogans were never heard in any western country. Moreover in the contemporary world it is obligatory that the treaties must be codified or reformulated in the Vienna Convention on the Law of Treaties concluded on 22 May, 1969. But long before this, the Holy Prophet attached great sanctitv to treaties and considered them binding.

Islam has not refuted the former religions rather it recognizes them and has left them undisturbed. The Holy Prophet maintained that every religion of the world was based on truth and it led to God provided no change had been made in it. He did not repel Christianity in his letters written to the contemporary kings or chiefs to accept Islam, instead the following verse was particularly included in them:[26]

> "Say: O People of the Book! Come to common terms as between us and you: that we worship none but God; that we associate no partners with Him; that we erect not, from among ourselves, lords and patrons other than God."

Again it was ordered:[27]

"Let there be no compulsion in religion." Still again it was observed:[28]

"To you be your way, and to me mine."

Here it seems appropriate to mention Abyssinia of the first century of the Islamic era. Muhammad (P.B.U.H.) is reported to have said, "Leave the Abyssinnians in peace, so long as they do not take the offensive."[29] So the Muslim state refrained from attacking it. Thus Muhammad(P.B.U.H.) ordained to co-operate with non-Muslim state, in terms of peaceful co-existence, and refrain from any violation of the territorial integrity of another state. These commitments recall those state Article 2/1.3.5 of the Charter of the United Nations. The basis of faith in Islam is thought, common sense and meditation in the above-mentioned verses of God and not the compulsion, obligation and force. There is no parallel example of freedom of belief in history. When Muhammad's (P.B.U.H.) mission was endangered by the Jews, he took them to task. He was so noble and polite that he spared them when they differed with him in religious matters. Similarly he did not interfere in Christianity unless the Christians clashed with him in politics in Arabia. It is vivid that the position which he entrusted to the Christians and the Jews in the political polity of Islam, possible great result was exerted on Islamic cultural progress in general.[30]

Islam has recognized the freedom of the non-Muslims rather they were given key posts, as Amr bin Umaysh Damari was the earliest ambassador of the Muslim State sent to Abyssinia in 2 A.H. He was still a non-Muslim. The treaties concluded with them not only recognized the freedom of their person and property but also of the freedom of their faith and traditions. It was ordered:[31]

"Say, 'The Truth is from your Lord': Let him who will believe, and let him who will reject (it)."

In this very context it was clarified:[32]

"Know ye that it is Our Apostle's duty to proclaim (the Message) in the clearest manner."

The Muslim army captured in booty several copies of the Torah during the battle of Khyber but Muhammad (P.B.U.H.) returned them to the Jews on their request.

Just compare it with the incident when the Romans conquered Jerusalem in 70 A.C. when they burnt all the holy books of the Jews. Again the Crusaders destroyed an immense library at Tripoli, in Palestine. The General, finding that the first room of the library contained the Holy Quran only, ordered the whole library to be burnt.

The Holy Prophet waged Jihad in order to strike at the strength of the unbelievers so that they might not obstruct his mission. But his wars were humane and bloodless. He fought for the redress of the depressed and the uplift of the human rights. His battles were purely defensive in nature. When the Quraish invaded Medina, he defended in Badr. Then he defended in Uhad and saved the Muslims. When in the battle of the Ditch the Makkans joined hands with the Jews, Muhammad (P.B.U.H.) adopted the defensive method of war by digging a ditch around Medina. From Medina the Muslims could pose a threat to the life-line of the Meccans whose only trade route to Syria passed from that region. In the beginning the Holy Prophet demanded the Meccans not to traverse this zone otherwise their caravans would be captured. He took the initiative of consolidating the Muslim power by entering into alliances with the non-Muslim Arab tribes living around Medina especially on the caravan route. Thus he created a chain of buffer-states and gradually encircled the Meccans. After the battle of Uhad, their trade remained closed because the route of *Rahla tush Shatta* had been closed upon them. Now they deviated a bit from their traditional route through Najd which, later on, was also closed upon them. When the Muslims got effective control over these routes, all those tribes were unemployed which got their livelihood by serving their caravans. Due to this economic depression the tribe of Ashjah sent its deputation to Medina and entered into an alliance with Muhammad (P.B.U.H.).[34]

It was his practice that he considered the allies of a nation to be his allies with which he concluded a treaty. And if the other nation concluded a treaty with him then he regarded it his ally by including that nation in the treaty. Thus the fighting nation was regarded as belligerent. On this plea he invaded upon Mecca because when he had concluded a treaty of cease-fire for ten years with the Meccans, Banu Bakr bin Wile entered upon this pledge on the side of the Meccans. On the contrary, Banu Khaza'ah signed the treaty with Muhammad (P.B.U.H.) and thus entered upon this pledge.[35] Muhammad (P.B.U.H.) laid great emphasis on forming alliances with the Christians of the north in comparison to the southern part of Arabia. 'Perhaps he proposed a united front against the Persians, and followed this up with propaganda emphasizing what Muslims believed that was also held by the Christians. Or perhaps he tried to gain the support of the Christian Arabs by siding with the monophysites among them against the orthodox. His letter to Bishop Dughatir is an example of this type of diplomatic approach.'

It is appropriate to compare the Treaty of Hudaibiyah, a masterpiece of the foreign policy of the Holy Prophet, with the Treaty of Versailles which is a specimen of modern diplomacy. Abu Jandal appeared on the scene of negotiations while the Treaty of Hudaibiyah was being concluded. He had embraced Islam but was in the confinement of the Quraish. Suhail bin Amr, the Quraishite plenipotentiary, demanded his extradition and threatened that otherwise the treaty would not be concluded. Muhammad (P.B.U.H.) extradited Abu Jandal and advised him to be patient. Similarly Abu Busair was extradited in accordance with the stipulations of the Treaty on his reaching Medina. The Holy Prophet could easily occupy Mecca with force during the parleys at Hudaibiyah. But he did not. And when he conquered Mecca he did not demand any reparation from his fierceful enemies. Because nothing can be more disastrous in diplomacy than short temper. The world recalls with horror occasions when diplomats have lost their temper. Napoleon flung his hat on the carpet in the Marcoloni Palace at Dresden while negotiating with Metternich. Sir Charles Smith tore up a treaty with the Sultan of Morocco in the imperial presence. Count Tattenback lost his temper at the Algeciras Conference and exposed his country to a grave humiliation.[36]

The Treaty of Versailles was signed on 28 June, 1919 after the World War I. Germany was held solely responsible for war. Her forces were disarmed. The German delegates were presented disgracefully before the representatives of the Allies. They were kept standing like criminals during the drafting of the Treaty. Consequently heavy reparations of 25,000,000,000 were imposed upon Germany. The Treaty demanded intolerable sacrifices of Germany and that it could not be carried out without wrecking its economic life.[37] This is the reason that H. G. Wells regarded it the "Treaty of Victors."

In the contemporary age diplomacy has been defined as the science of fraud and favours. Uptil the nineteenth century an ambassador was thought to be an honest man sent to lie abroad for the good of his country." Today the ambassadors are assassinated without keeping in view their status. But the diplomacy of Muhammad (P.B.U.H) was another name for the practice of Divine Injunctions. It was without bitterness, suspicions and misunderstandings. It did not be-devil human relations. 'Wahshi received, as the ambassador of the Quraish, the treatment unexpected and unparallelled in the annals of human history in spite of the fact that he had barbarously murdered Hamza, the Prophet's uncle, in the Ghazwa of Uhad. When the envoys of Musailima, the Liar, came to him, he asked them, "Which faith do you follow?" They replied, "We do the same as Musailima." Upon this Muhammad (P.B.U.H.) said, "Had you not been envoys, I would have ordered you to be beheaded."[38] Similarly once the Quraish sent Abu Raf'i as their envoy to Medina for negotiating peace. During his stay at Medina he was influenced by the Islamic teachings and expressed his intention for conversion to Islam. The Holy Prophet admonished him as he was an ambassador at that time. He was asked to go back to Mecca and embrace Islam as a common Muslim later on.

Every injunction of Islam demands to sacrifice the smaller for the greater. Present sentimentalism is sacrificed for the permanent construction of future. Its vivid example is that of the Treaty of Hudaibiyah. There was a military pact between Khyber and Mecca. Medina was between two fires and it was not easy to cope simultaneously with both. The

Holy Prophet made the Quraish neutral in the case of the Jews with great sagacity. It is a great manifestation of his political and diplomatic success. After two weeks he marched towards Khyber and displayed such a diplomatic policy that the people of Khyber were left helpless. Nobody came to their rescue. Even their Ghatfan allies shut their doors and enjoyed the situation. After the subjugation of Khyber further friendships were sought. This was the time when the relations with Bahrain and Oman were started. And when the Quraish were left alone, Mecca was occupied without bloodshed.

After three months of the conquest of Mecca Declaration of Discharge was proclaimed in the season of pilgrimage in Zul Hijja 9 A.H. which was the foundation of the Islamic Commonwealth. Due to this Islam spread rapidly. It touched the boundaries of Yemen, Yamama, Oman on the one side and spread to Iraq and Syria on the other in 9-10 A.H. In these territories the Arabs had established great kingdoms before the advent of Islam. Even at that time they were under the suzerainty of two grand empires of Rome and Persia. However, Islam continued to march forward without the company of sword under the shadow of peace and tranquillity. Weak and feeble Arabs dominated over East and West with the force of monotheism. The teachings of Islam extended to the courtesies of life. The historical paramountcy of the Great Roman Empire and the centuries old veneration of the Romans was swept by the mighty scymitar of the Arabs. 'The creation of the political power of the Muslims was so sudden that it took the world by surprise.' It crumpled up the grand empires of Jamshed Nushirwan, Chosroes and Rustum at the knock of their unfaltering hand at their doors. ' The revolution was brought about in a short span of 10 years under conditions of extreme scarcity of means and in the teeth of maximum opposition from all around. Within a century the Truth was recognized from Aden to Antioch, and from Seville to Samarkand. No nation could lit its lamp in front of the blazing sun of their glory. 'It crushed the false prophets that always follow in the wake of true one, as the jackals do the trail of a lion! It remoulded the sole of races and built up a whole world the world of Islam. The world was immersed in darkness, moral and social, before Islam but now all the disjointed fragments were brought together to the worship of Allah. The warring tribes were galvanised into one Ummah. The genius of the Holy Prophet 'gave them unity, discipline and enthusiasm as an army.' The Arabs earned a good name in learning, arts, industry and technology alongwith conquests. Those who took pride in ignorance and illiteracy became the teachers of the world. Muhammad (P.B.U.H.) 'raised the wild children of the desert from the abyss of degradation to the zenith of civilization and prosperity. He emancipated them from, the clutches of ignorance, superstition, idolatry and moral depravity.' Islam emerged into the civilized outer world, not as the crude superstition of marauding hordes but as a moral force that commanded respect and coherent doctrine that could challenge on their own ground the Christianity of East Rome and the Zoroastrianism of Iran.[39] But it was only possible due to the following principles of foreign policy framed by the Holy Prophet.

1) The Islamic State should not deceive the other states neither it should accept those responsibilities which it does not intend to fulfil. Cordial love and affection should be the basis of mutual relation.
2). It should abide by its pledges.
3). It should not invade upon its neighbours without any solid reason.
4). It should not encourage intrigues (for its benefits) in other countries, leading to rebellions.
5). It should not encourage and assist any other state in oppression and coercion.
6). It should avoid retaliation when it overcomes an enemy because it breeds contempt and obstacles for the future.
7). Ambassadors must not be killed or disrespected.
8). Trade and commerce should be carried on equal terms.

2

Preaching of Islam

(A) Letters To The Kings :–

Judaism and Christianity were most prominent religions before the appearance of Islam but they could not get any roots in the soil of Arabia. Judaism is pessimistic in its approach and instead of teaching ethics or expectations it itself is a tragic story of keen regrets and sorrows. The Jews regard themselves a chosen nation and that God belongs to them alone. At the advent of Muhammad (P.B.U.H) the Christian cloak had been torn to pieces. The theory of Trinity had been propounded at that time. Christianity not only regarded Jesus Christ as the son of God but it also added the concept of nunship.

Muhammad (P.B.U.H.) is the last Prophet of God therefore the sphere of his teachings was neither national nor territorial in nature. He did not say that his mission was only the emanicipation of the Israelites as Jesus Christ was "not sent but unto the lost sheep of the house of Israelites". The Vaid was revealed for the Indians, Zindavesta for the Persians, the Torah for the Jews, the Gospel for the lost sheep of Israil, Hud and Saleh for 'Aad and Thamud tribes. On the contrary, Muhammad (P.B.U.H.) claimed that the emancipation of the whole mankind from the shackles of un-Godly slaveries was his mission. Islam regarded the world as a great country for the mankind. It believes in the universality of the Divine call with which the Holy Prophet was commissioned. He is the reformer of the whole mankind. He did not call to worship the god inhabiting the Himalayan Valleys or the heights of Sina but he exhorted to bow before God of this whole universe Who is Omnipotent. Islam believes in divine universal nomocracy. Its aim is the proselytization of the whole mankind. This mission is to be achieved through the Prophethood of Muhammad (P.B.U.H.). God says in the Holy Quran:–

1. "We have not sent thee but as a universal (Messenger) to men, giving them glad tidings, and warning them (against sin)."[2]
2. "We sent thee not, but as a Mercy for all creatures."[3]
3. "It is He Who has sent His Apostle with guidance and the Religion of Truth, that he may proclaim it over all religions."[4]
4. "Say: 'O men! I am sent unto you all, as the Apostle of God' "[5]

Muhammad (P.B.U.H.) had clarified in the very beginning that his message was for the whole of mankind. He said:[6]

1. "I am apostle of God not only for the Arabs but also for all the members of mankind."
2. "I have been commissioned to all the people - - - white or black."
3. Before me every prophet was sent to his particular nation or country but I have been commissioned for the whole mankind.

Once he said with all clarification: "I have been entrusted with the keys of the world."[7] Again he said, "God has given me the control over the whole earth. I have seen the eastern and western hemispheres where the government of my Ummah will be established." Once he said, "I have been endowed with five special attributes, namely:[8]

Firstly: I have been helped solely with terror upto one month's journey. "I will soon cast awe in the minds of the unbelievers."[9]

Secondly: The whole of the earth has been made pious and serves as a mosque for me.

Thirdly: Before me the spoils of war were not legal for any prophet.

Fourthly: I have been given intercession.

Fifthly: Previous prophets were national prophets sent to particular peoples, while I have been sent for the whole of mankind.

Muhammad (P.B.U.H.) invited all men to confess the

Kalimah that there is no god but Allah and Muhammad is His Messenger. His teachings are eternal as he was last of the Prophets. After a few centuries the world was to be shrunk into one entity due to modern technology. Islam raised the slogan of internationalism 1400 years ago. Consequently it was not difficult even in the material age to unite the mankind in one relationship mentally, theoretically, morally and objectively. Muhammad (P.B.U.H.) discovered the respect for mankind. He told such secrets in the international affairs from which even the present civilization has sought guidance. This has been acknowledged even by some orientalists. His teachings changed the world in a short span of 23 years. The degraded man was elevated before whom the crowns of Caesars and Chosroes were to bow. In his very life the waves of the ocean of Islam began to touch the neighbouring states of the Arabian Peninsula.

Almost major part of the Arabian Peninsula had embraced Islam from the start of his mission to the Treaty of Hudaibiyah. Now the Holy Prophet decided to invite, 'in his bold uncompromising way', those kings, rulers and chiefs of the states to embrace Islam, for the correctness of international problems, who ruled the neighbouring territories of Hijaz. Some of them were sovereigns and others paid tribute either to Rome or Persia.

The grip of royal system was so tight in these countries that the people could enjoy their liberties whatever their sovereigns liked. These sovereigns crushed humanity under their feet with the co-operation of pontiffs and religious leaders. The motto of Islam was to eliminate the distinctions between red and white, black and white. It predicted a glorious and bright future for the mankind. It taught freedom, equality and fraternity regarding collective, social, political, mental and spiritual aspects of the human life. Before this the concept of human fraternity advocated by Jesus Christ was based upon that concept of theocracy which was prevalent among the Jews. Consequently his movement failed. To preach oneness of God and universal fraternity Muhammad (P.B.U.H.) invited these rulers to embrace Islam in accordance with the principle that the people follow the religion of their kings. He despatched envoys to invite the neighbouring sovereigns and subjects to convey his message. He kept in view all such international protocols while writing these letters to these heads of states which have been included in the modern diplomatic protocols. It is notable that during the life of the Holy Prophet there was a regular Foreign Service which was run by the well-read men. Preference was given to those who knew court etiquette, but only their merit was kept in view while appointing them. The ambassadors were well-versed in the languages of the territory to which they were deputed and they had already visited these countries so that they could preach satisfactorily. They were asked to work with patience to give good tidings to the people and not to incite hostility towards this mission. On the top of these letters three words of Allah, Apostle and Muhammad were written in three lines respectively. For this purpose a silver pearled ring was prepared in which these words were carved. He started to seal the letters first of all in Arabia.[10] He addressed them "Great al-Rome," "Great al-Persia" and "Great al-Coptic." The sentence "embrace Islam, you will be safe" was particularly written in these letters. It was his political sagacity because this sentence also means that "pay allegiance, you will be safe." And between lines there is also a threat of punishment in case of refusal. They were told that religiously, they should keep in mind that they were also responsible for their nations and God would punish them in the world hereafter. Politically they should be ready to see their doomsday in case of refusal. This is a best example of modern diplomacy. He did not intend to cheat them rather it is his sagacity and discernment that two meanings could be understood from these sentences.

Through the despatch of these letters the neighbouring rulers came to know that Arabia no more remained a neglected land as before. But a regular system was evolving there under which an organized government had been established there.

There are two views about the start of the journey of these ambassadors. Some are of the view that they set out on Ist Muharram 7 A.H./11 May 628 A.C. on Wednesday.

But some think that they started their journey on different dates. History has recorded some 250 to 300 letters which Muhammad (P.B.U.H.) despatched to his contemporaries. But the actual number must be far more than this because his empire covered a vast area of 10 lakh square miles and he had to perform the duties of rulership for ten years.[11] The letter written to Muqauqis is still safe in library of Egypt in its original form. Similarly his letter to the Caesar of Rome is safe in a library of Istanbul. It is remarkable to note that the following verse was particularly written in the letters written to the Christian sovereigns:[12]

"Say: 'O people of the Book! come to common terms as between us and you: that we worship none but God; that we associate no partners with Him;that we erect not from among ourselves, lords and patrons other than God."[13]

In the following some important letters and the results which they bore are discussed :

1. To The Negus:

The title of the Abyssinian sovereign was the Negus and his name was Asham or Ashamah bin Al-Jabr. He was a Christian and a protected ruler of the Eastern Roman Empire. The Muslims, earlier, had migrated to Abyssinia from Makkah and they were welcomed there. 'Amr bin Ummayia al-Dhamri was the ambassador designated to him who was warmly welcomed. According to the Muslims Asham was not the same Negus whose funeral prayer was led by Muhammad (P.B.U.H.). Ibn-Hazm is also of the view that the Negus to whom the letter was written did not embrace Islam. 15 But Ibn-Ishaque, Waqdi and Ibn-Sa,d are of the view that he had embraced Islam[16] and he had corroborated the truth of Prophet's teachings. The letter of Muhammad (P.B.U.H.) was as under :–

"In the name of the Most Merciful and Beneficent God. From Muhammad, apostle of God, to Negus al-Asham, the king of Abyssinia. Peace. First of all I praise Allah, the King, the Holy, the Peace, the Faithful, the Watcher. I bear witness that Jesus, son of Mary, is the spirit of Allah and His word which He cast to Mary, the Virgin, the good, the pure, so that she conceived Jesus. God created Christ from His spirit and His breathing as He created Adam by His hand and His breathing. Now I call you to God, the Unique, without partner and to His obedience. Always submit to Him and follow me and believe in that which came to me, for I am the apostle of God. Before this I have already sent to you my cousin Ja'far with a number of Muslims. Take care of them. Negus! leave pride because I invite you and your court to Allah. Mind it that I have accomplished (my duty) and my admonitions. Now it is better for you to receive my advice. Peace upon all those that follow true guidance.,,

According to Ibn Sa'd two letters were written to Negus.[17] In his second letter he had asked for his marriage with Umm-i-Habiba, daughter of Abu Sufyan bin Harb. She had migrated to Abyssinia in the company of her husband Obaidullah b. Jahash Al-Asadi who embraced Christianity in that country and thereafter died there. It is said that Negus did the same and paid four hundred dinars as Mahr or nuptial gift on his behalf.[18]

Here it is necessary to refute the idea of certain orientalists and other writers that why did the Muslims not attack Abyssinia? Or why did Negus embrace Islam? Among the orientalists Budge is prominent.[19] Similarly Abul Hasan Muhammad bin Abdul Hadi has stated the reason, why Muhammad (P.B.U.H.) did not invade upon Abyssinia in these words:

"The real reason was the barrenness, treeless, mountains and uneven valleys of Abyssinia. Moreover, there was sea between the Muslims and Abyssinia."[20]

Muhammad (P.B.U.H.) did not mention any sort of political power in his letter. He, only, mentioned the right position of Christ. The Holy Prophet is reported to have said, "Leave the Abyssinians in peace, so long as they do not take the offensive."[21] It was only keeping in view their honesty, courage and rightfulness. Thus the Muslims did not attack Abyssinia for centuries. Relations with it were friendly though Abyssinia was not part of Daru'l Islam. Abyssinia also extended friendship to the Muslim State. They penetrated only into that land peacefully, particularly in the 18th and 19th centuries when the trade of the Red Sea was under their control.

In the light of these facts the statements of Budge and

Abul Hassan nullify that Negus accepted the invitation of Muhammad (P.B.U.H.) to embrace Islam because he feared the downfall of his political power. On the other hand, the fact is that he was affected by Islam. Therefore, he embraced Islam in the hands of Ja'far Tayyar and sent a detailed letter to Muhammad (P.B.U.H.) in this context. Moreover, he sent his son Arha as his ambassador and asked if it was necessary for him then he would come himself. Similarly this view of Abul Hasan has no ground that the geographical position and the physical characteristics of Abyssinia did not attract the Muslims. Because what was the attraction for the Muslims in the desert of Libya or were not Cyprus, Sicily or Sardinia surrounded by sea? The message of Islam is for the whole universe. The Finalty of the Prophethood of Muhammad (P.B.U.H.) is not proved unless his message is not conveyed to all the corners of the world.

2. To The King Of Bahrayn :

Bahrayn was a tributary territory of Persia. The Arabs were, also, inhabiting the land in a large majority. Among them Abul Qais, Bakr bin Wa'il and Tamim were prominent tribes. At that time Mundhir b. Sawa represented Persia as a ruler of Bahrayn. Alla b. Al-Hadramiy acted as the ambassador of Muhammad (P.B.U.H.). The feudal lord accepted Islam with his co-religionists. As a result a major portion of his subjects also embraced Islam. Mundhir b. Sawa wrote to the Holy Prophet, "Some people have liked Islam and the others have shown abomination to it. In Bahrayn there are also Jews and the Magians, also direct about them." The Holy Prophet replied as follows:

> "Salutations! If you keep up prayer and give zakat, and show sincerity towards Allah and His Apostle, and give *ushr* on dates and half *ushr* on grain, and will not convert your progeny into magians then you will remain owner of all those things which were in your possession at the time of embracing Islam. But Allah and His Apostle will have their right on fire temple. If you refuse from it then you will have to pay Jizya."8

Ibn Tulun also mentions the following letter written

by the Holy Prophet:

"So long as you will do good things, you will not be terminated from services. And those who do not leave Magian religion and Judaism will be levied upon Jizya."[23]

The amount sent by 'Ala b. Al-Hadramiy as Jizya and Zakat was approximately 80 thousand.[24] Dr. Muhammad Hamidullah is of the view that Abu Hurairah was sent to Bahrayn to collect the amount.25

3. To The Kings Of Oman :

Oman was under the joint rule of the two brothers named Janaifer and Abd of the Azd tribe. They were the sons of al-Julundi.26Amr b. Al-Aas went to them with a letter of Muhammad (P.B.U.H.) inviting them to Islam. But some are of the view that Abu Zaid Al-Ansari and 'Amr-b. Al-'Aas both took the letter to these brothers. Ibn Sa'd thinks that only Amr b. Al-Aas performed the duties of the ambassador.[27] This letter was written by Ubbay b. Ka'b and was sealed. Amr b. Al-Aas visited Janaifar and Abd in Suhar on the sea-shore[28] and delivered the epistle letter to them. The Holy Prophet had written :

"In the name of the Most Merciful and Beneficent God. From Muhammad, the Apostle of Allah, to both the sons of Julunda, Janaifer and Abd. He may be in peace who follows the right path.

Salutations! I invite both of you to embrace Islam. You both should embrace Islam, you will be in peace. I have been sent as apostle of Allah to the whole mankind so that I may frighten them from the opposition of God and the management of God may be completed for infidels. If you both embrace Islam, you will remain the rulers of your country otherwise you will have to lose your kingship. My cavaliers will enter into your land and my Prophethood will dominate your kingship."

Both the brothers enquired about several questions relating Islam from the ambassador of Islam. At the end they embraced Islam. The Holy Prophet let remain their kingship intact according to his promise. He, however, attached to them 'Amr b. Al-'Aas as resident there[29] who occupied with the affairs of the Muslim subjects, teaching, etc. With the embracing of Islam by these brothers the prestige of the Muslim State increased as this region had numerous ports and international annual fairs were held here. After the death of the Holy Prophet Azdi apostatized. The first Caliph Abu Bakr despatched a detachment against them under 'Akrama b. Abu Jahl who set them right. The leader of the Azdis, Laqeet b. Malik Zultaq, escaped to Dubba. Some writers are of the view that he escaped to Duma which is a place in Dubba.[30]

4. To Heraclius:

Heraclius was the king of the eastern branch of the Roman Empire and was known as Caesar. A successful coup d etat had brought him to power in Constantinople. There are two sayings about the messenger of the Holy Prophet :

(a) Dihya b. Khalifa Al-Kalbi Al-Khazraji[31] himself delivered the letter to Heraclius in his court; or

(b) The letter was delivered to Heraclius through his Resident at Busra.[32]

According to Muslim[33] and Tabqat Ibn Sa'd[34] this letter was delivered to Heraclius through the ruler of Bŭsra probably in 627 A.C. Caesar was at that time at Hims elated by his victory over the Persians who had suffered a decisive defeat at Ninevah in December 627. From Hims he walked on foot in thanks to God for what He had restored to him, so that he could pray in Jerusalem.[35] Still he came so magnificently that ground was carpeted and aromatic herbs were thrown on them.[36] The letter ran as follows :

"In the name of Allah, the Most Merciful and Beneficent. This letter is from the Servant and Apostle of Allah to the King of Rome. Peace be upon him who follows guidance. After this it may be clear that I invite you to embrace Islam. If you embrace Islam you will be safe. If you embrace Islam God will give you double reward. But if you turn back the sin of the husbandmen will be upon you. O Scriptuaries! Come to an equitable proposition between ourselves and yourselves that we shall not worship any deity besides Allah, that we shall not set up any partner with Him, nor, some of us will take others of us as lords besides Allah.

So if the Scriptuaries turn away, then say: we bear witness that we are those who owe allegiance to God."

Caesar looked at the letter and then put it between his thighs and his ribs.[37] Then he ordered to summon any Arab in his court to investigate further. It was a chance that Abu Sufyan, alongwith several other merchants, was staying at Gazah. The agents of Heraclius escorted the merchants from Gazah to Hims. Heraclius held a magnificent court in which clergymen, ecclesiasts and priests were standing in rows. Abu Sufyan was one of the bitterest enemies of Muhammad (P.B.U.H.) at that time. Heraclius tried to acquaint himself better with the character of the men who had sent him the message. Therefore he interrogated about Islam and the Holy Prophet from Abu Sufyan. "What are the doctrines Muhammad advances?" asked Heraclius of Abu Sufyan. "He bids to abandon idolatry and adore one God; to observe truth and purity, to abstain from fornication and vice; to flee abominations and to bestow alms." He further asked if followers of Muhammad (P.B.U.H.) were increasing in number, or if they were falling off? Abu Sufyan replied, "his adherents are increasing incessantly, none of his followers had left him." Then Heraclius asked about his genealogical line. "He comes of a noble blood," was the reply.

Abu Sufyan was forced to speak truth before Heraclius. Moreover, the elites of the Quraish hesitated to tell a lie. After this conversation Heraclius uttered graciously, "I knew that a Final Prophet is about to appear but I did not know that he will be born in Arabia. If you have told me the truth about him he will conquer me on the ground that is beneath my feet, and I wish that I were with him and that I might wash his feet." Now the letter was read. Upon this the courtiers kicked up a row, they brayed like wild asses, grunted like camels and took up the Cross.[38] When Heraclius saw their resentment, he pacified them by assuring that he had only test of firmness of their religion in view. Now all the courtiers fell down in obeisance.[39] It is said that Heraclius wrote to the Holy Prophet, "I am a Muslim." But the Holy Prophet remarked, "He is a liar he still believes in Christianity."[40] Moreover, Heraclius himself encountered the Muslims in the battle of Mutah.

5. *To The Ruler Of Alexandria And Egypt :*

Alexandria and Egypt were a semi-sovereign part of the eastern Roman Empire and Jarih b. Hatti, known as Muqauqis, was its ruler. He was a Christian and leader of his Coptic nation. Hatib b. Abu Balta'a Al-Khami delivered the letter of Muhammad (P.B.U.H.) to him. The letter was as follows .

> "In the name of the Most Merciful and Beneficent God. From Muhammad, the Servant and Apostle of Allah to Muqauqis, the Coptic king. He is in peace who follows the right path. After this I invite you to embrace Islam. Embrace Islam, you will be in peace and Allah will give you double reward. And if you do not embrace Islam then you will be held responsible for all the miseries suffered by the Coptics. O Scriptuaries! Come to that which is common between you and us, viz; should not worship anyone but Allah and we should not associate anyone with Allah. We should not make god one another amongst us except Allah. So if the Scriptuaries do not accept then clarify upon them that they should stand witness that after all we are Muslims."

It is said that Hatib himself convinced Muqauqis besides delivering the letter of the Holy Prophet.[41] Muqauqis received the messenger with great honour and put the letter in a box of ivory after sealing it and placed it in the national exchequer. Although he did not embrace Islam yet he wrote a letter to Muhammad (P.B.U.H.) besides sending some gifts. The reply of Muqauqis to this letter runs as below :

"To Muhammad, son of Abdullah, from Muqauqis, the chief of the Copts. Peace be upon you. As for next, I have read your letter and understood what you have mentioned therein, and to which you have invited. We know that a Prophet will come and I thought that he would come out at Syria. I have honoured your messenger and sent you two girls who have got a high position among the Copts and a robe as presents. I sent you one mule[42] that you may ride thereon. And peace by on you."

Muhammad (P.B.U.H.) accepted these gifts but said that Muqauqis showed to be miser in connection with his empire though it is mortal.[43] Anyhow the bond of friendship was for ever cemented between Egypt and Hijaz.

6. *To The Ruler Of Yamama* :

Yamama was known as Jauv but afterwards it was called Al-Yamama. Its connotation was that a woman named Al-Yamama daughter of Murr, who belonged to the tribe of Jadlees, was hanged on one of its gates. Hauda b. Ali Al-Hanfi was the ruler of Yamama. Suleet b. Qais known later on as Al-Khazraji delivered the letter of Muhammad (P.B.U.H.) to him. The letter ran as follows:

"In the name of the Most Merciful and Beneficent God. From Muhammad, the Apostle of Allah, to Hauda b. Ali. He may be in peace who follows the right path. Know, that my religion will spread to that corner where the horses and cattle can go. So embrace Islam, you will be safe. Whatever is in your control we will let you the master of it."

Hauda gave Suleet some gifts and Hajr-made clothes. He wrote to Muhammad (P.B.U.H.) :

"To what you invite is very good. I am a poet and orator of my nation. The Arabs are afraid of my grandeur, so delegate some powers to me then I will follow you."

Muhammad (P.B.U.H.) read the letter and said, "No, I swear the Greatness of God, never. O God, save me from his vice."[46]

It is further mentioned in Tabqat Ibn Sa'd that Muhammad (P.B.U.H.) said after reading the letter, "If he had asked the flow of water from me, I would have not granted it. He has been destructed alongwith whatever is in his hands."[47]

Hauda died after sometime when Muhammad (P.B. U.H.) had conquered Makkah and was on his way back to Medina.

7. *To The Ruler Of Ghassan:*

Mundhir b. Harith was the governor of Syria. The epistle despatch was carried by Mubbarak Shuja b. Wahab Al-Asadi probably in 628 A.C. He had written:

> "In the name of the Most Merciful and Beneficent God. From Muhammad, the Apostle of Allah, to Harith bin Abi Shimer. He may be in peace who follows the right path, and believes in Allah and testifies it. I invite you to believe in Allah, Who is Unique, no one is His associate, then your country remains yours."

Shuja was able to see Harith after several days because he was busy in the hospitality of Heraclius who was to arrive in Jerusalem from Hims to give his offerings. Shuja tore the letter to pieces after reading it and shouted at, "Who can snatch my empire from me? I myself will go to him (Muhammad) whether he may be in Yemen. Otherwise I will send for him."[48] Later on, he wrote all the events to Heraclius who asked him to come to Jerusalem. Shuja was seen off with honours; he was given one hundred misqal gold. On his arrival in Medina, Shuja narrated all the events to the Holy Prophet who remarked, "His empire is devastated." Harith died in 8 A.H.

8. *To Kesra :*

Khusro Pervaiz Hermzan Nosherwan, known as Chosroes, was the king of half eastern world of that time. His court was so grand and splendour that Saif bin Zenzun Humairi stood stunned there for a longwhile. Ruby, topazes and pearls were studded in his crown and throne. The Persians were Zororastrians. Abdullah bin Huzafah As Salmi delivered Muhammad's (P.B.U.H.) letter to the Kesra. He had written :

"In the name of the Most Merciful and Beneficent God. From Muhammad, the Apostle of Allah, to the Kesra, the King of Persia. He may be in peace who follows the right path, believes in Allah and the Apostle and testifies that no one is worth worship other than Allah and Muhammad is His Servant and Apostle. I invite you to the Message of Allah. And I am Apostle of Allah. I have been deputed towards all the mankind to warn those who are alive. Embrace Islam, you will find peace. If you deny then upon you are the sins of the Magians."

Khusro Pervaiz was amazed at the audacity of the fugitive of Makkah in addressing him on terms of equality so he tore the letter to pieces. He was enraged in a fit of rage, he shouted: "He has the audacity of addressing the king of kings and writes his name before my name." He drove the emissary from his presence with contumely. When this incident was narrated to Muhammad (P.B.U.H.) he remarked, "It is thus that God will tear his kingdom and reject his supplication." The fulfilment of the prophecy is engraved on the pages of history. "A brief prophetic verdict eternally sealed the fate of an empire that had existed for more than 4,000 years and in front of whose glory and might once trembled the Romans and the Greeks like cowering captives."

Kesra wrote to Badhan, his Yemen viceroy, to make arrangements to bring the Prophet before him under arrest. Badhan sent two stout fellows named Babawayh and Khar Khasrah to Medina for compliance of the orders of his master. 50 Some writers opine that Khar Khasrah was a military officer and the local officer accompanying him was Baniya whose duty was to study the life of Muhammad (P.B.U.H.) and the people at Medina.51

Ibn Sa'd has mentioned only one name, viz; Qahrmana. Anyhow when these emissaries reached Tayef, a wave of jubilation swept the hill-city as the elites of that city thought that now Muhammad (P.B.U.H.) would certainly be devastated.[52] The two went straight to the Holy Prophet upon reaching Medina and explained the purpose of their arrival. He asked them to come the next day. And on the next day he surprised them with the news that in the very night the Chosroes had been assassinated by his own son (10 Jamadi-ul-Awwal 7 A.H./Februrary 628 A.C. at 7 O' clock. 53 Babawayh was completely upset by this shaking piece of information. Both emissaries repaired for Yemen where they came to know about the truthfulness of the information. Kesra had been slain by his son Shirawayh who had himself ascended the throne. It is remarkable that the apostle gave Kharkhasrah a girdle containing gold and the silver which one of the kings has given him.

Now Badhan completely investigated about the Holy Prophet and his teachings and after satisfaction he embraced Islam alongwith a vast section of Yemeni population. It was an end of Kesra's suzeranity over Yemen and first step towards throwing off the foreign yoke of imperialism from Arabia.

9 To The Ruler of Ma'an :

Farwah bin Amr Al-Juzami was a feudatory over Balqa'a. Ma'an was his capital. Adjacent area of Palestine was also included in the kingdom of Farwah. It is said that the Holy Prophet also invited him to Islam but Ibn Sa'd[55] and Ibn Ishaque[56] opine that he did not despatch him a letter rather Farwah himself sent his emissary, Masood bin Sa'd, and informed the Holy Prophet about his embracing Islam. Farwah also sent some gifts to Muhammad (P.B.U.H.) which included a white mule, some clothes and a quilted garment of silk embroided with gold' who accepted them and also replied his letter. He gave twelve *auqia* gold and presents to Masood. He wrote to Farwah:

"Salutations! From the Apostle of Allah to Farwah bin Amr. Your emissaries came to me. They delivered your gifts to me and informed about you and your embracing

Islam. Do good things and obey Allah and His Apostle. Keep up prayers and give zakat. This is good for you."

When the Caesar came to know about Farwah's embracing Islam, he summoned him to his court. He convassed him to renounce Islam but when he sternly refused, he sent him behind the bars. Later on, he was put to the gallows on the bank of a pond named Ifra'a. Farwah recited the following verse before his death :

"Inform the leader of the believers about me. Even my body and my bones are surrendered to my Lord and my position is an obedient position.

10. To The Chief Of Busra:

Busra was a place near Damascus. Harith bin Amr went to him with the letter of Muhammad (P.B.U.H.). He was assassinated, against all international rules, at Muta by Shurahbil bin Amr - - - the chief of that place. "This wanton outrage on international obligations became eventually the cause of that war which placed Islam in conflict with the whole of Christendom."[58]

11. To Dhu'l-Kula' Hamairi:

The Holy Prophet sent Jurair bin Abdullah with a letter to the chiefs of the tribe Hamair named Dhu'l-Kula' bin Naqur. This letter was written by Khalid bin Saeed. This tribe was famous for its military strength. Dhu'l-Kula' forced people to bow before him as he was their god. But after reading the letter of Muhammad (P.B.U.H.) he embraced Islam alongwith his wife. He liberated eighteen thousand slaves on the day of embracing Islam. During the reign of Umar he shifted to Medina and led a devoted life.

12. To The King Of Ghassan:

Muhammad(P.B.U.H.) also invited Jablah bin Al-Ayham, the King of Ghassan, to embrace Islam.Consequently he embraced Islam in 7 A.H. and informed Medina about his conversion. He also sent some gifts to the Holy Prophet.

But Jablah deviated from Islam during the reign of Umar.

13. To Ma'di karb bin Al-Barha.

The Holy Prophet also invited Ma'di karb bin Al-Barha to embrace Islam and told him that all his belongings would remain his after embracing Islam.

14. To The Tribe Of Lakhm:

Abdullah bin Zaid wrote the the following letter, for Muhammad (P.B.U.H.), to the tribe of Lakhm:

"Whosoever will embrace Islam, keep up prayer, give Zakat and the share of Allah and His Apostle, leave the side of the polytheists then he is without fear and in the shelter of Allah and Muhammad. And who will deviate from it then Allah and Muhammad have no responsibility. If any Muslim stands witness to the embracing of Islam of anyone then he will be in the shelter of Allah and Muhammad and he will be from amongst the Muslims."

15. To Khalid bin Damad Al-Azdi:

The letter to Khalid bin Dhamad was written by Mubarak Ubbay bin Ka'ab. It was written:

"If you embrace Islam, the land you own will remain yours. Keep up prayer, give Zakat, keep fast during the month of Ramdan and perform Haj. Do not give shelter to any heretic. Do not doubt the truthfulness of Islam and support Allah and His Apostle. Then Allah and His Apostle will be responsible for you."

16. To Abd Yaghus bin Ilta Al-Harithi:

This letter was written by Arqam bin Abi Al-Arqam Al-Makhzoomi for Muhammad (P.B.U.H.) to Abd Yaghus bin Ilta Al-Harithi. The contents of the letter were:

"If you embrace Islam then your land and oasis will remain yours and for your nation provided you keep up prayer, give zakat and pay *khumus* out of booty of Jihad. *Ushr* will not be levied upon you."

17. To Musailima, The Liar:

When the deputation of Bani Hanifa returned from Medina to Yamama, Musailima[59] proclaimed to be a prophet. And after this proclamation he began to utter rhymes in *saja'*and speak in imitation of the style of the Quran: 'God had been gracious to the pregnant woman; He has brought forth her a living being that can move; from her very midst.' He permitted them to drink wine and fornicate, and let them dispense with prayer.[60] One of his companions Rajjal bin Unfaw endorsed his claims and declared that Muhammad had joined Musailima in his prophethood. Several people began to follow Musailima. When Muhammad (P.B.U.H.) came to know about this he sent Amr bin Umayya tul 'Al-Damri to Musailima inviting him to embrace Islam who replied through his emissary Abada bin Al-Harith. This letter was written by Amr bin Abi Jarood Al-Hanfi and was delivered to Muhammad (P.B.U.H.) by Musailima's two emissaries.[61] Their names were Abdullah bin Nawah and Ibn Uthal.[62] Musailima had written:

> "From Musailima, the apostle of God, to Muhammad, the Apostle of God. Peace be upon you. No doubt I have been made partner with you in authority. To us belong half the land and to Quraish the other half But the Quraish are a grasping people, not given to justice."[63]

Muhammad (P.B.U.H.) asked his emissaries to say, "There is no god but Allah and Muhammad is His Apostle." But they said, "There is no god but Allah and Musailima is His apostle." He, further, asked them whether they endorsed Musailma's sayings. They, both, replied in affirmation. Upon this Muhammad (P.B.U.H.) replied, "By God, were it not that heralds are not to be killed I would behead the pair of you."

Now Muhammad (P.B.U.H.) despatched a letter to Musailima through Habib bin Zaid. This letter was written by Ubayyi bin Ka'b. It opened with these words:

"In the name of God, the Merciful and Compassionate. From Muhammad, the Prophet of God, to Musailima, the Liar. Peace be upon him who follows the guidance. The earth is God's.[64] He lets whom He will of His creatures inherit it and the result is to the pious."[65]

Musailima arrested Habib notwithstanding the fact that the person of an envoy was always considered inviolable. He asked him, "Do you testify that Muhammad is the Apostle of Allah?" Habib replied, "Yes." Then he asked, "Do you testify that I am apostle of Allah?" Habib replied, "I do not hear." So Musailima began to mutilate him to pieces member by member until he expired.[66]

18. *To Abu Dabiyan Al-Azdi :*

Abu Dabiyan Al-Azdi belonged to the tribe of Ghamid. Muhammad(P.B.U.H.) despatched a letter to him inviting him to embrace Islam. Abu Dabiyan embraced Islam along-with a part of his tribe which was at Makkah at that time. Among the prominent converts were Abdullah and Zubair. These people came to Medina to see the Holy Prophet after some time.

19. *To The Chiefs Of Himyar:*

When Muhammad (P.B.U.H.) returned from his journey from Tabuk, a letter of the chiefs of Himyar; Harith bin Kulal, Nu'aym bin Kulal and Naaman Dhi Ru'ayn, was delivered to him by their emissary. They had mentioned about their embracing Islam. Muhammad (P.B.U.H.) wrote in reply:

"In the name of the Most Merciful and Beneficent God. From Muhammad, the Apostle of Allah, to the Chiefs of Himyar; Harith bin Kulal, Nu'aym bin Kulal, Dhi Ru'ayn[67] and to Naaman; the Chiefs of Hamdan and Ma'afir. I praise God and the only God unto you. Your messengers reached me on my return from the land of the Byzantines and conveyed your message and your news and informed us of your Islam and of your killing the polytheists. God has guided you with His guidance. If you do well and obey God and HisApostle and perform prayer, and pay alms, and God's fifth of booty and the Apostle's share[68] and selected part, and the poor tax which is incumbent on believers from land, namely a tithe of that watered by fountains and rain; of that watered by the bucket a twentieth; for every forty camels a milch camel; for every thirty camels a young male camel; for every five camels a sheep; for every ten camels two sheep; for every forty cows one cow; for every thirty cows a bull calf or a cow calf, for every forty sheep at pasture one sheep. This is what God has laid upon the believers. Anyone who does more is to his merit. He who fulfils this and bears witness to his Islam and helps the believers against the polytheists he is a believer with a believer's rights and obligations and he has the guarantee of God and His Apostle. If a Jew or a Christian becomes a Muslim he is a believer with his rights and obligations. He who holds fast to his religion, Jew or Christian, is not to be turned from it. He must pay the poll - - for every adult, male or female, free or slave, one full dinar calculated on the valuation of Ma'afir or its equivalent in clothes. He who pays that to God's Apostle has the guarantee of God and His Apostle, and he who with holds it is the enemy of God and His Apostle."[69] Ibn Hisham has added the following portion too: "The Apostle of God, Muhammad the Prophet has sent to Zur'a Dhu Yazm: When my messengers Mu'adh bin Jabal and Abdullah bin Zayd, and Malik bin 'Ubada, and Uqba bin Nimr, and Malik bin Murra and their companions come to you I commend them to your good offices. Collect the alms and the poll tax from your provinces and hand them over to my messengers. Their leader is Mu'adh bin Jabal, and let him not return unless satisfied. Muhammad witnesses that there is no god but Allah and that he is His servant and apostle. Malik bin Murra al-Rahwai has told me that you were the first of Himyar to accept Islam and have killed the polytheists and I congratulate you and order you to treat Himyar well and not to be false and treacherous, for the Apostle of God is the friend both of your poor and your rich. The alms tax is not lawful to Muhammad or his household; it is alms to be given to the poor Muslims, and the wayfarers. Malik has brought the news and kept secret what is confidential and I order you to treat him well. I have sent to you some of the best of my people, religious and learned men, and I order you to treat them well, for they must be respected.

Peace upon you and the mercy and blessings of God."

Muhammad (P.B.U.H.) sent Mu'adh bin Jabal to Yemen to receive one year old cow for every thirty cows, one full grown cow for every forty cows, and one dinar or its equivalent calculated on the valuation of Mu'afir from every adult.[70]

This despatch was sent through Ayyash bin Abi Rabiah. The Holy Prophet gave instructions to Mu'adh: "Deal them gently and not harshly; announce good news and do not repel people. You are going to the people with Scripture who will ask you about the key of heavens. Tell them it is the witness that there is no god but Allah Who has no partner."

20. To Bani Anseeb:

Rifa'a bin Zayd came to Muhammad before the conquest of Khayber and embraced Islam. He presented a slave to the Holy Prophet who gave the following letter to him addressed to his nation:

"To Rifa'a bin Zayd whom I have sent to his people and those who have joined them to invite them to God and His Apostle. Whosoever comes forward is from the party of God and His Apostle, and whosoever turns back has two months' grace period."[71]

Bani Anseeb embraced Islam.[72]

21. To Hilal, Ruler Of Bahrayn:[73]

The Holy Prophet sent the following letter to the ruler of Bahrayn:

"You are peace-loving people so I praise that God unto you as none deserves to be worshipped except Him. He has no associate. I invite you to embrace the Oneness of God, submit and come in the circle of the Apostle. It is better for you. Peace be upon him who follows the right path."[74]

22. To Dughatur, the Bishop:

The Holy Prophet sent the following letter to Dughatur (autocrator). It was delivered by Dihya bin Khalifa Al-Kalabi Al-Khazraji. He had written:

"Peace be upon him who embraces Islam. Salutations! Jesus son of Mary is the spirit and word of Allah which He cast to Mary, the Pious. I believe in Allah and that which He revealed on us - - - on Abraham, Ishmael, Ishaque, Jacob and their descendants. That which has been revealed to Moses and Christ. That which have been revealed by God to the prophets. We do not differentiate between any of them. We are to bring Islam for Allah and he will be in peace who follows the right path."[75]

According to another narration Dihya had gone with the letter to Heraclius who told Dihya: "I have read about your prophet in our book. I go in fear of my life from the Romans; but for that I would follow him. Go to Dughatur, the bishop and tell him about your master, for he is greater among the Romans than I and his word counts for more than mine. Accordingly Dihya went to Dughatur and explained the situation. Dughatur said, "No doubt! your prophet is a true prophet. We know him by his descriptions and we find him mentioned by name in our scriptures." Then Dughatur went inside and discarded his black clothes and put on white garments and took his staff and went out to the Romans who were assembled in church and said:

"O Romans, a letter has come to us from Ahmad in which he calls us to God and I bear witness that there is no god but Allah and that Ahmad is his servant and apostle."

Hardly Dughatur had uttered these words that the crowd leapt upon him with one accord and beat him until he was dead.

Now Dihya came back to Heraclius and told the whole incident. Heraclius said, "I had told you that we feared death at their hands and Dughatur was greater among them and his word counted for more than mine."[76]

23. To The Chiefs Of Ailah:

The Holy Prophet wrote a letter to Yuhannah bin Royah and other chiefs of Ailah in the following:

> "You people are peace-loving. I praise that very God unto you as none deserves to be worshipped except Him. I am not going to wage war against you unless I invite you to embrace Islam. So embrace Islam or pay Jizya. Submit to Allah, His Apostle and his messengers and respect them. Make them wear proper dress befitting Mujahidin. Make wear Zayd most proper dress. If my messengers are satisfied, I will be satisfied. You know Jizya. If you want that there should be peace on land and sea then submit to Allah and His Apostle. You will be prevented from the right due to you from Arabia and Persia except the right of Allah and His Apostle. If you send back my messengers without their satisfaction, I will not take anything from you unless I fight with you. I will arrest the children and kill the grown ups because I am the Apostle of God to deliver truth. I believe in Allah, His Books and His apostles. Jesus son of Mary is the word of Allah. I believe in him as the apostle of Allah. You should embrace Islam before an evil reaches you. I have advised my messengers about you. Give three *wasaq* of barley to Hermlah. He has made a recommendation for you. Had it not been the case, I would have not written the letter and invaded upon you. If you submit to my messengers then Allah, Muhammad and their representatives will be your guardians.
>
> Sharjil, Hermlah, Ubbay, Harith bin Zayd Al-Tai are my messengers. What they settle with you, I will be

satisfied. Your responsibility will be lying with Allah and Muhammad. If you submit then you will be in peace. Provide the necessities to the people of Maqna so that they may go to their country."[77]

24. To Bani Zuhair bin Uqaish:

Bani Zuhair bin Uqaish was a branch of Uskal. The Holy Prophet sent the following letter to this clan:

"In the name of the Most Merciful and Beneficent God. From Muhammad the Prophet, to Bani Zuhair bin Uqaish. If you bear witness that there is no god except Allah and Muhammad is His Apostle, segregate yourself from the polytheists and admit the right of fifth and reserved and common share for Muhammad out of booty; then you have the shelter of Allah and His Apostle."[78]

This letter was written on a piece of leather.[79]

25. To Ahbiyeen:

Habib bin Amr, who belonged to Ahbiyeen, came to the Apostle and was given the following letter:

"In the name of the Most Merciful and Beneficent God. From Muhammad to Habib bin Amr and anybody of his clan who embraces Islam, performs prayer and gives Zakat. Their property and water (well) belong to them in the cities and the deserts.

This is the promise of Allah and responsibility of His Apostle."[80]

26. To Bakr bin Wail :

The Holy Prophet sent the following letter to Bakr bin Wail :

"Salutations! Embrace Islam, you will be in peace."[81]

Tabiyan bin Marthad Al-Sadusi delivered the Apostle's letter.[82]

27 Nahshil bin Malik Al-Wailee:

The Apostle's letter to Nahshil bin Malik Al-Wailee was written by Usman bin Affan. The letter ran as follows:

"With the name of Allah. From Muhammad the Apostle to Nahshil bin Malik and his companions of Bani Wail who embrace Islam, perform prayer, give zakat, submit to Allah and His Apostle, pay fifth for Allah and share for the Prophet out of booty, bear witness to his embracing Islam, segregate from polytheists, then they are in the protection of Allah. Muhammad will save him from every sort of cruelty. These people have the right that neither they should be exiled from their country nor *Ushr* be exacted from them. Their administrator shall be appointed from among them."[83]

28 To Hajar :

The Apostle sent the following letter to the people of Hajar :

"In the name of the Most Merciful and Beneficent God. From Muhammad, the Prophet, to the people of Hajar. You have been given peace. I praise God as none deserves to be worshipped except Him.

After this I advise you for God's sake and for yourselves not to deviate from the right path. I have been informed what you have done. Whosoever among you remains of noble character will not be responsible for the sins of wrong-doers.

When my grandees approach you then you should submit and help them in the path and duty of God. Whosoever among you shall do good deed will not be wasted by God and me.

Your deputation came to me. I did nothing unpleasant with them despite the fact that if I tried to get my full right, I would have exiled you from Hajar. I have given concession to your absentees and been kind with the present ones. So mention the blessings of God bestowed upon you."[84]

The Holy Prophet sent his messengers to the nobles of Kesra who were in Hajar but they did not embrace Islam. So he levied one dinar as Jizya on each of them.[85]

29 To The People of Najran :

The Christians of Najran were highly organized in religious matters. The Holy Prophet wrote to the people of Najran:

"With the name of God of Abraham, Ishaque and Jacob. After salutations! I invite you to worship God instead of men. If you refuse then you will have to pay Jizya, I will declare war against you. And peace be upon you."[86]

30 To Nufatha ad-Di'li:

Muhammad wrote a letter to the king of Samawa, a region situated in the south-east of Hira. But the details of this letter are not known. Being of Arab origin, there is greater chance of his having embraced Islam, to liberate from the Iranian grip. But one cannot be sure of that.

This policy of despatching letters bore far-reaching effects. The message of Islam was conveyed to the gigantic states of the Arabian Peninsula. Their inhabitants came to know that a revolution was going to be staged in Arabia which stood for the *Oneness of God* and equality of man. Several rulers of these states took refuge in Islam. Their subjects followed them. Those who did not accept Islam and adopted a satirical attitude towards the Holy Prophet was really the echo of their frustration and disappointment which had taken place out of their cruelties. Their so-called system was about to die because the life of despotism is always short. Chosroes was assassinated by his own son. Can there be a more sorrowful end than this? When he tore the Apostle's letter into pieces, the Apostle had said, "In fact he has smashed his own state by tearing my letter." Ponder over these words which contained the tragic end of

Chosroes. After a few years the ancient grand empire of Persia yielded before the Arab bedouins.

The beginning of this period of internationalism also helped in creating solidarity inside the country. The ideal of the Islamic State was widened. From this point the Apostle determined the lines of his state which was actually the goal of his prophethood. The Muslims were prepared to fight in the path of Allah. They did not engage themselves in any sort of leisure after the conquest of Makkah, rather they got impetus from it.

The companions of the Holy Prophet acquired experience and expertness in diplomatic affairs. They got an opportunity to visit splendid courts and thus availed the chances to know in detail their rulers and their subjects. Muhammad (P.B.U.H.) selected such ambassadors who were acquainted with the language of the country where they were being sent. In this way a tendency to learn foreign languages was inculcated among the Muslims. New vistas of knowledge were opened upon them. In the years to come they lit the lamps of knowledge throughout the world beneficiary even to the non-Muslims.

(B) The Year of Deputation

The year 10 A.H. (April 630-April 631) is noted for the embassies which flocked into Medina to render homage to the Holy Prophet. Upto this time almost whole of Arabia had embraced Islam. After subjugating all the negative tendencies the Islamic State, now, had stepped forward from the stage of city-state to the nation-state. The treaties were being concluded with the nomadic tribes. The insurgents had been smashed in the battlefields. Now the non-Muslims were also included in the Islamic State who had accepted the Islamic suzerainty by paying Jizya. This year several deputations visited Medina and embraced Islam. This period was spread over three years, viz; 8, 9, 10 A.H. after the conquest of Makkah. There is difference of opinion about the number of deputations. Ibn Ishaque has mentioned only fifteen deputations while Hafiz Ibn Qayyim and

Qastlani think that their number was thirtyfour. Demati, Mughaltai and Zain ud Din Iraqi agree with Ibn Sa'd who has mentioned seventy deputations. Only Shami mentions their number as one hundred and four.

It is due to the majority of the number of the deputations that God said to His prophet, "When God's help came and the victory, and you saw men entering into God's religion in batches, then glorify God with praise and ask His pardon for He is most forgiving."

A deputation coming from a certain tribe does not mean that the whole of the tribe became Muslim, for often the deputation would represent nobody but themselves.[1]

There used to be a Master of Ceremonies who instructed the envoys in the local formalities previous to their reception by the Holy Prophet. He used to receive foreign envoys in the Great Mosque where the pillar of Embassies still commemorates the place. He and his Companions are said to have usually put on fine dress at the time of the ceremonial reception of envoys.[2] He is reported to have expressed his wish on his death-bed that his successors should award gifts to the envoys as he himself used to do during his life time.[3] Generally his companions entertained them in their houses and were lodged in the house of Ramlah, daughter of Harith, which was the State Guest House. When they increased in number tents were pitched for them. On departure they always received an ample sum for the expenses, additional gifts, corresponding to their rank. Once he gave an envoy from Uman 500 drachmas, on another occasion gold and silver girdles, and at other times other things.[4]

A few deputations visited Medina even before the Year of Deputations. We start from there:

1. *Muzaynah Deputation :*

Muzaynah seems to have been immediately north of Medina. This deputation visited Medina in Rajab 5 A.H. Noa'man b. Maqran. a famous companion of the Holy Prophet, belonged to this tribe. This deputation consisted of 400 persons notable among them were Bilal b. Al-Harith,

Noa'man b. Maqran, Abu Asma, Usama, Ubaida b. Barda, Abdullah b. Darra, and Bishr b. Lamahtazr. When the members of the deputation desired to migrate, the Apostle said to them, "You people are *Muhajirin* wherever you dwell. So go back to your households."[5] These people embraced Islam and returned to their territory. At the time of conquest of Mecca Noa'man b. Maqran was the standard-bearer of Muzaynah and later on he came to be known as the conqueror of Ispahan.[6]

The Apostle gave them money for journey.[7]

2. *Sa'd bin Bakr Deputation:*

Bani Sa'd b. Bakr sent Dammam b. Tha'laba as their envoy to Medina in Rajab 5 A.H. The way in which Dammam performed his duties as envoy depicts the real simplicity and fearlessness of the Arabs.[8] He came to the Holy Prophet riding on the back of a camel asking loudly:

"Who among you is the son of Abdul Muttalib?"

Muhammad (P.B.U.H.) replied: "I am son of Abdul Muttalib."

He asked: "Are you Muhammad?"

The Apostle replied: "Yes."

Now Dammam said: "O son of Abdul Muttalib! I am going to ask you a harsh question, so don't take it amiss."[9]

The Holy Prophet told him to ask what he liked and he would not take it amiss.[10]

He asked: "I adjure you by God your God the God of those before you and the God of those who will come after you, has God sent to us an apostle?"

The Apostle replied: "Yes."

Now Dammam said: "I adjure you by God. Has God ordered you to order us to serve Him alone and not to associate anything with Him and to discard those rival deities which our fathers used to worship along with Him."

The Apostle replied: "Yes God has ordered me this."

Afterwards Dammam mentioned all the ordinances of Islam one by one and repeated the above-mentioned words every time. At the end he read out the Kalima (I bear witness that there is no God but the one God Who is without associate, and that Muhammad is His servant and apostle).

On his return to his people, he smashed all the idols. His tribesmen tried to frighten him but he said, "By God, neither they can give profit nor loss."

All the people embraced Islam before evening.[11]

3. *Ashjah Deputation:*

This tribe had taken part in besieging Medina in the battle of the Ditch. This deputation consisted of one hundred persons and it came to Medina under the leadership of Masood b. Rukhaylah in 5 A.H. The deputation was lodged at Mohallah Sha'ab Salaa. The Apostle went to them himself and instructed that they should be entertained with dates.[12] They said, "We don't want to fight with you but we do wish to make an armistice with you."[13] Consequently the Holy Prophet concluded a peace treaty with them.

Another Ashja' deputation, consisting of seven hundred men, visited Medina after the expedition of Bani Quraiza and embraced Islam.

4. *Khushni Deputation:*

When the Apostle was about to march towards Khyber Abu Thalaba Al-Khushni came to him and embraced Islam. He also accompenied him in the expedition of Khyber. Afterwards another deputation consisting of seven hundred persons visited Medina.[14] It was lodged at the house of Abu Thalba. After embracing Islam the deputation returned to their country.

5. *Al-Ash arin Deputation:*

The members of this depuation belonged to an honourable tribe of Yemen. They visited Medina in 7 A.H. A renowned companion of the Apostle Abu Musa *Al-Ash'ari* was also among them. Upon hearing the ministry of

Muhammad (P.B.U.H.), the Al-Asha'reen (53 in number) boarded on a ship en route to Medina. But anti wind took them to Abyssinia where they came across Ja'afer Tayyar who escorted them to Arabia via Jeddah. This was the time when Khyber had been conquered and the Holy Prophet was still staying there. When the Al-Asha'reen entered Medina they were reciting the following verses:

"Tomorrow we will meet our friends Muhammad and his group." When Muhammad (P.B.U.H.) saw them he said, "These people are weakhearted and faith is only to be found in Yemen." He further said, *Asha'reen* among the people are as fragrance is in the bag."[16] The deputation asked the Holy Prophet, "O Apostle of God! What was the beginning of the world?" The Apostle replied, "God was there first of all. There was none except Him. His Throne was on water and He has written everything in the Book."

6. *Daus Deputation:*

Tufayl b. Amr Dausi was a noble and sharp-witted poet. Once he visited Makkah where some elites of the Quraish tried to present a distorted picture of Muhammad (P.B.U.H.) before him by saying, "This man is shattering our unity. It is better for you that neither you should have talks with him nor give attention to what he says." They put so much insistence on their advice that Tufayl determined that he would act upon their advice. He told later on, "I put stuff cotton in my ears."[18] One morning he went to the Holy Mosque and there he saw Muhammad (P.B.U.H.) praying near the *Ka'aba.* Tufayl stood near him then he thought that why should he not listen what Muhammad (P.B.U.H.) said. So he followed him upto his home after his prayer and told him what people had said to him. Muhammad (P.B.U.H.) recited the Holy Quran before him. After his recitation he was so very over-whelmed with its charming diction that he embraced Islam. As he was a man of authority among his people so he asked the Apostle to say prayer for him to God for his success in preaching Islam. The Apostle prayed, "O God, give him a sign."

On reaching his home Tufayl said to his aged father, "I have become a Muslim so I have nothing to do with you or you with me." He invited his father to embrace Islam which he did. Then his wife also embraced Islam. Now Tufayl invited his tribesmen to embrace Islam but people did not pay heed to his call. Being disheartened he went to the Apostle in Makkah and said to him, "My nation is indulged in fornication, so invoke a curse on them."[19] But the Holy Prophet prayed, "O God, guide Daus."[20]

Now Tufayl succeeded in his mission. He visited Medina in 7 A.H. as the leader of a deputation of Daus which consisted of seventy or eighty persons.[21] Among them Abu Huraira and Abdullah bin Uzair were also included. At that time the Apostle was at Khyber and the deputation visited him there. He also gave them their share out of booty.[22] Then they came to Medina accompanying the Apostle where they learned the injunctions of Islam.

7. *Judham Deputation:*

Before the conquest of Khyber Rifa'ah bin Umayr bin Ma'bad Al-Judhami came to Medina and presented a slave to the Apostle. The Judham used to worship Jupiter. Rifa'ah embraced Islam. On his return, the Apostle gave him a letter addressed to his people inviting them to Islam. It ran as follows:

> "This is a letter from Muhammad, the Messenger of God, to Rifa'ah b. Zayd and to his tribe and to those who follow with them; he calls them to God, he who accepts is in the party of God *(hizb Allah);* he who refuses has two months' security."[23]
>
> The people of Judham accepted Islam.

8. *Juhayna Deputation:*

In this deputation were included Abdul Uzza bin Badr, Akhaifi and Abu Roha. The name of their valley was Ghawi. The Holy Prophet changed its name to Guidance.

Similarly he changed the name of Abdul Uzza to Abdullah. On the day of conquest of Makkah he was one of the standard bearers.[24] These people were also given a tract of land for construction of a mosque. This was the first mosque of Medina for which a tract of land was given.[25]

Another person of the same tribe named Amr bin Murra Al-Juhayni heard about the teachings of Muhammad (P.B.U.H.) smashed his idol, came to him and embraced Islam.[26] On the instruction of the Apostle he returned to his people and invited them to Islam. All the people embraced Islam except one.

9. *Tha'laba Deputation:*

In 8 A.H. when the Holy Prophet returned from Ji'rana a deputation consisting of four men came to him. They embraced Islam and told him about their poverty. They stayed for some days in Medina and on their return each of them was given five *Auqia* silver by Bilal on the instructions of the Holy Prophet. (P.B.U.H.)

10. *Bani Abd-ibn-'Adiy Deputation:*

Harith bin Utban, Rabia bin Mullath, Habib bin Mullath, Awaimar bin Al-Akhram and several others were included in this deputation that came in 5 A.H. They belonged to Makkah. They said, "O Muhammad! We are the mightiest of all those who live in Makkah. We don't want to fight you. If you are on war with anyone we are ready to help you except against the Quraish. If anyone of us is killed by you unintentionally, you will be responsible for the blood-money. Similarly if anyone of your companions is killed by us unintentionally, we will be responsible for his blood-money.

The Apostle agreed with them and then the deputation embraced Islam.

11. *Bahla Deputaion:*

After the conquest of Makkah Mutrif bin Al-Kahin

Al-Bahli came to the Holy Prophet and after embracing Islam he got a peace-letter for his people.[27] The Holy Prophet mentioned to him the duties of Zakat.

The Nahlthil bin Malik Al-Wayli came to the Holy Prophet. He also belonged to Bahla and had come as an emissary of his people like Mutrif. He also embraced Islam and got a letter from the Apostle in which the descriptions of the injunctions of Islam were written.

12. Sada Deputation:

In 8 A.H., when the Apostle came back from Ji'rana he sent Qais bin Sa'd a' the head of four hundred Muslims to fight with Sada in Yemen. But when a man named Zayd bin Harith came to him from Sada he sent back his army. Later on, Zayd bin Harith came with a deputation of fifteen members and embraced Islam. The members of the deputation complained the scarcity of water in a well during summer in their land. The Apostle gave them seven pebbles and asked them to throw in the well on by one in the name of Allah. On their return they did so and the level of the water in the well came up.[29] The Apostle gave them dress to wear as they needed besides entertaining them.[30]

Islam spread fastly among the people of Sada. One hundred men of this tribe came to attend the Farewell Pilgrimage.[31]

13. *Abd Al-Qais Deputation;*

This tribe was settled in Bahrayn and it was a branch of Rabia. There were fourteen members of this deputation.[32] Among them were Abdullah b. Auf Al-Ashja'h Al-Aasri, Mazida b. Malik Maharbi, Ubaida b. Hamam Maharbi, Sahar b. Abbas Al-Mazi, Amr b. Makhzoom or Merjoom Al-Aasri, Harith b. Junab, Harith b. Shuaib Al-Aasri and a nephew of Ashja' named Munqiz b. Hayyan. Jarud b. Amr was the leader of the deputation who was a Christian.[33] The deputation visited Medina in 8 A.H./630 A.C.[34]

Munqiz b. Hayyan was a trader in sheets and dates and used to come to Medina from Hajar. Once on a mercantile transaction he halted at Medina and met the Holy Prophet who asked him, "Munqiz! how is your nation?" Then the Apostle counted some prominent names of his people.[35] Seeing this miracle Munqiz immediately embraced Islam. The Apostle gave him a letter addressed to Abd Al-Qais. Once his wife, who was the daughter of Ashja'h[36] told her father about Munqiz's prayers and ablution. Now Munqiz and Ashja' exchanged their ideas. Ashja' liked the teachings of Islam so he took the Apostle's letter and went to his people. They were also inclined to Islam therefore they decided to send a deputation to Medina.

Boarding arrangements of the deputation were made at the house of Ramlah, daughter of Harith, where it stayed for ten days. The Apostle advised its members to act upon four things:

1. Oneness of God and bear witness of the apostleship of Muhammad;
2. Keepup prayer;
3. Give Zakat; and
4. Keep the fasts of Ramdan.

According to some traditions the Apostle also advised them to give fifth out of booty. He also advised them to avoid the use of all such pots in which wine was prepared. He asked them to convey all the instructions to the people and ask them to visit Medina. On their return he bestowed upon them different gifts. Abdullah Al-Ashja was given twelve and a half *auqia* silver.[37]

The first mosque after that of Medina - - - where Friday prayer was celebrated was at Juwatha, in the territory of the tribe of Abd al-Qais. This region had also great economic importance. The annual fairs held in Mushaqqar and Daba had international attraction. Daba was one of the two major ports of Arabia. Ibn Khaldun is of the view that after the death of the Holy Prophet some of the Abd Al-Qais apostatized[38] but there is no such mention in other books.

14. *Sulaym Deputation:*

Qais b. Nusaiba of Bani Sulaym came to the Holy Prophet and when he invited him to Islam, he embraced it.

On his return to his locality he invited his people to accept Islam. In the year of the conquest of Makkah some seven hundred persons met the Apostle at Qadid and embraced Islam. Then a deputation of Sulaym came to Medina. Prominent among the members were Abbas b. Mirdas, Anas b. Abbas and Rashad b. Abdriba. These people also took part in the conquest of Makkah, battles of Hunain and Tayef.

There is a tradition that Qadr b. 'Ammar came to the Holy Prophet and embraced Islam. He promised that he would bring one thousand horsemen to the Apostle to embrace Islam.[39] On his return he informed his people and then set out with nine hundred men and left one hundred persons behind. On his way he died but he left a will for them that they should proceed to Medina. Consequently they continued their journey and narrated the whole incident to the Apostle in Medina. He enquired them about the other one hundred men. They told him that they expected an attack by Kinanah so they had been left behind. The Apostle told them that they should ask them to visit Medina as they had no danger of any unpleasant accident that year.[40] Subsequently the remaining persons also visited Medina. Maqnah b. Malik was their chief. These people met the Holy Prophet at Hudda.

15. *Hawazin Deputation:*

Until the campaign of Hunain in January 630 A.C. the Holy Prophet had no contact with Hawazin. They roamed towards the south-east of Makkah and had for their favourite idol the goddess Lat, located at Tayef. After the siege of Tayef the Holy Prophet proceeded to Makkah to perform Umra. On his way he stayed at Ji'rana. Six thousand women and children captives and innumerable cattle had not been distributed yet. It was at Ji'rana that fourteen members[41] of Hawazin, under the leadership of Zuhair b. Hirwan came to the Apostle. Among them was also his foster-uncle Abu Barqan. The members of the deputation embraced Islam. Then they requested, "O Apostle of Allah! We are root and branch also. The origin of the tribes is from us and the branches which have become clans and families also owe their origin to us. You are well aware of the disaster which has befallen on us. Be kind to us, Allah will be kind to you." Then Zuhair stood up in his place and said, "O Apostle of Allah, in the enclosures are your paternal and maternal aunts and the women who suckled you and who used to look after you. Had we acted as foster-parents for Harith b. Abu Shimr or Nu'man b. Mundhir and then got into the position in which you hold us we could hope for his kindness and favour and you are the best of trustworthy men."[42]

The Apostle enquired of the deputation, "Which are dearest to you? Your sons and your wives or your cattle?" The deputation replied, "So far as concerns what I and the Banu Abdul Muttalib have they are yours. But so far as the share of the *Muhajirin* and the *Ansar* is concerned, I tell you that when I have prayed the noon prayer with the men then get up and say, 'We ask the Apostle for our sons and our wives'. "43 The deputation did the same. The *Muhajirin* and the *Ansar* agreed to give back the captives but Aqra b. Hisn and Abbas b. Mirdas refused to do so. But afterwards they also handed over their share of their own accord.

Then the Holy Prophet said, "He who holds to his right to these captives shall have six camels for every man from the first booty I take."[45]

Shima, the Apostle's foster-sister, was also included among the captives. He paid a great reverence to her. She embraced Islam and the Holy Prophet sent her back with presents and a slave.

16. *Mustaliq Deputation :*

The Apostle sent Walid b. Uqba to Banu Mustaliq for the collection of Zakat When he was in the suburbs, people rode out to welcome him. But Walid misunderstood it and went back to the Apostle who consulted with his companions over this issue. In the meanwhile a deputation from Banu Mustaliq came to the Apostle and explained the situation, saying, "We heard about your messenger when you sent him to us and we went out to meet him to show him respect and to pay Zakat that was due, but he went back as far as he could. Now we hear that he has alleged that we went out to kill him. By Allah we did not go out with such intent".[46] So God sent down the following verse about this incident[47]: "O ye who believe! If a wicked person comes to you with any news, ascertain the truth, lest ye harm people unwittingly, and afterwards become full of repentance for what ye have done."

17. Thumala Deputation:

This deputation came to the Apostle under the leadership of Abdullah b. Unais after the conquest of Makkah. The deputation embraced Islam and paid allegiance on behalf of their people. The Apostle gave the deputation a letter in which the precepts of Zakat were mentioned. It was written by Thabit b. Qais and Sa'd b. Ubada and Muhammad b. Maslama signed the document as witnesses.

18. Al-Haddan Deputation:

This deputation[48] also came to the Apostle after the conquest of Makkah. Musailat-ul-Hazzan was its leader. The deputation embraced Islam and paid allegiance on behalf of their people. The Apostle gave the deputation a letter in which there were precepts of Zakat. The letter was written by Thabit b. Qais and Sa'd b. Ubada and Muhammad b. Maslama signed it as witnesses.

19. Banu Tamim Deputation:

In the expedition against Banu Tamim the Muslims arrested eleven men and eleven women[49] and thirty children in Muharram 9 A.H. They were brought to Medina. Now the following chiefs of Tamim came to Medina: Utarid b. Hajib, Hutat b. Yazid, Zibrqan b. Badr, Qays b. Asim, Aqra b. Habis, Qays b. Al-Harith, Nu'aym b. Sa'd, Amr b. Al-Ath'am, Uyayna b. Hisn and Ribah b. Al-Harith. Ibn Sa'd is of the view that some eighty or ninety persons were accompanying them.[50] These people stood at the door of the Apostle who was in his apartments at that time. They called out rudely, "O Muhammad! come out." At this time people were waiting for the Apostle for noon prayer. He came out and led the prayer. After the prayer he paid heed to them. Utarid b. Hajib, a prominent orator, got up and said: "Praise belongs to God for His favour to us and He is worthy to be praised, Who has made us kings and given us great wealth wherewith we are generous, and has made us the strongest people of the east and the greatest in number, and the best equipped so who among mankind is our equal? Are we not the princes of men and their superiors? He who would compete with us let him enumerate what we have enumerated. If we wished we could say more, but we are too modest to say much of what He has given us and are well known for that. I say this that you may bring forward the like and anything better."[51]

After his speech Utarid sat down. Now the Apostle asked Thabit b. Qays to speak on his behalf. He said: "All the praise is due to Allah Who created heavens and earth and established His rule therein and His knowledge includes His throne; nothing exists but by His bounty. By His power He made us kings and chose the best of His creation as an Apostle and honoured him with lineage, made him truthful in speech, and favoured him with reputation, and sent down to him His book and entrusted him with it above (all) He had created. He was God's choice from the worlds. Then He summoned men to believe in him, and the emigrants from his peoples and kinsmen believed in God's Apostle; the most noble men in reputation, the highest in dignity, and the best in deeds. The first of creatures to answer respond to God when the Apostle called them were ourselves. We are God's helpers and the assistants of His Apostle, and will fight men and they believe in God; and he who believes in God and His Apostle has protected his life and property from us; and he who disbelieves we will fight in God unceasingly and killing him will be a small matter to us. These are my words and I ask God's pardon for myself and the believers both men and women. Peace be upon you."[52]

Next there was contest regarding poetries. Now again Zibrqan got up and recited some verses in reply of which Hassan recited a few verses. This was repeated by both the sides once again. Then Aqra b. Habib said, "By my father, this man has a ready helper. His orator and his poet are better than our and their voices are sweeter than ours."[53]

After this acknowledgement the members of the deputation embraced Islam. It is about them that God sent down the following verses:[54]

"Those who shout out to thee from without the Inner Apartment most of them lack understanding."

The Holy Prophet released all their captives and gave them valuable gifts on their return.[55]

20. 'Uzrah Deputation :

'Uzrah was a famous place of Syria. It is quite possible that the locality came to be known so after the name of this tribe. This deputation consisted of twelve persons and it visited Medina in Safr 9 A.H. Prominent among them were Dummra b. Nu'man, Saleem b. Malik, Sa'd b. Malik and Malik b. Abbi Riyah. The members of the deputation were lodged at the house of Ramlah daughter of Al-Harith.

The Apostle asked the deputation, "Who are you?" They replied, We are brothers of Qusayy (from mother's side). We had helped Qusayy and ousted Khuzzah and Bani Bakr from Makkah."

Upon hearing this the Holy Prophet said, "Welcome whole heartedly. What prevented you to salute in the Islamic way?" They replied,"We had come for the sake of our nation."

Then the Apostle invited them to Islam and they embraced it. He gave them the good tidings of the conquest of Syria. On their return he gave them gifts and put on a sheet on one person.[56]

21. Bali Deputation:

Politically the territory of this tribe was very important.

A deputation from there visited Medina in Rabi'ul Awwal 9 A.H. The members of the deputation boarded with Ruaifah b. Thabit who also came of this tribe. He escorted the tribe to the Holy Prophet and introduced them. The Apostle welcomed Ruaifah and his tribesmen who then embraced Islam. TheApostle said:

"All the praises are for Allah Who has guided you to embrace Islam. Whosoever shall die following a religion other than Islam will go to hell."

One member of the deputation named Abu Khubayb enquired about different problems, about fast and other religious matters. After a while when they were with Ruaifah at his residence, the Holy Prophet himself brought dates for them. They stayed for three days in Medina. On their return the Apostle gave them gifts.[57]

22. Hamdan Deputation:

This tribe was settled in Hamdan. At first the Apostle sent Khalid b. Walid to Yemen to preach Islam but he could not succeed even for six months. Then Ali was sent there for the same purpose and he was so successful in his efforts that the whole tribe embraced Islam in only one day.[58] When the Holy Prophet came to know about this he thanked Allah and said, "Peace be upon Hamdan". A deputation of Hamdan visited Medina in 9 A.H. after the return of the Apostle from Tabuk. Prominent among the members were Malik b. Uz, Abu Thaur known as Dhu'l-Mish'ar, Malik b. Anfah Al-Salmani, Amr b. Malik Al-Kharifi, and Dimam b. Malik. They were wearing robes of Yemeni clothes and turbans of Aden. They were riding on Mahri and Arhabi camels with wooden saddles. They were reciting the following verses:

Hamdan has the best of princes and of subjects;
It has no equal in the universe.

High is its position, and from it come warriors and chiefs with goodly wealth therein.

Hassan b. Yaqub Hamdani is of the view that this deputation consisted of one hundred and twenty members.[59]

The Apostle wrote a letter for them and gave them several gifts.[60] The letter ran as follows: "To the district of Kharif and the people of the high country and the sand hills with their envoy Dhu'l-Mish'ar Malik b. Namat and those of his people who are Muslims. theirs is the high ground and the low ground so long as they perform prayer and pay zakat they may eat its fodder and pastures on its herbage. For this they have God's promise and the guarantee of His Apostle and their witnesses are the Emigrants and the Helpers."

Malik b. Uz was appointed their leader by the Holy Prophet

23. Kinanah Deputation:

This tribe was closely allied to the Quraish politically and by blood, besides the star Aldobaran, it served the goddess 'Uzza', represented by a tree, at Nakhla. When the Apostle was about to leave for Tabuk, Wathla b. Al-Asqah came to him and embraced Islam. Then he returned to his relatives. His father became angry with him but his sister accepted his invitation. Now Wathla marched out towards Tabuk. The Holy Prophet sent him to Ukaider with Khalid b. Walid where he took part in the fighting.

24. Thaqif Deputation:

This deputation visited Medina in Ramadan 9 A.H. Urwa b. Mas'ud was the first Thaqifite to embrace Islam after the battle of Hawazin. Urwa had acted as the plenipotentiary of the Quraish at the time of Treaty of Hudaibiya. After embracing Islam he desired to preach Islam among his people. The Holy Prophet warned him that his people would fight with him.[61] But Urwa replied that he was dearest to them than their first born. Upon his insistence the Apostle allowed him. He immediately ran among the bigoted of his city to call them to Islam. The next day his people took counsel among themselves and killed Urwa while he was praying.

His blood blossomed and after some time a deputation

visited Medina in 9 A.H. under the leadership of Abdu Yalil. It consisted of nineteen members.[62] Notable among the members were Kinanah b. Abdu Yalil, Rabia b. Abdu Yalil, Shurjil b. Ghaylan, Hakm b. Amr, Uthman b. Abu'l-'As and Numayr b. Kharasha. Abdu Yalil took these persons as a precautionary measure as he feared that on his return he would meet the same end as that of Urwa. But each man on his return could secure the attention of his clan.

In Medina they stayed in Qanat where they found Mughira b. Shu'ba who ran to inform the Apostle. On his way he met Abu Bakr whom he informed that the Thaqifites intended to accept Islam provided that they could get a document guaranteeing their people and their lands and their animals. Abu Bakar implored Mughira to let him be the first to tell the Apostle about the news. Mughira agreed and Abu Bakr informed the Apostle about the arrival of the deputation of Thaqif. Meanwhile Mughira returned to the deputation and spent the time there until evening. During this time he taught them how to salute the Apostle but when they went to him they did not act upon his advice.[63] A tent was pitched for them near the mosque so that they could hear the recitation of the Holy Quran.[64]

Khalid b. Saeed acted as intermediary between them and the Apostle. The parleys continued till they got a document from the Apostle. It was written by Khalid b. Saeed. During this time when meal was served, the members of the deputation would not eat until Khalid ate some.[65] They begged for a short respite for Lat, undestroyed for three years. But the Apostle refused. They requested for a year or two. But the Holy Prophet was immovable. Finally they asked for a month after their return home but this request was again turned down. Anyhow the Apostle agreed to this extent that Abu Sufyan b. Harb and Mughira b. Shu'ba would accompany them to smash the idol. ('Al-Mughira assembled the Ta'ifites to see the ceremonious destruction of the fetish, and after giving the first blow feigned to suffer'[66]). Similarly the deputation begged for a remission of some of the daily prayers. The apostle replied that there could be no good in the religion in which there was no prayer.[67] Then they asked that they should be excused from Jihad and Zakat. The Apostle accepted it and told his Companions that they would perform these two injunctions gradually under the influence of Islam. It is remarkable that before the death of the Holy Prophet they began paying Zakat, and after some time they sent contingents of armed volunteers to Medina, to participate in suppressing the rebellion of apostates that had broken out in certain regions.

The Holy Prophet appointed Uthman b. Al-'As over them. Mughira b. Shu'ba (a nephew of Urwa) and Abu Sufyan accompanied the deputation to their territory where Mughira smote Lat with an axe amidst uproarious cries of despair and grief from the women of Tayef.[68] The jewell beeds and gold which Mughira thus collected settled the debts of Urwa and Aswad by the orders of the Apostle.[69]

25. Asad Deputation:

This tribe was apparently closest to the Quraish. It worshipped Mercury. Its deputation of ten persons came to the Holy Prophet in 9 A.H. Prominent among them were Wabsa b. Ma'bad, Talha b. Khuwaylid,, Hadhrami b. Amir, Drar b. Al-Azdr, Qatada b. Al-Qayif, Salma b. Juraysh, and Naqda b. Abdullah b. Khalaf. At the time of the arrival of the deputation the Apostle was in the mosque. The people of the Bani Asad were as proud as the common Arab of those days. Hadhrami b. Amir told the Holy Prophet that they bore witness to Oneness of God and his apostolate despite the fact that he did not send any representative to them. Moreover, they had come themselves. It was at this time that the following verse was revealed:[70]

> "They impress on thee as a favour that they have embraced Islam. Say, 'Count not your Islam as a favour upon me, nay God has conferred a favour upon you that He has guided you to the Faith, if ye be true and sincere.' "

The members of the deputation asked about the languages of animals and omens. The Apostle forbade them from this. Then they asked about geomancy which the

Apostle said to be a knowledge no doubt.

Ibn Sa'd thinks that some people of Bani Al-Zinah were also with this deputation who were the descendants of Malik b. Malik b. Tha'laba b. Dudan.[71] During the caliphate of Abu Bakr a man named Talha b. Khwalid claimed to be a prophet. He belonged to Bani Asad.

26. Fazarah Deputation:

A deputation of Bani Fazarah came to the Apostle after his return from Tabuk in 9 A.H./January 631. To Hafiz Ibn Qayyim the number of the members of the deputation was more than ten.[72] But Ibn Sa'd tells that they werenineteen in number.[73] They were riding on weak camels. Prominent among them were Kharijah b. Hisn and Hurr b. Qays. Latter is described by Hafiz Ibn Qayyim as Hassan Qais.[74] They were the brother and nephew of Uyyania b. Hiseen respectively. Their boarding arrangements were made at Ramlah daughter of Al-Harith's house. They accepted Islam. The Apostle enquired of them about their territory. They told that cattle had died due to drought and the gardens had become barren. So they had to face starvation. The Holy Prophet prayed for them on their request. It rained torrently for six days and it stopped when the Apostle prayed.

27. Dhi Murra Deputation:

A deputation consisting of thirteen persons headed by Harith b. Auf came to the Apostle on his return from Tabuk in 9 A.H. Harith revealed to him that they were the descendants of Luwy b. Ghalib so had relation with him. He smiled and asked where had they left their family? They replied that it was stationed at Silah. Then he asked about their country. They requested for rain-prayer as there was drought. The Apostle prayed for them and asked Bilal to give ten *auqias* silver to each of them and twelve *auqias* to Harith. The deputation stayed for some days in Medina and on their return to their country they saw that it had rained and there was fertility everywhere.

28. Kilab Deputation:

It visited Medina in 9 A.H. and consisted of thirteen men. Prominent among them were Labid b. Rabia and Jabbar b. Salma. They were boarded at the house of Ramlah daughter of Al-Harith. As Jabbar and Ka'b b. Malik had friendly relations therefore he gave some gifts to Jabbar and entertained them. He escorted them to the Holy Prophet to whom they saluted. They told him that they had embraced Islam through Dahhak b. Sufyan who had gone there to preach Islam on behalf of the Holy Prophet.

29. Qasheer b. Ka'b Deputation:

A deputation of Bani Qasheer came to the Holy Prophet before the Farewell Pilgrimage and after the battle of Hunain. Notable among them were Thaur b. Urwa, Qarata b. Hibara and Hayda b. Mu'awiya. The Holy Prophet gave Thaur a piece of land and a letter.[75] He gave Qarata a sheet of cloth and ordered for his appointment as Zakat-collector of his people.[76]

30. Bani Al-Bakka Deputation:

This deputation visited Medina in 9 A.H. and it consisted of three persons. They were: Mu'awiya b. Thaur, Bishr b. Mu'awiya and Fajih b. 'Abdullah.[77] The Apostle entertained them and gave them white sheep.[78] Besides he gave Fajih the following letter:[79]

> "From Muhammad to Fajih and his followers who embrace Islam, keep up prayers, give zakat, submit to Allah and His Apostle, give fifth of booty for Allah, help the Apostle of Allah and his companions, bear witness to Islam and leave the polytheists, they are in the custody of Allah and Muhammad."

31. Baihraa Deputation:

This deputation consisted of thirteen persons and it came in 9 A.H. from Yemen. They drove their ridings till they stopped in front of the house of Miqdad b. Amr in Bani Jizila Mohalla. Miqdad received them and entertained them with Haish.[80] Miqdad sent some food for the Apostle who took a little and returned the remaining. Now Miqdad presented the same dish at both times to these people but it was still sufficient. When the members of the deputation asked the reason, Miqdad told them that it was due to the fingers of the Holy Prophet which had touched the meal.[81] Upon this the members of the deputation embraced Islam immediately. On next day Miqdad escorted them to the Apostle.[82] They stayed for a few days in Medina and on their return the Apostle gave them some gifts.[83]

32. Taye Deputation:

Bani Tayi belonged to the Persian sphere of influence rather than the Byzantine. This tribe used to worship Canopus. Its deputation visited Medina in 9 A.H. under the leadership of Zaydu'l Khayl. It consisted of fifteen members. Notable among them were Wazr b. Jabir, Qabisa b. Al-Aswad, Malik b. Abdullah and Qa'een b. Jadilah. They met the Holy Prophet in the mosque. They embraced Islam on the invitation of the Holy Prophet who named Zaydu'l Khayl as Zaydu'l Khayr.[84] On their return the Holy Prophet gave each one of them five *auqia* and Zayd twelve and a half *auqia* silver. Moreover, he allotted to him Fayd and some lands with it and gave him a deed accordingly.[85] Zayd died of fever at Farda.[86] His wife tore the deed into pieces and burnt it in the fire.[87]

Later on the Holy Prophet sent Ali in the company of two hundred[88] cavalrymen to destroy the idol "Nabit" of this tribe. It was in July/August 630. He did so and brought with him several captives among whom was Sufana, daughter of Hatim Tayi. Adi made his way to Syria. Medina released all the captives. Sufana proceeded to her home and told her brother of the nobleness of Muhammad (P.B.U.H.) Adi hastened to Medina to embrace Islam. In Medina he was astonished to see the faithfulness of the Muslims and preparedness for Jihad. He could not decide whether Muhammad was a king or prophet. At the same time a free woman came with a certain problem and the Apostle immediately went with her to help her. On his return, he asked Adi:

"Adi! Perhaps you do not accept Islam because the Muslims are not rich. By God! I am sure that the time is not far off when there will be abundance of wealth among the Muslims and there will not be anybody to take it (even by search). Moreover, you don't embrace Islam because you see the enemy is in large number and the Muslims in lesser numbers. By God! (I am sure) that time is not far off when you will hear that a woman shall travel on a camel all alone from Qadisya and go to see the *Bait'ullah* without any danger. Perhaps you don't embrace Islam because the Muslims are not the rulers. By God! (I am sure) that the time is not far off when you will hear that the Muslims had conquered the white palaces of Babylonia."[89]

Upon this Adi embraced Islam and the Holy Prophet appointed him the alms collector of his people.

33. Tujeeb Deputation:

This deputation consisted of thirteen persons and it visited Medina in 9 A.H.[90] Its members brought with them the amount of alms due to them. The Holy Prophet advised them to take them back and distribute the amount among the destitutes of their people. They submitted that it was balance after such distribution. They were very much anxious to go back to tell their people about the teachings of Islam and at the same time keen to learn them. On their return every one of them was given presents.[91] The Holy Prophet asked them that had there been left anyone from among them? He came to know that a boy was there with their luggage. He asked them to send for him. That boy came and requested, "You, O Apostle have been kind to the representatives of my nation. Kindly give me something."

The Apostle asked him, "What is your need?" He replied, "Pray for my remission and God make my heart rich." The Apostle prayed for him and gave him gifts.[92]

In 10 A.H. the Holy Prophet went to perform pilgrimage. In Mina sixteen persons belonging to Tujeeb met him. He enquired them of that boy. They told that they had not seen anyone more contented than that boy.[93] Upon this the Holy Prophet wished that everyone of them should meet his end like this.[94]

When after the death of the Holy Prophet there was apostacy it was only due to the efforts of this youth that none apostatized in Yemen.[95]

34. Harith b. Ka'b Deputation:

In Rabiu'l Awwal 10 A.H.[96] the Holy Prophet sent Khalid b. Walid to Najran to preach Islam. Four hundred persons accompanied him. He directed him to invite people thrice to accept Islam before fighting.[97] These people embraced Islam and when the Holy Prophet was informed about this he summoned a deputation of them in Medina.[98]

Khalid himself escorted their deputation to Medina. Prominent among its members were: Qays b. Al-Haseen Dhu'l-Qussa, Yazid b. Abdul M'adan, Abdullah b. Abdul M'adan, Yazid b. Muhajjil, Abdullah b. Qurad, Shaddad b. Abdullah Al-Qanani, Amr b. Abdullah.[99] They lodged with Khalid. They had conquered those who fought with them in the pagan period. The Holy Prophet enquired of them its reason. They told that they were united and had no dissentients and never begun injustice. The Apostle, appointed Qays b. Al-Husayn their leader.[100] He gave each of them ten *auqia* and to Qays b. Al-Husayn twelve and a half *aquia* of silver.[101] The deputation returned to their country towards the end of Shawwal.[102]

35. Khulan Deputation:

This deputation consisted of ten persons and it visited

Medina in Sha'ban 10 A.H. They told that they were the representatives of their people and had travelled on camels' backs for Muhammad's sake. The Apostle told them that whosoever visited Medina to see him would be his neighbour on the Day of Resurrection.[103]

The Holy Prophet asked about Umm-i-Anas (an idol which they worshipped). They replied, "It was the cause of a great evil for us. There was drought. A share for Umm-i-Anas was taken out of cattle and agricultural products. Once we slaughtered one hundred oxes in one day for it and left the meat for beasts ignoring our own dire need for it." They continued and said, "Now only one old man and an old woman adhere to it but we, on our return, will demolish it."[104] The Apostle advised them particularly to:

i) fulfil the promise;
ii) always return the deposits for custody;
iii) best treatment with the neighbours; and
iv) not to oppress anybody.

The deputation stayed at the house of Ramlah daughter of Al-Harith. On its return, each member was given twelve and a half *auqia* of silver.[105] First thing which they did on reaching their land was to demolish Umm-i-Anas.[106] During their stay in Medina they told the Apostle "We used to take our disputes to Umm-i-Anas and it spoke." The Apostle said that they were the devils which spoke to them.[107]

36. Amir Deputation:

This deputation visited Medina in Ramadan 10 A.H. It consisted of ten persons.[108] It stayed for a few days in Medina to learn the injunctions of Islam.

37. Ghamid Deputation:

This deputation visited Medina in Ramadan 10 A.H. It consisted of ten men. The arrangements for its boarding were made at Baqih Al-Gharqad. When its members came to the Holy Prophet, he enquired whom they had made the custodian of their luggage? They replied that a young boy was left behind. The Apostle told them that after their departure he had gone to sleep and a thief made off with a horse-bag. One of them said that the horse-bag belonged to him. Now the Apostle told that he should not be anxious as the boy had awakened and he made noise and thus the thief was caught red-handed.

When these people returned the boy narrated the same incident. Upon this they embraced Islam alongwith that boy. Ubbay b. Ka'b taught them the Holy Quran. The Apostle gave them a deed in which the injunctions of Islam were written. He gave them gifts on their return as usual.[109]

38. Ghassan Deputation:

It consisted of three members[110] and it visited Medina in Ramadan 10 A.H. It stayed at the house of Ramlah daughter of Al-Harith. The members embraced Islam. The Holy Prophet gave them gifts on their departure.[111] On their return to their country they invited their people to Islam but they could not make any headway.

39. Salaman Deputation:

This deputation visited Medina in Shawwal 10 A.H./ January, 632 A.C. It comprised of seven persons among whom Habib b. Amr was prominent. They embraced Islam. They asked, "Which is the best act?" The Apostle told them, "To say prayer in time." They complained that drought had struck their land and requested him to pray for rain. The Apostle raised his hands in supplication. The deputation stayed for three days in Medina. On its return, the Apostle gave each member five *auqia* of silver.[112] Bilal excused that as there was not abundance of silver so they could not be given more than this.[113] The deputation on their return found their lands irrigated with a plentiful rain which had fallen on the day of the prayer.[114]

40 Ubas Deputation:

This deputation visited Medina in 10 A.H. It consisted of Maisra b. Masrooq, Harith b. Al-Rabeeh, Qinan b. Darm, Bashir b. Al-Harith, Farwah b. Al-Haseen, Abdullah b. Malik, Hadm b. Masa'da, Sibah b.Zayd and Abu'l Hasan b. Luqman. They embraced Islam. The Apostle appointed Talha b. Ubaidulla, over them as *ushr* collector and gave him a standard. Three of them came to the Apostle later on, and told him that they had sold their property and cattle for migration so that their conversion to Islam might be completed. The Holy Prophet told them that they should fear God wherever they lived.

41. Muharib Deputation:

Comprising of ten persons this deputation visited Medina in 10 A.H./631 A.C. Prominent among them were Sawa b. Al-Harith and his son Khazima. They were the representatives of their nation. They were made to stay at the house of Ramlah daughter of Al-Harith and Bilal was appointed their minister-in-waiting.

This tribe was very harsh in its treatment with the Holy Prophet when he used to preach among tribes. Now the Holy Prophet recognized one of them who had been very rude to him but he forgave him. That person asked the Apostle for his remission. The Holy Prophet replied, "Islam cancels all the sins of the pagan days."

42. Azud Deputation:

This deputation visited Medina in 10 A.H. and it consisted of nineteen persons. Prominent among the members were Ṣurad b. Abdullah. It lodged with Farwah b. Amr for ten days. Surad became a good Muslim. The Apostle put him in command of those of his people who had accepted Islam. He instructed him to preach among the tribes of Yemen. On their way back they stayed in Jurash where they invited the people to embrace Islam. When they refused, they besieged Jurash. The siege continued for one month without any success and at last the Muslims lifted the siege. The people of Jurash took it as the defeat of the Muslims and pursued them. A severe fight took place but the Muslims were successful

Now the people of Jurash sent two men to Medina. The Apostle told them the victory of Surad.[115] On their return they narrated the whole account to their people. Now a deputation comprising of seven men visited Medina. The Holy Prophet was pleased to see their manners and style. He said to them, "You are good in look, true in meeting, pious in conversation and great in trust. You are mine and I am yours."[116] They replied, "O Apostle of Allah! We have fifteen characteristics:[117] Five characteristics are those for which your preachers asked us to believe in, viz;

1. Belief in Allah;
2. Belief in angels;
3. Belief in heavenly books;
4. Belief in the prophets; and
5. Belief in the Hereafter.

"We have been advised to act upon the following:

1. To say that there is no god but Allah;
2. To keep up the prayers five times a day;
3. To pay Zakat;
4. To keep the fasts during the month of Ramadan;
5. To perform the *Haj* (incumbent upon a man of means).

Following five things we knew before embracing Islam:

1. To thank God in prosperity;
2. To be contented in distress;
3. To be patient in troubles;
4. To contend with fate; and
5. Not to be happy over the loss of the enemy."

The Holy Prophet further advised them to inculcate five characteristics:[118]

1. Don't collect those things which you have not to eat;
2. Don't construct that house in which you have not to live;
3. Don't compete in those things which you have to leave the next time;
4. Trust in God before Whom you have to be present; and
5. Like those things which will be useful for you in the Hereafter where you will live for ever.

These people fully acted upon his instructions. The Holy Prophet demarked their areas for limitation and protection purposes.[119]

43. Kinda Deputation:

A deputation of Kinda comprising of nineteen men[120] visited Medina in 10 A.H. under the leadership of Al-Ash'ath b. Qays. They had combed their locks and blackened their eyes with kohl and they wore striped bordered with silk.[121] When the Holy Prophet asked them not to wear such dress they tore it off and threw it away.[122] On their return he gave each member ten and to Ash'ath twelve *auqia* of silver.[123] Kinda deputation had come in the company of Hadramut deputation.[124]

44. Hadramut Deputation:

This deputation visited Medina in 10 A.H. Its members were the descendants of Waliah. Their leaders Jamad,[125] Makhus and Mashrah were also with them. They embraced Islam. Makhus complained of his stammering and requested for prayer. The Holy Prophet prayed for him and gave some grains to the members out of the annual products of Hadramut.[126]

Makhus's face was paralysed on way to Hadramut. Some persons came back and enquired of the Apostle its cure. He asked them to take a hot needle and turn both the eyelids of Makhus, and he will be cured. He, further, asked them what had they uttered at the time of their departure.[127]

Makhus was cured with this treatment.

45. Hanifah Deputation;

This deputation consisted of nineteen persons and it visited Medina in 10 A.H./632 A.C. It was headed by Salama b. Hanzala.[128] Other prominent persons were Rajal b. Unfuh, Talaq b. Ali, Hamran b. Jabir, Ali b. Sanan, Aqhas b. Salama, Zaid b. Amr and Musailma b. Habib commonly known as Musailma the Liar.

The deputation was lodged in the house of Ramlah daughter of Al-Harith. They were served with two times meals.[129] During their stay they learnt the Holy Quran from Ubbay b. Ka'b. Each member was given five *auqia* of silver on return.[130] In addition, the Holy Prophet gave them a leather bag for carrying water in which there was a small quantity of water left after his ablution. He instructed them to demolish their idol-temple and construct there a mosque after washing that place with this water.[131] They executed his instructions.

After some time Musailma claimed to be a prophet in Yammama. He acknowledged Muhammad (P.B.U.H.), too, as a prophet because he wanted to save himself from the opposition of the local Muslims. Talaq endorsed his prophethood. It was in the caliphate of Hadrat Abu Bakr that a force was sent against this false prophet and he was killed by Wahshi.[132]

46. Najran Deputation:

Najran was situated at a distance of one hundred and fifty miles in north of San'a. It was a centre of Christianity and the Christians used to come here for pilgrimage from far off places.

Two deputations from Najran visited Medina in 10 A.H. Before this the Apostle had invited the people of Najran to embrace Islam. When the bishop read the letter from Medina he sent for Shurahbil b. Wadah as their national problems were not settled without him.[133] He asked his opinion who told him that God had promised Abraham to cherish his generation with prophethood. He further said that it was quite possible that he might be the same person. But at the same time he told that he had no opinion about prophethood. Now the bishop sent for Abdullah b. Shurahbil who gave the same opinion. This person was a notable of Humayar. Then he summoned Jabbar b. Qays, a notable of Bani Harith b. Ka'b, who was also agreed upon with the formers.

Now a conch was rung on his orders to assemble all the people of the valley.[134] The bishop informed the assembled populace about the problem. All agreed upon that Shurahbil b. Wadah, Abdullah b. Shurahbil and Jabbar b. Qays should visit Medina and collect information.

Subsequently the deputation went to Medina. When it reached in the suburbs of Medina, the three members of the deputation clad themselves in silk garments and put gold rings on their fingers. Then they came to the Holy Prophet and saluted him but he did not reply.[135] The members of the deputation had acquaintance with Hadrat Othman b. Affan and Abdul Rehman due to trading so they turned towards them. Both these gentlemen told them that their precious dress was the cause of the displeasure of the Holy Prophet, and advised them to change their dress.[136] They acted upon their advice and then visited the Apostle. He replied their salutation.[137] After this the parleys took place. The members of the deputation enquired of his opinion about Christ. Upon this Allah sent down the following:[138]

> "The similitude of Jesus before God is as that of Adam; He created him from dust, then said to him: "Be": And he was. The Truth (comes) from God alone; so be not of those who doubt. If any one disputes in this matter with thee, now after (full) knowledge hath come to thee, say: "Come! let us gather together, – our sons and your sons, our women and your women, ourselves and yourselves: then let us earnestly pray, and invoke the curse of God on those who lie!"

The members of the deputation refused to admit these verses therefore the Apostle took Hasan and Hussain in his lap for *Mobahalah.*[139] Fatima, his daughter, also came and stood behind him. Now Shurahbil said to his companions, "Had this man been a king the Arabs would have reproached him first of all and his message could not reach us. Furthermore, cruel people would have been his advisers. And if this man is an apostle, we will be annihilated completely after his curse."[140]

After consultation with his companions, Shurahbil told the Holy Prophet that they did not want to resort to cursing. He further asked him to decide what was better for them.[141] Next day, the Holy Prophet wrote a peace-treaty for them.

After the return of this deputation, came another deputation from Najran. It consisted of sixty persons.[142] Prominent among them were Abu'l Harith,[143] Al-Ayham,[144] and Abdul Masih.[145] In addition to them twenty-four famous chiefs were also included in this deputation.[146] These people reached Medina in the late afternoon and began to pray facing towards the east. Some Muslims tried to prevent them from this but the Holy Prophet let them continue.[147]

Some Jews also came to see these people. One of them said that Abraham was a Jew. In reply a Christian said, "No he was a Christian." Upon this Allah sent down the following verses:[148]

> "Ye people of the Book! Why dispute ye about Abraham, when the Law and the Gospel were not revealed till after him? Have ye no understanding? Ah! Ye are those who fell to disputing (even) in matters of which ye had some knowledge! But why dispute ye in matters of which ye have no knowledge? It is God Who knows, and ye who know not! Abraham was not a Jew nor yet a Christian; but he was true in Faith, and bowed his will to God's (which is Islam), and he joined not gods with God, without doubt, among men, the nearest of kin to Abraham are those who follow him, as are also this Apostle and those who believe: and God is the Protector of those who have faith."

One of the Jews asked the Apostle, "Do you want that we should worship you as the Christians worship Christ? Upon this one member of the Najran deputation repeated the same question. The Apostle replied, "I seek protection of Allah if I worship anybody other than Allah or I order to worship anybody other than Allah."

On their return the Holy Prophet gave them a deed. The members of the deputation requested that an able man should be sent with them to do justice. Consequently Abu Ubaida b. Jarrah was sent with them and due to his efforts whole of Najran was blessed with justice.

47. Aish Deputation:

This deputation visited Medina four months before the death of the Holy Prophet. Its members asked, "We have heard that you, O Apostle of Allah, have ordered that Islam is not perfected without migration. We have property and cattle too. But if there is no perfection of Islam without migration then is there any benefit of these things? We have sold them and have come to Medina." The Holy Prophet replied, "Wherever you are settled now remain there as you are and do action for pleasure of Allah."

They learnt the teachings of Islam for a few days and then returned to their country.

48. Zubayd Deputation:

This deputation visited Medina in 10 A.H. under the leadership of Amr b. Ma'di Karb. It consisted of ten persons. It was lodged with Sa'd b. Ubada who entertained its members. Then they visited the Holy Prophet and embraced Islam. After some days they returned to their country. Each member was given gifts.[149] Banu Zubayd counterfeited Amr and embraced Islam. After the death of the Holy Prophet these people apostatized but again turned towards Islam.[150]

49. Waa'il b. Hajar Deputation:

In 10 A.H. Waa'il b. Hajar came from Hadramut and told the Holy Prophet that he had come to Medina for migration and conversion to Islam. He prayed for him and put his hand on his head. He was lodged with Mu'awiya and people were called to congregational prayer to celebrate the rejoicings of his arrival in Medina. On his return, the Apostle gave him the following deed:

> "This deed is from Muhammad (P.B.U.H.) to Waa'il b. Hajar, the king of Hadramut. It is stated that you embraced Islam. I have allotted to you the lands and forts which are at present in your possession. One tenth will be received from you fixed by a judge. I have this for you. You should not reduce it. The Prophet and the Muslims are your helpers until the religion remains."[151]

50. 'Amir b. Sa'sa'ah Deputation:

The tribe of 'Amir b. Sa'sa'ah was a part of Hawazin. A deputation consisting of 'Amir b. Tufayl, Arbad b. Rabia[152] and Hayyan b. Muslim[153] came to Medina in 10 A.H. These people belonged to Banu 'Amir. They were evil doers. 'Amir intended to assassinate the Holy Prophet treacherously.154 During his meeting with him 'Amir asked him to hand over the government to him after his death. The Holy Prophet said, "It is neither for you nor for your nation. It is upto Allah to give it whom He likes." Now 'Amir asked, "All right you give me the forests and plains and appropriate for yourself the populated areas and cities." The Holy Prophet told it was impossible and said, "I give you the necks of horses because you are a good rider." When 'Amir heard this he said sternly, "By God I will fill the land against you with horses and men."[155]

Saying this 'Amir turned away. The Holy Prophet prayed, "O Allah, guide'Amir."and make Islam fearless of 'Amir."

Amir was still on his way to home that he suffered from plague in his neck. A thunder bolt consumed Arbad and his camel.

After this incident his rival 'Alqama b. Ulatha, Hodha b. Khalid alongwith his son came to Medina and embraced Islam. 'On the whole Muhammad was successful in winning 'Amir b. Sa'sa'ah to his side. They do not seem to have become Muslims, however, until comparatively late, and then only a few.'[156]

51. Sa'd Hudhaim Deputation:

Bani Sa'd Hudhaim belonged to the tribe of Quza'ah. When this deputation came to Medina, the Holy Prophet was leading a funeral prayer. These people sat aside and when the Apostle was free he asked them that were they Muslims? They replied in affirmation. Now he asked them that why had they not taken part in the funeral prayer of their religious brother? They replied that they thought that before homage to him they were not entitled to do anything.

The Holy Prophet told them, "You are Muslims from the time you embraced Islam." On their return he ordered Bilal to give each of them some *auqias* of silver. He, further, directed them to appoint a chief from among themselves.

The whole tribe embraced Islam due to the efforts of these people.

52. *Rawa'as b. Kalab Deputation:*

'Amr b. Malik came to Medina and embraced Islam. On his return, he preached Islam among his people but his nation had enemity with Bani Aqeel b. Ka'b and it did not want to embrace Islam before taking vengeance. Even 'Amr b. Malik went to take revenge and he killed a man named Rabia. His companions drove with them the cattle of Bani Aqeel, Now 'Amr b. Malik was repentant, he tied his hand with his neck and came to the Holy Prophet. When he was informed he said, "If 'Amr b. Malik comes to me, I will indeed strike upon his collar."[157]

Now 'Amr b. Malik untied his hand and came to the Apostle and saluted him. But the Holy Prophet turned over his face. 'Amr b. Malik went from the right side and the Apostle again turned over his face. Now he went from the left side and said humbly, "If Allah is supplicated He is pleased. Allah may be pleased with you, you should be pleased with me." Now the Holy Prophet was pleased with him.

53. *Jathan Deputation:*

Prominent among the members of this deputation was Abu Wahab Al-Jathani. The deputation enquired of a local-made wine of Yemen. The Apostle asked them, "Is one intoxicated by it?" They replied, "Yes, if taken in abundance." The Apostle said, "Then its small quantity is unlawful because every thing which intoxicates is unlawful."

54. *Aqeel b. Ka'b Deputation:*

Rabih b. Khafaja, Muttraf b. 'Abdullah, Anas b. Qays were included in the first deputation of Aqeel b. Ka'b. They embraced Islam. The Holy Prophet gave them the following deed written on red leather:[158]

> "In the name of Allah, the Most Merciful and Compassionate. It is a document which Muhammad, the Apostle of Allah, has given to Rabih, Muttraf and Anas. Uqiq[159] has been given to them provided they keep up prayer, give zakat and remain submissive."

After this Laqeet b. 'Amar visited Medina and paid homage on behalf of his people. The Holy Prophet gave him a watering place named Nazeem. After sometime Abu Harb b. Khwailid came, whom the Holy Prophet invited to accept Islam. He said, "Let me draw lots by casting arrows." He did it thrice and then embraced Islam. Last of all his brother Uqal came to Medina and embraced Islam.

55. *Ju'da Deputation:*

Raqad b. 'Amr came to Medina as the representative of his people. The Holy Prophet gave him a property in addition to a document.[160]

56 *Hilal Deputation:*

It consisted of Abd Auf b. Isram, Qabisa b. Al-Makhraq

and Zayad b. Abdullah. The Apostle enquired of the name of Abd Auf and on his reply said that he was Abdullah. Qabisa b. Al-Makharaq requested for monetary help as he was indebted. The Apostle promised him some money when the Zakat would be received.[161]

57. *Ju'fi Deputation :*

It consisted of Qays b. Salamah and Salamah b. Yazid. Both embraced Islam. The Apostle enquired of them, "Don't you eat heart?" They admitted. The Apostle said, "To consider lawful as unlawful is incomplete Islam." Then he sent for roasted heart and gave Salama b. Yazid to eat. With trembling hands he ate.[162] He gave a document to Qays b. Salamah by which he was appointed administrator of his people, 'those who perform the worship, give the zakat, and contribute *sadaqa* of their wealth and purify it.'

Then they said, "Our mother, Maleeka, used to liberate the captives and feed the indigents but she buried one of her girls alive. Tell us in what condition she will be now?" The Apostle told them that she would be in the hell. Upon this they were displeased, they got up and went away saying, "The man, who made us to eat heart and informed us that our mother will be in hell does not deserve obedience."[163] They met a companion of the Holy Prophet on their way who was coming with some camels of the zakat collection, they tied him with a rope and drove away the camels.[164]

After some time Yazid b. Malik visited Medina alongwith his two sons - - - Barra and Aziz. They embraced Islam. They also belonged to the Ju'fi tribe. The Apostle changed the name of Aziz to Abdu'l Rehman and conferred upon him the valley of Hurdan.[165]

58. *Bani Muntafiq Deputation:*

This deputation consisted of Laqeet b. 'Amir and Naheek b. Aasim.[166] They met the Holy Prophet at the morning prayer. On the enquiry of Laqeet, the Apostle told them that five things are known to Allah alone: death, child in the abdomen, time of the rainfall, what to happen tomorrow and the time of the Resurrection. They pledged to keep up prayer, give zakat and not to associate anybody with Allah.

Laqeet asked, "Will we both have authority in East and West?" Upon this the Apostle drew back his hand and said that how could he bargain on such a thing which Allah was not going to give them.[167] Laqeet replied, "I may go wherever I like. There may not be any check except his intention and soul." Now the Apostle pulled out his hand and took their pledge. He also discussed with them the topics like Resurrection, Paradise, Hell, Prophets and the Ancients.

59. *Tariq b. Abdullah Deputation:*

Tariq b. Abdullah used to narrate that one day he was standing in the market of 'Ukkaz that all of a sudden a man came there. He was saying loudly that "O people! say that there is no god but Allah. You will get happiness." At the same time another man appeared on the scene who was throwing stones at him saying, "O people, don't confirm him, he is a liar."

Tariq enquired of the two. Both belonged to Bani Hashim: One was Muhammad who claimed to be a prophet and the other was his uncle - - - Abdul Uzza.

Tariq continued and said, "After several years we went from Abza to Medina to purchase dates. With the intention of changing our dress we stayed in the suburbs of Medina. In the meantime a man, who had worn ordinary dress, came and after salutation asked us from where had we come from? We told him our intention and further told that we had a red camel with us. That man asked would we sell that camel? The reply was in affirmation."

Now that man held the string of the camel and marched towards the city. When he disappeared, we were repentant that we had handed over the camel without getting its price. In the caravan there was a lady sitting in a litter who at once uttered that there was such a gleam on his face as if moonlight. If that man does not pay the price, I will pay it."[168]

Tariq continued to narrate the incident and said, "We

were still busy in discussion that a man came and told that he had been sent by the Apostle of Allah who had given dates as the price of the camel in addition to the dates for your feast. He, further, asked us to weigh the dates of the price of the camel. We ate the dates and then weighed the remaining dates.[169] When we were satiated, we entered the city. At that time the Apostle was sitting in the mosque and he asked us "Give alms, it is better for you. It is good to give than to take."

Tariq and his companions embraced Islam.

60. Bakr b. Waa'il Deputation:

It consisted of Bashir b. Al-khasasitah, Abdullah b. Martad, Hassan b. Hawt and Abdullah b. Aswad. The latter lived in Yammama from where he migrated to Medina after selling out his property. He brought a provision-box made of dates-wood for the Holy Prophet who prayed for his safety and prosperity.

61. Taghlib Deputation:

The Taghlibites had established themselves in Mesopotamia. Their deputation consisted of sixteen Muslims and Christians. They were boarded at the house of Ramlah daughter of Al-Harith. The Christians had put golden crosses on their chests. The Holy Prophet concluded a peace-treaty with the Christians on the condition that they might remain Christians but would not teach their descendants Christianity. He gave the Muslim members some gifts on their return.

62. Sheeban Deputation:

Qeela daughter of Makhrama was married with Habib b. Azhar who died in the early days of Islam. Her two daughters were snatched by Aswab b. Azhar, her husband's younger brother. Now Qeela went out in search of the Holy

Prophet. At the time of her departure, her daughter Hudaibah began to weep so she took her with her. Aswab snatched her forcibly. Qeela went to her sister's house who was married in the tribe of Sheeban. One night she overheard the conversation of her brother-in-law and sister who were thinking of marrying Qeela with Hureeth b. Hasban Al-Sheebani who used to go to the Holy Prophet as a representative of Bakr b. Wa'il. Qeela searched out Hureeth and went to the Holy Prophet in his company. She requested him to write a document concerning a place known as Dahna which might forbid the people except the travellers or neighbourers to proceed beyond this place. When the Holy Prophet ordered to write a document for Qeela, she spoke out, "This is my country and my home. But Bani Tamim also reap advantage from it." When the Holy Prophet heard it, he stopped the deed to be written and said, "Muslims are brethren unto one another. Water and trees are for the utilization of the both."[170]

The Holy Prophet gave a document to Qeela and her daughters. It was written on the red leather. He had written: "They may not be deprived of their rights. They may not be forced to marry. Every Muslim is their protector. You women should also do good things and not resolve on mischief."[171]

63. Murad Deputation:

Farwah b. Musayk al-Muradi separated himself from the kings of Kinda and came to Medina where he lodged with Sa'd b. Ubada and learnt the injunctions of Islam. Shortly before Islam there had been a battle between Murad and Hamdan in which the former suffered a severe defeat. This battle was known as "Youm-ur-Rome."

When Farwah came to the Holy Prophet he asked him, "Are you upset at what befell your people on the day of al-Rome?"

Farwah replied, "Such a tribal defeat as that would distress any man."

The Apostle said, "If that were so Islam could bring them only good." Then he gave Farwah twelve *auqias* of silver, a camel of good line and a pair of Oman-made dress.[173] He was also appointed the governor over the tribes of Murad, Madhhij and Zubayd.[174] Khalid b. Saeed was sent with him as incharge of the Zakat. Farwah was also given a document in which were written duties regarding Zakat.

64. Sadaf Deputation:

It consisted of nineteen persons.[175] They came and sat in the mosque. The Apostle asked them were they Muslims? They replied in affirmation. Then the Apostle asked that why had they not saluted? Now they got up and saluted. He replied their salutation and asked them to sit down. Then he discussed with them the timings of prayers.

65. Kalb Deputation:

'Abd 'Amr b. Jabla and Aasim came to the Holy Prophet and embraced Islam. Then another deputation of Banu Kalb consisting of Haritha b. Qatan and Hamal b. Sa'dana visited Medina and embraced Islam. The Apostle gave a standard to Hamal b. Sa'dana and gave a document to Haritha b. Qatan.

66. Jarm Deputation:

Asqah b. Shuraih and Howda b. 'Amr came to Medina and embraced Islam. The Holy Prophet gave them a document. After it some other persons of the same tribe came and embraced Islam. They asked the Apostle that who should lead their prayers. He replied, "That person from among you should lead the prayers who has learnt the Holy Quran more than all of you." On their return, they appointed 'Amr b. Salma their Imam though he was much younger in age. 'Amr b. Salma used to say that he learnt the Holy Quran from the camel drivers.

67. Sa'd Al-Asheera Deputation :

A man named Dhabab of Sa'd Al-Asheera came to the Holy Prophet after smashing the idol[176] of the tribe and embraced Islam. He fought on the side of Hadrat Ali in the battle of Siffin.

68. Ans Deputation:

A man named Rabiah of this tribe came to the Apostle in the evening when he was taking his dinner. He also served him with the dinner. After taking dinner he saluted the Apostle who asked him, "Have you come due to greed or fear?"

Rabiah replied, "By God! You have not wealth for which I may covet. I live in such a city where your forces cannot reach so I should not be afraid of you. I have embraced Islam due to the fear of punishment of the Hereafter."

Rabiah stayed for a few days in Medina and on his return the Holy Prophet gave him travelling expenses.[177] He also advised him that in case of any disease he should take refuge in a nearby village. Rabiah was on his way to his home that he suffered from a severe fever. He took refuge in a nearby village and died there.

69. Aslam Deputation:

This deputation visited Medina under the leadership of 'Umaira b. Afsa. After embracing Islam the members requested the Holy Prophet to fix for them such a dignity that the people of Arabia should know their superiority. Accordingly he prayed to Allah for the safety of the Aslam. He also gave them a document in which there was mention of zakat.[178] It was written by Thabit b. Qays and Abu Ubaida b. Jarrah and Umar Farooq signed it as witnesses.

70. Mahra Deputation:

This deputation visited Medina under the leadership of Mahri b. Al-Baid and embraced Islam. The Holy Prophet gave the deputation a document. After some time Zuhair b. Qardam came to Medina. He also belonged to the same tribe. He embraced Islam. On his return, the Apostle gave him a document.

71. Himyar Deputation:

Malik b. Marat Al-Rahadi came to Medina in Ramadan 9 A.H. as the representative of the kings of Himyar. He was lodged with Bilal. On his return, the Holy Prophet gave him a document addressed to the Kings of Himyar in which the basic injunctions of Islam were mentioned.

72. Barq Deputation:

This deputation embraced Islam after its arrival in Medina. The Holy Prophet gave it a document in which he had written:

> "From Muhammad, the Apostle of Allah, to Barq. Neither their fruits will be cut nor cattle shall be grazed in winter or summer without their permission. Any Muslim who has no pasture or grass growing of itself for grazing happens to pass nearby will be the guest of Barq for three days. If ripen fruits of the Barq fall, a traveller will have the right to take it to satiate himself."

This document was written by Ubbay b. Ka'b and Abu Ubaida b. Jarrah and Hudaifah b. Al-Yamani signed it as witnesses.

73. Dareeyeen Deputation:

This deputation consisted of ten persons and it visited Medina after the expedition of Tabuk. Prominent among its members were Tamim, Naeem (both sons of Aus b. Kharja), Yazid b. Qays, Alfakh b. Numan, Jabla b. Malik, Abu Hind, Tayyab (both these were sons of Abdullah b. Razeen), Aziz, Hani b. Habib and Murra. The members embraced Islam. The Holy Prophet changed the names of Tayyab to Abdullah and Aziz to Abdur Rehman. Hani presented to the Holy Prophet a leather bag of wine, few horses and a golden-embroidered silky gown. He accepted horses and the gown but rejected the leather-bag.

Tamim requested to the Holy Prophet, "There is a nation of Rome in our neighbourhood. If Allah gives you victory over the country of Syria then give me their villages of Jara and Bait Ainum as gift." The Holy Prophet promised him the same.

74. Bajila Deputation:

In 10 A.H. Jareer b. Abdullah came to Medina with one hundred and fifty[179] men of his tribe. They embraced Islam and took the pledge. Jareer stayed with Farwah b. Amr Al-Biadi. The Holy Prophet asked him how were his tribesmen. He told him that the tribes had demolished their respective idols.

The Holy Prophet asked about Dhul Khalsa (an idol). Jareer replied that it was still there and by the will of Allah it soon would be got rid of. The Holy Prophet deputed him to perform this noble duty and gave him a standard. Jareer dismembered the idol with the help of his companions. Then he came back and informed the Apostle who prayed for him.

75. Azda'man Deputation:

With the efforts of 'Ala b. Hadrami a deputation of the people of Umman came to Medina. Prominent among its members was Asad b. Pabrah Al-Tahi. After being blessed they requested that a person should be sent with them to administer their affairs. So the Apostle sent Mudrak b. Khowt.

After this another deputation came to Medina under the leadership of Salama b. Ayaz. It enquired of the Apostle about his teachings. He told them that they should believe in the Oneness of Allah. Futhermore, he taught them other injunctions of Islam. He prayed for them and then they accepted Islam.

76. *Ghafiq Deputation:*

Juleejah b. Shajjar was the head of this deputation. He told the Holy Prophet that, "We are the middle-aged persons of our tribe. We have accepted Islam but our alms are lying in the plains."

The Apostle replied that they had the same rights and duties as other Muslims had. Upon this another member of the deputation said, "We pronounce belief in Allah and obedience to His Apostle."

77. *Madhhaj*[180] *Deputation:*

This deputation consisted of fifteen members and visited Medina in 10 A.H. It was boarded at the house of Ramlah daughter of Al-Harith. The Holy Prophet himself went to see the deputation.[181] The deputation presented a few gifts to the Holy Prophet including a horse known as Mirdaj.

78. *Khasa'm Deputation:*

After demolishing Dhulkhalsah (an idol) Ashas b. Zahr and Anas b. Mudrik came to Medina and embraced Islam.

79. *Tin'ah Deputation:*

There was a lady named Tainet d. of Kulaib in the Tin'ah tribe of Hadramut. She sent her son Kulaib b. Asad to Medina with a dress for the Holy Prophet. He embraced Islam after his arrival in Medina. At this time he was reciting some verses in which it was admitted that Muhammad was the same prophet who had been divinely inspired in Torah and the prophets had given good news about him.[182]

The Holy Prophet prayed for Kulaib.

80. Nukha Deputation:

It was the last deputation which visited Medina in the middle of Muharram in 11 A.H. from Yemen. It consisted of two hundred members. They were boarded at the house of Ramlah d. of Al-Harith. They had taken pledge through Mu'adh b. Jabal.[183] Dhurarah b. Amr was also included among them. He told his four dreams to the Apostle who interpreted them. This deputation came to affirm its conversion to Islam.

Before this deputation Artat b. Sharajil and Arqam had come to Medina who informed the Holy Prophet that their people had embraced Islam. Both of them converted to Islam and the Holy Prophet prayed for their welfare.

3

Relations Regarding Treaties

(A) Principles of Treaties

Before Islam there was the rule of arrogance and obstination. It was prevalent in thought and faith, collective relations and system of government. Actually infernal sentiments and heinous passions were active forces of the world. These were the basis of mutual relations. There was law of jungle everywhere. Everyone was afraid of others and no life was safe. As big fish eat small fish in the ocean and the beasts tear out other animals in the jungle, similar were the characteristics of the human life. In short, force and vengeance, violence and magnificence, and rapine and plunder were governing every aspect of human life.

These were the circumstances when Islam appeared on the scene. It taught to respect humanity. It invited mankind to unity other than disobedience and aggression. It was based on the feelings beyond that of nationality. It also preached justice and fraternity. The teachings of Islam were and still are exempted from the concept of kinsmen and strangers, unknown from the differentiation of friends and enemies, and free from the discrimination of vigorous and feebles. It is to this reality that the Holy Quran points out.[1]

> "O ye who believe! stand out firmly for God as witnesses to fair dealing, and let not the hatred of others to you make you swerve to wrong and depart from justice. Be just; that is next to piety and fear God."

And at another place it is said :[2]

> "O ye who believe! stand out firmly for justice, as witnesses to God, even as against yourselves, or your

parents, or your kin."

These were the two principles ––unity of mankind and frank practice in the light of which the principles of relations were carved out between the Muslims and the non-Muslim nations. Muhammad (P.B.U.H) abided by both these principles firmly and he elaborated all the rules and regulations of international relations.

There are two aspects of treaties:

1. The principles which to Islam are the basis of concluding peace with any person, group or nation.
2. The injunctions of Islam about the observance and annulment of the treaty.

Islam has formulated certain rules and regulations which cannot be violated in any case unless a dire need demands so. Such injunctions are there in the Holy Quran.[3] Certain injunctions are not compulsory but only desirable. The observance or non-observance of such rules is left to the discretion of the individuals.

The Kinds Of Treaties After The War.

1. Such a treaty which fixes the time and place of peace. It is concluded during war or on a battlefield so that the parties may negotiate mutually, bury their dead bodies or take safety measures from flood, storm or earthquake.
2. A treaty may be unlimited in respect of time but the place is fixed.
3. A general treaty which is for a fixed time. It is normally for armistice purposes. All sorts of belligerent measures are prohibited during such a peace time. It is quite possible that the general peace, which is for a fixed time, may be a completed peace and not to get simply a chance for negotiations. The example of such a treaty is Peace Treaty of Hudaibiya which fixed a period of ten years for the Muslims and the Quraish. In such a case each party is free to invade upon the opposite party without any information on the expiry of time.
4. A treaty may be unlimited both in place and time.

Normally such a treaty is concluded on the end of a battle when one party is defeated or is fed up of fighting.

The Methods To End War:

A. The parties may cease hostilities without any mutual alliance or fixing the time limit. Its reason may be that the parties are fed up of fighting; or if a party is successful but does not want to prolong the fighting because it wants to complete the work of subjugation. It is generally in that case when a weak party has won the battle. Its examples are: Badr, Uhad, the Trench and Muta. The belligerents departed without determining the nature of their relations.

B. When a non-Muslim enemy accepts Islam. It is not necessary that it may be included in the Islamic State or the unity of the new Islamic State may come into existence. The letters which the Holy Prophet wrote to the chiefs of Ghassan, Bahrain and Oman simply invited them to accept Islam. These letters also contained the message that in case of embracing Islam they would remain in power. Negus, the king of Abyssinia accepted Islam so his state was not incorporated in the Islamic State. Rather the Holy Prophet ordered not to invade upon Abyssinia unless the people of that country invaded upon them.[4]

C. When the country of the enemy is occupied after its subjugation. Its prominent examples are Mecca, Khyber and the conquest of several other places. Generally there is no need of negotiations and treaties in such cases. The Apostle did not conclude any treaty in Mecca but negotiated about the protection of the lives and property of the enemy. The stipulations of the treaty were accepted.

D. When the enemy accepts the suzerainty of the Islamic State. Its examples are Najran, Taima, Fidak, Ailah and several other city-states. In several cases fighting did not take place.

E. To remove differences through peace treaty when

both the parties want to maintain their freedom.

The context of the treaty is determined by the consequences of the war. Generally a temporary alliance is concluded to reach at the basic points, after which the military activities are prohibited immediately. In this kind of treaty it is also mentioned that damaging the lives and property of enemy is prohibited. At a later stage the other details are settled and a final shape is given to the treaty.

Nature Of The Treaty :

Sometimes the message for future friendship is contained in a peace treaty and co-operation and amity as a result of settled terms. Generally hostilities cease in this way and it is tried to establish the cordial relations. Similarly the weaker party pays the reparations and tributaries. The Holy Prophet agreed upon to give one third of the products of the oases of Medina to Ghatafan by an unendorsed treaty, provided they lift the siege of the city and conclude a separate treaty with the Islamic State immediately.[5]

Affection, affability, reconciliation, tolerance, justice and fraternity are separate things.[6] If the Muslims think proper they may conclude a peace treaty with the infidels according to the injunctions of Islam.[7] As the nucleus of the Islamic State is the Oneness of God therefore it is impossible to maintain the perpetual alliance with the non-Muslims. When the Holy Prophet laid down the foundations of the Islamic State after his *Hijrah,* he was agreed upon to establish a confederation with the Jews. Besides this he concluded treaties of mutual military assistance with the pagan tribes living around Medina, particularly with those in the direction of Yanbu‘ from where the caravans of the Quraish passed while going to Iraq, Syria or Egypt, to and fro.‘ These treaties were without the time limit. They added to the dignity of Medina and at the same time struck at the Quraish economically. Between lines another intention of these treaties was that the Quraish should not pursue them to Medina as they had done in the case of Abyssinia. In the meantime the Muslims wanted to gain so much power that the Quraish be forced to conclude a treaty with them. The development of their religious values was in addition to this.

Another aim of these treaties was to impress the Jews of Medina and adjacent areas because they had violated the Medina Treaty notwithstanding the fact that they were a party to it. They were always busy in instigating the extinguished sparks of the enmity between Aus and Khazraj. It was necessary to make them believe that a central government had been established in Medina and they could easily be punished.

Only those infidels could be treated affectiona‑ ‑y or politely who were not at daggers drawn with the Mus ‑ms.[8] Then the Holy Quran said :[9]

> "O ye who believe! Take not for protectors your fathers and your brothers if they love infidelity above Faith; if any of you do so, they do wrong."

The Holy Prophet proclaimed a declaration in a ‑ord-ance with the injunctions of the Holy Quran[10] th‑ ‑ all the treaties which were for the contracted time would remain applicable for the same period. But the treaties concluded with the pagans, which were not for contracted time, were declared null and void on the notice of four months.[11]

Several tribes remained firm on their treaties after the conquest of Makkah. Some of them were for a fixed period and others were open. There were many a tribes with which no treaty had been concluded. The pagans with whom existed no fixed-time treaty were informed that the Muslims would not desire to continue the treaty. They were given a respite of four months so that either they should join the Islamic Community or vacate the centre of Faith and Oneness of Allah or be ready for a fight.

Effects Of A Treaty Of Peace:

Such a treaty bears the following effects :

1. The subject over which hostilities had broken out is settled.
2. The rights of belligerency, i.e., killing, capturing, plun-

dering, occupying, and other things described before, are brought to an end.

3. If there is no mention in the treaty, the treaty will be effective uptil its end.
4. As the prisoners of war are exchanged or otherwise released, therefore generally terms are determined for this purpose.
5. As soon as the peace is established, the suspended treaties of the war-time and those which need no revival, are revived themselves. And the treaties concerning the manners during the war become null and void.

Elements Of The Treaty :

The Holy Quran ordains that the treaty should be written.[12] This was also the practice of the Holy Prophet. Shaibany and others say that a treaty must be in black and white. Majid Khadduri interprets Shaibany differently. According to him the writing as well as the signing and dating (in certain cases the witnessing) of the treaty are not necessarily legal pre-requisites, they are merely to indicate that an agreement has been reached, as well as to record the actual terms of the treaty and its duration.[13] There is explicitly mention of the date and the period of its enforcement. There is also mention of general matters such as cessation of fighting, settlement of conditions created by war and the causes creating hostilities. The treaties include solemn promises for the observances and execution of the treaty, the signature of the duly authorized persons, and the sanction for execution, such as hostages, etc. Sometimes annexes and supplements and even some secret sections are also included in the prominent treaties.

Actually, there is no limit to the subject-matter of the treaties.

Ratification Of The Treaties :

Generally, treaties are concluded, temporarily, by the representatives of the states. Ultra vires matters are presented to the central government. Khalid b. Walid wrote to the Holy Prophet from Yemen and asked instructions.[14] It is just possible that the whole treaty may be declared null and void. The Apostle himself concluded a treaty on the condition that it would be ratified after consultation with his companions. These terms were not accepted and consequently the text was affected.[15] It means that :

1. Islam does not allow any nation or group to conclude such a treaty which affects the fundamentals of Islam;
2. Islam considers only that treaty true and worth observance which is concluded freely and satisfactorily by the parties.
3. It is necessary that every treaty to be concluded should be explicit and non-ambiguous document. In it the rights and duties and other stipulations are clearly determined so that the other party may not interpret it according to its wishes. Islam does not accept any such treaty which may cause disgrace to Islam, such as: to declare legal decisions contrary to the injunctions of Allah; or give such rights to the non-Muslims which the Muslim government is not entitled to give them. Similarly Islam does not justify any such treaty which might have been concluded under force and coercion. It, also, does not recognize a treaty which may be the result of a clever diplomacy and deprives the other party from its rights and wealth.

The Holy Prophet said about these rules and regulations:

> "The stipulation which is not mentioned in the Holy Quran is false."

In this connection there are clear manifestations in the Holy Quran, such as:

1. "Nor take your oaths to practise deception between yourselves, lest one party should be more numerous than another; for God will test you by this."[16]
2. "And take not your oaths, to practise deception between yourselves, with the result that someone's foot may slip after it was firmly planted."[17]

In these verses by oaths is meant either those pledges

taken at the time of the ratification of treaties or promises which are to be fulfilled. Similarly the word *dakhl* means deception, hypocrisy, forgery and intrigues.

In the contemporary world deception is considered to be wisdom and the key to the successful life in the diplomacy. But Islam regards this kind of deception accursed after the ratification of a treaty.

Amendment Of Treaty :

Treaties can be amended in view of the mutual consent according to the circumstances instead of concluding a new pact.

Interpretation Of Treaties :

Shaibany writes, "There are things which may be taken for granted by the Muslims even without express mention of them, but other nations may not imply that. Such things must be expressly mentioned, otherwise the contracting party may conclude that there is an infringement of the pact. And, as we have mentioned, the document must be written in a way to bear witness against the contracting parties and no accusation of perfidy should be possible."[18]

In another passage, the same writer says that if a besieged fortress surrenders on the condition that the free people will not be molested and that the ownership of the slaves will be transferred to the conquering army, and the parties differ regarding the status of certain individuals, the presumption will be that they are free people, since originally every man is free."[19]

Denunciation Of Treaties:

Sometimes a treaty becomes impracticable with the passage of time and it is necessary to revive it in the changing times. The Muslim jurists opine that if a Muslim ruler announces the denunciation of a former treaty, he cannot do anything contrary without informing the other party until reasonable time has passed. It helps to guess that the central government of the other party has been informed.[20] A treaty was concluded between the Muslims and the pagans that nobody would be stopped to enter the House of Allah and frightened in this holy city. To end it Surah "Repentance" was sent down by Allah in 9 A.H. In this treaty the time and period were not fixed.[21]

When this was proclaimed, the period of four months was completed from that day so that every nation might go to its place of safety or to its cities. After this the Muslims were not bound by any treaty with any pagan nation except with whom the period had not ended.[22]

Hostages And Pledges :

For the safety of the hostages the Holy Quran lays down the following principles :

1. "Every soul draws the meed of its acts on none but itself; no bearer of burden can bear the burden of another."[23]
2. "Who receiveth guidance, receiveth it for his own benefit: who goeth astray doth so to his own loss: no bearer of burden can bear the burden of another: nor would We visit with Our Wrath until We had sent an apostle (to give warning)."[24]
3. "Nor can a bearer of burden bear another's burden. If one heavily laden should call another to (bear) his load, not the least portion of it can be carried (by the other), even though he be nearly related."[25]
4. "No bearer of burdens can bear the burdens of another. In the End, to your Lord is your Return, when He will tell you the truth of all that ye did (in this life)."[26]
5. "Namely, that no bearer of burdens can bear burden of another."[27]

If Muslim hostages are killed, the Muslims cannot kill their non-Muslim hostages because it was not their fault. Anyhow, they can be forced to become non-Muslim subjects because they cannot go back until the Muslim hostages return, or their murder makes their return impossible. So they are bound to stay permanently in the Islamic State.

Observance Of Treaty :

The Preamble of the Vienna Convention stresses upon that good faith and *pacta sunt servanda* are universally recognized. Article 26 provides that all treaties are binding on the parties thereof, and must be performed by them in good faith. Long before the Vienna Convention this principle was laid down in the Holy Quran. In his hey-days the Holy Prophet did not forget to respect the treaties, and pledges. Sometimes in observing the terms of treaties, he had to forego the advantages of his infant Commonwealth.

But long ago the Holy Quran laid great emphasis on abiding by the treaties and pacts :

1. "O ye who believe! Fulfil (all) obligations."[28]
2. "For the worst of beasts in the sight of God are those who reject Him: they will not believe. They are those with whom thou didst make a covenant. But they break their covenant every time, and they have not the fear (of God). If ye gain the mastery over them in war, disperse with them, those who follow them, that they may remember. If thou fearest treachery from any group, throw back (their Covenant) to them, (so as to be) on equal terms: for God loveth not the treacherous."[29]
3. "A (declaration) of immunity from God and His Apostle, to those of the Pagans with whom ye have contracted mutual alliances. Go ye, then, for four months, backwards and forwards, (as ye will), throughout the land, but know ye that ye cannot frustrate God (by your falsehood) but that God will cover with shame those who reject Him."[30]
4. "(But the treaties are) not dissolved with those Pagans with whom ye have entered into alliance and who have not subsequently failed you in aught, nor aided anyone against you. So fulfil your engagements with them to the end of their term: for God loveth the righteous."[31]
5. "And fulfil (every) engagement, for (every) engagement will be enquired into (on the Day of Reckoning)."[32]

But despite this Declaration

1. Muslims cannot break their pledges;
2. They cannot change the treaty;
3. They cannot do any wrong to any pagan with whom they have a treaty;
4. They are bound to admit and carry out the treaty till the prescribed time.

Muslims are made to believe that Allah considers the pious men His friends. In other words, to respect the treaties is piety though they are with the odious people.

5. "The Believers must (eventually) win through those who humble themselves in their prayers; who avoid vain talk; who are active in deeds of charity; who abstain from sex, except with those joined to them in the marriage bond, or (the captives) whom their right hands possess, — for (in their case) they are free from blame, but those whose desires exceed those limits are transgressors; those who faithfully observe their trusts and their covenants."[33]

Islam does not like a treaty which is like a spider's web in which weakers are entangled but the powerful can break it. Allah sent down the verses about those pagans who had not violated their pledge: "(But the treaties are) not dissolved with those pagans with whom ye have entered into alliances and who have not subsequently failed you in aught, nor aided any one against you. So fulfil your engagements with them to the end of their terms."[34]

Then again it is said about those who break their pledges "But when the forbidden months are past, then fight and slay the Pagans wherever ye find them, and seize them, beleaguer them, and lie in wait for them in every stratagem (of war); but if they repent, and establish regular prayers and practise regular charity, then open the way for them."[35]

Again Allah sent down the following verses about these treacherous and faithless pagans :

"How can there be a league, before God and His Apostle, with the Pagans, except those with whom ye made a treaty near the Sacred Mosque? As long as these stand true to you, stand ye true to them: for God doth love the righteous. How (can there be such a league), seeing that if they get an advantage over you, they respect not in you the ties either of kinship or covenant? With (fair words from) their mouths they entice you, but their hearts are averse from you; and most of them are rebellious and wicked."[36]

Then again Allah says about them:

"In a Believer they respect not the ties either of kinship or of covenant! It is they who have transgressed all bounds. But (even so) if they repent, establish regular prayers, and practise regular charity, ––they are your brethren in Faith: (thus) do We explain the Signs in detail, for those who understand. But if they violate their oaths after their covenant, and taunt you for your Faith, ––– fight ye that chiefs of Unfaith: for their oaths are nothing to them: that thus they may be restrained. Will ye not fight people who violated their oaths, plotted to expel the Apostle, and took the aggressive by being the first (to assault) you? Do ye fear them? Nay, it is God Whom ye should more justly fear, if ye believe! Fight them, and God will punish them by your hands, cover them with shame, help you (to victory) over them, heal the breasts of Believers."[37]

There are several traditions of the Holy Prophet which prohibit the pretext, violation of pledge and doing wrongs to the people with whom treaties have been concluded. It is a worst sin in Islam. Abdullah b. Amr narrates that the Holy Prophet said:[38] "Whosoever shall kill a person with whom an agreement has been made, he will not have even the smell of paradise whereas its smell is felt from a distance of forty years."

In another Hadith Abdullah b. Amr states that:[39]

"There are four characteristics of a pure hypocrite. Firstly when he speaks, tells a lie. Secondly when he makes a promise, breaks it. Thirdly when he makes a treaty, violates it. Fourthly when he quarrels, he abuses."

Then the Holy Prophet said, "There will be a standard on the Day of Resurrection to declare the unfairness of every faithless (treacherous) person which will be equal to his treachery. Remember that if the head of a nation commits treachery, there is no treacherous greater than him."[40]

Again Abu Rafai narrates:

"The Quraish sent me to Muhammad. When I saw him, I was impressed by Islam. I requested, 'O Apostle of Allah! I will never go back to them now. The Holy Prophet said, 'I don't break the treaty nor can I arrest the ambassadors. At this time you should go back and if your sentiments remain the same then come back.' So at that time I returned to the Quraish and then again I went to embrace Islam."[41]

If the enemy of Islam concluded a treaty with any Companion of the Holy Prophet, he would let it remain in force (for a limited time). Its example is that Hudhaifa and his father concluded a treaty with the infidels that they would not fight against them in the company of the Apostle. The Holy Prophet let it in force but said, "You both should go back. Fulfil the promise which you have made. We need only the help of Allah in facing the infidels."

Islam puts so much emphasis on the observance of a treaty that there is its accountability in this world and the Hereafter. The Holy Prophet himself will complain to Allah on the Day of Resurrection about those who break the pledges. He said, "Listen to me attentively that whosoever will oppress those with whom agreement has been made or reduce their rights or burden them more than their patience or take anything from them without their willingness, I will file a suit against him as a plaintiff on the Day of Resurrection."[42]

If we analyse these above-mentioned verses and traditions, we conclude:

1. The Muslims should fight against those who break their pledges. Those infidels are also included in this category who take oath of allegiance with the Muslims and then rebel against the Islamic State.
2. The people with whom treaty has been made and their attitude is based on enmity, Islamic State feels a constant danger from them. It is necessary to serve them a notice, at once, for the annulment of the treaty. And after that they should be dealt with severely.

3. The people who are habitual violators of their pledges and are incredible, have no respect for morality and humanity should be fought on a permanent basis. A peace treaty with them is only possible when they renounce their behaviour and embrace Islam. Otherwise killing, arrest, siege and such other war-like tactics would have to be adopted to save Islam and Dar-us-Salam from their influence.

Kinds Of Breach Of Treaty :

There are two kinds of breach of treaty :

1. When the Muslims suspect that the other party is not sincere in its observance of the treaty or will commit treachery whenever gets an opportunity. In this case the Muslim Government is allowed to take a measure itself and declare the treaty null and void. The condition is that it should not keep quiet after breaking the treaty but it should inform the other party of its decision immediately. This very situation has been described in the Holy Quran :[43]
"If thou fearest treachery from any group, throw back (their Covenant) to them, (so as to be) on equal terms : for God loveth not the treacherous."
2. When the circumstances might have changed than the circumstances when the treaty was concluded, and now the treaty is a loss for the Muslim Umma, and the evils and harms are numerous in number than the safeguards which are being secured through it. In this case it is incumbent upon the Muslim Government to break the treaty and inform the other party. The following verse guides us in this connection :[44]
"And a proclamation from Allah and His Messenger to all men on the day of the Greater Pilgrimage that Allah is free from obligation to the idolaters, and (so is) His Messenger."

This declaration of the cancellation of the treaties was made against all those tribes who were always busy in hurting Islam and the Muslims in spite of the treaties and whenever they got chance they were in open opposition.

If the infidels do not stick to the treaties of peace and break it and are inclined to sedition and rebellion, then Allah says :[45]

"But if they violate their oaths after their covenant, and taunt you for your Faith, —— fight ye the chiefs of Unfaith: for their oaths are nothing to them: that thus they may be restrained. Will ye not fight people who violated their oaths, plotted to expel the Apostle, and took the aggressive by being the first (to assault) you? Do ye fear them? Nay, it is God Whom ye should more justly fear, if ye believe!"

After the breach of the treaty the responsibility of the Muslims is over and they are not bound to abide by the treaty. They have the right to wage war with them and prolong it until their power is paralysed. In other case if the treaty is for a fixed time then its limit should be completed. In this connection Allah ordains :[46]

"(But the treaties are) not dissolved with those Pagans with whom ye have entered into alliance and who have not subsequently failed you in aught, nor aided any one against you. So fulfil your engagements with them to the end of their terms."

This exception is concerned with the above-mentioned general information and it has been conditioned by that stipulation that the nation (with which an agreement has been made) may not be engaged in open anti-Muslim activities. Rather it might have fulfilled the pledge. But on the whole this treaty may be for greater loss of the Muslim Umma. Therefore it is advisable to wait till the fixed time-limit is over.

Characteristics Of Treaties :

The policy of Islam to enforce and annul the treaties contains in itself the merits which create good-will and peace at the international level. A just-minded person will certainly admire them.

The treaties concluded during the reign of the Holy Prophet bore the following characteristics:

1. Generally these treaties were brief and general in nature. Greater attention was given on providing the details and it was managed, particularly, to abide by the settled stipulations. The texts were simple and balanced.
2. Every treaty was started with "the name of Allah, the Most Merciful and Compassionate. And then were written the names of the representatives of the parties with their titles. All the treaties, with the exception of treaty of Hudaibiya, which the Holy Prophet concluded bore the words 'Apostle of Allah' with his name. At the end there were the names of those persons as witnesses who used to be present at the time of concluding the treaty.
3. The contents of the treaties were different according to the aims. In some of the treaties religious aims were mentioned (particularly in the early Islamic treaties). Political or economic motives were written in the treaties concluded in the years to come.

Basic Aim Of Treaties :

The basic aim of the treaties, concluded by the Holy Prophet, was the welfare of the mankind, establishment of peace, end of oppression and achievement of economic, political and collective rights of the people under the guidance of Islam. A Muslim State is a universal state and it works for the establishment of international relations in this position. But it does not abandon the real aim due to these treaties.

Treaties And Religious Tolerance :

These treaties not only depict the preliminary relations of the Muslims and non-Muslims but we also come to know that how clear were these relations. The Holy Prophet put great emphasis on tolerance with those people who claimed to be Scriptuaries. The first and foremost aim of his invitation was that people should admit the Oneness of Allah. The Scriptuaries had faith in Allah but did not admit

Muhammad (P.B.U.H.) as His Apostle. But when they accepted his pacts it meant that they had recognized his strong heavenly position without recognizing his apostleship. He went on accepting compromise with them on this hope that it would have good impact on these semi-Muslims and they would become true believers gradually. This is the reason that he did not impose on the Scriptuaries any social or other discriminatory condition except Jizya.[47]

All nations of Arabia, except the Jews of Hijaz, accepted the supremacy of Islam of their own accord. Islam took all the responsibility of the protection of their lives, property, honour, respect and religion and imposed only a trivial amount, viz; one dinar per annum on every capable sensible adult. It was not necessary to pay it in coins. The non-Muslims could pay in kind whatever was produced or manufactured in their respective territories.[48]

The Holy Prophet reconciled, first of all, with the Jews of Khybar, Fidak, Wadi-ul-Qura and Taima in 7 A.H. Uptil that time Jizya was not heavenly ordained. Consequently the terms reached at with mutual willingness were abided by after the revelation of the verse about Jizya.[49] The real condition was that they would be subjects and take half the products themselves and the other half taken by the government.[50]

Jizya was imposed in 9 A.H. and afterwards all the treaties were concluded accordingly. The Christians of Najran came to Medina and requested for a compromise which was accepted. The stipulations were: "They will give two thousand clothes annually to the Muslims in two instalments —— one in the month of Safar and the other in Rajab. If there is any rebellion or disturbance in Yemen, they will lend thirty armours, thirty horses, thirty camels and thirty weapons of every kind. The muslims will be responsible for their return. On return neither their churches will be demolished nor their priests be ousted; moreover, they will not be converted from their religion, provided they do not do their business with interest or stage a rebellion."[51]

Several Christian and Jewish families were inhabited in the confines of Syria. In 9 A.H. the Christian and Jew landlords of Daumatu'l Jandal, Ailah, Maqna, Jurba, Azrah, Tabalah and Jursh did not accept Islam and consented to pay Jizya. Each adult man had to pay one dinar per annum. It was also incumbent upon them to entertain the Muslims who would happen to pass through their lands.

The Jews of Yemen, who did not embrace Islam, had to pay Jizya in the same quantity. They were given the facility that if they could not give in cash they were allowed to give it in equivalent Mua'fri clothes.[52] Similar terms were presented to the Magians of Bahrain.

The lands, trade and industry of the Dhimmis were let remained intact. Nothing was done contrary to the treaty and exacted more than what was settled. Islam gave them full protection. The Holy Quran lays down the following injunctions in this connection which show the scrupulous respect of treaties concluded with the non-Muslims :

1. "But if the enemy incline towards peace, do thou (also) incline towards peace, and trust in God."[53]
2. "Let there be no compulsion in religion."[54]
3. "To you be your Way, and to me mine."[55]

The Holy Prophet said :

"Several sons of the Companions of the Holy Prophet narrate postulately with reference to their fathers that whosoever oppress those with whom the treaties have been made or reduce in the treaty or put more burden than his patience or exact anything without his willingness, I will be his pleader on the Day of Resurrection."[56]

If we compare these principles of treaty-making with the most advanced nations of the modern age, an open reality comes forth that their treaties are not for the protection of the weaker nations but a rich morsel for them. They have thrown the world into the hell of adversity instead of benefitting it with prosperity and welfare.

(B) Treaties

Ibn Sa'd[1] has quoted Yazid b. Rooman that the Holy Prophet preached for three years in Makkah secretly. It was in the fourth year that he began to preach openly. In the tenth year of his ministry he began to preach at the fairs like Ukaz.[2] Majna[3] and Zu'l Majaz[4] to the half-traders and half-pilgrims. These fairs had great importance in the social, political and literary life of Arabia. 'It was the only occasion on which free and fearless intercourse was possible between the members of different clans'. There he discovered to them the destination of real happiness. In 3 A.H. he invited fifteen different groups to Islam in Mina. Prominent among them were: Banu Amir b. Sa'as'a, Muharib b. Khasfa, Fazara, Ghassan, Murra, Hanifa, Sulaym, Abas, Bani Nazr, Bani Al-Bakka, Kinda, Kalb, Harith b. Ka'b, Azra and Hadarama. But nobody paid heed to him. His inveterate enemy and uncle Abu Lahb, always, pursued him wherever he went and said, "O people! this man is a liar and apostatizer."[5] Thus he spoiled everything by his taunts and insults. And when Muhammad (P.B.U.H.) talked outside the ubiquitous Abu Lahb was no less obnoxious. The Quraish had a predominance over the tribes of Arabia and were a trustee of the Ka'ba so they enjoyed respect throughout the Peninsula. It meant that people were fascinated by the oily tongue of Abu Lahb. He called him a driveller and a maniac-poet. So the Makkans treated him with contemptuous indifference. Umm-i-Jameel, his wife, was the most inveterate of Muhammad's (P.B.U.H) persecutors. She strew thorns in his path. Refuse was thrown at his door. When he went to prostrate the infidels put the entrail of camel on his back. And once Aqba b. Abi Mu'eet wound his sheet of cloth up like a rope and put it round the neck of the Holy Prophet when he went prostrate. The converts were exposed to the burning heat of the desert on the scorching sand. They were thrown into prisons, starved and then beaten with sticks. But they stood steadfast and did not budge an inch from their Faith.

Thus the number of the converts could not increase in the uncultivated valley[6] of Makkah whereas Medina[7] was fortunate enough to embrace Islam, as if Allah had managed for the victory of his family.[8] There were two tribes named Aus and Khazraj in Yathrib.[9] Both these tribes were the descendants of Qahtan. They were agriculturalists by profession. Jews were also inhabited in that city. They were traders. The mutual relations of Aus, Khazraj and Jews were not fast. Occasionally they were at war with one another. The causes of this tension were :-

Firstly : There was conflict for power between the Jews and the different tribes of Yathrib. They needed a master who could unite them. He should be sincere, true and a man of strong determination so that he might be able to put an end to their social evils.

Secondly : The Jews were wealthy as they were traders. The members of Aus and Khazraj, generally, borrowed money from them at interest which was compound in nature. Consequently, the Jews led a comfortable and prosperous life.

Thirdly : These tribes were at war with one another. The Jews instigated their disputes. Actually they were dreaming to become the rulers of Yathrib.

Fourthly : The Jews were Scriptuaries. They wanted that the Arabs should acknowledge their religious paramountcy. They had become accustomed to the idea of a prophet. They used to say to Aus and Khazraj, "A prophet will be sent soon. His day is at hand. We shall follow him and kill you by his aid as 'Ad and Iram perished." The reality is that the Jews were waiting for a prophet who might be as great as Christ, Elijah or Moses. There were many predictions which declared that this prophet would be responsible for the vast propagation of Judaism. The Aus and Khazraj could not predict anything as they were not the Scriptuaries.

These were the four elements which made room for the Aus and Khazraj to embrace Islam. It was in the tenth year of the ministry of Muhammad (P.B.U.H.) that a caravan of

Khazraj came to Makkah. As usual one day (620 A.C.) he came upon a group of six persons at Aqba.[10] He asked them who were they?

They replied, "We belong to Khazraj."

He asked, "Are you friends of the Jews?"

They replied, "Yes"

He asked, "Will you not listen to me calmly?"

They replied, "Why not."

Now the Apostle recited to them a passage of the Holy Quran and mentioned the Greatness and Glory of Allah. He made them feel aversion from idols.

Although these men were idolaters yet they knew that a prophet was going to appear.[11] This was due to their relations with the Jews. Upon his invitation one of them said, "By God! This is the very prophet of whom the Jews warned us. Why not steal then the priority?"[12]

In short, these men were struck by his earnestness so they embraced Islam. They requested, "Our unity has been shaken due to our dissensions. These may be put to an end with your presence."[13]

The names of these fortunate persons were :[14]

1.	Abu Umama Asad b. Zurara	Bani al-Najjar.
2.	Auf b. Harith (known as Ibn-i-Ifra).	Bani al-Najjar.
3.	Rafi' b. Malik	Bani Zurayq.
4.	Qutba b. Amir	Bani Salima.
5.	Uqba b. Amir	Bani Haram b. Ka' b.
6.	Jabir b. Abdullah	Bani Ubayd b. Adi .

Now they returned to Medina and became the great preachers of Islam. They were so successful in their mission that there was not left a single house of the Aus and Khazraj which had not embraced Islam.[15] Thus the Holy Quran was recited first of all in the Zurayq mosque of Yathrib. Waqdi opines that Abu Umama Asad b. Zurara and Dhakwan b. Qays had embraced Islam before this event.[16]

First Pledge Of Aqba :[17]

One year lapsed in fear and hope. Next year (621 A.C.)

twelve[18] Yathribites came to Makka for pilgrimage. Five of them were the same who had embraced Islam last year but the other seven were new.[19] They were :

Asad b. Zurara	Bani al-Najjar.
Auf b. Harith	Bani al-Najjar.
Mu'adh b. Harith	Bani al-Najjar.
Rafi' b. Malik	Bani Zuraq
Dhakwan b. Abdul Qays[20]	Bani Zuraq
Ubada b. Samit	Bani Auf b. Khazraj.21
Yazid b. Tha'laba	Bani Auf b. Khazraj.
Abbas b. Ubada	Bin Amir b. Auf.
Uqba b. Amir	Bani Salima.
Qutba b. Amir	Bani Sawad.

These ten persons belonged to the Khazraj.

Abu'l-Haytham Malik b. Al-Tayyiham	Bani Abdul-Ashhal.
Uwaym b. Sa'ida	Bani Amr b. Auf.

These two persons belonged to Aus.

They swore allegiance to the Holy Prophet about the following :

1. They will ascribe nothing as partner unto God.
2. They will refrain from theft.
3. They will commit adultery nor fornication.
4. They will not kill their offsprings (daughters) for fear of penury.
5. They will abstain from calumny and slander.
6. They will obey the Holy Prophet in every aspect that is right and will be faithful to him in weal and in sorrow.[22]

After the oath the Holy Prophet told them, "If you stick to your pledge, Paradise will be yours. And if you commit any of these sins it was for God to punish or forgive as He pleases."[23] Asad b. Zurarah led the Friday prayer in Medina.[24] At that time Yathrib was divided into hostile camps. Aus and Khazraj could not bear to see one of their rivals take the lead in prayer.[25] Both tribes had been at war in the battle of Bu'ath (615 A.C.). Aus, with the help of their Jewish allies, Banu Qurayza and the Banu Nadir, inflicted a crushing defeat upon the Khazraj. Probably this was the reason that both Aus and Khazraj might have written to the Holy Prophet that someone should be sent to Medina to teach them the Holy Quran. Accordingly, Hazrat Mus'ab b. Umayr, was sent for this purpose.[26] Now Mus'ab[27] began to lead the prayers in Yathrib.[28]

The delegate of the Holy Prophet performed his duty of preaching with utmost efforts. His high manners, pleasant speech, and sincerity compiled very far-reaching effects on the Yathribites. He lodged with Asad b. Zurarah who was a leading wealthy figure of the city. People took pledge in troops on his hands. Within a few days he came to be known as 'The Reader'. He was happy as he was successful in his mission as many dignitaries embraced Islam. Banu Abdul-Ashhal and Banu Zafar were two main branches of Aus. Sa'd b. Mua'dh[29] was the chief of the former. Usaid b. Hudair was the chief of Banu Zafar. Their conversion was so effective that all the members of their tribes except Amr b. Thabit embraced Islam. He embraced Islam on the Day of Uhad and was martyred even without a single prostration. The Holy Prophet remarked about him that his practice was a little but compensation great.

As Islam was yet in its infancy therefore the conditions of the Pledge were very simple. Moreover, the Yathribites embraced Islam immediately and they did not feel necessity to debate with the Holy Prophet. This is the reason that these conditions bore the moral teachings notwithstanding the fact that before this incident the Christians and the Pagans used to interrogate with him in a topsy-turvy way.

One of the conditions of this Pledge was the prohibition of killing the daughters. This depicts the position which Islam gave to the woman from the very beginning. It gave her an elevated position in the society whereas the Arabs looked down upon her. The other conditions were about theft, fornication and slandering. The Arabs were proud of these things. The Arab poets mentioned these things in their verses and got pride. They were ignorant and proud of ignorance. Imrau'l-Qays used to say, "Look, no body should do wrong with us because we become the greatest of the ignorants on such occasions." On the contrary, Islam gives the lesson of forgiveness and humbleness.

These persons took pledge and gave a best example of practice to the world. These words of the Holy Prophet, after the Pledge was taken, are worth consideration : "If you stick to your pledge Paradise will be yours. And if you commit any of these sins it is for God to punish or forgive as He pleases." Islam is a complete code of life. If it frightens us from the punishments of the Hereafter, at the same time its laws have mandatory force too. The Muslim State had not been established at the time of the First Pledge of Aqba, therefore, it was enough to point out only such punishments of the Hereafter. And when after the migration of the Holy Prophet Muslim State came into being, laws were formulated about fornication and theft. The punishment was in the form of lashing, stoning to death and amputation of hands. The reason for the severity of the punishment is to continue smoothly the business of the State which is otherwise impossible.

Next year Mus'ab came to Makka in the month of Rajab and discussed the advancement of his mission with the Holy Prophet. He told him that Yathrib could be Islamized as the circumstances were favourable and the converts brave. "So prepared was the ground, so zealous the propagation, and so apt the method, that the new faith spread rapidly from house to house and from tribe to tribe."

Muhammad (P.B.U.H) compared these circumstances with the unbearable tortures given by the pagans of Makkah where Islam seemed stationary, and its followers were silent and reserved. The temperament of the Makkans was hard like the barren land of Mecca. Whereas the Yathribites were cordial and the land of Yathrib was cultivable. They had presented to the Holy Prophet such a place where Islam seemed to get completion. The six persons who embraced Islam before the First Pledge of Aqba had requested him, "We endorse your apostleship and put faith in you. We are at daggers drawn with one another and the Jews. If we are united through you, no body will be more dearer to us than you."[30] He knew that his companions could not face the Quraish. A few of his relatives, i.e., Abbas b. Abdul Muttalib, certainly, helped him but they could not make the Quraish angry at the cost of Muhammad (P.B.U.H.).

An effect to seek a political centre for the Muslims was also contained in the First Pledge of Aqba. No doubt, the Muslims twice migrated to Abyssinia and the Negus had welcomed them there. But the situation of Yathrib was more in the favour of the Muslims than Abyssinia. Their religious brothers could help them in Yathrib whereas it was quite impossible for them to go to Abyssinia and help them.

This Pledge was the first military success of Muhammad (P.B.U.H.) outside Makkah because Islam began to be spread fastly in Yathrib. An army thus prepared there which could be trusted upon during war and other critical times.

Second Pledge Of Aqba :

Next year (in the 12th year of the Ministry or 622 A.C.) another caravan from Yathrib came to Makkah to perform pilgrimage. Many families of Yathrib had embraced Islam by that time.[31] Several non-Muslims were, also, included in this caravan.[32] Its total number was five hundred.[33] Its Muslim members visited the Holy Prophet in Makkah. He promised to meet them in the stillness of night when all the hostile elements appeared slumbering at Aqba on 21 Dhu'l-Hijja of the days of Tashriq.[34] He advised them not to disturb the sleeping ones or await any one who was absent.[35]

Accordingly these persons reached at the fixed place in the late night. Their idolatrous companions remained quite ignorant of their movement. The Holy Prophet came in the company of his uncle Abbas b. Abdul Muttalib. The Yathribites were 75 including 2 women.[36]

Their names were:[37]

Usayd b. Hudair[38]

Salma b. Salama b. Salama[39] Bani Abdul - Ashhal

Abu'l Haytham b. Tayyaham[40]	
Zuhayr b. Rafi'	
Abu Burda b. Niyar[41]	Bani Haritha b. Al-Harith
Nuhayr b. al-Haytham	
Sa'd b. Khaythama[42]	
Rifa'a b. Abdul-Mundhir[43]	
Abdullah b. Jubayr	
Ibn Tha'laba[44]	Bani Amr b. Auf
Ma'an b. 'Adiy[45]	
Abu Ayub Khalid b. Zayd[46]	
Mu'adh b. al-Harith[47]	
Auf b. al-Harith[48]	
Mu'awwih b. al-Harith[49]	Khazraj b. Al-Harith
'Umara b. Hazm[50]	
As'ad b. Zurara[51]	
Sahl b. 'Atik[52]	Bani Amr. b. Mabdhul
Aus b Thabit[53]	
Abu Talha[54]	Amr b. Malik55
Qays b. Abu Sa'sa'a[56]	
Amr b. Ghaziya	
Sa'd b. al-Rabi[57]	
Kharija b. Zayd[58]	
Abdullah b. Rawaha[59]	
Bashir b. Sa'd[60]	Banu al-Harith b. Khazraj
Abdullah b. Zayd[61]	
Khallad b. Suwayd[62]	
'Uqba b. Amr[63]	
Ziyad b. Labid[64]	
Farwah b. Amr[65]	Bani Bayada b. Amir
Khalid b. Qays[66]	
Rafi' b. Malik[67]	

Dhakwan b Abdu Qays[68]	
Ubada b. Qays[69]	Bani Amir b. Zurayq
Harith b. Qays[70]	
Bara b. Ma'rur[71]	
Bishr b. Al-Bara[72]	
Sinan b. Sayfi[73]	
Tufayl b. Nu'man[74]	
Ma'qil b. al-Mundhir[75]	Banu Salma b. Sa'd
Yazid b Mundhir[76]	
Masud. b Yazid	
Dahhak b. Haritha[77]	
Jabbar b. Sakhr[78]	
Tufayl b. Malik[79]	
Yazid b Khazzam	
Ka'b b. Malik	Bani Sawad
Saleem b. Amr[80]	
Qutba b. Amir[81]	
Yazid b. Amir[82]	B. Ghanam
Abu'l Yaseer[83]	
Sayfi b. Sawad	
Tha'laba b. Ghanama[84]	
Amr b. Ghanama	
Abs b. Amir[85]	
Abbullah b. Unays	Bani Nabi b. Amr
Khalid b. Amr	
Abdullah b. Amr[86]	
Jabir b Abdullah[87]	
Mu'adh b. Amr[88]	
Thabit b. al-Jidh[89]	
Umayr b al-Harith[90]	
Mu'adh b. Jabal[91]	
Anas b. Ubayd	Bani Haram b. Ka'b
Ubada b. Samit[92]	

Abbas b. Ubada[93]
Amr b. al-Harith[94]
Abu Abdul Rehman Yazid b. Tha'laba
Rifa'a b. Amr[95]

Bani Sulaym b. Ghanam[97]

Malik b Walid[96]
Sa'd b. Ubada[98]
Mundhir b. Amr[99]
Nusayba d. of Ka'b[100]
Umm Asma d. of Amr

B. Salima

When these people visited the Holy Prophet, Abbas b. Abdul Muttalib, who was at that time a polytheist, started the conversation. He said, "O group of Khazraj.[101] Muhammad (P.B.U.H.) holds respect among the Hashimites. He is safe in his city but refuses to live with anyone else except you. If you assume the burden you have undertaken, then we have no objection. And if you intend to hand him over to the enemy or intend to abandon his help then he is safe where he is. In this case abandon his help just now."[102] Now Bara' b. Ma'rur said, "What you have said, we have heard. O Apostle of Allah! now you should speak. Whatever you will make us to vow, we are present."

After this the Holy Prophet, first of all, recited the Holy Quran and then invited them to embrace Islam. This recitation was in his melodious voice. Then he said to them, "I invite your allegiance on the basis that you protect me as you would your women and children."[103] Upon this Bara' b. Ma'rur pledged at the hand of the Holy Prophet and said, "By Him Who sent you with the Truth we accept these terms. We are men of war."[104] While Bara' was speaking Abu'l Haytham interrupted him and said, "O Apostle of Allah! We have special ties with the Jews. We will severe them. But thou wilt not leave us in the hour of prosperity to return to thy people?"[105]

The Holy Prophet smiled and said, "Nay never; blood is blood and blood is not to be paid for. I am yours, you are mine. I will war against them that war against you and be at peace with those at peace with you."[106]

Imbued with grand teachings of the Holy Prophet they swore allegiance to him and his Allah. Abbas b. Ubada[107] stepped forward and said, "O men of Khazraj, do you realize to what you are committing yourselves in pledging your support to this man? It is to war against all and sundry. Give him up, then do so now, for it would bring you shame in this world and the next. If you are loyal to your undertaking then pledge at once. But O Apostle of Allah! What return we will get for it?"[108]

The Apostle promised them paradise.

Now they asked that he should take pledge from them. The Holy Prophet took out his hand. First of all Bara' b. Ma'rur pledged his word.[109] As he did not shake hand with the ladies therefore he simply made them to confess. After this he said to them, "Go now, I have taken allegiance from you."[110] The following gentlemen were elected as the delegates upon the instructions of the Holy Prophet :[111]

Abu Umama As'ad b. Zurara
Rafi' b. Malik
Ubada b. Samit
Sa'd b. Rabi
Abdullah b. Rawaha — Khazraj
Bara' b. Ma'rur
Abu Jabir Abdullah b. Amr
Sa'd b. Ubada
Mundhir b. Amr

Usayd b Hudayr
Sa'd b. Khaythama
Rifa'a b. Mundhir[112] — Aus

After this election the Apostle asked them, "You are the sureties for your people just as the disciples of Jesus, Son of Mary, were responsible to him." He, further, told them that it was just the beginning of a great programme. So they should try to inculcate ability to act upon that programme.

All these proceedings took place in the quite stillness

of full-moon night at Aqba. When they were going to be off from this place Abu Lahab's voice came floating on the air. Unverifiable rumour had somehow reached him. He was calling out the Quraish for help. He was saying, "O people of the stations of Mina! Do you know that Muhammad and his irreligious companions have planned to war against you."

When Abbas b. Ubada heard this voice he asked the Apostle, "If you wish it we will fall on the people of Mina tomorrow with our swords."[113] But the Holy Prophet said, "No. We have not been commended to do that; but go back to your tents."[114]

The next morning the elites of the Quraish met the notables of Yathrib in their encampment and said to them, "We don't want to fight with you but why have you concluded a war treaty against us with Muhammad." Abdullah b. Ubayy replied, "Nothing of the kind has happened and my nation cannot do so without my order." It is notable that he was dreaming of the rulership of Yathrib. As the Quraish addressed only the pagans of Yathrib therefore the Muslims kept quiet. Now the Quraish went away but they verified the incident after the departure of the people from Mina. They pursued the Yathribites but found no clue. Accidentally they caught hold of Sa'd b. Ubada, one of the Twelve Disciples, who was delivered a violent blow in the face. They put him, later on, in the jail in Mecca. At last Jubayr b. Mut'im and Harith b. Umayya made his release feasible. These two gentlemen were the neighbourers of Sa'd b. Ubada in Yathrib and were indebted to him.

The Pledges of Aqba were, simultaneously, religious pacts and political treaties. They laid down the magnificence of Islam. They fully depicted the vigour, rare faith and complete steadiness of Muhammad (P.B.U.H.). On one side there were exessive injustices of the Quraish and on the other the rays of hopes were splitting through the pitch darkness. William Muir has aptly remarked about these events :[115]

"Mahomet, thus holding his people at bay, waiting, in the still expectation of victory, to outward appearance defenceless, and with his little band, as it were, in the lion's mouth, yet trusting in His Almighty power whose messenger he believed himself to be, resolute and unmoved -- presents a spectacle of sublimity parallelled only in the sacred records -- by such scenes."

The Makkans, who were his relatives, were all thirsty for his blood. But some had sympathy with him, as Abbas b. Abdul Muttalib, who had to take part in the battle of Badr against him by compulsion. It was far-sightedness for knowledge of men that he sought beauties in him which were a blessing for Islam. This is the reason that he had brought Abbas with him at the time of the Second Pledge of Aqba. He was only two years older than Muhammad (P.B.U.H). He was so dauntless that being a pagan he accompanied him in the pitch darkness of the night far from the city and did not care for the expected dangers.

The Second Pledge of Aqba inculcated love and fraternity in the hearts of the Yathribites. Before this they were thirsty for one another's blood. The battle of Bu'ath, which the Aus and Khazraj fought against one another, continued for one hundred years. The destiny of the people, who were habitual to flood the land with the human blood, was changed within no time. Now the Bani Qeela[116] forgave the murders due to them.

This Pledge was full of political spirit. The Quraish were depressed in spirits. They had tyrannized the Holy Prophet and his companions. They had, socially, boycotted the Bani Hashim for three years,[117] but his steadiness did not tremble. The Quraish hoped that the Muslims would convert to paganism one day or the other if they stayed in Makkah. But the Second Pledge of Aqba changed the whole state of affairs. This treaty paved the way to welcome a huge shift of population from Makkah to Medina. The Yathribites were convinced that with their coming-in the power would increase boundlessly. This thing was also felt by the Quraish who were afraid of the possible vengeance at the hands of the Muslims. Moreover, it became clear upon them that the future of their gods was dark.

There was also a war clause in this treaty contrary to

the First Pledge of Aqba. They took an oath to assist Muhammad (P.B.U.H.) even by arms against the possible attacks and outrages of his enemies. They, also, pledged to protect him just as their children and women. They accepted this condition without any hesitation. After this pledge the Muslims of Makkah were allowed to migrate to Yathrib so that they might worship freely Allah Who has no associate.

This treaty made the Yathribites bound to his submission in poverty, opulence, happiness and helplessness. The Holy Prophet was himself a party to the treaty. He said, "Your war is my war, your truce is my truce and I am now from you." It was a sort of social contract.[118] This Pledge stood stable both in misfortune and authority. When the Holy Prophet prayed to Allah on the mountain of Safa after the conquest of Makkah, the Yathribites suspected he might stay there in Makkah. They expressed this suspicion with one another. But when he got clue of it he ended all their doubts by saying, "My life and death are related with your life and death."[119]

This Pledge proved to be the foundation of the foreign policy of Muhammad (P.B.U.H.). It regarded Yathrib as the Centre of the Muslims as it laid the foundation of a collective order. Political construction began through this treaty and not by using force. Yathrib got fame. But all this became possible only when the Yathribites acknowledged the basic aims of the Islamic teachings. These basic aims are part and parcel for both the establishment of peace and unity of the scattered parts of the world. Uptil that day the Holy Prophet was only an apostle but now he achieved the paramountcy of the Ummah.

Migration of The Apostle :

The Quraish persecuted and oppressed the Muslims, seducing some from their religion, and exiling others from their country. Earlier one band of the Muslims had migrated to Abyssinia. After the Second Pledge of Aqba, the Apostle allowed them to migrate to Yathrib because he feared a general massacre. So quietly by twos and threes they escaped to Yathrib. The inhabitants of that city were the embodiment of truth and purity. They were modest and civil. Even the airs of that city were the guardians of chastity. The Holy Prophet remarked about Yathrib and the Yathribites, "Allah has provided you such brothers and such a home in which you will be living fearlessly."

There were best chances of propagation of Islam in Yathrib. The Muslims could express their faith openly. After the order to migrate,the Muslim men and women began to migrate gradually. The migration took place on such a large scale that entire quarters of the city thus became deserted. Utba b. Rabi'a, at the sight of these vacant abodes, once so full of life, sighed heavily and recited the following verse :

> "Every dwelling-place, however long its prosperity lasts, will one day be overtaken by misfortune and trouble."

The fury of the Quraish was now unbounded. They constituted a committee consisting of twelve leaders of different clans. It met in all despatch in the town-hall *(Dar-un-Nadwa).* Assassination of Muhammad (P.B.U.H.) by selected stalwarts of different families was proposed by Abu Jahl so that the blood recompense might not fall on one household alone. On the night of 12th September, 622 A.C. Muhammad (P.B.U.H.), in the company of Abu Bakr, left Makkah where his voice was in the wilderness eluding the vigilance of the Quraish. At the time of his departure he cast a glance at Makkah and sighed, "O Makkah! thou art dearer to me than the whole world but thy sons don't let me live here."

The fugitives reached Yathrib on Friday (24th September, 622 A.C.) where they were received with acclamation. Its ancient name was changed to Medina. It was declared to be a *haram.* Now history began to write a new and novel chapter with the migration of the Holy Prophet. It marked an event of paramount importance and was a manifestation of excellent wisdom. In Medina the Faith gathered fresh strength. The Muslims were surrounded by the enemies from all sides before the migration. The Quraish inflicted terrible sufferings on them but the migration gave them freedom and a refuge of independence. There they found the people who loved them and who gave them so much affection which they could not dream of. Economically they became sound. They got the status of free and respectable citizens of the city state of Medina.

The Quraish had become an iron obstacle in the propagation of Islam. People were hesitant to hear the message of the Holy Prophet but after the migration it was possible to unite them on one platform. Now the Apostle began to strive universally for the achievement of his motto and he made Arabia its centre. He sent his delegates to the chiefs of tribes, appointed *naqeebs* and despatched emissaries with letters to the kings of different states. At the same time he received the credentials from the several emissaries. He concluded treaties and waged war against fifth column.

After the migration people came to the Holy Prophet without any fear and returned after embracing Islam. His chief aim was to gain friends so that when he went on expeditions, they could move about freely without fear of being molested. Islam spread fastly and the whole of the Arabian Peninsula embraced Islam within ten years. The Holy Prophet got the full opportunity to formulate the Islamic economic system according to the divine orders. Several problems, which related to the civilization and collective life of the Muslims, could be solved only in Medina. The Muslims became members of such a society, instead of being a few oppressed and scattered individuals who followed Oneness of Allah. Now they had their own civilized and cultural system.

After the migration all the Muslims were concentrated on one centre. The Holy Prophet got the opportunity to constitute a political system in the safe and secure atmosphere. This political system was so strong and organized that within ten years the whole of Arabia lauded the suzerainty of the Apostle. The people who believed in tribal ethnocentrism became an invincible force. Thus all those elements of collective policy became apparent responsible for the constitution and progress of the Muslim Umma. It made the use of the new means of political expansion possible. Thus the

Islamic movement could be able to reach in the far off corners of the world after coming out from narrow territorial atmosphere.

Hijrah (migration) was that starting point from where the real achievements of Islam began. It put an end to the helpless and oppressed life of the Muslims and it gave them a new life. When the second Caliph Hadrat Umar Farooq instituted the Islamic calendar he started it from the *Hijrah* and not from the birth of the Apostle or his ministry.[120] The Hijrah proved that, to the Muslims, the country is not the entity to be worshipped. Rather country is a land where the Muslims may lead a life according to the Islamic principles in a pleasant atmosphere. Almighty Allah has appreciated migration and mentioned several benefits of it.[121] The *Hijrah* smashed the concept of territorialism and it explained to the Muslims that the foundation of nationalism in Islam is to believe in the Oneness of Allah and the finality of Muhammad's (P.B.U.H.) prophethood. It was due to the difference of beliefs that Abu Jahl and Muhammad (P.B.U.H) could not become members of one nation notwithstanding the fact that both belonged to the Quraish. "Whereas formerly Muhammad merely endeavoured to preach righteousness and the fear of God to an unbelieving city, he was now to wage wars, to subdue rebels, to reconcile rivals, to make treaties, to withstand a siege, to lead a nation to conquest."[122]

Charter Of Medina :

No area of the world was more torn by strife, more poisoned by age-old hatreds, more strewn with the seeds of potential conflict than Yathrib. Yathrib 'itself was honeycombed by sedition and treachery.' It was a hot-bed of disturbances, internecine quarrels and long-standing wars. It was a city of multi-factions following different religions. Before Christianity the Jews and the converted Jews ruled over this city but after the fifth Christian century they ruled over Yathrib with the collaboration of Aus and Khazraj. These tribes had migrated from south Arabia. The

Jews were proud of being the Scriptuaries. Moreover, their financial position was very sound. Their settlements were scattered far and off. They had domineered over the neighbouring Arab tribes. They lent money to the Aus and Khazraj and exacted heavy compound interests from them. Thus they had made them economically weak. They were, also, always busy in conspiring against them. "For more than a century the inhabitants of Medina -- the two tribes of Aus and Khazraj -- -- had been interlocked in bitterest enmity, and lived in a state of incessant warfare."[123] Its result was the battle of Bu'ath in which human blood was shed ruthlessly. The Aus were defeated but the real benefit was acquired by the Jews than the Khazraj whose past glory was revived. Now Aus and Khazraj forgot their inveterate and mortal feuds. Under this feeling they decided to set up their own government and for this purpose they searched out Abdullah ibn Ubayy who aspired to rule over the whole of Yathrib. He was considered trustworthy by several quarters. It is notable that after the Second Pledge of Aqba when the Quraish complained to him he had replied, "Nothing of this sort has happened. My nation cannot do anything without my order."[124] Preparations were going on to crown him the king of Yathrib and even his crown was with the artisans under making.[125] 'Had the Jews been converted to Islam, this dream might have come true in part.' Abdullah ibn Ubayy embraced Islam to kill it from within. His was the role of an adroit saboteur in the garb of a follower.'

These were the circumstances under which Muhammad (P.B.U.H.) arrived in Yathrib. He felt the following exigencies in that city keeping in view the circumstances :[126]

1. Determination of the rights and duties of himself and local inhabitants;
2. Arrangements for the living of the *muhajirin;*
3. Conciliation with the non-Muslims particularly the Jews;
4. Management of political organization and military defence of Medina;
5. Reparation of the mortal and financial losses of the *muhajirin* at the hands of the Quraish.

The six persons, who embraced Islam before the First

Pledge of Aqba, had requested to the Holy Prophet, "We endorse your apostleship and have faith in you. We are often at daggers drawn with one another and the Jews. If God unites us through you, then no man will be more dearer to us than you."[127] Keeping these demands in view one of his first acts after his arrival in Medina was to weld together the heterogeneous and conflicting elements of which the city and its suburbs were composed, into an orderly confederation. He granted a Charter to the people after some months of his migration in 1 A.H. The Jewish tribes of the Bani Nadir, Bani Qainuqa and Bani Quraiza were not at first included in this Charter; but after a short time they, too, gradually accepted its terms. This treaty is the most important chapter of history from the point of comprehensiveness. "Despite later troubles, the Prophet's diplomacy and statesmanship in the early Medina period was to set the seal on Muslim attitudes towards non-Muslim minorities. The pattern established by the Prophet in his famous *Ummah* document, and the spirit of tolerance which it expressed, was to characterise, for the most part, the policies of succeeding generations of Muslim rulers down the ages."[128]

The illustrious charter had the following fifty three clauses :[129]

In the name of the Most Merciful and Beneficent God.

1. From the Apostle of God, for those of the Quraish and the inhabitants of Medina who accept Islam and adopt the Faith; and for those who are subservient to them when participating in a war (an alliance, defensive or offensive).

   They shall constitute one political "Ummah", or entity against the whole world.
2. The Quraish emigrants will be responsible for their own wards. They will pay blood-money on a co-operative basis and they will ransom their prisoners out of their own pockets, so that relations between them and the Believers in Faith may be based on justice and equality.
3. The people of the Banu 'Auf will be responsible for their own wards and, like the previous tribes, pay blood-

money themselves, every tribe ransoming its own prisoner so that relations between them and the Believers may be based on justice and equality.

4. And the people of the Banu Harith will be responsible for their own wards. Like the previous ones, they will pay their own blood-money and every tribe shall ransom its own prisoners so that relations between them and the Believers may be based on justice and equality.

5. And the Banu Sa'ada will be responsible for their own wards and will pay blood-money like the previous ones; and every tribe will ransom its own prisoners so that relations between them and the Believers may be based on justice and equality.

6. And the Banu Jasham will be responsible for their own wards and will pay blood-money like the previous ones; and every tribe will ransom its own prisoners so that relations between them and Believers may be based on justice and equality.

7. And Banu Najjar will be responsible for their own wards and will pay blood-money like the previous ones; and every tribe will ransom its own prisoners so that relations between them and the Believers may be based on justice and equality.

8. And the Banu Amr b. Auf will be responsible for their own wards and will pay blood-money like the previous ones; and every tribe will ransom its own prisoners so that relations between them and the Believers may be based on justice and equality.

9. And Bani al-Nabit will be responsible for their own wards and will pay blood-money like the previous ones; and every tribe will ransom its own prisoners so that relations between them and the Believers may be based on justice and equality.

10. And Banu Aus will be responsible for their own wards and will pay blood-money like the previous ones; and every tribe will ransom its own prisoners so that relations between them and the Believers may be based on justice and equality.

11. The Believers are to make a point of going to the rescue of anyone who has fallen badly into debt so that relations between such a person and the Believers may be based on justice and equality.
12. No Believer will enter into direct relations with any person who has already entered into contract with another Believer.
13. The pious Believers in Faith will unanimously rise against anyone who rebels, or who commits fornication, or any offence or tyranny, or who attempts to stir up mischief amongst them; and they are to make a common cause against such a person, even though he be their son.
14. And no Believer will assassinate a Believer on behalf of an infidel; nor is he to render any help to a non-Believer against a Believer.
15. The responsibility of a Believer to God (because it is God's kingdom) is such that should even the lowest amongst the Believers offer refuge to somebody, then every Believer in Faith would be under an obligation to defend and respect him. The Believers are brothers and constitute one unit against the whole world.
16. Whosoever from amongst the Jews would follow us will receive our help and be treated as our equals. They would not be tyrannized and no help would be offered to anybody against them.
17. The Believers would be one community (act in a body) while making peace. While fighting in the way of God, no Believer would make peace with an enemy, leaving aside his fellow Believer, as long as the peace is not unanimously resolved upon.
18. Those tribes who fight shoulder to shoulder with us will be allowed a day's respite from fighting each in its turn.
19. The Believers will unanimously wreak vengeance on anyone who fights against them in the path of God.
20. Verily the Faithful and the Pious have the best and the straightest path.
21. None of the non-Muslim subjects may offer refuge

to the life and property of the Quraish, nor cross the path of a Believer in this respect.

22. Whosoever kills a Believer, intentionally and deliberately, and has his crime established against him shall be subjected to retaliation unless the guardian of the assassinated person agrees to accept blood-money. All the Believers will obey this and this alone will save them.

23. And none of the Believers who has given an undertaking to abide by the covenant of this mandate, and who has accepted God and the Day of Resurrection as an article of Faith, will offer to harbour any murder or abet him in any way. Whosoever does so will bring down on himself the wrath and curse of God. No penalty or indemnity would be accepted of him.

24. Should any differences crop up amongst you, you should turn for guidance to God and Muhammad (P.B.U.H.)

25. And the Jews are to shoulder the expenditure, along with the Muslims, as long as they fight side by side with them on the battlefield.

26. The Jews of the Banu 'Auf are recognized as being in a political alliance with the Muslims and at one with them. Whether it is the Judaism of the Jews or the Faith of the Muslims, both Jews and Muslims, together with their annexes (alliances) are to offer reciprocal respect for the two religions. Whosoever is responsible for any aggression or for the breach of any treaty, will precipitate none save himself or his household into the abyss of degradation.

27. The privileges of the Jews of the Banu-Najjar are similar to those of the Bani 'Auf.

28. The privileges of the Jews of Bani al-Harith would also be identical with those of the Bani 'Auf.

29. The privileges of the Jews of Bani Sa'ada would also be identical with those of the Bani 'Auf.

30. The privileges of the Jews of the Jusham would also be identical with those of the Bani 'Auf.

31. The privileges of the Jews of Al-Aus would also be identical with those of the Bani 'Auf.

32. The privileges of the Jews of Tha'laba would also be identical with those of the Bani 'Auf. Whosoever commits aggression or any breach of treaty would let fall into the abyss of degradation none save himself or his household.
33. And Jafinah which is a branch of the Jhafna would enjoy the same rights as the Jhafna themselves.
34. The Banu Al-Shutayba will have the same privileges as the Jews of the Banu 'Auf, provided they remain faithful and display no treachery.
35. The annexes of Tha'laba would have the same rights as the Tha'laba themselves.
36. The following tribes of the Jews would have the same rights as they enjoy themselves.
37. And none of these would declare war or proceed on a military campaign save only with the permission of Muhammad (P.B.U.H.).
38. No obstacle or impediments would be placed in the way of anybody who had received a bruise or minor injury, should he wish to retaliate. Whosoever causes bloodshed shall be held responsible himself and his tribe with him, otherwise it would be an act of tyranny. God's will is with those who obey the injunction of the mandate most scrupulously.
39. And the Jews will be responsible for their own expenses and the Muslims for theirs.
40. Whosoever wages war against the people of this covenant will be unanimously resisted by them (the Jews and the Muslims). There shall be mutual love and concord amongst them.
41. There shall be fidelity of faithlessness and the oppressed will be helped in every case.
42. And the Jews shall share the expenses with the Muslims so long as they fight shoulder to shoulder with them.
43. The valley of Yathrib will be taken for a Sanctuary by these covenanters.
44. The same treatment will be meted out to the refugee as to the one who has offered him refuge. Neither will any harm accrue to him nor will he (himself-

protector) break his covenants.

45. No refuge will be offered except with the permission of the people of that place, i.e. the refugees will have no right to offer refuge to others.

46. If there takes place any dispute or murder amongst the people of this covenant, and further mischief is feared, then guidance will be sought from God or His Apostle. God's will is with that person who obeys the injunctions of the mandate with the best of intentions and fidelity.

47. The Quraish will not be offered any refuge, nor their abettors.

48. These Jews and Muslims will mutually help each other if somebody contemplates an invasion of Medina.

49. If the Muslims are invited to make peace, the Jews shall also accept the same terms and stick to them. And if the Jews invite the Muslims for a similar purpose, it will be incumbent on the Muslims to behave similarly. The only exception will be in the case of a religious war.

50. Every group would then be responsible for defence against flank which falls right opposite to it.

51. The Jews of the 'Auf tribe (whether themselves or their collaborators) will enjoy the same rights as the people of the covenant. They should offer fidelity not faithlessness. Everyone will receive the fruits of his personal acts.

52. God is with him who offers himself in all sincerity and fidelity when acting upon the various clauses of this Charter.

53. And this Charter will offer no protection to a tyrant or to one who commits a breach of contract or promise. Those on this front along with those in Medina should aim at establishing peace, otherwise they will be dubbed tyrants and breakers of the Covenant. May God protect him who carefully and faithfully observes his promise and Muhammad (P.B.U.H.) will also be pleased with such a person.

Charter of Medina was not only a charter but a written

constitution. The word scripture has been used for it. It was the first written constitution of world.[130] It had two major parts : first related to *Muhajirin* (emigrants) and *Ansar* (Helpers), and the second related to the Jews. *Muhajirin* and *Ansar* had embraced Islam and *Ansar* had taken the Pledge of Aqba. So far as the Jews are concerned Dr. Muhammad Hamidullah opines that it is not understandable that the Jews might have confederated with the Muslims in that prelimi-nary period. But the second part of the constitution is related to the period falling after the battle of Badr when they were awed by the tremendous victory of the Muslims.[131] The Holy Prophet concluded several treaties with the neighbouring tribes, such as Banu Madlaj, Bani Damra and Johaina, as a link of the Charter of Medina.

As there were several tribes in Medina so each tribe lived in one place only. In each locality there were *Naqeeb* (chief), *'Areef* (deputy chief) and *Saqifa* (meeting place). *Ansar* were familiar with this division. As the *Muhajirin* did not know this system therefore they were also regarded as a tribe for judicial and social purposes. Further, the Charter decided that if a committee of a locality was not capable of fulfilling the responsibilities of any one of its inhabitants then the other committees would help it. It was also elaborated that if there is a client in a tribe then he would have no right to differ with his locality. Similarly nobody would make a person his client who is the client of another person without his permission.

Another aim of the Charter was to exalt the truthfulness of Islam. It was why the Muslims were directed, under one clause of the Charter, that if any of their non-Muslims relatives was killed by a Muslim, they should not insist upon *diyat*. They should not help any non-Muslim against a Muslim.

The nucleus of the treaty was war and truce. It was regarded essential that while waging war or making truce whole of Medina would be kept in view. It would not be appreciated that a few people should fight or make truce. Rather it was regarded individual and collective responsibility. War service was declared essential. It was, also decided that each group, which had accepted the treaty, would fight and take rest by turn in the actual hostilities. Only one group was not going to bear the burden.

The Charter regarded Medina a *haram* and consequently it was prohibited to shed blood there from the point of religion. The parties agreed that they would do their utmost to uplift its *hurmat* (reverence) for ever even if they had to, offer sacrifices. Politically it maintained that the inhabitants living within the bounds of the *haram* constituted one party upon which were imposed all laws of the government. If they got some rights, they were also asked to carry out certain duties. Small minarets were constructed on the boundaries of the *haram* under the supervision of Ka'b b. Malik to determine its limits. It was a political achievement of Muhammad (P.B.U.H.) that he made the Jews to recognize a semi-Arab city a *haram*.[132]

The Charter did not content with only the problem of war and peace but it solved the problem of *diyat* on very modern lines on the whole. The problem of quarter has been discussed in it. The right of giving quarter by an individual was recognized according to the ancient custom. The most important thing was that this right was bestowed upon everyone indiscriminately. But this liberty was conditioned in a way that the parties to the Charter would not give quarter to the lives and property of the Quraish. Moreover, they would not cause hinderance if the Muslims do any harm to the lives and property of the Quraish in connection with their belligerent rights. Some writers opine that this clause was not included in the preliminary Charter and it was added to the original text after the battle of Badr when treaties were concluded with the Jewish tribes or on another occasion.[133]

The Jews accepted the treaty but their participation in the army was conditioned with the permission of the Holy Prophet. The pagans of Makkah could ask help against the Muslims from the Jews only. But they were deprived of this after this Charter. This is a separate issue whether it was acted or not. But the Jews were convicted to be at fault because they had accepted the treaty. 'It elaborates the revolutionary concept of a State whose foundations are laid on faith but which bestows oneness of community on those who do not belong to the same faith but are loyal to it in the political sense.' It made the parties bound to respect it more than anything. It laid down the foundation of a centralized government in the Arabian Peninsula for the first time. Before this there was tribalism in which every tribe was in the state of war with one another. 'The Treaty abolished the local, territorial and tribal alliance so conspicuous in the history of Arabia'. "A death-blow was thus given to that anarchic custom of the Arabs, which had hitherto obliged the aggrieved and the injured to rely upon his own or his kinsmen's power in order to exact vengeance, or satisfy the requirements of justice. It constituted Muhammad the chief magistrate of the nation, as much by his prophetic function as by a virtual compact between himself and the people."[134]

Muhammad (P.B.U.H.) made the Confederates one community as against mankind. 'He rid himself, at one stroke, of the old Arab conception which had kept back the Makkans themselves from adopting a drastic policy of suppression and repression against him. And with it he dissolved the old ties, broke down the old barriers, and placed every Muslim under the protection of the entire community of the Faithful -- a protection which even extended to blood revenge .... as regards bloodshed for the cause of God, the Faithful are avengers of each other's blood.[135] He was not only a Prophet but head of a government and in this capacity he always looked forward that nobody should do any wrong with anybody. He granted a Charter of tolerance to non-Muslims and allowed them freedom to worship their own religion, and to retain their own laws and institutions.

The importance of this document was, even, deeply felt by the orientalists. How beautifully Nicholson has written, "Ostensibly a cautious and tactful reform, it was in reality a revolution. Muhammad didst not strike openly at the independence of the tribes, but he destroyed it, in effect, by shifting the centre of power from the tribe to the community; and although the community included

Jews and pagans as well as Muslims, he fully recognized, what his opponents failed to foresee, that the Muslims were the active, and must soon be the predominant partners in the newly founded State."[136]

The parties to the Charter acknowledged that all powers would be vested in Muhammad (P.B.U.H.) and that his decisions would be last and final. "On the religious side it meant the acceptance of Muhammad as prophet, and on the political side the acceptance of him as arbiter between the opposing factions in Medina."[137] There was absolutely no question of materialism because it was admitted, at the same time, that the real source of power is only Allah Who sent Muhammad (P.B.U.H.) as His Apostle. He guided him Himself and, therefore, his decisions could not be wrong. Although he was the head of a State but was not above law. There was complete supremacy of law. He was the final court of appeal but, again, ancient system of insurance was explained and endorsed for the payment of damages and blood-money.[138] Blood money and blood revenge were fully explained in this great document. In brief, justice took place in every sphere of life. To fulfil the demands of justice it was prohibited even to save the skin of the real son.

At one point, the word *'deen'* has been used in this document. It points out that Islam does not believe in any discrimination between religion and politics. Although religion was predominant yet there was a great room for tolerance in the Muslim State. There were certain people in Medina who made their children Jews after making a vow. In a specific clause it was clarified about them that if they inclined to be submissive and co-operative, they would enjoy the equal rights with the Muslims.

This was the first Islamic treaty in foreign affairs which gave great impetus to complete the aims of the Islamic society. Besides the Muslims, the Holy Prophet himself was satisfied that there would not be any pressure of opposing group. Now every issue was going to be settled after general consensus. The available sources in the state were set for its safety. We cannot agree with historian Spranger who thinks that the Islamic State of the first century of Hijra was "a purely military state not unlike the old Sparta --- only Islam recognized no aristocracy."

Now the question arises that why the non-Muslims of Medina acknowledged the position of Muhammad (P.B.U.H.)?

It is necessary to know the circumstances of Medina to elaborate the above-mentioned reality. The two major tribes -- Aus and Khazraj -- of Medina had seen the bloodshed in the battle of Bu'ath. In this battle the Khazraj were victorious. Aus were so much depressed that they decided to leave Medina and settle somewhere else. For this purpose they chose Makkah and asked the permission from the Quraish elites who refused to permit them to settle in Makkah They also refused to help them in actual hostilities. Now the Aus turned towards the Bani Quraiẓah. When the Khazraj came to know about these steps of the Aus, they took forty Jewish youths as hostages. This step was as an assurance of their impartiality. At last they were killed. This incident took place in 10th year of the Ministry. Thus a coalition was formed between Aus and the Jews. After the battle of Bu'ath they felt a need to form a government to avoid inter-fightings. For this purpose the personality of Abdullah b. Ubayy emerged. He belonged to the Khazraj and he had prohibited the Khazraj from killing the Jewish youths. On this plea he did not take part in the battle of Bu'ath. Consequently the Jews liked him. But if we go into the details we know that not a single tribe wanted to crown him as a king. Aus did not like him on the above-mentioned reason. The third party, the Jews, was not ready to accept the paramountcy of any pagan.

It was during the pilgrimage that the Yathribites were introduced to Muhammad (P.B.U.H.) and in him they saw their lost destination. He, himself, was indeed a stranger for the Yathribites but his government was not at all stranger because the Yathribites were themselves running the government. Secondly, the tribesmen had to accept his paramountcy after the Yathribite chiefs had embraced Islam because it was a characteristic of tribalism. This contractual state of Medina came into being not through sword but after the negotiations of the concerned individuals. This state was the manifestation of an evolution in which the integrity of the whole country was kept in view.

We come across ten tribes in this treaty. Each signatory had complete religious freedom. The customs of each group were let remained intact. As there was no tyranny in it from any angle therefore the Jews, even, accepted that Muhammad (P.B.U.H.) would perform the duties of Superme Court. He used to decide their disputes according to their personal law. 139 The Jews had not participated in the Confederation as a unit but each tribe was a unit itself in its place. This was the reason that whenever the Muslims fought against a Jewish tribe or any of them was expelled from Medina, the other tribes not only remained silent but on certain occasions they helped the Muslims. 140

The Charter laid the foundation of an Islamic State which was the result of several verbal and written treaties. 'It appears that he considered it as a government of Makkah in exile, a de jure government.' Several of the treaties were in the form of fealties while others were defensive concluded with the non-Muslims, e.g. with the Jewish tribes of Medina or the Christians of Najran.

In the beginning three Jewish tribes, i.e. Banu Nadir, Banu Qainuqua and Banu Quraizah, which were settled in the vicinity of Medina, were not party to the Treaty. But after a short while they also became a party to it, as it was a flexible and practicable constitution.[141] As the Treaty was international in nature therefore the Holy Prophet intended to include the neighbouring tribes of Medina in it due to two reasons:[142]

(a) to end the inter-tribal civil wars;

(b) to save the contracting parties from the instigation of the Quraish against the Muslims.

Keeping in view these two aims he concluded treaties with Bani Damra b. Bakr in 1 A.H., with the people of Mountain Buwat in Rabi'ul Awwal in 2 A.H., and with Banu Mudlaj in Jamadi'ul Akhar 2 A.H.

He recognized the economic lives of the people. A destitute could get financial aid from a rich person in paying his debts by accepting his demand for blood-money. He was a statesman of universal qualities. 'The document reveals the Man in his real greatness -- a master-mind, not only of his own age, as Muir calls him, but of all ages.'

The Charter is the Magna Carta of the Islamic constitutional history. It was enforced in the form of a duty and order because the Book carries the same meaning.[143] It is the 'first charter of freedom of conscience.'[144] This Treaty was concluded with those people who were (in Quranic words) swift-paced in 'oppression and sin.' They were accustomed to tell a lie, daring in taking ill-gotten things, usurer capitalists, and illegally took the belongings of the poor.[145]

Muhammad (P.B.U.H.) kept the following aims while concluding the Treaty :

1. Defence of Islam from foreign aggressions and the struggle for its survival at every cost;
2. Fullest success in propagation of Islam;
3. To sacrifice everything in the path of Allah.

He laid the foundation of such a society which claimed universal mankind. It brought tribal anarchy to an end. 'The Charter was a revolutionary step in so far as securing one's right ceased to be the concern of an individual of his clan.' The Treaty began with these words: "In the name of Allah, Who is Most Merciful and Beneficent." Had the Jews abided by the Treaty the world would have seen how peacefully different nations were leading their lives in the State of Medina. This Document provided the guiding principles to the Muslim rulers to come that how they should treat their non-Muslim subjects. This was the first and foremost constitution of the mankind. All constitutions which followed, including the Charter of the United Nations, are its immitation.

The Treaty Of Juhaynah :

This tribe was settled in the hilly tract of "Dudwa" in Yanbu'. This place was at the three stages journey from Medina. Muhammad (P.B.U.H.) sent a detachment of thirty *Muhajirin* under Hamza in the seventh month of the first year of Hijra, to shut the road upon a Quraish caravan, which consisted of three hundred persons. Abu Jahal was leading the caravan from Syria to Makkah.

The Muslim detachment reached the sea-shore enroute to Aa'is[147]. Majdi b. Amr the chief of Juhayna, was ally of both the Muslims and the Quraish. When both the parties encountered one another, Majdi used his good offices and succeeded in it. No fighting took place,[148] and the Quraish stole away to Makkah.

Ibn Sa'd has described the following different forms of the treaty concluded with the different branches of Juhayna :[149]

a) He wrote for Bani Dhara'a and Bani Al-Rabah that "they have safety for their lives and property. Whosoever oppresses them or fights with them, they will be helped against them except when that oppression and war is about children or their families. Their nomads will enjoy the same rights which their citizens, provided they are noble and pious. And help is sought from Allah."

Dr. Muhammad Hamidullah writes about the words children and families in the treaty that "they are not clear. It seems that they have been incorporated at a later stage. Or it may mean the civil war of the tribe itself ..... It would have been futile unless they were assured help against Majdi b. Amr. It was necessary to save them from the aggression of the Quraish besides Majdi. And probably they had accepted to seek the help of the Muslims because they had tensioned relations with Majdi."[150]

b) He wrote Aaosja b Harmalah al-Jahni who lived in Dhi Al-Marwah:[151]
"In the name of Allah, Most Merciful and Beneficient. The Apostle of Allah has granted Dhi Al-Marwah[152] to Aaosja b. Harmalah and this document relates to that. he has been given the area lying between Balkatha to Madha Jaflath to the mountain of Qabla. No one will cause hindrance to them in this connection. And if anyone causes hindrance, it will be unlawful. The right will be of Aaosja.

Witness: Uqba.

c) He wrote for Bani Shamkh:
In the name of Allah, Most Merciful and Beneficient.. This is a document granted to Bani Shamkh of Juhayna by Muhammad. He has granted them the land of Sufaina, they demaracted it and .cultivated it. Whosoever will cause hindrance to them will have no right and their claim will be true.
Witness: Ala' b. Uqba.

d) He wrote the following peace-treaty for Bani Al-Jurmaz b. Rabia:
They have peace in their localities. All the wealth and belongings which they had at the time of embracing Islam, are theirs.
This treaty was written by Mughira.

Treaty Of Abwa or Banu Damrah:

In Safar 2 A.H., the Holy Prophet went to Waddan in his expedition of Abwa. No fighting took place but he concluded a treaty with Makhsi b. Amr Damrahi who was the chief of Banu Damrah. Its clauses were:[153]

In the name of Allah, the Most Merciful and Beneficient.

1. This is the writ of Muhammad, the Apostle of Allah, in favour of the Banu Damrah.
2. They have been assured the security of their persons and their properties.
3. That they may count on (his) help if anybody takes aggressive action against them, except in case of fight in the name of religion.
4. This assurance is valid so long as the sea wets the shells.
5. Similarly, when the Prophet requires it of them, they will help him; and they pledge for that Allah and His Apostle. To help them will depend upon their loyalty and piety.

The historian Jauhri has written in Futuhul-Arab that

this treaty was concluded in the battle of Bawat whereas Ibn Sa'd opines that the treaty concluded in Bawat was with Banu Madlaj.

Abwa is the place were the mother of the Holy Prophet was buried. The central place of Abwa was Fara'a which was an important town situated at a distance of eighty miles from Madina. The tribe of Damrah was settled in the same direction. Situated in the south-west of Medina this place was also important because the Quraish trade caravans passed through his passage to Syria and Egypt. This treaty gave a severe blow to the trade of the Quraish. Further, Medina could get information about the Quraish well in time. Thus this treaty is the bearer of first political expedition of the city state of Medina. This treaty, also, contains the real aim of establishing peace and the claim that every Islamic treaty should be according to the basic aim.

Treaty Of Buwat :

In Rabiu'l Awwal 2 A.H., the Holy Prophet went to the Mountain of Razwi and concluded a treaty with the people living there. This treaty was an extension of the Charter of Medina.

Treaty Of Banu Madlaj :

Banu Madlaj was the same tribe to which Suraqa b. Malik belonged. He had tried to arrest Muhammad (P.B.U.H.) at the time of his Migration from Makkah to Yathrib to get the heavy prize announced by the Quraish.

In Jamadi'ul Thani 2 A.H., (October 623 A.C.) the Holy Prophet set out from Medina to obstruct a trade caravan of the Quraish. This expedition is called Ghazwa-i-Ushayra. He reached Ushayra in Sukhayrat in search of the caravan after passing from the valley of Yanbu'. The caravan slipped away by the sea-side and no fighting took place. Anyhow, he concluded a treaty with Banu Madlaj at this place. This tribe was an ally of Banu Dhamara which was a signatory of the Charter of Medina. It is why that it accepted terms easily. The second reason was the policy of non-interference in the others' religious affairs.

Treaty Of Ashjah :

Banu Ashjah was a branch of the Ghatfan tribe,. It was settled adjacent to the trade route. When the Muslims blocked the Quraish it badly affected the economy of Banu Ashjah, because its total earnings depended upon the income which it got by serving the carvans. When they were hard pressed their deputation visited Medina. A treaty was concluded with them. It was written by Ali.[155]

In the name of Allah, Most Merciful and Beneficient This is that pledged-treaty which Naeem b. Masood Al-Ashj'ai has concluded. He has concluded it on the condition of help till the mountain of Uhad remains on its place and the sea wets a shell.

This tribe embraced Islam in 5 A.H., before the Ghazwa of Trench. The whole tribe had not embraced Islam at the time when treaty was concluded. Prominent among the converts was Naeem b. Masood. The basis of the treaty was the "wide relations of help and support, goodwill and cordiality."

Treaty Of Banu Ghifar :

This tribe was inhabited near the sea-coast of the Red Sea. It was a branch of Banu Damrah. The famous companion of the Holy Prophet, Abu Dhar Ghifari, belonged to this tribe. The people of this tribe were highwaymen. A treaty was concluded with it almost at the same time when Ghazwa Badr was fought. The treaty was as follows :[156]

"That these people are Muslims. They have the same rights as the Muslims. Same is incumbent upon them as the Muslims. Help is assured to them if anybody attacks them aggressively. If the Prophet requires their help, they will help him, and it is incumbent upon them to help him, except in wars waged in the name of religion. This is valid so long as a sea wets a shell. Whosoever prevents anybody to practise upon it will be sinner."

The beginning of the treaty shows as if these people

were Muslims. It seems strange. It is possible that any later writer might have added in it intentionally. Because another clause of the treaty is impediment to accept them Muslims at the time when the treaty was concluded, i.e. in which they have been allowed to remain neutral in the religious wars. So they might have embraced Islam gradually or at one time at a later stage.

Treaty with ainiya b. Hisn :

In Rabi'ul Awwal 5 A.H. the Holy Prophet set out for Daumatul Jandal. No fighting took place, anyhow he concluded a treaty with ainiya b. Hisn that he would graze his animals in Taghlmeen to Al-Marad and its environs.

The need of the background of this treaty was that the villages of ainiya were suffering from drought whereas it had rained locally in Al-Marad. Taghlmeen was situated at the distance of two miles from al-Marad and the latter was at thirty-six miles from Medina. Muhammad (P.B.U.H) accepted their request and concluded a treaty with them.[157]

Efforts For A Truce With The Chiefs Of Ghatfan :

The Muslims had to face many difficulties during the siege of the Ghazwa of Trench. It was the tenth day of the siege that the Holy Prophet sent a message to ainiya b. Hisn and Harith b. Auf that if they withdrew their forces from the scene he was ready to give them one-third of the harvest of Medina. 158 The Chiefs of Ghatfan agreed to sign such a treaty. Even the treaty was drafted but not signed.

After the preliminary stages the Holy Prophet sought the advice of Sa'd b. Abada and Sa'd b. Muadh. They told him that they had no objection if he was pleased to do so. And if Allah had ordained him for this then it should be carried out. The Holy Prophet told them that it was only his opinion.

When Sa'd b. Mu'adh heard this he said, "When we were pagans, these people were bent upon to eliminate us. Now Islam has given us honour and we have become stronger due to you, how is it possible that we hand over our goods to them. We do not need these conditions at all. Only sword will decide amongst us."

Now Muhammad (P.B.U.H.) said, "All right take this draft-treaty." Sa'd b. Mu'adh erased it saying that they wanted to govern and extort from us.[159] When this conversation was going on Naeem b. Masood Al-Ashj'ai appeared on the scene. Both parties had cordial relations with him. He caused discord among the attacking parties and they returned without fighting.[160]

This treaty was a process-verbal.

Treaty With St. Catherine :

In the sixth year of Hijra, the Holy Prophet granted a writ to the bishops and all Christians of St.Catherine near Mount Sinai. This writ is an excellent example of freedom and rights. He wrote :[161]

> "Whatever goods, little or abundant (movable or immovable) they have of their churches, monasteries and bishopric and those who are neighbours of Allah and His Apostle, will remain in their possession. (Nothing will be extorted from them despite the fact that they have not embraced Islam). No bishop is to be driven out of his bishopric. No monk is to be expelled from his monastery. No change will be made in their rights or kingdom or anything in their possession provided they remain well-wishers. And they will reform their rights incumbent upon them. Neither they will be oppressed nor they will oppress."

Mughira wrote this treaty which is a great charter of freedom, tolerance and equality in letter and spirit. History of the world has no parallel example in this respect. It granted the Christians such privileges and immunities which they did not possess under sovereigns of their own creed. It regarded a Muslim as a violator of Allah's testament and a transgressor of His commandments if he violated this treaty. The Holy Prophet undertook himself to protect the Christians and same was enjoined on his followers.

They were not to be unfairly taxed. Their churches were not to be pulled down for the sake of building mosques. It was further emphasized that the Christian women married to the Muslims were to enjoy their own religious rights. The Muslims were, further, ordained that they would give assistance to them in repairing their churches or monasteries.

Treaty Of Hudaibiyah :

It was after one year and five months of the Hijrah that Qibla was changed from Jerusalem to Ka'ba in the beginning of the month of Rajab. It increased the sentimental attachment of the Muslims particularly the Muhajirin. Muhammad (P.B.U.H.) had taken part in the construction of the holy sanctuary before his ministry. He was fortunate enough to fix the Black Stone in its place. After the Hijrah the Muslims were busy in the Ghazwas of Badr, Uhad and the Ditch and the other expeditions. Consequently they were deprived from the visit of the Ka'ba and other holy places due to the enemity of the Quraish. The exiles had left their families in Makkah and they yearned sadly for them. They were also worried about them lest they should remain pagans or those inclined towards Islam might deviate from it. They had their movable or immovable properties left in Makkah. Moreover, there was climatic difference between Makkah and Medina. Several of them suffered from a seasonal fever so they could not perform their religious duties. The Muslims were hard-pressed and tortured in Makkah that they had migrated to Medina. But above all this reality remained there that they had a great love for their country. They did not hesitate to leave their country for Islam but loved every inch of Makkah. In Medina the love increased for the place of their nativity. The most persecuted was Bilal for whom novel methods had been devised for torture. Whenever he recollected his memories, he recited the following verses :[163]

> "Alas! Can that day ever come again when I pass a night in the valley of Mecca and Adhkhar and Jalil (a kind of grass) be by my side. And will that day come that I land by the side of springs of Majna and I see Shama and Nakheel?"

That was a happy morning in the year 6 A.H. for the Muslims when the Holy Prophet told them a dream that they were going around the Ka'ba after entering peacefully in Makkah. When the Muslims heard this they became very eager to visit the Ka'ba. Although the Holy Prophet had not pointed out any exact date yet his companions guessed that the visit would be in the same year. Then one morning he told them the glad tidings of making an *Umrah*.[164] He gave out his intent. People responded to his call. At last he set out for *Umrah* in the company of fourteen hundred persons 165 in Dhi Qa'da 6 A.H. (March, 628 A.C.). He left Medina in charge of Numela b. Abdullah Laithi.[166] It was necessary to show that they did not aim at fighting so they donned the pilgrim garb. They were all perfectly unarmed. The Holy Prophet took seventy camels with him for sacrifice.[167] "His march from Medina to Makkah displayed the peaceful and solemn pomp of a pilgrimage; seventy camels, chosen and bedecked for sacrifice, preceded the van; the sacred territory was respected; and the captives were dismissed without ransom to proclaim his clemency and devotion."168

When the Muslims reached Usfan, a place at two stages journey from Makkah, the Holy Prophet was informed by Bishr b. Sufyan of Banu Ka'b that the Quraish had got a clue of his arrival. He, further, told that they had pledged not to allow him to perform Umrah. At this time the Quraish sent a contingent of about 200 cavalry under Khalid b. Walid. Soon he reached at Kura'u'l-Ghamim, a wadi about eight miles from Usfan. From here the Holy Prophet changed his course and went by Thani'atul Murar, a camping -ground of the army, which finally led to the declivity of Hudaibiyah where he encamped.[169] Hudaibiah, a well in the outskirts of Makkah was about twelve miles from Makkah

Immediately after his arrival in Hudaibiyah diplomatic activities began. First of all Budayl b. Warqa al-Khuza'i came with some companions.[170] He asked the aim of his arrival and told him, at the same time, that the Quraish were bent upon not to let him and his companions enter in Makkah He told him that they had come only to visit the House of Allah and to venerate its sanctity and not to fight.[171]

Budayl explained the situation to the Quraish on his return but they maltreated him. The animosity of the Quraish, however. was not yet extinguished and they still obstinated.[172] Now they sent Mikraz b. Hafs to the Holy Prophet.[173] Upon this the Holy Prophet said, "This is a treacherous fellow!"[174] He repeated the same intention to him which he had told to Budayl. After Mikraz the Quraish sent Hulays or Ibn Zamman[175] for negotiations. Their intention was that if Hulays was rejected by Muhammad (P.B.U.H.) his tribe would become their ally. But when the Apostle saw him he said, "This is one of the devout people, sacrificial animals should be shown to him." [176] So greatly was he impressed by what he had seen that he tried to convince the Quraish to allow the Muslims to enter Makkah to perform *Umrah*. The Quraish were so much indignant that they abused him. But when he threatened to take away the black troops to the last man, they requested him not to do so until they obtain for themselves acceptable terms.[177] Now the Quraish sent Urwah b. Mas'ud al-Thaqafi,[178] a very old and revered leader, to Hudaibiyah. After hearing the intention of the Muslims he said to Muhammad (P.B.U.H.), "Do you want to destroy your own nation? Your companions will desert you.[179] Remember that the Quraish are clad in leopard skins and they will not allow you to enter in Makkah"[180] At this juncture Urwa and Hadrat Abu Bakr exchanged hot words. During his visit Urwa was struck with the profound reverence and love shown to the Holy Prophet by his followers. Whenever he performed his ablution they ran to get the water he used. Urwa, on his return, told the Quraish that he had seen sovereigns like the Chosroes,, the Caesar and the Negus, surrounded with all pomp and circumstance of royalty, but he never witnessed a sovereign in the midst of his subjects receiving such veneration as was paid to Muhammad by his people. It was better for them to revise their decision.[181]

Now Muhammad (P.B.U.H.) guessed that there was some thing wrong with the Quraish envoys. It was possible that they might not have apprised the situation fully so he should send his own envoy. Subsequently he sent Khirash b.

Umayya to Makkah mounting him on one of his camels called Tha'lab. The Quraish hamstrung his camel and intended to kill him too but could not do so on the interference of the black troops.[182] Simultaneously, the Quraish posted a large army, some miles in advance of Makkah, to bar the way of the Muslims. The same night some forty or fifty youths of Quraish attacked a Muslim camp with stones and arrows with the avowed object of killing the Muslims. They were also abusing. At last they were caught hold of but the Holy Prophet pardoned and released them,[183] notwithstanding the fact that one of his companions named Zaneem was killed by one of their arrows.[184] But the Holy Prophet foiled the tactics of the Quraish of instigating war.

After this incident the Apostle decided to send Hadrat Umar Farooq to Makkah to explain the point of view of the Muslims. Umar requested, "The indignation of the Quraish about me is not hidden from you. There are none of Bani Adiy in Makkah. I recommend Othman b. Affan because he holds veneration in Makkah."[185] The Holy Prophet liked this suggestion and subsequently sent Othman b. Affan, one of his closest associates and son-in-law, to Makkah for negotiation with the Quraish leaders among whom Abu Sufiyan was prominent. Before entering into Makkah Othman came across Abban b. Saeed who gave him quarter in Makkah. When Othman conveyed the Apostle's message to the Quraish, they offered him that if he wanted to go round the Ka'ba he could do so. But Othman did not accept the offer without the company of the Holy Prophet. Upon this the Quraish detained Othman in Makkah.[186] His long stay created misgivings and a rumour got about that he had been killed. It made the Holy Prophet to say that they would not leave until they fought the enemy decisively.[187] He sat under an acacia tree and demanded a Covenant of Fealty from the Muslims. The response was spontaneous. Hadrat Umar was holding his hand.[188] First of all Abu Sanan b. Wahb Al-Asadi made an undertaking.[189] There was so much fervour among the Muslims that Salama b. Alakwa'h pledged thrice——in the beginning, in the middle and in the last.[190] Only Jadd b. Qays did not pledge and stuck to his camel's side cringing as he tried to hide himself from the men.[191] The Holy Prophet himself pledged on behalf of Hadrat Othman by placing one hand of his (symbolising Othman's) on his other hand.[192] It was at this moment that Allah sent down this verse.[193]

Later on, it was known that the news of killing of Hadrat Othman were false. But the immediate effect of this Pledge was that the Quraish were embarrassed. They sent Suhail b. Amr[194] for the renewal of the negotiations but conformed him not to accept, in any case, the condition of performing *Umrah* that year.[195]. Negotiations were resumed immediately after the arrival of Suhail. There was deep disappointment in the Muslim camp. Hadrat Umar Farooq is said to have protested on the conditions of the treaty. First of all he expressed his views with Abu Bakr and then with the Holy Prophet himself. He replied to Umar, "This is the command of Allah and I will not go against His commandment."[196] When the treaty was going to be written 197 according to the direction of the Holy Prophet, Ali wrote down, "In the name of Allah, the Compassionate, the Merciful ". Suhail, at once, objected and said, "We do not recognize this. You should write 'in the name of Allah.' Muhammad (P.B.U.H.) directed Ali to do so. Then he asked him to write "This is that treaty which Muhammad, the Apostle of Allah, concluded with Suhail b. Amr." Upon this Suhail again objected and said, "If we witnessed that you were God's Apostle we would not have fought with you." The Holy Prophet directed Hadrat Ali to write accordingly but he felt reluctant, so he himself erased the words 'Apostle of Allah' and wrote Muhammad b. Abdullah.[198]

After protracted negotiations both the parties agreed upon the following stipulations :[199]

1. All hostilities should cease for ten years. During this period people were to enjoy peace.
2. That Muslims should retrace their steps on this occasion. Next year they will come having their scimitars in sheaths. They will put on no weapon. They will stay for three days in the *Haram*.
3. And that the animals of sacrifice brought will be slaughtered in Hudaibiyah. They shall not be allowed to be slaughtered in Makkah.

4. The rights and duties shall be equal and reciprocal between the Muslims and the Quraish.
5. Whosoever of the companions of Muhammad comes to Makkah for pilgrimage, *Umrah* or trade will be in the quarter of the Quraish. And whosoever of the Quraish passes through Medina enroute to Egypt or Syria[200] for trade, his person and property shall have the protection.
6. If any person of the Quraish comes to Medina without the permission of his warden Muhammad will be responsible for his extradition. But if any of the companions of Muhammad escapes to Makkah, he will not be extradited to Medina.
7. And that between us is a tied-up breast (i.e., bound to fulfil the terms), and that there shall be no secret help violating neutrality, and no acting unfaithfully.
8. And that whosoever likes to enter the league of Muhammad and his alliance may enter into it; and whosoever likes to enter the league of the Quraish and their alliance, may enter it.[201]

The following persons signed the treaty:

Muslims : Abu Bakr Siddique, Umar Farooq, Abdur Rehman b. Auf, Abdullah b. Suhail b. Amr. Sa'd b. Abi Waqqas, Muhammad b. Maslama.

Quraish : Mikraz b. Hafs.

Scribe and Witness : Ali b. Abi Talib

Dr. Muhammad Hamidullah has quoted Ibn Sa'd and Sarkhasy that two copies of the treaty were prepared,[203] one was kept by the Apostle and the other was handed over to Suhail. Immediately after the concluding of the treaty Banu Khaza'ah announced their loyalty with the Muslims whereas Banu Bakr stood for the friendship of the Quraish.204

The treaty was still under preparation that a persecuted convert named Abu Jundal b. Suhail suddenly, appeared on the scene walking in fetters, having escaped to the Apostle to beg for protection and asylum. When Suhail saw his son, he stepped forward and hit him in the face.[205] Suhail sternly demanded his immediate surrender, saying, "This is the first person about whom the decision has to be taken, because the agreement between us was concluded before this man came to you." So the Holy Prophet extradited him in compliance with the sixth stipulation of the treaty. He said to Abu Jundal, "Allah will provide relief and means of escape for you." He, further, said, "This treaty is like a joint of threshold between us. If a part is separated the whole affair will be spoiled."

After the treaty the Holy Prophet slaughtered the camels and shaved his head. Khirash b. Umayya shaved him.[206] Then he went on his way back to Medina.

The Treaty of Hudaibiyah shows us that how the dream of the Holy Prophet was interpreted by Allah as He Himself says.[207]

Muhammad (P.B.U.H.) could neither perform Haj nor *Umrah*. But his three days' stay shows that it was a fair of I'd or happiness for the Muslims. Allah made them content out of their complete sincerity, faithfulness and acquiescence of fate. They were above greed of any kind. This is why that when the Syrian Christians observed their manners they said, "These people are most excellent than those who had the honour to support Jesus Christ."[208] Allah promised them a reward. They pledged on the hand of the Apostle actually which they did on the Hand of Allah. Some individuals had left behind in accepting his invitation, about whom Allah sent down :[209]

> "Those who lagged behind (will) say, when ye (are free to) march and take booty (in War): 'Permit us to follow you.' They wish to change God's decree : Say : 'Not thus will ye follow us : God has already declared (this) beforehand."

At first glance the stipulations of the treaty seem to be insulting as face-saving clauses were inserted. But it is a fact that there is hardly an example most excellent than this in the history of foreign relations. This treaty depicts Muhammad's (P.B.U.H) excellent sagacity. He had devoted companions with him and a balance had been created, temporarily, in force. But still the Quraish were powerful. Moreover, the treaty with the Jews had been abrogated. The Government of Medina wanted to weaken the economic position of the Makkans by sealing off their trade route of Syria. Therefore the parties were desirous of a peace truce at least for sometime.[210] Had Muhammad (P.B.U.H.) been emotional and stepped to enter Makkah victoriously there would have been tremendous bloodshed. The Quraish[211] might have got a pretext to prove to the Arab tribes that the Muslims did not care even for the sacred months. Thus the conquered tribes would have bent upon taking revenge and an endless chain of wars might have started contrary to the mercifulness of the Holy Prophet. Therefore the adjournment of war is the kernel of the treaty. He had taken the non-Muslims in his company in this journey with the intention that if the Quraish tried to confront him, none of the Arabs would support them or oppose the Muslims. He undertook this journey in the month of Dhi Qa'da in which the Arabs, according to the inter-tribal law and time-honoured custom, did not stop their bitterest enemy even the murderer from the visit of the *Haram;* and they did not attack him. But the Quraish not only violated the inter-tribal law but a few refractories attacked the Muslims. Thus the sagacity of the Holy Prophet disgraced the Quraish in the eyes of the Arabs who supported the cause of the Muslims because their swords were in their sheaths, the sacrificial animals with them and they wore garments of pilgrims but the gates of Makkah were closed upon them! This journey was, at the same time, religious and political. Therefore it became a great challenge for the Quraish. Actually the Holy Prophet displayed great moderation and magnanimity in concluding this treaty. "Surrounded by a surging sea of emotionalism he rises to rare heights of objectivity and uses language which, in contrast to his surroundings, appears amazingly staid and devoid of all sensationalism and over-statement."[212]

It seems appropriate to review the strategical conditions of that time. Medina had confrontation with the Quraish besides the Jews who had great fortfications in the north of Medina. Medina was not in a position to face them simultaneously. As the state of Medina was the common enemy of both the Quraish and the Jews therefore there was a great possiblity of a defence pact between them and thus they could easily sandwich Medina. Being different in nature "there was a military pact between Khyber and Makkah–(one in the North, the other in the South of Medina)–and that if the Prophet set out against one of these regions, the other should attack Medina."[213]

It was the requisition of statesmanship to make peace with any one enemy and make it friend or at least impartial in comparison with the other.[214] The Muslims preferred Makkah over Khyber because it was their native homeland. Many of their relatives lived there and above all the Makkans were gifted with many virtues than the Jews. After the sealing off their trade routes of Syria, Iraq, Yamamah, and even Yemen, surrounded on all sides by Islamicized tribes (for instance, Khuza'ah in the south of Makkah) brought great economic pressure on the Quraish and they actually suffered by drought. After making them realise the importance of Medina Muhammad (P.B.U.H.) lifted the ban (during this period the Quraish widened their trade to make up the deficiencies). He, also, contributed a handsome amount of 500 gold coins towards the famine fund of the Quraish.[215] This was the time when the Romans had defeated the Persians at Nanevah. It made easy for the Government of Medina to let make acknowledge its suzerainty from the Persian provinces of Yemen, Oman and Bahrain. The Muslims were, now, knocking at the doors of Oman and Bahrain because the people of Yamamah had embraced Islam. It was not difficult for them to reach Yemen after repelling the Quraish. It is on the record of history that the pagans of Makkah were disheartened without fighting and their chances of remaining in power were lost. And this was the excellence of Muhammad's art of belligerency.

Now the Quraish admitted the right of the Muslims to visit Ka'ba. In other words Islam was recognized as a religion. It is a great proof of the statesmanship of Muhammad (p.b.u.h) that the Quraish agreed upon not to wage war for the next ten years. When the war menace was over, the Muslims got the opportunity to propagate Islam whole-heartedly. Now elites of the Quraish began to visit Medina in connection with trade and family relations. They were impressed by the morality and teachings of the Muslims. Open discussions about Islam started and even that who held Islam secretly became apparent. Zuhri opines that there was not so great a victory in Islam before the treaty of Hudaibiyah. Whenever people encountered one another, a war was certain. But when this treaty was concluded, war was stopped. People became safe from one another. They visited one another and exchanged their ideas. Its result was that when a person talked about Islam, he understood it and embraced it. The number of the Muslims increased and it was doubled only in two years.[216] Now the Holy Prophet invited the different chieftains and kings of the neighbouring states to embrace Islam besides the general masses. After this treaty two prominent generals of the Quraish –– Khalid b. Walid and Amr b. Al-A'as — embraced Islam. Rate of conversion increased enormously through the pacific contacts between Makkans and the Muslims. The whole of the Arabian Peninsula yielded to Islam only in three years and the Islamic State spread over three continents only in fifteen years. In this context the Holy Quran says :

1. "Verily We have granted thee a manifest Victory."[217]
2. "And that God may help thee with powerful help."[218]

This treaty proved an index of a Great Victory. It proved a blessing in disguise. "The treaty was thus favourable to Muhammad's long-term strategy, but for the moment left him to deal with the disappointment of his followers at the apparent failure of the expedition."[219] The Holy Quran regarded it a victory in the near future. To Ibn Hisham it meant the conquest of Makkah.[220] Hafiz Ibn Qayyim writes that some people thought it to be the conquests of Iran and Rome and to others it meant a chain of conquests over the world horizons after the conquest of Khyber.[221]

Apparently the most defective clause of the treaty was that "If any person of the Quraish comes to Medina without the permission of his warden Muhammad will be responsible for his repatriation. But if any of the companions of Muhammad escapes to Makka, he will not be repatriated to Medina." Muhammad (P.B.U.H.) explained it that the runaway from Medina would be apostate and there was no need of insisting upon him to live in Medina. But Allah would provide relief and means of escape for the runaways from Makka. Nobody came from Medina to Makka but Abu Jandal started propagating Islam in Makka and only in one year he made as many as 300 conversions. At last the Quraish turned Abu Jandal and his companions out from Makkah. As they were not allowed to come to Medina, therefore, they made their abode on a hill near the trade-route of the Quraish. They subsisted by attacking upon the trade caravans of the Quraish and gave a severe blow to their economy. (They were not aware of the Islamic teachings on the point).

One of the Muslim prisoners of Makka was Abu Busair who managed to make his way to Medina. Azhar b. Abdu 'Auf and Akhnas b. Shariq wrote to the Holy Prophet about him and sent a man of Banu Amir b. Lu'avy accompanied by a freed slave on his heels to demand his extradition. The Holy Prophet handed Abu Busair over to them in accordance with the treaty.[22] He said to him, "Go, for Allah will bring relief and a way of escape for you." These individuals stayed at Dhu'l-Hulayfa, at a distance of about six miles from Medina, to take rest. Abu Busair desired to see the sword of Amiri which he showed to him. Abu Busair unsheathed it and dealt him a blow that killed him. His companion ran off to the Apostle and narrated the whole event. In the meantime Abu Busair also reached there and said, "Now your obligation is over and I am also free."[223] Now Abu Busair went off until he halted at al-'Is in the region of Dhu'l-Marwa by the shore of Red Sea. Trade caravans of the Quraish were accustomed to take to Syria by that route. The runaways from Mecca attached themselves to him till their number reached seventy.[224] Abu Jandal was also one of these runaways. They hard-pressed the Quraish trade caravans by attacking them. 'As these men were not officially members of his community he had no responsibility for their actions'. At last the Quraish begged the Holy Prophet to re-open parleys in order to get the clause rescinded.[225] Moreover the one-sided extradition proved expensive and inconvenient to the Quraish. The Holy Prophet asked them to request in black and white. Consequently it was done so. Subsequently all the newly-converts were called to Medina. With the passage of time the other clauses of the treaty became effectless. It is remarkable to note that the women were excluded from this clause of extradition and the Quraish reluctantly gave way. Umm Kulthum, a daughter of Uqba b. Abu Mu'ayt - -·- a chief of Makka, escaped to Medina. Her both brothers Ummara and Walid came for her repatriation. The Holy Prophet prohibited her repatriation as Allah forbade it:[226]

> "O ye who believe! When there come to you believing women refugees, examine (and test) them: God knows best as to their Faith: if ye ascertain that they are Believers, and send them not back to the unbelievers. They are not lawful (wives) for the unbelievers, nor are the (unbelievers) lawful (husbands) for them. But pay the unbelievers what they have spent (on their dower). And there will be no blame on you if ye marry them on payment of their dower to them. But hold not to the guardianship of unbelieving women: ask for what ye have spent on their dowers, and let the (unbelievers) ask for what they have spent (on the dowers of women who come over to you). Such is the command of God: He judges (with justice) between you. And God is Full of Knowledge and Wisdom. And if any of your wives deserts you to the unbelievers, and ye have an accession (by the coming over of a woman from the other side), then pay to those whose wives have deserted the equivalent of what they had spent (on their dower). And fear God. in Whom ye believe."

With the revelation of these above two verses Hadrat Farooq divorced his two pagan wives namely Qurayba d. Abu Umayya b. al-Mughira and Umm Kulthum d. Jarwal.[227]

In brief, the Quraish recognized the suzerainty of Muhammad (P.B.U.H.) over Medina. Before the Treaty of Hudaibiya they did not consider him more than a rebel. After the Pledge of Ridwan, revolutionaries gathered in large numbers around him who were praiseworthy devoted persons. At the time of this treaty the Muslims were fourteen hundred in number and this number was the fruit of thirteen years of

Makkan and six years of Medinite life of continuous struggle. After the Treaty of Hudaibiyah people were impressed highly by the highest morals and the lofty ideals of Islam. They embraced Islam in troops and it was only after two years that their number touched the peak of ten thousand at the time of conquest of Makkah. The top-brass of the Quraish came to Medina and embraced Islam because they came to reckon Islam as a real force to deal with. (They rose to greater heights of honour and magnanimity in dealing with the Quraish). Prominent among them were Khalid b. Walid, Amr b. al-A'as and Othman b. Talha. When they embraced Islam the Holy Prophet aptly said, "The Quraish have handed over pieces of their liver to us." He held their opinions in high esteem in the State affairs. In Medina was established a democracy through consultations where steps were taken according to the Divine Book. His political sagacity and leading vigilance determined the path for the guidance of the people to come by concluding this treaty. The Muslims had to conclude a peace treaty keeping in view the growing Zionist menace in the north of Medina so that they got opportunity to strike it with full force. Otherwise this menace could endanger the integrity of Medina itself. "It was a masterpiece of diplomacy. The growing fervour and fever of the Quraish was made to leak from the safety valve of this truce. Exactly at that time a suggestion of a new powerful siege of Medina, by a union of the Jews of Khyber and the Quraish of Makka, was stopped. Because the Quraish had promised, after meeting out their requested conditions and opening the north trade route, neither to wage war against the Holy Prophet for ten years nor to support anyone secretly or openly. Rather they would remain completely neutral in the wars of the Muslims. With this truce new avenues of foreign policy were opened to Muhammad (p.b.u.h.) Within a month the centre of danger - - - Khyber - - - was eliminated for good."[228]

The Treaty of Hudaibiyah was not a political defeat but a political success. It established an equilibrium. We can analyse its consequences as follows:

1. The Muslims were recognized as an equal party with the

Quraish. It was the first declaration by the bitterest and most powerful enemy of Hijaz about the Islamic Government.

2. Now the Holy Prophet got a wide field for concluding treaties with the tribes who were reluctant before this because they were afraid of 'the Quraish who enjoyed a special position due to the Ka'ba. Naturally their religious sympathies were with the Quraish.
3. A separation was created between the Quraish and their Jewish allies who were busy in instigating the tribes against the Holy Prophet. He was able to crush them effectively at Khyber within a short period of time.
4. The Muslims got confidence and respite for the propagation of Islam whole-heartedly in wider circles. He wrote epistles to the kings and chiefs of different countries inviting them to embrace Islam.
5. The Muslims got success in their armed protection. Generally they became safe and peaceful.
6. It paved the public opinion for them because the Quraish had committed a great blunder in not allowing them to visit the Sacred Mosque. Several tribes were inclined towards Islam and above all certain persons from among the Quraish sympathized with the Muslims. It also influenced the adjacent areas of Makka. All these elements, practically, made easy the conquest of Makka
7. The Makkans could easily visit Medina and thus they got more opportunities to come in contact with the Islamic culture. They were impressed by it, and it made them inclined to embrace Islam.

In brief, 'it was a victory not on the battlefield but on the diplomatic and strategic levels.' Anyhow "the treaty is silent regarding the property of the Muslim refugees, appropriated by the Makkans,[229] as the Muslims had fled to Medina, the property of Muhammad not excluded. And tacitly the Muslims accepted the *status quo* regarding the validity of the enemy occupation."[230]

Treaty Of Khuza'a :

The Khuza'a was a tribe of Qahtani blood which was

settled in the adjacent areas of Makka. Abdul Muttalib, grand-father of the Holy Prophet, had concluded a permanent alliance with this tribe. It was only to this reason that Banu Khuza'a had informed the Holy Prophet about the preparations of. a siege (in the battle of Trench) only in four days.

Banu Khuza'a leapt up at the time of the Treaty of Hudaibiyah and said, "We are in a bond and agreement with Muhammad." Banu Bakr leapt up and said the same with regard to the Quraish.[231] On this occasion the Holy Prophet renewed the old alliance of Abdul Muttalib and said, "Islam strengthens every friendship of the Ignorance."[232]

Treaty Of Khyber:

In Muharram 7 A.H. (May 628 A.C.) the Holy Prophet besieged the Jews of Khyber in their fortresses of Watih and Sulalim. Before this he had occupied the villages of Shaqq, Nattat and Kaita.[233] When they were assured about their defeat, they requested for a truce.[234] He accepted their request and the following treaty was concluded[235] on condition of good conduct:

1. Their murders may be forgiven;
2. Their women and children may not be taken captives;
3. They will be exiled from Khyber;
4. They, in return, will leave their land, gold and silver, and belongings for the Muslims except the goods on their bodies;
5. And that they will not hide anything from the Muslims.

Muhayyisa b. Mas'ud and brother of Banu Haritha acted as intermediaries between the Holy Prophet and the people of Khyber.[236] When their surrender was over they requested the Apostle to let them live in Khyber as tenants of the State lands, saying, "We know more about it than you and we are better farmers." He accepted their request and concluded a treaty with them on the half of the produce of fruits and grains."[237] Muhammad replied, "I let you remain here till God let you remain."[238] The Jews were given complete religious freedom. As they were exempted from the payment of regular taxes therefore they had to pay half of their produce in return of protection for which the Muslims were responsible.[239]

Every year at the time of division of cultivation, the Holy prophet used to send Abdullah b. Rawaha to Khyber. Once the Jews, mischievously, complained to the Apostle about the product estimate made by Abdullah b. Rawaha and on the other hand, they tried to give gold, which they had collected from the ornaments of their ladies, in bribe to Abdullah b. Rawaha.[240] Abdullah rejected their offer despisely and said, "I hate you more than the monkeys and pigs but I will not abstain from justice." Upon this the Jews said, "The world and the skies are standing only due to this justice."[241]

Treaty Of Fidak:

During the siege of Watih and Sulalim the Holy Prophet sent Muhayyisa b. Mas'ud to the people of Fidak to invite them to Islam. Yousha b. Noon was the chief of the people of Fidak. His emissaries came to the Holy Prophet and delivered his message in which he had said, "Spare our lives and we would leave our property."[243] The Holy Prophet accepted their request and a truce was concluded on the condition of half produce like the people of Khyber.[244] Ibn Hisham opines that a stipulation was attached with this treaty, i.e. 'when we will desire to expel you, we will do.'[245]

As the Muslims had not driven horses or camels against Fidak therefore it was declared to be the property of the Apostle whereas the spoils of Khyber were distributed among the Muslims.

Treaty Of Wadi-ul-Qura:

After the conquest of Khyber the Holy Prophet set out for Wadi-ul-Qura and conquered it. The spoils were distributed among the Muslims and the lands and gardens were given to them for cultivation. The Holy Prophet concluded a treaty with them on the same lines as with the people of Khyber.[246]

Treaty Of Taima :

Taima was a place situated near Medina and some think that it was located near Syria. It was inhabited by the Jews. When they heard about the downfall of the Wadi-ul-Qura they requested for a truce.[247] The Holy Prophet appointed Yazid b. Abu Sufian the governor of Taima. He had embraced Islam on the very day of the conquest of Taima.[248] Muhammad (P.B.U.H.) concluded the following treaty with the people of Taima.[249]

> "In the name of Allah, Most Merciful and Beneficent. This is a writ from Muhammad, the Apostle of Allah, to Banu Aadia. Their responsibility lies with us and they will have to pay Jizya. They will not be oppressed or exiled. Night will extend this treaty and the day enforce it."

This treaty was written by Khalid b. Saeed.

Treaty Of Banu Aareez And Banu Ghazia :

The Holy Prophet concluded a treaty with the Jews of Banu Aareez and Banu Ghazia of Bahrain. They agreed upon to submit and pay Jizya provided they confirm to their religion.

Annulment of the Treaty of Hudaibiyah And the Treaty of Makka.

There was enmity between Banu Khuza'a and Banu Bakr from the days of Ignorance.[250] The former had sided with the Muslims and the latter opted for the Quraish at the time of the treaty of Hudaibiyah. According to one stipulation of the Treaty both the parties had to avoid war for ten years. Banu Waile of Banu Bakr availed of the opportunity and intended to get blood-money from Banu Khuza'a for the revenge of Banu Aswad b. Razzan whom they had killed.

Naufil b. Muawiya, the chief of Banu Wail, attacked the Banu Khuza'a by night with the help of his tribesmen.[251] Banu Khuza'a were lying at their spring named

Wateer. One of their members was killed. Banu Khuza'a had to leave that place. Fighting was resumed again. On the other hand, the Quraish not only supplied Banu Bakr with the weapons[252] but Tabri writes according to a narration of Waqdi that Safwan b. Ummaya, Ikrama b. Abu Jahl and Suhail b. Amr (who had signed the Treaty of Hudaibiyah on behalf of the Quraish), alongwith their supporters and soldiers attacked, by night in disguise.[253] Banu Khuza'a were forced to seek asylum in the *Haram*. Banu Bakr asked Naufil b. Muawiya to cease hostilities due to the sacredness of the *Haram* but he said proudly, "Today, I have no God. I don't admit anyone today. O Banu Bakr step forward and get your revenge."[254] Consequently Banu Khuza'a were ruthlessly massacred even in the *Haram*. Now they took refuge in the houses of Budail b. Warqa and Rafa'i in Makka.

Amr b. Salam Al-Khuza'ai came to Medina to inform the Holy Prophet about this bloody incident in which the Quraish, also, had taken part. At that time the Holy Prophet was sitting in the mosque that, suddenly, someone shouted loudly: "O God! Let me recollect Muhammad the old friendship of his father and my father. I refer to it. O Apostle of Allah! help us and send for the servants of Allah for our help."[255]

After this Budail b. Warqa came to Medina with some companions and narrated the events to the Holy Prophet who was hurt to hear.

Now the Quraish sent Abu Sufiyan to Medina for the renewal of the Treaty of Hudaibiyah but the Holy Prophet kept silent. Then Abu Sufiyan visited Hadrat Abu Bakr,Umar Farooq and Ali turn by turn and emphasized upon them to convince Muhammad (P.B.U.H) to renew the Treaty. But none of them assured him to do so. When he persisted, Hadrat Ali asked him to go in the presence of the people, declare the renewal of the Treaty and depart for Makka. Abu Sufiyan did so. On his return, he told the Makkans the whole affair. They were astonished to hear and said to Abu Sufiyan that it was futile as Ali had cut a joke with him. In reply Ibn Sufiyan said that he could do nothing more than this.[256]

Now the Holy Prophet ordered the people to set out for Makka. He reached Makka on Friday on 20 Ramadan, 8 A.H. (11 January, 630 A.C.) with a huge army. He made a public declaration :[257]

1. "He who enters Abu Sufiyan's house is safe;
2. He who locks his door is safe;
3. He who enters the Sacred Mosque is safe;
4. He who surrenders is safe; and
5. He who enters the house of Hakim b. Hazam is safe."

It was the sagacity of the Holy Prophet which made the Quraish to think. So far as the blood-money of the murdered was concemed, their number was too much that both the Quraish and Banu Bakr were not in a position to pay it. The Arabs attached a great importance to the relation of an ally and it was thicker than the blood-relation. The Quraish were prominent among the Arab tribes, how could they leave their ally and earn ignominy and disgrace for them. Therefore, they announced the annulment of the Treaty of Hudaibiyah. Afterwards they were repentant over their decision but now they had lost their reputation.

Some orientalists have written that Muhammad (P.B. U.H.) himself created the chance of the annulment of the treaty. This point of view is based on prejudice. Had he intended to occupy Makka, who could stop him from this when he came to perform *Umrah* and the Quraish had evacuated the city and gone to near-by hills. But he did not make injury to anything in Makka.

Treaty Of Mozayna :

The tribe of Mozayna was inhabited in the west of Medina towards sea-shore on a distance of only twenty miles from the trade-route of the Quraish leading them to Syria.. Muhammad granted the mines of Qabliya to a chieftain of Mozayna as a feoffe so that he might prove an ally to the Muslims in sealing off the trade route of the Quraish.

The people of Mozayna embraced Islam in Rajab 5. A.H. A deputation of Mozayna, consisting of four hundred individuals, visited Medina and desired to migrate. The Holy Prophet replied, "Wherever you live, you are *Muhajir.* So return to your properties." He, also, granted a feoffe of agricultural land to their chieftain. This writ was written by Muawiya.

Treaty Of Jurash :

Jurash was an important place in the south of Tayef in Yemen. Surd b. Abdullah Al-Azdi had besieged Jurash, on the directions of the Holy Prophet, after the conquest of Makka but probably before the embracing of Islam of the Tayefites. The people of Jurash requested for truce and concluded a treaty with the Muslims. The Holy Prophet let their, who embraced Islam, *status quo* remain. Every adult, from among the scriptuaries, was levied upon one dinar as Jizya. It was also made incumbent upon them to give travelling expenses to the Muslim wayfarers.[259]

Ibn Hisham and Tabari both are of the view that the Holy Prophet fixed a pasture for their horses, camels and agriculture near their dwellings. He, further, decided that if anyone else other than the people of Jurash grazed his animals there, his action would be unlawful.[260] He gave them a writ in which he wrote, "The pasture which they had at the time of embracing Islam will remain safe for them. Nobody else will graze his animals there without their permission. Whosoever does not admit it, his property is excluded and anybody can take possession of it."[261]

The Holy Prophet appointed Abu Sufiyan over them.[262]

Treaty Of Aslam :

There are different traditions about the treaty of Aslam and Ibn Sa'd thinks that Aslam were a branch of Khuza'a. This is how the document reads :[263]

1. "It is for Aslam who are a branch of Khuza a. It is for those who have embraced Islam, keep up prayers, give zakat and are wellwishers about the *din* (religion) of Allah.

2. They will be given assistance against those who attack upon them all of a sudden out of oppression.
3. It is incumbent upon them to assist the Holy Prophet whenever he needs it.
4. Their nomads have the same rights and duties which the people of their dwellings have.
5. And they are *Muhajirin* wherever they live.

Ibn Sa'd thinks that this treaty was written by Al-Ala' b. Hazrami. He also stood witness to it. Waqdi is another writer who has mentioned this treaty. He says that when the Holy Prophet encamped near the pond of Ghadir Al-Ashtat, a cheiftain named Bureeda b. Al-Khaseeb came to him and informed him that he and his tribe had embraced Islam. He also told that some people had migrated to Medina and the others intended to migrate. The Holy Prophet asked them to stay there and not to migrate.

It is said that Aslam were a branch of Khuza'a which might be a dwelling in the north of Medina.[264]

Dr. Muhammad Hamidullah thinks that it is very difficult to decide whose statement should be preferred. There is a mention of Khuza'a in Ibn Sa'd. And in the name given by Waqdi a vowel point on the name may be the fault of the copyist.[265]

The same writer writes that the orders to migrate were abrogated after the conquest of Makka, and if there is an exception it can be before 8 A.H. So this writ might have been written before that year. Ibn Sa'd. mentions about zakat whereas a regular department for zakat was established in 9 A.H. but the mention of unfixed voluntary zakat was there from the very beginning of Islam.[266]

Treaty Of Thaqif:

A deputation of Banu Thaqif visited Medina under the leadership of Abd Yaleel in Ramadan 9 A.H. They were lodged in the cupola of the mosque. A writ was given to them written by Khalid b. Saeed :[267]

"In the name of Allah, Most Merciful and Beneficent. This is a writ from Muhammad, the Apostle of Allah, for Thaqif. They are given the responsibility of Allah Who has no associate and the responsibility of the Prophet Muhammad b. Abdullah about that which is written in this writ. Undoubtedly the valley is unlawful to them and the whole is forbidden for Allah. The use of wild thorny trees, to game, to suppress, to steal or commit any other vice is forbidden there.

Banu Thaqif have the foremost right to (this valley) Wajj. Their fort will not be crossed and no Muslim can go there and build a building in their fort or valley. They will not be asked to assemble for military service. They will not be charged Ushr or Zakat. They will not be extorted in property or person.

They constitute a group of the Muslims. They can move freely amidst the Muslims wherever they like. The captives which they have belong to them. They will have the right, more than anybody else, on them and to decide about them.

If they have to receive a debt on the security of mortgage and the time of its payment approaches, it is interest and acquittal from Allah and a debt on the security of a mortgage due after the season of Ukaz, its net principal may be paid at the time of Ukaz.[268]

And Banu Thaqif will get from people whatever due according to their ledgers on the day of embracing Islam.

And Banu Thaqif will get whatever due from people the deposit or wealth, or men (bondmaid and bondsman) which the depositors had got in booty or lost it will certainly be returned.

If some persons or things of Thaqif (now) are absent, will have the same peace which the present-ones have. Their goods in Liah will be safe as those in Wajj.

An ally or business partner of Thaqif will be having an undisputed chieftain like the Thaqif. If anyone blames Thaqif or oppresses them he will not be credible either about their things or person. The Holy Prophet and all the Muslims will assist Banu Thaqif against him who oppresses. And from amongst the people whom they dislike to come, he will not be allowed to come to them. And the business will be conducted in the bazars and the courtyard of the houses. Their chieftain will be from amongst them only and nobody else. Same will be true in the case of Bani Malik and their successors. And if the Banu Thaqif will water the fields of the Quraish, the watering-man will get half of the produce. The interest will not be charged from them on the loan due on the surety of a mortgage. If the masters of a mortgage are in a position to pay, they will. And if they cannot pay immediately then they will return it by next Jamadi-ul-Awwal. And whosoever does not return on the time fixed, it will be considered that he has received interest thereof.

And the loan due from these people will not be more than original principal capital. And if they have a prisoner in their possession sold out by his master, he will have the right of his buying and selling. And if not sold out his ransom will be six female camels, by dividing in equal share of three (well-nursed, fatty and nice.) And if he had purchased it, then he will have the right of buying and selling it."

Treaty Of Daumat ul-Jandal:

It is also known as the Treaty of Ukaidir and was concluded in Shawwal 9 A.H. During the *Ghazwa* of Tabuk the Holy Prophet felt that the Romans had retreated of their own accord and the chieftains of the border area had succumbed to Medina except Ukaidir b. Malik Al-Kindi (a Christian ruler) who had inclination towards Heraclius and might join hands with him. So the Holy Prophet sent Khalid b. Walid who had embraced Islam just 16 months before, in charge of 500 soldiers towards Daumat-ul-Jandal[269] to 'crush him. The Holy Prophet told Khalid b. Walid that he would find Ukaidir hunting wild cows.[270] Khalid b. Walid found Ukaidir alongwith his wife hunting the wild cows on the roof of the fort. Some other members of his family were also present there. It was a summer night with a bright moon. The wild cows were rubbing their horns against the gate of the fort all the night. Meanwhile Khalid arrived there alongwith his cavalry. During the fight Hassan, Ukaidir's brother was killed. Ukaidir was arrested. Hassan was wearing a gown of brocade covered with gold. Khalid stripped him of this and sent it to the Holy Prophet. Khalid spared Ukaider of his life and escorted him to Medina where he embraced Islam. He was given the following charter :[271]

> "In the name of God, the Most Merciful and Beneficent. This is a rescript of Muhammad, the Apostle of Allah, in favour of Ukaidir who has embraced Islam for forsaking the false gods and idols; and for the people of Duma. That portion of the ponds situated outside the population, barren lands and forests, uninhabited lands, coats of arms, armours, weapons, the solidungular animals for means of conveyance, and small forts are for us. To you the walled palm groves and the running water in the cultivated lands. Your grazing animals will not be driven away from the pastures. The beasts which are more than the prescribed number will not be counted at the fixation of the time of zakat. And your plants will not be checked from growing. You will have to say your prayers in time and pay zakat accordingly. In return you will be assured of bonafides and scrupulous observance. You deserve our sincerity and performance of promise. Allah and the present Muslims stand witness to it."

Ibn Sa'd opines that the Holy Prophet concluded this peace-treaty on the collection of two thousand camels, eight hundred horses, four hundred coats of mail and four hundred lances. After the death of the Holy Prophet, Ukaider deviated from the treaty and stopped sending alms to Medina. In Hira a building was constructed on his orders which was named Duma after Dumatul Jandal. Meanwhile, his brother Hureath embraced Islam. Abu Bakr, the first caliph, ordered Khalid b. Walid (who was fighting a battle at Ainul Muter) to crush Ukaider. Consequently he was killed in a fight against the Muslims and thus Dumatul Jandal was again subjugated by the Muslims.

Treaty Of Ailah :

Ailah was situated on the end of the bay of 'Aqabah (the biblical Elath). It is the modern 'Aqabah on the Red Sea. The Holy Prophet sent a letter to Yuhannah b. Ru'bah the governor of Ailah. He came in person to Medina after receiving the letter.[272] He was treated as a guest alongwith his companions. The Holy Prophet treated him with regard and bestowed upon him a cloak.[273] After negotiations[274] the following treaty was concluded :[275]

> "In the name of God, Most Compassionate and Beneficent. This is a writ of protection from God and Muhammad, the Prophet and the Apostle of God, in favour of Yuhannah b. Ru'bah and the people of Allah for their ships and their caravans by land and sea. They and all that are with them, men of Syria and Yemen, and seamen, all have the protection of God and the protection of Muhammad, the Prophet. Should any one of them break the treaty by introducing some new factor then his wealth shall not save him; it is the fair prize of him who takes it. It is not permitted that they shall be restrained from going down to their wells or using their roads by land or sea!"

This charter was written by Juhaim b. Al-Salat and Shurahbil b. Hasana. Buladhri opines that one dinar was imposed upon every adult of that territory as Jizya thus making the collection of three hundred dinars. Furthermore, they were considered to be bound that they would entertain every Muslim passing through their land.[276]

Every clause of this truce depicts a system which is the torch bearer of affability, peace and prosperity. It means that a non-Muslim government can equally be the share holder of the system of peace. It also nullifies the charge that Islam got power through sword. Islam and the Islamic government only want to establish peace. If the world-powers realize this truth, they will admit this reality that Islam aims none other than the welfare of the humanity.

Treaty Of Jarba :

In the ninth year of the Hijra, the Holy Prophet

marched towards Tabuk. The peoples of that land were not in a position to face the Muslims, so they came to the Holy Prophet. The people of Jarba were one of those visiting deputations. They declared to be loyal with the State of Medina and intended to pay one dinar per head as Jizya.[277] The Holy Prophet wrote a charter for them.[278]

Treaty Of Adhruh :

During the *Ghazwa* of Tabuk the people of Adhruh came to the Holy Prophet and expressed their willingness to pay Jizya. He agreed upon to receive 100 dinars from them in every Rajab.[279] They were also granted a charter like the people of Jarba.[280]

Treaty Of Maqna :

Maqna was a port city near the gulf of Aqba. Its inhabitants were Jews of B. Janbah. The following treaty was concluded with them in 9 A.H.[281]

"In the name of Allah, the Most Compassionate and Beneficent. It is from Muhammad, the Apostle of Allah, to Bani Habiba and the people of Maqna. You may be in peace. I have come to know that you people are going back to your village. When this letter of mine comes to you, you are in security. You have the *dhimmah* of God and the *dhimmah* of His Messenger. The Messenger of God pardons you for your evil deeds, and all your faults. Towards you is no wrong and no enemity. After today you will not be subjected to oppression or violence. And the Apostle of Allah will save you from all these things from which he saves himself.

Besides the things exempted by the Apostle of Allah or his representatives your woven clothes, slaves, horses and the armours are for the Apostle of Allah. One fourth of the products of your oases, fishing by your boats and whatever is spun by your wives is meant for us. And the rest is yours.

Furthermore, the Apostle of Allah has exempted you from everykind of Jizya and compulsory labour. If you hear and obey it will be incumbent upon the Apostle of Allah to honour the honourable men of you and to pardon the wrong-doer.

Whosoever from the the Bani Habiba and the people of Maqna will be kind to the Muslims he will, also, be treated as such. And whosoever will harm the Muslims he will have to face the same. Nobody will be your chief except the person from among you or member of the family of the Holy Prophet."

This treaty was written by Hadrat Ali.[282]

Treaty Of Najran :

Muhammad (P.B.U.H.) concluded the following treaty with the people of Najran in 10 A.H.[283]

"In the name of Allah, the Most Compassionate and Merciful. This is the document written by Muhammad, the Apostle of Allah, for the people of Najran. Although he had the power to take his share from their fruit, gold, silver, iron (arms) and the slaves yet he left all these things for them provided they pay two thousand garments of stipulated value every year —— one thousand in Rajab and the other one thousand in Safar. Each garment will be equal to one *Auqia.* More or less than this will be calculated. The armours, horses or carriages offered will be calculated too. It will be the duty of the people of Najran to manage the boarding and lodging for my messengers. No messenger will be detained for more than one month. If there is some disorder in Yemen, the people of Najran will have to lend thirty armours, thirty horses and thirty camels. In case some casualty occurs or something is destroyed, the people of Najran will be compensated for it. To the Christians of Najran and the neighbouring territories, the security of God and pledge of His Prophet are extended for their lives, their religion, and their property —— to the present as well as the absent and others besides; there shall be no interference with the practice of their faith or their observance; nor any change in their rights or privileges; no bishop shall be removed from his bishopric; nor any monk from his monastery, nor any priest from his priesthood, and they shall continue to enjoy everything great and small as heretofore; no image or cross shall be destroyed; they shall not oppress or be oppressed; they shall not practise the rights of blood-vengeance as in the days of ignorance — the era before the advent of Islam; no tithes shall be levied from them nor shall they be required to furnish provisions for the troops.

If anyone demands his right from you, justice will be maintained between you. Neither you will be oppressed nor you will be allowed to oppress others. Whosoever from amongst you will take usury after this,[284] is excluded from my security. No one will be held responsible for others' crime. Whatever is mentioned in this statement is the quarter of Allah, and Muhammad is responsible for that untill Allah sends a new command if they are loyal and perform their obligations well, not being burned by wrong."

The following persons signed this treaty as witnesses :

Abu Sufiyan b. Harb, Ghilan b. Amr, Malik b. Auf, Aqra' b. Habis and Mughira b. Shu'ba.

The treaty was written by Abdullah b. Abu Bakr. The treaty of Najran carries a remarkable position. It conferred on the non-Muslims, living in the Islamic State, autonomy, both religious and administrative. It is unforgettable milestone, in the early Muslim history, for tolerance, politeness and high-mindedness. "This document," observes Syed Amir Ali, "has furnished the guiding principle to all Muslim rulers in their mode of dealing with their non-Muslim subjects, and if they have departed from it in any instance the cause is to be found in the character of the particular sovereign. If we separate the political necessity which has often spoken and acted in the name of religion, no faith is more tolerant than Islam to the followers of other creeds. Reasons of State have led a sovereign here and there to display a certain degree of intolerance, to insist upon a certain uniformity of faith; but the system itself has ever maintained the most complete tolerance. Christians and Jews, as a rule have never been molested in the exercise of their religion, or constrained to change their faith. If they are required to pay a special tax, it is in lieu of military service, and it is but right that those who enjoy the protections of the State should contribute in some shape to the public burdens. Towards the idolaters there was greater strictness in theory, but in practice the law was equally liberal. If at any time they were treated with harshness, the cause is to be found in the passions of the ruler or the population. The religious element was used only as a pretext."[285]

Treaty Of Tabala :

The people of Tabala embraced Islam without any fighting. Muhammad (P.B.U.H.) concluded a treaty with them in 10 A.H. according to which their status quo was maintained. One dinar was imposed as Jizya on every adult of the Scriptuaries and it was made obligatory for them to furnish supplies for the Muslims.[286]

Treaties With Bani Al-Harqa
And Bani Al-Jurmuz :

Muhammad (P.B.U.H) gave assurance to Amr b. Ma'bad Al-Jahni, Bani Al-Harqa and Bani Al-Jurmuz through a charter on agreeing the stipulations for peace after embracing Islam i.e. to say prayers, pay tithe and land revenue. They should pay 1/5 of spoils to the centre. They should receive principal and give up interest thereof after breaking their relations with their non-Muslim relatives. The individuals, who merge themselves in this tribe, will enjoy the same facilities which this tribe enjoys.

Dr. Muhammad Hamidullah opines,[287] after quoting Ibn Tulun, Tirmidhi and Tiyalsi that the Holy Prophet sent a directive to this tribe "one or two months before" his death emphasizing that the animals which die their natural death, nothing should be gained from their dead bodies as they are impure and carrion.

4

Ghazwas and Expeditions

(1) Ghazwas and Expeditions against the Quraish

The Islamic community could become one Ummah only after the Hijrah which drew a line differentiating between the ancient and the new values. It erased the communal differences. As it was against the temperament and beliefs of the Quraish therefore their two chieftains Abu Sufiyan and Ubayy b. Khalaf gave the following ultimatum to the people of Medina :

"Your breaking off relations with us is very woeful to this much extent that had any Arab tribe broken its relations with us, it would have been not so important. But the step you have taken has deteriorated our inter-relations. You have granted quarter to that person who was one of the elites of Makka. Henceforth we have been forced to intervene and warn you not to poke your nose in our affairs. If that person is noble we are in a better position to reap benefit from him as we know him better than you. And if he is a malefactor we know better to punish him for his bad deeds."

After this the Quraish sent a despatch to Abdullah b. Ubayy asking him that Muhammad (P.B.U.H.) should be repatriated otherwise they would invade Medina, kill the Medinites and take possession of their women. Abdullah b. Ubayy remained silent.

The Quraish wrote the third letter to the Jews and sought their assistance. They promised to assist them at the proper time.

It was under these circumstances that Muhammad (P.B.U.H.) sent different expeditions at different times because the Muslims became well acquainted with the routes surrounding Medina which led to Makka, particularly the trade route of the Quraish from Makka to Syria. The Quraish depended economically on it. The Muslims, also, came across those tribes who either controlled these routes or lived in this territory. Consequently, they concluded friendly alliances with them.

Now the Muslims proved that they were strong and could face the Makkans and the neighbouring tribes. They could safeguard their faith accordingly. Moreover, they could propagate Islam freely. They made some of the neighbouring tribes their allies.

Muhammad (P.B.U.H.) invented quite a novel thing to keep the enemy in dark, viz; the secret letter –– letter of Maktum. Thus the enemy could not get such information which otherwise could be useful for them strategically.

In the present age Germany used this method as an art during the World War II.

The Quraish were merchants. Muhammad (P.B.U.H.) adopted the most effective method to destroy their economy. The Muslims created an effective sphere around their trade routes. The geographical situation of Medina was such that the Quraish had to pass within about 80 miles from it even if the Quraish tried to keep as close to the Red Sea as possible. This situation was favourable to the Muslims and dangerous for the redoubtable Makkans, who could not dare to pass through these routes. At the same time there was every possibility that the Quraish, with the help of other pagans, might make the supply of all sorts of goods to Medina impossible (as it was done during the battle of Ditch.) This economic blockade could become tense. Thus Muhammad (P.B.U.H.) was forced to take step because the Quraish could not be defeated politically so he preferred the war.

Expedition Of Hamza

(Ramadan, 1 A.H./March, 623 A.C.)

This expedition is also known as Saif al-Bahr. The Holy Prophet sent thirty *Muhajirin* riders under the command of

Hamza b. Abdul Muttalib towards sea-shore in the neighbourhood of Al-'Is, in the seventh month of Hijra. The underlying purpose was to obstruct the trade caravan of the Quraish coming from Syria. This caravan consisted of three hundred persons and Abu Jahl was leading the caravan. The Muslims marched forward with a white flag held by Abu Marthad Kinaz b. Hissen Ghanvi. They approached the sea-shore of Yanbu' after crossing the clump of trees and made themselves ready for encounter. But Majdiy ibn Amr, who was an ally of both the parties, intervened with mediations[1] and separated them without fighting.

Expedition Of Rabigh
(Shawwal, 1, A.H./April, 623 A.C.)

During the first year of the Hijra in the month of Shawwal, the Holy Prophet sent Ubayda b. Al-Harith in the company of sixty[2] persons towards the valley of Rabigh. Not a single one of the *Ansar* was included in this detachment.[3] The Muslims had a white flag which was carried by Mistah b. Athatha. They encountered the enemy near a spring which was situated below the mountain of Thaniyatu'l-Murra. This spring was situated at the distance of ten miles from Jahfa. There were two hundred persons in the Quraishite caravan.[4] There is difference of opinion about its command. Ibn Hisham opines that Ikrima b. Abu Jahl was in command of the Quraish. But Ibn Qayyim has mentioned the name of Abu Sufiyan b. Harb as its leader (Waqdi agrees with Ibn Qayyim).[5]

No fighting took place in this expedition except that Sa'd b. Abi Waqqas shot an arrow on that day. It was the first arrow to be shot in Islam. Another remarkable thing is that Al-Miqdad b. Amr Al-Bahrani and Utba b. Ghazwan fled from the polytheists and joined the Muslims. They had accepted Islam and migrated to Abyssinia. From there they returned to Makka and now got a chance to come to Medina.

Expedition Of Kharrar :
(Dhi Qa'da, 1 A.H./May, 623 A.C.)

In Dhi Qa'da 1 A.H. the Holy Prophet sent Sa'd b. Abi Waqqas with some emigrants towards Kharrar in the

Hijaz. Miqdad b. Amr was the flag-bearer in this expedition. The Muslims travelled during the night. On the fifth day they reached Kharrar but the caravan of the Quraish had passed from that place one day earlier. So the Muslims returned without fighting.

Ghazwa of al-Abwa or Waddan:
(Safar, 2 A.H./August, 623 A.C.)

In Safar 2 A.H. the Holy Prophet himself set out from Medina for the purpose of Jihad against the Quraish and Banu Damra. He left Medina in charge of Sa'd b. Ubada. Two hundred persons were accompanying him. Hamza was carrying a white flag. The Holy Prophet went as far as Abwa where his mother was buried. Waddan and Abwa were situated at a distance of six miles from each other. No fighting took place with the Quraish but a peace-treaty was concluded with Makhshi b. Amr al-Damri, the chief of Banu Damra.

The Ghazwa of Abwa is called the first of Ghazwas.

Ghazwa of Buwat[7]
(Rabi'ul-Awwal, 2 A.H./Sep., 623 A.C.)

In Rabi'ul Awwal 2 A.H. the Holy Prophet set out from Medina in the company of two hundred persons in order to obstruct a trade caravan of the Quraish. In this detachment both the *Muhajirin* and *Ansar* were included. During his absence from Medina, he appointed Sai'b b. Uthman his deputy.[8] The Holy Prophet marched until he reached Buwat in the neighbourhood of Radwa. The Makkan caravan was led by Ummaya b. Khalaf. It consisted of one hundred swordsmen and a herd of 2500 camels.[9] The enemy got wind of the Muslims' movement and escaped from the scene.

Ghazwa Of Bahran :
(Rabi'ul-Awwal, 2 A.H./Sept., 623 A.C.)

In Rabi'ul-Awwal 2 A.H. the Holy Prophet proceeded to Bahran, a mine in the neighbourhood of Al-Furu (a village near Medina). Ibn Umm-i-Maktum was appointed as his deputy in the capital. The Holy Prophet remained there for the rest of Rabi'ul Akhar and some part of Jamadi ul-Awwal. Then he returned to Medina without fighting.[10]

Ghazwa Of First Badr :
(Rabi'ul-Awwal, 2 A.H./Sept., 623 A.C.)

This Ghazwa is also known as Ghazwa of Safwan. In Rabi'ul Awwal Kurz b. Jabir al-Fihri, a freebooter of the neighbouring region, raided the pasturing camels of Medina and stole away some of them. When the Holy Prophet came to know about this incident, he gave Medina in charge of Zaid b. Harith and went out himself in search of Kurz until he reached Safwan, a place in the neighbourhood of Badr. Kurz escaped and could not be overtaken. Then the Holy Prophet returned to Medina.

Ali was the flag-bearer of this detachment which consisted of seventy persons.

Ghazwa of Al-Ushayra :
(Jamadi'ul Akhar, 2 A.H./December, 623 A.C.)

In the last days of Jamadi ul Akhar 2 A.H. the Holy Prophet came to know that a Makkan trade-caravan was proceeding to Syria under the command of Abu Sufiyan. Medina was left in charge of Abu Salama b. Abdul Asad Al-Makhdhumi. The Holy Prophet proceeded in the company of 150 or 200 emigrants to obstruct the Makkan caravan. Hamza was the flag-bearer of this detachment which was of a white colour. The Holy Prophet led this detachment by traversing an unknown path until he reached Sukhayrat al-Yamam. Then he camped at al-Ushayra, a place in the valley of Yanbu' where he came to know that the Makkans had escaped. During his stay at al-Ushayra he made a treaty of friendship with Banu Mudlij.

Expedition Of Nakhla : (Rajab 2 A.H. January, 624)
(Rajab, 2 A.H./January, 624 A.C.)

The Holy Prophet sent Abdullah b. Jahash al-Asadi, on his return from the First Badr in Rajab 2 A.H. (November, 623 A.C.), towards the valley of Nakhla. Some sources say the date was the end of Rajab, others make it the beginning. Eight emigrants[11] accompanied Abdullah b. Jahash who was given the title of Amir-ul Mumineen.[12] The names of his companions were :[13]

1.	Abu Hudhayfa b. Utba	Bani Abd Shams b. Abd Manaf
2.	Ukkasha b. Muhsin	Bani Asad b. Khazha.
3.	Utba b. Ghazwan	Bani Naufal.
4.	Sa'd b. Abu Waqqas	Bani Adiy.
5.	Amir b. Rabia'a	Nakhr b. Wa'il (a branch of Bani Adiy).
6.	Waqid b. Abdullah	Bani Tamim.
7.	Khalid b. Bukayr	Bani Sa'd b. Layth.
8.	Suhail b. Baidar	Bani al-Harith b. Fahr.

All the members of this detachment were emigrants and it was meant for collecting information. The Holy Prophet gave a sealed letter of instructions to Jahash and ordered him not to open it until he had jouneyed for two days. He did the same. It ran as : "When you have read this letter of mine proceed until you reach Nakhla between Mecca and Tayef. Ambush there a Meccan caravan and find out for us what they are doing."[14] Having read the letter Abdullah said, "To hear is to obey." Then he informed his companions about the text of the letter and said, "If anyone wishes for martyrdom let him go forward, and he who does not, let him go back. So far as I am concerned I am going on as the Prophet has ordered." All his companions agreed with him so they continued their journey until they reached at a mine called Bahran above al-Furu'. Here Sa'd and Utba lost their camel so they stayed behind to look for it. Abdullah and the rest of them went on to Nakhla. The Makkan caravan carrying dry raisins, wine, leather and other merchandise passed by them. Amr b. Al-Hadrami, both the sons of Abdullah b. Mughira --Othman and Naufal, Hakam b. Kaysan, freedman of Hisham b. Mughira were among them. The Muslims took counsel among themselves and said, "This is the last day of Rajab. If we fight, we will be enervating the sacred month. And if we leave them alone tonight they will get into the sacred area and will be safe." At last they decided to fight. Waqid shot Amr b. Hadrami with an arrow and killed him. Uthman and al-Hakam surrendered. Naufal escaped and eluded the Muslims who took the two prisoners and the merchandise to Medina. Abdullah set apart for the Holy Prophet a fifth of the booty.[15]

The Holy Prophet showed his displeasure when he came to know that the Muslims had fought in the sacred month. He refused to take *Khumas* and held the caravan and the two prisoners in suspense. (But eventually a revelation justified this action. Al-Quran 2 : 214-217). After some time the Quraish sent a deputation to Medina to arrange the return of their captives. The Holy Prophet said, "We will not let you redeem them until our two friends Sa'd and Utba come, for we fear for them on your account. If you kill them, we will kill your two friends."[16]

After some time Sa'd and Utba turned up, the Holy Prophet let them redeem charging 1600 Dirhams as ransom. Al-Hakam embraced Islam but Othman b. Abdullah died as an unbeliever.

Great Ghazwa Of Badr :
(Friday 17 Ramadan, 2 A.H./13 March, 624 A.C.)

The reasons underlying the Great Ghazwa of Badr were religious, political and economic. The throne of the idolatrous system of the Quraish had started tottering by the progress of Islam which was increasing day by day. The Quraish were hearing quite clearly the bell of danger. They considered themselves on the right path. They tortured the newly-converted persons under the impression of the haughtiness of their might. Their aim was to make the Muslims either to relinquish Islam or to bid farewell to Makka. The properties of the Muslims were confiscated in the name of Lat and Uzza to reduce them to great straits. The Quraish, also, did not like that the Muslims might lead a peaceful life even in Medina or Abyssinia after their exile from Makka. It was under this purpose that they continuously induced the notables of Medina and Abyssinia not to give asylum to these "apostatized" people.

Now the Muslims could tolerate no more. They decided to strike at the economy of the Quraish and they chalked out a programme of obstructing their trade caravans. By this step the Quraish became anxious because there was no way of escape. Had they chosen anyother route it would have been lengthy.. Furthermore, the possibility of food scarcity and supply could have added to their difficulties in their case.

Those who were arrested or killed in the expedition of Nakhla were elites of the Umayyads, e.g. Amr b. Al-Hadrami was the son of Abdullah Al-Hadrami who was an ally of Harb b. Umayya (grandfather of Ameer Mu'awiya). Harb enjoyed a great respect among the Quraish and had become the chief of the city-state of Makka after the death of Abdul Muttalib. Both the captives were the grandsons of Mughira who was father of Walid and grandfather of Khalid. His position was second to that of Harb. The Makkans took this incident as an insult and thus a stage was set for blood vengeance.

It was the time that Holy Prophet heard that Abu Sufiyan was coming from Syria at the head of a big, richly laden caravan. It was said to be worth 50,000 dinars. It was defended by a guard of the Quraish. Besides consignment of merchandise, it was bringing munitions of war.[17] It consisted of forty persons[18] among whom Makhrama b. Naufal and Amr b. Al-As were notable. Now the Holy Prophet summoned the Muslims and said, "This is the caravan of the Quraish containing their property. Go out to attack it, perhaps God will give it as a prey." The people answered his summons. Then the Holy Prophet deputed Talha b. Ubaidullah and Saeed b. Zaid to collect information about the Makkan caravan. They kept themselves lie in wait at Jaura in the house of Kasha al-Juhni. When the caravan passed nearby, they rushed to Medina to inform the Holy Prophet who had got wind of it already. On the other side, Abu Sufiyan was, also, aware of the current movements. As precautionary measures he sent a courier -- Damdam b. Amr al-Ghifari -- to Makka with a S.O.S. message. When he reached near Makka he cried out loudly. as he stood upon his camel, having cut its nose, turned its saddle round, and rent his shirt. He said, "O Quraish! Your caravan is in danger.

Muhammad and his companions are lying in wait to invade upon it. I do not think that you will overtake it. Who is that brave fellow who will save Abu Sufiyan?"

Now Abu Jahl provoked the Quraish in such a way that every citizen became furious and bent upon to take revenge. The whole of Makka was thus aroused and soon came to be gripped by war hysteria. Anyhow there were a few persons who thought the alleged step of the Muslims right because they had been subject to the oppressions of the Quraish. This cruel attitude had forced them to migrate first to Abyssinia and then to Medina. But such people could be counted on fingers while the majority was anxious about its share in the merchandise. All the leading Makkan merchants and financiers had an interest in it. It is just possible that smaller caravans might have joined together for greater safety from the Muslims. The Quraish were, also, afraid of Banu Kinanah lest they invade upon them in the rear out of enmity. When Malik b. Ju'them al-Mudliji, one of the chiefs of Banu Kinanah got clue of this, he made the Quraish satisfied on his side, that even if the Makkans were denuded of defenders, they would not be attacked by Banu Kinanah which had a blood-feud with them. Now Abu Jahl and A'amir Hadrami mustered courage and they planned to mount a naked aggression against the nucleus of Islam. Soon Abu Jahl marched towards Medina, responding to Abu Sufiyan's message, leading one thousand fast-moving iron-clad warriors. This march was a measure of their annoyance keeping in view the above-mentioned facts.

The Apostle set out on 12 Ramadan 2 A.H. with 313 devoted companions[19] leaving Medina in the charge of Ibn Maktum.[20] He gave one flag to Ali called al-'Uqab and one to Sa'd b. Mu'aadh. Both these flags were black. The third flag was given to Mus'ab b. 'Umayr which was white. The Muslims had three horses — al-Sabal belonging to Marthad; Ba'zaja belonging to Miqdad b. Amr al-Bahrani and al-Ya'sub belonging to Zubayr b. al-Awwam. Besides these horses the Muslims had seventy camels on which they rode in turn. When the Muslims reached a valley called Dhafiran the Holy Prophet was informed that the Quraish had set out from

Makka to protect their caravan. Now he conferred with his companions. First of all Abu Bakr got up and spoke well. Then Umar and Miqdad b. Amr assured him of their assistance. Now the Apostle sought the opinion of the *Ansar* as they formed tne majority. In reply Sa'd b. Mu'adh assured the Apostle and extended full co-operation of the *Ansar*. Upon this the Apostle was delighted and said : "Forward in good heart, for God has promised me one of the two parties,[21] and by God, it is as though I now see the enemy lying prostrate."[22]

Now the Holy Prophet marched forward and reached the vicinity of Badr -- an oval plain surrounded by the mountains. Its length was about five miles and width four miles. The Red Sea was only at a distance of ten miles from this place. To some people it was a well owned by a person named Badr, who belonged to Bani Ghifar. Still some people think that Badr was the site of one of the Arab fairs where they used to hold a market every year.[23] Now the Apostle sent Ali, Zubayr b. Awwam and Sa'd b. Abi Waqqas to scout information about the caravan of the Quraish. They brought with them two slaves -- Aslam and 'Arid Abu Yasar (slaves of B. al-Hajjaj and B. al-'As b. Sa'd respectively) and questioned them. They told that they were the watermen of the Quraish. This reply could not satisfy the Muslims so they beat them. After performing his prayers, the Apostle said, "When they told the truth you beat them; and when they lied you let them alone." After making inquiries himself, he guessed that the Quraish were between nine hundred and one thousand. Now he remarked : "Makka has thrown to you the pieces of its liver!" Among the aggressive elites of the Quraish were : Utba b. Rabiah; Shayba b. Rabiah; Abu'l Bakhtari b. Hisham; Hakim b. Hazam; Naufal b. Khawalid; Al-Harith b. A'amir; Th'ayma b. Adiy; Al-Nadr b. Al-Harith; Zama'a b. Al-Aswad; Abu Jahl b. Hisham; Umayya b. Khalaf; Nabih and Munabbih b. Hajjaj; Suhayl b. Amr and Amr b. Abdu Wudd.

One the other hand, the caravan clearly escaped. Abu Sufiyan sent a message to the Quraish to come back. At that time the Quraish had reached at Juhfa. Upon receiving the message of Abu Sufiyan the majority of the Quraish elites showed inclination to return but Abu Jahl cried out : "By God, we will not go back until we have been to Badr. There we will spend three days, slaughter camels and feast and drink wine and the girls shall play for us. The Arabs will hear that we have gathered together, and will respect us in future. So come on ! "[24]

Both the forces encamped at Badr. The Quraish occupied a soft plain in a haste. But it rained which turned the soft sand into a compact surface. Thus the movements of the Quraish were gravely restricted. They were one thousand in number led by Utba b. Rabiah. He wore an ostrich feather on his breast as a mark of bravery. Every soldier of the Quraish was completely clad in iron having abundant weapons. They had also decorated their horses with gold ornaments. They were so proud of their strength that when Aima b. Rahada al-Ghifari offered the Quraish arms and man power they said, "You have done all that a kinsman ought. If we are fighting only men, we are surely equal to them; and if we are fighting God, as Muhammad alleges, none is able to withstand Him."[25]

Hakim b. Hazam (who afterwards became a good Muslim) and Utba b. Rabiah persuaded the Quraish to return to Makka and avoid any fighting. But Abu Jahl raised a quarrel and excited Amir b. al-Hadrami to take revenge of his brother Amr b. Hadrami. He arose and cried out, "Alas for Amr! Alas for Amr! Subsequently the war was kindled.[26]

Al-Aswad b. Abdu'l Asad Al-Makhzumi was a quarrelsome ill-natured man. He stepped forth and said, "I swear to God that I will drink from the cistern of the Muslims or destroy it or die before reaching it." Hamza came forth against him and smote him and sent his foot and half his shank flying as he was near the cistern. But he crawled to the cistern and threw himself into it. Hamza followed him and smote him and killed him in the cistern.

Then after him 'Utba b. Rabiah stepped forth in the company of his brother Shayba and his son Walid. Three men of the *Ansar* advanced in to open space named Auf and

Mu'awwidh the sons of Harith and Abdullah b. Rawaha. Now 'Utba shouted, "O Muhammad! Send forth against us our peers of our own tribe." Now the Holy Prophet sent Ubayda b. Harith, Hamza and Ali who faced 'Utba, Shayba and Walid respectively. Within few moments Shayba and Walid were murdered. The combat between Ubayda and 'Utba was a remarkable one. Both inflicted heavy injuries upon each other that they became immovable. Now Hamza and Ali slew 'Utba and brought Ubayda to the Muslims' camp. His leg had been cut off and the marrow was oozing from it.

Now the two forces drew nearer to one another. The Holy Prophet ordered the Muslims not to attack until he gave the word. Then he dressed the ranks with an arrow.[27] After his departure to his hut a general melee developed. The Muslims appeared composed and determined. In his hut there was none except Abu Bakr. He fell prostrate on the ground beseeching his Lord for the help in these words : "O Lord, if this little band were to perish, there will be none to offer unto Thee pure worship."[28]

The first Muslim martyr was Mihja, a freedman of Umar. The second to fell was Haritha b. Suraqa whose throat was pierced by an arrow while he was drinking water from the cistern. Then Umayr b. Humam and Auf b. Harith were martyred. In the state of hopeless despondency the Holy Prophet took a handful of small pebbles and said turning towards the Quraish : "Foul be those faces!" and flung the pebble at them. After doing this he ordered the Muslims to charge. Within a short while the foe was routed. In this battle the angels, also, participated and their sign was white turbans flowing behind them.[29] When the Iblis, in Suraqa's form, saw them, he escaped. Abu Jahl, who was patrolling, immediately rebuked him, "Do not worry. He has been prompted by Muhammad to create fuss within your ranks. I swear Lat and Uzza! We will arrest the Muslims alongwith their prophet. Come on and attack severely upon the Muslims. Be watchful! Do not kill them. Capture them alive so that we may punish them severely."

But all was in vain because the crust of paganism had

cracked up as a dreadful plight confronted them. Abu Jahl fell a victim to his unruly pride. The Day of Badr "was a stormy winter day. A piercing blast swept across the valley." It seemed as if angels were riding on the wings of the wind, and driving the faithless idolaters before them in confusion.[30] Their loss amounted to 70 killed and 70 captured alive. Fourteen Muslim (6 *Muhajirs* and 8 *Ansar)* were martyred. Their names were :

1.	Mihja b. Salah	The Holy Prophet remarked about him that he was the leader of the martyrs.
2.	Ubayda b. Harith	Known as Abu'l Harith or Abu Muawiya. He was appointed as chief of the first Islamic expedition. He was 63.
3.	Umayr b. Abi Waqqas	Younger brother of Sa'd b. Waqqas. The Apostle tried to send him back as he was only 16 but he wept and was permitted.
4.	Aqil b. Bukayr	His brother Khalid was martyred in al-Raji.
5.	Umayr b. Abd	Known as Abu Muhammad.
6.	Auf b. 'Afra	Ansar
7.	Mu'awwidh b. 'Afra.	Brother of Auf.
8.	Haritha b. Suraqa	Maternal cousin of Anas b. Malik.
9.	Yazid b. Harith	Ansar Known as Ibn Fusham.
10.	Rafi' b. Mu'alla	Ansar
11.	Umayr b. Humam	Ansar
12.	Ammad b. Ziyad	Ansar
13.	Sa'd b. Khaythama	Naqeeb of the Apostle. Known as Abu Abdullah and Sa'd al-Khayer.
14.	Mubashir b. Abdu'l Mundhir	Ansar

God declared the Day of Badr as the Day of *Furqan,* 'that is, the coming of the promised calamity upon the unbelievers and the deliverance of the believers.' The people of Medina received the news of the victory on the 18th

Ramadan. God had already given the good news of this victory as it is clear from the Holy Quran :

1. "Then watch thou for the Day that the sky will bring forth a kind of smoke (or mist) plainly visible, enveloping the people : this will be a penalty grievous. (They will say :) "Our Lord! Remove the penalty from us, for we do really believe!" How shall the Message be (effectual) for them, seeing that an Apostle explaining things clearly has (already) come to them, yet they turn away from him and say: "Tutored (by others), a man possessed!" We shall indeed remove the penalty for a while (but) truly ye will revert (to your ways). One day We shall seize you with a mighty onslaught. We will indeed (then) exact retribution!"[31]
2. "Just as thy Lord ordered thee out of any house in truth, even though a party among the Believers disliked it."[32]

The day of Badr was a decisive one which had long been awaited : "Behold! God promised you one of the two (enemy) parties that it should be yours : ye wished that the one unarmed should be yours, but God willed to justify the Truth according to His words, and to cut off the roots of the unbelievers."[33]

When the war was over, the Holy Prophet ordered the Muslims to collect the booty. He laid down a systematic rule for its distribution. He conferred with Abu Bakr about the prisoners who was in favour of liberating them on ransom. The Muslim camp resounded with cries of revenge particularly Hadrat Umar demanded legitimately the execution of the captives as they were avowed enemies of Islam. The Holy Prophet replied, "These pagans of Makka are just like those who were before them. Noah had prayed, 'O God! Let no pagan be alive on the earth.' Moses had said, 'Destroy their wealth and harden their hearts.' Abraham had said, 'He belongs to me who follows me; and who disobeys me then God is Merciful and Compassionate. Christ had uttered, 'O God if You punish them then they are Your servants. And if You forgive them then You are Predominant and Wise." Now the Apostle addressed the captives in these words: "You belong to that nation which is used to kill the others by deceiving and cheating. No one amongst you will be liberated without paying ransom or he will be beheaded." Only Jubayer B. Mut'em, out of his own will, accepted Islam.

Thus four thousand dirhams were received from each prisoner. But this amount was enhanced for those who were wealthy. The Quraish had to pay more than 2½ lakh dirhams. It improved the financial position of the Muslims. The literate prisoners were allowed to go free as soon as they should have taught twelve lads the art of which they were ignorant. Among the notable prisoners were Al-Nadr, Uqba, Abbas b. Abdul Muttalib (the Apostle's uncle) and Abul-A'as b. Rabi (Apostle's son-in-law who was husband of Zaynab). Abu'l-As was liberated on this condition that he should let Zaynab come to Medina. Al-Nadr and Uqba had left no stone unturned to torment the Apostle and they did not repent upon their deeds. When the Apostle heard the cries of redresses of the daughter of Al-Nadr he became sad. Among the captives was Suhayl b. Amr who used to oppress the Holy Prophet and the Muslims mercilessly. When Umar saw him he said to the Apostle, "Let me pull out Suhayl's two front teeth; his tongue will stick out and he will never be able to speak against you again." But the reply was, "I will not mutilate him, otherwise God would mutilate me though I am a Prophet."

Thus the prisoners were treated with the greatest humanity contrary to all the usages and traditions of the Arabs. About this generous treatment William Muir bears testimony in these words : "In pursuance of Mahomet's commands, the citizens of Medina, and such of the refugees as possessed houses, received the prisoners, and treated them with much consideration. 'Blessings be on the men of Medina !' said one of these prisoners in later days; 'they made us ride, while they themselves walked; they gave us wheaten bread to eat when there was little of it contenting themselves with dates."[34]

Only two were executed notorious for their virulent animosity towards the Muslims. It will be appropriate to discuss two incidents about which the orientalists have presented distorted picture.

It is said that when Uqba b. Abu Mu'ait was being led to execution, he said, "Who will take care of my little children?" The Holy Prophet replied, "Fire of the hell."

This is a preposterous story as it is apocryphal. It is injustice to attribute such an incident towards Muhammad (P.B.U.H.) about whom Allah says : "We have not sent you but as a mercy for all the worlds." Generally a victorious nation loses its senses to rejoice the victory, but the Holy Prophet always admired God Almighty. How could it be expected from a man who was benevolent even with children. He inculcated love and protection of orphans as an absolute and noble duty. To think on these lines is a sheer foolishness. The reality is that he had addressed him, "Sibyat-un-Nar" (children of fire) and the children of Uqba were known as such. Uqba hailed from Ajlan. One of its clans was inhabited in the valley near Safra. These people were known as Bani-un-Nar (descendants of fire). On this ground the orientalists concocted this story.

The second so called incident is told that the Holy Prophet bitterly addressed the dead bodies of the idolaters on their burial. The reality is that the Holy Prophet stood on the side of the pit in which the pagans were buried. The name of each dead body was called out when the corpse was lowered. At the end the Holy Prophet addressed them in these words : "O my kindred! Have you found that what God promised you is true? I have found that what my Lord promised me is true. O people of the pit, you were an evil kinsfolk to your prophet. You called me a liar when others believed me; you cast me out when others took me in; you fought against me when others fought on my side." These words which were palpably meant to express pity, have been distorted to imply bitterness.[36]

The Muslims got victory despite their limited resources due to the following reasons:

God helped the Muslims and sent His angels who took part in the battle. 'The sign of the angels at Badr was white turbans flowing behind them.[37] The unity and the spirit of sacrifice of the Muslims were ideal. They were united by the bond of Islam. On the contrary, the Quraish were disunited and passionless. Those who took part were not whole-hearted supporters of Abu Jahl's policy. They were over-confident. Even their commander, Utba, was reluctant to fight. The warriors of Bani Zuhra withdrew when they had reached at Badr because their point of view was that when the caravan had escaped safely there was no sense of waging war. Similarly Bani 'Adi b. Ka'b did not participate in the war. Thus their number was reduced far below the original.

The strategic positions of the Muslims were also favourable for them being on strong and elevated points. Thus they seemed to the Quraish more than the actual number. On the contrary the positions of the Quraish were in declivity from there they seemed to be much less than their actual number. And when it rained these positions became muddy and swampy making their movement difficult. They sent Umayr b. Wahb al-Jumahi to estimate the number of the Muslims. He rode on a horseback round the camp and came back. He estimated that the Muslims were a little more or less than three hundred. But, immediately, he went again whether the Muslims had any in ambush or support. He went far and wide through all the corners of the valley and on his return he said, "I found nothing, but O people of the Quraish! I have seen camels carrying death. The camels of Yathrib are laden with death. These men have no defence or refuge but their swords. I think that a man of them will be slain till he slays one of you. And if they kill of you a number equal to their own, what is the good of living after that? Consider, then, what you will do?"[38]

The discipline within the ranks of the Muslims was praiseworthy. Muhammad(P.B.U.H.) himself straightened the ranks with an arrow. Credit goes to him for introducing this method among the Arabs. On the contrary, the Quraish had no battle arrays and the whole force did not look more than a crowd. Their warfare was ancient and obsolete. Consequently it was not an organized battle.

Every Muslim soldier was well aware of his motto and ready to risk even his life for it. They were intoxicated with the spirit of Jihad and martyrdom. It imbued in them great courage. They firmly believed that in case they are martyred God would be pleased. While the Quraish had only worldly aims to achieve. Muhammad(P.B.U.H.) himself was a gallant soldier and he fought bravely. His participation encouraged the Muslim soldiery. The leadership of the pagans was inexpert and even their commander, Utba, was not in a mood to fight. As a result, the movement of the Muslims and pouncing upon the enemy was very swift. But the Quraish's case was totally ruined, on the other hand.

Muhammad's(P.B.U.H.) generalship also won for the Muslims a tactical advantage. His strategic plans were so much effective that all the tricks of the pagans failed because the Apostle had forced the enemy to fight in the battlefield of his choice. We can easily judge their confusion and cowardice that when their defeated army reached Makka, many of their 'brave' leaders were absent. They had lost their ammunition and other goods. There was great panic and passion in the city. The people swore that they would not mourn their deads unless they took vengeance from the enemy.

The victory in this battle arranged far-reaching results for the Muslims. Their exploitation came to an end. The period of their persecution and torture, at the hands of the Quraish, was over. This victory frightened the superstitious Makkans and now they believed that they were now not in a position to cut jokes with Islam. Their military power was totally ruined and its grandeur was buried in the battlefield of Badr.

In Medina Muhammad's (P.B.U.H.) cause flourished mightily. It created a healthy respect for the new State of Medina among the nomadic tribes having friendly relations with Makka. The Zealots were confirmed in their faith, the waverers convinced, the disaffected overawed.[39] Medina became one of the greatest cities of Arabia. But the victory did not change the Apostle as a man. He remained the embodiment of humility and meekness. The spoils of the war corrected their economy and the ammunitions served their purpose for the future battles.

Ghazwa of Sawiq:
(Dhu'l-Hijja, 2 A.H./5th June, 624 A.C.)

When the Quraish fugitives returned from the battlefield of Badr there was a great passion and confusion in Makka. Abu Sufiyan swore solemnly to do nothing with oil or women till he had avenged himself on Muhammad and his followers. Accordingly he sallied forth two hundred horsemen scouring the country within 12 miles from Medina at Thayb. "His primary aims were doubtless to restore confidence among the Makkans and to show the world that the day of Quraish was not yet over."[40] In the pitch darkness of the night he came to Huyayy b. Akhtab and knocked at his door but he refused to open it as he was afraid of him. Subsequently he went to Sallam b. Mishkam who was the keeper of the public purse of Bani al-Nadir at that time. There he spent some time. Sallam entertained him with food and drink. He, also, delivered to him secret information about the Muslims and kept his arrival confidential. Abu Sufiyan rejoined his companions at the end of night and sent some of them to Medina. They reached Al-Urayd (an outlying place) and burnt one oasis[41] ravaging date-groves. They also killed Ma'abad b. Amr (one of the Ansar) and an ally of his working in the fields and then returned to Thayb.

On receipt of information the Holy Prophet went in pursuit with two hundred companions and got as far as Qarqratu'l-Kurd about eight posts distance from Medina. But the Quraish had went at full gallop and during this runaway course they had abandoned some excess provisions in order to lighten their beasts. It consisted mainly of sawiq (a dish of green grain made of parched wheat or barley, mixed with wheat or butter. It was 'drunk' as a sort of porridge) which the Muslims picked up for themselves.

The Holy Prophet had left Medina in charge of Bashir b. Abdul Mundhir, known as Abu Lubaba, during his absence.

Expedition Of Al-Qaradah:
(*Jamadi'ul-Akhar,* 3 A.H./November, 624 A.C.)

The Quraish used to take their trade caravans alongwith the coast of the Red Sea before the battle of Badr, but now they adopted the route of Iraq instead of their traditional route. In Jamadi'ul-Akhar the Holy Prophet got wind of a Makkan caravan led by Abu Sufiyan. He sent Zaid b. Harith with one hundred men. As the route was new therefore the Quraish hired a man from B. Bakr B. Wa'il, called Furat b. Hayyan, as a reliable guide. Zaid met this caravan at a watering place, in Najad, known as Al-Qarada. The pagans got away and the Muslims captured their merchandise - - - worth 100,000 dirhams.[42] A great deal of it was of silver. Furat was arrested. Later on he embraced Islam.

Ghazwa of Uhud:
(6th Shawwal, 3 A.H./23rd March, 625 A.C.)

The Quraish had to face extreme disaster at Badr and they had begun formidable preparations from the very first day. They were burning for revenge. They saved all their trade profit for the next battle to be fought. The caravan led by Abu Sufiyan had reached Makka quite safely. It had brought fifty thousand *mithqal* gold and one thousand camels as a profit. It was not distributed among the share-holders but was kept aside for war preparations. Besides it, public funds were raised for war against the Muslims. Now after the Badr the Muslims had occupied those routes leading to Syria and Iraq leaving to the Quraish only the unprofitable Abyssinian market. Naturally, their reactionary spirit was strengthened. Some ladies and poets (Amr Jumahi and Musafi') played an effective role in stirring them up for revenge. Some Jew poets (prominent among them was Ka'b b. Al-Ashraf), also, went from Medina to Mecca to instigate the infidels against Muhammad (P.B.U.H.). This was the time when the Quraish had prohibited the mourning of their deceased because they wanted to inflict revenge upon the Muslims. They declared that whosoever would mourn would be banished from the tribe. A committee was organized in Makka consisting of Abu Lahb, Abu Sufiyan and Safwan b. Ummayya; with the purpose of organizing the Makkans for war. The tribes of Kinanah and Tihamah, which were under the influence of the Quraish, were also bent upon to assist them in this revengeful campaign. The Quraish got war munition confidentially from different quarters but Abbas, the Apostle's uncle who was still residing in Makka, sent the latest information to Medina about the swiftly changing events in Makka.

The Quraish took with them their women to stir up their anger, to revenge their past ignominous defeats and prevent their running away. It was an ancient custom as before Islam "the presence of women on the field and the active share they took in the combat naturally provoked the bitterest feelings. If they were not engaged in finishing the bloody work of the men, their tongues were busy inciting them."43

The following women were prominent:

Hind d. Utba	wife of Abu Sufiyan
Umm Hakim d. Harith	wife of Ikrima b. Abu Jahl
Fatima d. Al-Walid	sister of Khalid b. Walid
Barza d. Mas'ud b. Amr.	daughter of the chief of Taif– Masu'd Thaqfi
Rayta d. Munabbih	wife of 'Amr b. Al-A'as
Sulafa d. Sa'd	with Talha b. Abi Talha
Khunas d. Malik	mother of Abi Aziz b. Umair. Also mother of Musa'ab b. Umair.
Amra d. Alqama.	

Hind repeatedly asked Wahshi to satisfy his vengeance and hers. (Wahshi was a negro slave of Jubayr b. Mut'im and could throw a javelin which seldom missed the target. Jubayr took him in order to take revenge of his uncle Tahama b. Adi and promised him to set him on liberty if he killed

Hamza. Wahshi had the title of Abu Dasma.). Hind was so revengeful that when the Quraish fled from the battlefield, the other women, under her leadership, opened their hair and tore out their dresses and their skin was naked.

In short, 3,000 well-equipped (of whom 700 had coats of mail; 3,000 camels and 200 horses) men set out from Makka under the relentless command of Abu Sufiyan on 11th March, 625 A.C. They went forward by easy stages until they halted at Aynayn on a hill in the valley of al-Sabkha of Qanat by the side of the wadi opposite Medina. 'They took possession of the pastures of Medina; luxuriant crops were cut down to secure as forage for the horses, and camels were let loose to graze in the fields and devastate them. When the Apostle was informed about them, he conferred with his companions but said, "If you think it well we should stay in Medina and if they attack, we can fight them therein." Abdullah b. Ubayyi, the hypocrite leader, also favoured this plan. He had an honourable place in the discussions of strategy. But he could not participate in Badr as he insisted upon to fight outside Medina. Now Abdullah b. Ubayyi again insisted to stay in Medina and the other side gave their arguments. Eventually the Holy Prophet went into his house and put on his armour. He decided on the second course. Now the people repented upon their insistence and requested the Apostle to remain inside Medina. He said, "It is not befitting for a prophet who has put on his armour that he should lay it inside until he has fought." Subsequently, he marched out of Medina with 1,000 companions. He left Medina in charge of Ibn Umm-i-Maktum.

When the Muslims had reached at Shaut, situated between Medina and Uhud, Abdullah b. Ubayyi deserted the Holy Prophet with 1/3 of the total number justifying his action by saying, "You have obeyed them and disobeyed me. We do not know why we should lose our lives here." Following him Banu Salma and Banu Haritha were, also, inclined to leave but refrained from their intention. The Holy Prophet did not mind Abdullah's action although it was a serious blow in the midst of battle. He continued to march forward with 700 persons. It was at that moment that the *Ansar* asked him to seek the help of the Jews (who were his confederates by the Charter of Medina) but he replied that there was no need of that.[44]

He continued to march until he came down the gorge of Uhud - - - a mountain situated at 3 miles distance from Medina. First of all, he appointed Abdullah b. Jubayr as commander of the fifty archers, distinguished that day by their white garments. He posted them on the top of the mountain and asked them not to let the enemy come on the Muslims from the rear whether the battle was in their favour or not. The Holy Prophet put on two coats of mail on that day. He delivered one standard to Mus'ab b. Umayr. Besides, he appointed Zubair b. Awwam and Mundhir b. Amr commanders of the two flanks. Striplings were asked to go back. They included Abdullah b. Umar, Usama b. Zaid, Usaid b. Zuhair, Barra b. Aazeb, Zaid b. Arqam, Zaid b. Thabit, Uraba b. Aus and Amr b. Hazam. But two looked stout and were allowed to participate in the battle. They were Samura b. Jundub and Raafi' b. Khadeej. Both were of 15 years.[45]

On the other hand, the Quraish had got the support of the Ahabish (they were the Arabs of Banu Kinanah). The Quraish emissaries had made extensive tours throughout Arabia and gathered volunteers. Among these emissaries were Amr b. Al-Aas, Amr b. Abdullah Jamhi, Musafa' b. Abd Manaf, Abdullah b. Az-Zibra and Habira b. Abi Wahb. They had mustered their troops about 3,000 men, among whom were 700 iron-clad mailed warriors and 200 horsemen. Their cavalry on the right flank was commanded by Khalid b. Walid and on the left by Ikrima b. Abu Jahl. Their standard bearer was B. 'Abdud-Dar who fought with great gallantry against overwhelming odds.

Now serious hand-to-hand fight started and the two sides glovered at each other. The Makkan ladies took tambourines which they beat behind the men to incite them. They inspired them to heroism. The girls sang war-songs and entertained the warlords who used to round off their rivalry by bouts of drinking and merry-making. They sang thus:[46]

We are daughters of the Star of the Morn (Tariq);
We tread softly on silken cushions;
Face the enemy boldly and we shall press you in our arms;
Fly, and we shall shun you, shun you with disgust.

The war-cry of the Muslims was 'Kill, Kill.' In the beginning the Muslims were overwhelming the infidels till they were about to be uprooted. 'They slew the enemy with the sword until they cut them off from their camp and theirs was an obvious rout.' But all of a sudden the situation changed when Amra d. Alqama took up the standard and raised it aloft for the Quraish who began to gather round it. From one hand to the other it finally went to Su'ab, the negro slave of Abu Talha. He fought until his hands were cut off then he knelt upon it and held the flag between his breast and throat until he was killed over it. Now the Makkan infantry took to their heels. And when the Muslims began to collect the booty, the archers hurried down the hill impatiently, forgetting the injunctions of the Holy Prophet. It proved a last straw which enabled Khalid b. Walid to fall upon the Muslims. Meanwhile, someone called out 'Muhammad has been killed. Now the Muslims began to scatter. The enemy got at the Apostle who was hit with a stone so that he fell on his side and one of his teeth was smashed, his face scored, and his lower lip injured. It was Utba b. Waqqas who pelted the Apostle while Abdullah b. Shihab al-Zuhri wounded his forehead. Ibn Qami'a wounded the upper part of his cheek bone so fiercefully that two rings from his helmet were forced into it. He fell upon one side. Ali took hold of his hand while Talha b. Obaidulla lifted him and made him to stand. Malik b. Sinan sucked the blood from his face and swallowed it out of love. Even at this precarious moment the Apostle did not curse his enemies rather he supplicated to God, "Lord, forgive my people because they know not."

A few Muslim devotees- - - seven *Ansar* and two Muhajirs - - surrounded the Apostle and managed to reach, by retreating, the heights of Uhud. The first to recognize him was Ka'b b. Malik who revealed the news to the Muslims who renewed the fighting at fearful odds. At the same time a group of the Makkans, led by Khalid b. Walid, followed them there. But Umar and a band of *Muhajirs* fought with gallantry until they drove them down the mountain. At the bottom of the mountain Abu Sufiyan taunted the Muslims in these words:

'Show your superiority, Hubal. Show your superiority. Hubal.'

The Holy Prophet asked Umar to get up and answer him and say, "Allah is Glorious, Almighty." Now Abu Sufiyan called out, "Our idol is Uzza and you have no Uzza." In reply it was said, "Allah is our Friend, not yours." Abu Sufiyan said, "Your meeting-place is Badr next year." In reply it was said, "Yes, it is an appointment between us.[47] Our deads are in paradise; your deads are in the hell."

Now Abu Sufiyan ordered withdrawal and both the fighting men and the baggage train moved off.' Before the final retreat Hind and her other pagan women barbarously mutilated the dead bodies of the Muslims. They cut off their ears and noses and made bracelets and necklaces. Then they were given to Wahshi who had killed Hamza. Hind tore out the liver of Hamza and chewed it but she was not able to swallow it so she threw it away. Then she mounted a high rock and shrieked at the top of her voice:

We have paid you back for Badr
And a war that follows a war is always violent.

In the battle of Uhud the following seventy Muslims were martyred[48] while forty got severe wounds:

1.	Hamza b.Abdu'l Muttalib	Wahshi killed him. Apostle's uncle. Title: Chief of the Martyrs.
2.	Abdullah b. Jahesh Al-Asadi	Apostle's cousin.
3.	Musa'b b.Umayr	Killed by Ibn Qami'a Al-Laythi. Migrated twice. Age: 40 years.
4.	Shammas b. Uthman	Migrated twice. Participated in Badr. Age: 34 years.

These four martyrs were the *Muhajirs* . The following were the *Ansar:*

5.	Amr b. Mu'adh	Participated in Badr. Brother of Sa'd b. Mu'adh. Age: 32 years.
6.	Harith b. Anas	
7.	Umara b. Ziyad	Got 14 wounds. Apostle made his foot a support for his head and he died with his face on the Apostle's foot.
8.	Salama b. Thabit	
9.	Amr b. Thabit	The son of Hudhayfa b. Yamman's sister.
10.	Thabit b. Waqsh	Brother of Rifa'a.
11.	Rifa'a b. Waqsh	Very old at the time of martyrdom.
12.	Husayl b. Jabir	Father of Hudhayfa. Was killed by the Muslims unwittingly.
13.	Sayfi b. Qayzi	Abu Haish b. Tayyihan's sister's son.
14.	Habab b. Qayzi	
15.	Abbad b. Sahl	
16.	Harith b. Aus	Took part in Badr. Nephew of Sa'd b. Mu'adh. Age: 28 years.
17.	Iyas b. Aus	
18.	Ubayd b. Tayyihan	Took part in Uqba and Badr.
19.	Habib b. Yazid	
20.	Yazid b. Hatib.	
21.	Abu Sufiyan b. Harith	
22.	Hanzla b. Abu Amir	His dead body was washed by the angels. He was killed by Shaddad b. Aswad Al-Laythi.
23.	Unays b. Qataba	Took part in Badr.
24.	Abu Hayya	Brother of Sa'd b. Khaythama by his mother.
25.	Abdullah b. Jubayr	Commanded the archers. Present at Uqba and Badr.
26.	Khaythama Abu Sa'd b. Khaythama	
27.	Abdullah b. Salama	
28.	Subay b. Hatib	
29.	Amr b. Qais	

30.	Qais b. Amr	Son of Amr b. Qais.
31.	Thabit b. Amr	Present at Badr.
32.	Amir b. Makhlad	Present at Badr.
33.	Abu Hubayra b. Harith	
34.	Amr b. Mutarrif	
35.	Anas' b. Thabit	Brother of Hassan b. Thabit, the poet of the Holy Prophet.
36.	Anas b. Nadr	Uncle of Anas b. Malik. Got more than 80 wounds. He killed many infidels.
37.	Qays b. Mukhallad	Present at Badr.
38.	Kaysan	
39.	Sulaym b. Harith	
40.	Nu'man b. Abdu Amr	Present at Badr.
41.	Kharija b. Zaid	Present at Uqba, Badr. His daughter was married with Abu Bakr. Her name was Habiba. Got more than 10 wounds.
42.	Sa'd b. Al-Rabi'	Present at Uqba, Badr.
43.	Anas b. Arqam	
44.	Malik b. Sinan	
45.	Saeed b. Suwayd	
46.	Utba b. Rabi'	
47.	Tha'laba b. Sa'd	
48.	Thaqf b. Farwah	
49.	Abdullah b. Wahb	
50.	Sakhra b. Amr	
51.	Naufal b. Abdullah	
52.	Abbas b. Ubada	Present at Uqba.
53.	Numan b. Malik	
54.	Mujadhar b. Ziyad	
55.	Ubada b. Hashas	
56.	Rif'a b. Amr	Present at Uqba, Badr.
57.	Abdullah b. Amr	Present at Uqba. Father of Jabir, the famous companion of the Apostle. The angels over-shadowed his funeral with their feathers. God talked with him.

58.	Amr b. Jamuh	
59.	Khallad b. Amr.	Present at Badr.
60.	Abu Ayman	
61.	Sulaym b. Amr	
62.	Antara	
63.	Sahl b. Qays	Present at Badr.
64.	Dhakwan b. Abdu Qays	Present at Uqba, Badr.
65.	Ubayd b. Mu'alla	

The following five names have not been mentioned by Ibn Ishaque:

66. Malik b. Numaila
67. Harith b. Addi
68. Malik b. Aiyas
69. Aiyas b. Addi
70. Amr b. Aiyas

The following Makkans were killed in the Ghazwa of Uhud:

1.	Talha b. Abu Talha	Standardbearer. Killed by Ali.
2.	Abu Saeed b. Abu Talha	Killed by Sa'd b. Waqqas or Ali.
3.	Uthman b. Abu Talha	Killed by Hamza.
4.	Musafi' b. Talha	Killed by Aasim b. Thabit.
5.	Julas b. Talha	Killed by Aasim b. Thabit.
6.	Kilab b. Talha	Killed by Qazman.
7.	Harith b. Talha	Killed by Quzman.
8.	Arta b. Abdu Shurahbil	Killed by Hamza.
9.	Abu Yazid b.Umanayar	Killed by Qazman.
10.	Su'ab	Killed by Quzman, Ali or Sa'd b. Abi Waqqas.
11.	Qasit b. Shurayh	Killed by Quzman.
12.	Abdullah b. Hamid	Killed by Ali.
13.	Abu'l Hakam	Killed by Ali.
14.	Siba b. Abdu'l Uzza	Killed by Hamza.
15.	Hisham b. Abi Ummiya	Killed by Quzman.
16.	Walid b. Al-Aas	Killed by Quzman.
17.	Abu Ummiya b. Abu Hudhayfa	Killed by Quzman.
18.	Khalid b. Al-A'lam	Killed by Quzman.

19. Amr b. Abdullah — Killed by the Holy Prophet.
20. Ubayyi b. Khalaf — Killed by the Holy Prophet.
21. Ubayda b. Jabir — Killed by Quzman or Abdullah b. Masud.
22. Shayba b. Malik — Killed by Quzman.

'The day of Uhud was a day of trial, calamity, and heart-searching on which God tested the believers and put the hypocrites on trial.' For the Muslims it was certainly a setback because:

In the beginning the Muslims pressurized the pagans, the archers (deployed at the top of the mountain) came down and began to collect the booty. The heathens exploited the situation and invaded upon them from the rear. It caused a dismay. On the whole the Muslims began to collect the spoils of the war immediately when the Quraish retreated. The Holy Prophet had advised the Muslims to avoid the individual combat which they did after breaking the rows. The Makkans could not boast of this victory because it was not according to their lofty expectations. The swiftness of Khalid could not bear fruit for them. By mutilating the deads of the Muslims the heathens proved themselves barbarous. The deities of Makka could not overcome God of Islam. The Quraish could not get a single prisoner of war. From military point of view it was not a defeat for the Muslims rather they were victorious in this battle. They had forced the invading army, successfully, to retreat. The Quraish could not achieve their end due to the following reasons:

a) The Quraish had not invaded upon the Muslims with the intention of fighting in the desert. Rather they thought that they would besiege the Muslims and the latter would also prefer to fight in the same way. Eventually the Quraish would destroy the Muslims with the help of the Jews and the hypocrites.
b) The Quraish could not get victory although they were large in number. Their morale was low. The night was approaching and the Quraish used to stop fighting before the prevailing of darkness.
c) Abu Sufiyan was not aware of the situation fully. The

intelligence service of the Makkans was not well-formed so they did not know the intentions and action of the Muslims accurately. On the contrary, the Muslims had evolved a well-organized intelligence service hence the Holy Prophet knew the intentions of the pagans.

d) Abu Sufiyan was a crazy man. Had he not ordered his army to withdraw that night or till the other day he would have annihilated the Muslims.

Despite the above-mentioned facts the prestige of the Muslims was shattered badly. The temporary defeat at Uhud eclipsed the victorious moon of Badr which became a part of history. The Arabs, Jews, Christians and the hypocrites were bent upon to oppose the Muslims because they thought their annihilation, at the hands of the Muslims, was temporary. Exploiting the weakness of the Muslim army the neighbouring nomads were prepared to attack the Muslim territories. They invited the Muslim preachers to visit them so that they could embrace Islam. Under this pretext they killed them. Bir-Ma'una is a prominent example in this connection. Seventy Muslim preachers were killed by Banu A'amir and Banu Sulaym treacherously. Another tribe was Mustaliq which raised the standard of rebellion under the leadership of its chief, Harith. But he had a wrong estimate of the power of the Muslims and was, consequently, killed in this campaign.

In brief, the defeat at Uhud did not have lasting effect on Muhammad (P.B.U.H.) as he attained another success in the battle of trench.

Ghazwa Of Hamra'u'l-Asad
(7th Shawwal, 3 A.H./March, 625 A.C.)

When Abu Sufiyan reached Rauha from Uhud he felt that the victory for the Quraish was not complete. On the other hand the Holy Prophet already feared that the Makkans might not attack again on the Muslims. Therefore he set out with almost 540 companions and marched upto Hamra'ul-Asad —— some eight miles from Medina. It was just a demonstration of strength — to show that the

Muslims were yet unbroken in spirit and too strong to be attacked with impunity. Banu Khuza'ah had not embraced Islam at that time but they had their sympathies with the Muslims. Their chief Ma'bad first visited Muhammad (P.B.U.H) and then went to Abu Sufiyan who revealed his intention of attacking the Muslims again. Ma'bad helped to lower the morale of the Quraish by exaggerating the number of the Muslims. He told him, "Muhammad has come out with his companions to pursue you with an enemy whose like I have never seen, burning with anger against you. . . . . Never have I seen anything like it." These words turned back Abu Sufiyan and his compatriots.

The result of this demonstration of the Muslims was that the Makkans did not dare to invade upon them immediately after the battle of Uhud.

Last Expedition To Badr :
(Sha'ban, 4 A.H./April, 626 A.C.)

In the battlefield Abu Sufiyan had threatened the Muslims to fight with them next year in Badr. So the Holy Prophet set out with 1500 companions in Sha'ban[49] to keep his appointment with Abu Sufiyan. Medina was left in charge of Abdullah b. Ubayyi.[50] The Holy Prophet bestowed upon Ali a standard. The Muslims went forth to Badr and stayed there for eight days and waited for the Makkans. On the other side, Abu Sufiyan also came forth with 2,000 followers including 50 horsemen. But when he reached Zahran, a valley near Makka, he addressed his companions in these words :[51]

"O Quraish! (From the point of warfare) only suitable year is a fertile year when you can pasture the animals on the herbage and drink their milk, whereas this is a dry year. I am going to return, and you must return with me."

So the Quraish returned to Makka. They called this expedition 'the porridge army,' saying that they, merely, went out to drink porridge. But the reality is that the Quraish had not fulfilled their promise. The Muslims called it the Second Badr.

Ghazwa Of Al-Ahzab or Trench:
(Shawwal, 5 A.H./2nd February, 627 A.C.)

This Ghazwa is also known as the Battle of the Allies. On the day of Uhud when the Jews saw the contemptuous attitude of the Makkans against the Muslims and heard the threat of Abu Sufiyan to fight next year, they rejoiced. But the Makkans could not fulfil their desire due to drought next year. It made the Jews of Medina desperate. Consequently their deputation went to Makka to instigate the Quraish against the Holy Prophet. It consisted of Sallam b. Abu'l Huqayq, Huyayy b. Akhtab, Kinana b. Abu'l Huqayq, Haudha b. Qays, Abu Ammar Al-Wa'ili, Sallam b. Mushkam and Kinana b. Rabi'. They instigated assiduously against Medina. The Quraish asked them, "You, O Jews, are the first scripture people and know the nature of our dispute with Muhammad. Which religion is best?"

The notables of the Jews replied, "Certainly your religion is better than his and you have a better claim to be in the right."

The Quraish were rejoiced to hear it. They responded gladly to their invitation and began the war preparations on a large scale. Now this deputation went off to Ghatfan and convinced them to wage war against Muhammad (P.B.U.H.) They also assured them of their assistance and as a result they were ready for a decisive battle. After this different Arab tribes were approached in this connection. Thus a formidable coalition was formed.

Eventually Abu Sufiyan set out with 4,000 soldiers from Mecca. The warriors of Banu Sulaim joined hands with them at Zahran. Then at different places Banu Asad, Banu Fazara, Banu Ashja, Banu Murra and Ghatfan joined hands with them making the total 10,000.[52] The whole army was divided into three parts. Banu Fazara was represented by Uyayna b. Hisn, Banu Murra by Harith b. Auf and Banu Ashja by Mis'ar b. Rukhayla.[53] Ibn Sa'd is of the opinion that Ghatfan was represented by Uyayna b. Hisn, Banu Asad by Talha while Abu Sufiyan was the supreme commander-in-chief.[54]

When the Holy Prophet came to know about the preparations of the Makkans he ordered to dig a trench around

Medina on the advice of Salman Al-Farsi.[55] It was an innovation, in Arabia, to defend oneself when the opponents were in large numbers. Credit goes to Muhammad (P.B.U.H) for introducing this new war technique. It was dug around the unprotected quarters of Medina facing Sala' mountain. It was 10 yards wide, 5 yards deep and 3½ miles in total length. The digging instruments were taken on loan from Banu Quraiza under an agreement. Several check posts were constructed along the trench in order to supervise its every part. It is noteworthy that the Holy Prophet, also, shared in the labour with an axe.[56] While digging the trench he was found saying :

"But for Allah, we would not have been guided,
Nor have been charitable, nor have prayed.
So on us, send down peace.
And make the feet firm if we meet.
Verily the first has against us rebelled
When they wished combat, we refused."

As a precautionary measure,he also ordered to bring every kind of agricultural products from without within Medina lest the Makkans could benefit from them. (This strategy was adopted by Russia against Germany during the Second World War when she brought all agricultural products from the fields and gardens into the rear of the German forces. Thus they could not utilize them).

Muhammad (P.B.U.H.) could only muster a body of three thousand men.[57] He left Medina in charge of Abdullah b. Umm Maktum. Women and children were left for safety in the fortified houses. It is appropriate to mention that the disaffected held back from digging the trench. Similarly Huyiy b. Akhtab had succeeded in wheedling Banu Quraiza after a long discussion. When the Holy Prophet came to know about this state of affairs, he deputed Sa'd b. Mu'adh Sa'd b. Ubada, Khawwat b. Jubayr and Abdullah b. Rawaha to collect the facts. They verified their breaking of the pledge. Similarly Bani Haritha asked his permission to go back to Medina on the plea that their houses were exposed to the enemy. In reality, they wanted only to escape. Seeing their unreliable attitude the Holy Prophet remarked thus,

"Allah-o-Akbar (God is Great): Be of good cheer, you Muslims. Calamity has become serious and hypocrisy has been exposed."

The Muslims had kept the mountain at their backs. The siege began on 31st March, 627 A.C. It lasted for about one month but there could be no fighting except for some shooting with arrows. Some horsemen of the beleaguering host made several assaults by night but every attempt was repulsed by eternal vigilance of Muhammad (P.B.U.H.) Anyhow on one occasion Amr b. Abdu Wudd, Ikrima b. Abu Jahl, Hubayra b. Abu Wahb Mukhzumi, Dirar b. Khattab succeeded to cross the trench. Ali with a contingent was there to hold the gap. He invited Amr to embrace Islam but he preferred to fight. Consequently Amr was killed in a single combat and the rest fled.

Conditions pressed upon the Muslims that the Holy Prophet offered a third of the dates of Medina to Uyayna b. Hisn and Harith b. 'Auf -- the chiefs of Ghatfan -- on the condition that they would go back. The negotiations were in progress but before finalization the Holy Prophet conferred with Sa'd b. Mu'adh and Sa'd b. Ubada. They said, "O Apostle of Allah! Is it a thing you want us to do or something God has ordered you to do which we must carry out? Or is it something you are doing for us? When we and these people were polytheists and idolaters then they could not dare to eat a single date except as guests or purchase. Now God has honoured and guided us to Islam, are we to give them our property without fighting?" The Holy Prophet said, "It was just my intention because the Arabs have shot at you from one bow and gathered against you from every side. I want to break their offensive against you." Now Sa'd b. Mu'adh took the paper and erased what was written, saying, "Let them do their worst against us!"[58]

In due course of time, Nu'aym b. Mas'ud came to the Holy Prophet and told him that he had embraced Islam but his tribe -- Ghatfan -- did not know of it and let him give what orders he would. The Holy Prophet asked him to awake distrust among the enemy to draw them off the Muslims if he could because war was a deceit.[59] Nu'aym, first of all, went off to B. Qurayza with whom he had been a boon companion in heathen days. He reminded them of his affection and said, "Quraish and Ghatfan are not like you : the land is your land, your property, your wives, and your children are in it; you cannot leave it and go somewhere else. If the invaders succeed they will make the most of it. But if things go badly, they will return to their homes and you will have to face the results. So do not fight along with these people until you take hostages from their chiefs who will remain in your hands as security that they will fight Muhammad with you until you make an end of him." Banu Quraiza accepted his advice.

Then he went to the Quraish and tried to make them understand saying, "I am your well-wisher therefore I think it my duty to tell you by way of warning, but regard it confidential. The Jews have regretted their action in opposing Muhammad and have sent to tell him, so saying; 'Would you like us to get hold of some chiefs of the two tribes Quraish and Ghatfan and hand them over to you so that you can cut their heads off.' Nu'aym further said, "Verify my disclosures. So if the Jews send to you to demand hostages, don't send them a single man."

Now Nu'aym went to Ghatfan and told them the same story as he had told the Quraish. Then he succeeded in frightening them about the Muslims.

In due course of time Abu Sufiyan and the chiefs of Ghatfan sent Ikrima b. Abu Jahl to B. Quraiza who persuaded them to fight against Muhammad. They replied that it was the Sabbath. They, further, continued by saying, "We will not fight against Muhammad alongwith you until you give us hostages whom we can hold as security until we make an end of Muhammad." The Quraish and the Ghatfan refused to do so but still made them convince to fight alongwith them.

In this way God sowed distrust among them. Their horses were perishing fastly and provisions becoming scanty. In the darkness of winter night, amidst a storm of wind and rain, their tents overthrown, their lights put out. The chilly month of January coupled with a tempest also played some role in their decision to lift the siege.[60]

Muhammad (P.B.U.H.) deputed Hudhayfa b. Yaman to collect information about the Makkans who told him about their return. Consequently, next morning he also (alongwith the Muslims) left the trench and returned to Medina.

Thus Medina was saved from a total destruction despite two opposing forces — Jews within and the Makkans outside Medina. It was all due to :

That the leadership of the pagans was divided. Every clan had its own chief. On the contrary the Muslims had an ideal leadership. Muhammad (P.B.U.H.) had a democratic instinct. He accepted the advice of digging a trench around the city. Furthermore, he himself participated in this manual work. Discipline and cohesion were so ideal that none could leave his place without permission how much his need might be. The results of the battle of the trench was a fresh victory of organization over sheer mass power.[61] "The whole was a battle of wits in which the Muslims had the best of it. Without cost to themselves they weakened the enemy and increased the dissension."[62]

'On the military side the reason for the Makkan failure was the superior strategy of Muhammad (P.B.U.H.) and probably also his superior information service and secret agents.'[63] Digging of a trench was a novel strategy of warfare for the Arabs. About Salman Farsi who suggested this technique, the Holy Prophet remarked, "Salman is one of the members of my family". The underlying purpose of these remarks was the encouragement of a modern thought, annihilation of territorial prejudices and encouragement of those working for the betterment of the general welfare. The Makkans could not get fodder for their horses as the grain had been harvested a month before their arrival.

The Holy Prophet knew at that time the importance of propaganda and rumour and the extent up to which they could affect the morale of the enemy. On his initiative Nu'aym succeeded in creating suspicion within the ranks of the Confederates. It is remarkable that the Holy Prophet had a superior information service and secret agents.

The Confederates lost their spirits. They could not manage such a big force time and again. Weary and dispirited, they decided to retire to Makka in the darkness of the night.

In brief, if the Trench threw the Makkans out of calculation, want of discipline among the Bedouins, inclemency of the weather, untiring defence and vigilance of the Muslims did the rest.[64] All these factors gave the *coup de grace* to the morale of the besiegers.

The following Muslims were martyred in this battle :[65]

1.	Anas b. Ans	Took part in Uhud.
2.	Abdullah b. Sahl	Took part in Badr.
3.	Tha'laba b. Utmah	Present at Uqba, Uhud.
4.	Tufayl b. Malik	Present at Badr, Uhud. In Uhud he got 31 wounds.
5.	Ka'b b. Zayd	Present at Badr. He was the only survival of Bir Mau'na.
6.	Sa'd b. Mu'adh	He was wounded by a random arrow. The Holy Prophet nursed him himself. He remained alive for one month. Upon his death the Throne shook.

Three pagans were killed in the battle of Trench.[66]

Expedition Of Amr b. Umayya :
(Shawwal, 6 A.H.)

A Makkan secretly came to Medina with the intention of assassinating the Holy Prophet. He was deployed by Abu Sufiyan for this purpose.[67] But he was so much impressed by his pleasing manners that he embraced Islam. The Holy Prophet deputed Amr b. Umayya and Salma b. Aslam to kill Abu Sufiyan. After fastening their camels in the valley of the mountains, they entered Makka in the pitch darkness of night. First of all they went round the Ka'ba and performed their prayer. Afterwards they set out for the completion of their mission. On their way one of the the inhabitants of Makka named Amr recognized Amr b. Umayya. Upon this they made off with full speed and climbed the mountain. They took refuge in a cave where they spent the night. In the morning they saw a Quraishite coming with a laden horse with crops. They thought that he would leak out their presence so they killed him and ran away.

Ghazwa Of Hudaybiya :
(Dhu'l-Qa'da 6 A.H./March, 628 A.C.)

In Dhu'l-Qa'da 6 A.H. the Holy. Prophet, in the company of 1400 Muslims, set out from Medina to perform Umra. He, also, took animals with him for sacrifice. When he reached Usfan, Bishr b. Sufiyan Al-Ka'bi informed him that the Quraish had got wind of the coming of the Muslims. Moreover, they were bent upon not to allow the Muslims to visit the Ka'ba. Their cavalry led by Khalid b. Walid had reached Kura'u'l-Ghamim. Now the Holy Prophet adopted another route which led by the pass of al-Murar to the declivity of al-Hudaibiya and encamped there. After the negotiations with Suhail b. Amr the truce of Hudaybiya was concluded.

Expedition Of Al-Is : (Safr, 7 A.H.)

The Muslims who were left in Mecca had to face great tortures at the hands of the Quraish. Many of them succeeded to flee and took refuge on a mountain located on the route of Makka and Syria, in region of Dhu'l-Marwa by the sea-shore. Gradually their number rose to 72. Among them were Abu Jandal and Abu Busair. They used to loot the trading caravans of the Quraish. In Safr 7 A.H. an incident of the same nature occurred but the Holy Prophet ordered them to return the looted goods. In this incident some nine persons of the Quraish were injured.

Umrat-ul-Qada. (Dhu'l-Qa'da, 7 A.H.
March, 629 A.C.)

It was a visit of accomplishment according to Hudaybiya pact. In Dhu'l-Qa'da, 7 A.H., the Holy Prophet showed his intention to perform the rites of *Umra.* This was the month in which the Makkans had prevented him from performing pilgrimage. He named it the 'fulfilled *umra.*' Eventually he set out from Medina in the company of two thousand persons, one hundred horses and sixty animals for sacrifice. He ordered that all those who were in Hudaibiya should accompany him. During his absence he gave Medina in charge of Uwayf b. Al-Adbat al- Dili.[68]

On hearing the arrival of the Muslims the Makkans evacuated the city and said among themselves, "Muhammad and his companions are in destitution, want and privation."[69] The Quraish lodged at Darul Nadwa (the assembly house). When Muhammad reached Yejudge, all weapons were laid there by his orders. Here he put on the *ahram* and said, "God have mercy on a man who shows them today that he is strong."[70] Then he performed the *Umra.* On the third day Huwaytib b. Abdul Uzza came to him, with some other Makkans, and asked, "Your time is up, so leave Makka."

The Holy Prophet asked for the extension of three days' limit and said, "How would it harm you if you were to let me stay and I gave a wedding feast among you and we prepared food and you came too." (He had married Maymuna, daughter of Al-Harith in this journey). But the extension was not granted by the Quraish and they replied, "We don't need your food so leave Makka for us." Upon this the Holy Prophet left Makka after a sojourn of three days.[71] "It was surely a strange sight," says Muir, with an unconscious thrill, "which at this time presented itself in the vale of Makka, —— a sight unique in the history of the world. The ancient city is for three days evacuated by all its inhabitants, high and low, every house deserted; and, as they retire, the exiled converts, many years banished from their birthplace, approach in a great body, accompanied by their allies, revisit the empty homes of their childhood, and within the short allotted space, fulfil the rites of pilgrimage. The outside inhabitants, climbing the heights around, take refuge under tents, or other shelter among the hills and glens; and, clustering on the overhanging peak of Abu-Qubeys, thence watch the movements of the visitors beneath, as with the Prophet at their head they make the circuit of the Ka'aba, and the rapid procession between As-Safa and Marwah;

and anxiously seen every figure if perchance they may recognize among the worshippers some long-lost friend or relative. It was a scene rendered possible only by the throes which gave birth to Islam."[72]

Had this incident occurred in the contemporary age, the incoming people would not have vacated the city when the inhabitants had left it. 'He could utilize the opportunity to make treacherously a permanent occupation of the city, from which nobody could oust him, least of all the Quraish, especially when they had left the city.' But the Holy Prophet did not. "The self-restraint and scrupulous regard for their pledged word displayed by the Believers created a visible impression among the enemies of Islam."[73] This is why many of the pagans professed Islam in due course. They were men of position and influence. Among them prominent were Khalid b. Walid and Amr b. Al-'Aas.

Expedition Of The Coast : (Rajab, 8 A.H.)

Abu Ubayda was the chief of this expedition. He was sent to the coast in the company of three hundred horsemen in pursuit of a trading caravan of the Quraish. The Holy Prophet furnished them with a supply of dates. Abu Ubayda began to ration them until the dates finished. He divided the dates among them and a man lacked even a single date. Then they caught a whale from the sea which they ate. They stayed along the coast for about twenty days and then returned to Medina.

The purpose of this expedition was to divert the attention of the Quraish.

Submission Of Makka : – (20th Ramadan. 8 A.H.)
(11th January, 630 A.C.)

The Quraish violated the Treaty of Hudaibiya. They defeated Bani-Khuza'a by supporting Bani Bakr. Bani Khuza'a were in alliance with the Muslims. They took refuge in the Haram but they were massacred even there. Suhail b. Amr, who had signed the Hudaibiya Treaty, himself took part in aggression in disguise. One representative of Bani Khuza'a approached the Holy Prophet and appealed for help. He was shocked to hear it. Subsequently he sent his delegates to the Quraish asking them to accept any of the following conditions:

1. Pay blood money of the killed persons of Bani Khuza'a;
2. Stop supporting Bani Bakr;
3. Announce that the Treaty of Hudaibiya was no more in force.

The Quraish accepted the third condition but soon repented upon it. They sent Abu Sufiyan to Medina who negotiated for the orientation of peace, but all was in vain because the violation could not be tolerated with impunity. Soon after Abu Sufiyan's departure from Medina, the Holy Prophet ordered preparations to be made for a grand expedition. He took precautions to secure a large measure of secrecy. But one Hatib b. Abu Balta'a sent a woman of Muzayna with a letter to the Quraish. Another narration is that she was a freed woman of Banu Muttalib and her name was Sara. She concealed the letter on her head and then plaited her locks over it. When she set out for Mecca, God informed the Holy Prophet who sent Ali and Zubair b. Awwam in her pursuit. They caught hold of her at Khulayqa of Bani Abi Ahmad - - - at twelve miles distance from Medina. They took the letter to the Holy Prophet who sent for Hatib and asked him the reason for such an heinous act. He replied, "I believe in God and His Apostle. But I am not a man of standing among the Quraish. My family resides in Makka. So I had to deal prudently with them for their sake."[74] The Holy Prophet forgave him but at the same time a bid to deliver information was foiled.

The Holy Prophet put Abu Ruhm Kulthum b. Husayn Ghifari over Medina and himself set out from the city in the company of ten thousand persons on 10th Ramadan, 8 A.H., on Monday. This force included contingents from Muzaynah, Sulaym, Aslam, Ghifar, Juhaynah, Ashja, Khuza'a (sc. Ka'b), Damrah, Layth, Sa'd b. Bakr, Tamim, Qays and Asad. He closed the frontiers so the news could not reach the Makkans. The march was executed swiftly and secretly.

On the other hand, Abbas b. Abdul Muttalib migrated from Makka alongwith his family and joined the Muslim army at Juhfa. When the Muslim army camped at Marr al-Zahran, Abbas thought that he should go to Makka and convince the Quraish for seeking asylum. On his way he came across Abu Sufiyan and Budayl b. Warqa a bit beyond Arak. He persuaded Abu Sufiyan to come to the Holy Prophet and then escorted him. Upon seeing him Umar flared up because one of the greatest enemies of Islam was standing there helplessly. He demanded the penalty of death for his past record and said to the Holy Prophet, "O Apostle of God! Let me take off his head". But the Holy Prophet not only forgave him but declared, "All those persons are safe who enter the courtyard of Ka'ba or the house of their chief, Abu Sufiyan, or who shut the doors of their houses or lay down their arms."[75] Now Abu Sufiyan intended to go back but Abbas detained him in the narrow part of the valley where the mountain projected so that he could see God's armies passing from there.

When the Holy Prophet gave amnesty to the chiefs of the Quraish, a few people objected that it was all due to the love of his homeland and family. Upon this he summoned the *Ansar* and said to them, "Taking side of my homeland and family is not my aim. I am Apostle and Messenger of God. The place which I like will be your place, and the place where I die will be yours". Upon hearing this the people were overcome by feelings and began to weep.

Now Abbas took Abu Sufiyan on the top of a mountain. Besides them thousands stood in clusters to see the Holy Prophet. Whenever a tribe passed nearby Abu Sufiyan asked, "Abbas, which is this tribe?" Abbas told him, "This is Sulaym and that is Muzayna." At last the Holy Prophet passed with his greenish-black squadron.[76] It consisted of the *Muhajirin* and the *Ansar*. On its left flank was posted Zubair b. Awwam. While Khalid. b. Walid was posted on the right flank. Sa'd b. Ubada was the chief of the *Ansar* and the *Muhajirin* were led by Abu Ubaida b. Jarah. Zubair b. Awwam was ordered to enter Makka from the north, Khalid b. Walid from the south, Sa'd b. Ubada from the west and

Abu Ubaida from the north-west. Abu Sufiyan was surprized to see this splendid formation and he uttered, "Abbas! No one can combat with these people. I see that a grand state of your nephew will be established in the near future." Abbas replied, "This is prophethood." Then Abu Sufiyan replied, "Then I have nothing to say against it."[77]

Now Abu Sufiyan hurried to his people on the advice of Abbas. He stood in the Ka'ba and cried at the top of his voice, "O people of the Quraish! Muhammad has come. You are not in a position to resist him. So enter my house you will be safe." The people surrounded him. Meanwhile his wife, Hind, came in and seized his moustaches by saying, "Kill this fat greasy bladder of lard! What a rotten protector of the people!"[78]

Abu Sufiyan warned the Quraish that they should not let that woman deceive them. He told them the same three ways to save them which the Holy Prophet had told him. So the Quraish did the same.

Muhammad (P.B.U.H.) entered Makka on Thursday, 20th Ramadan. Zubair b. Awwam entered from the side of Kuda with his detachment. Khalid b. Walid had been ordered to enter from al-Lit, the lower part of Makka. While Abu Ubayda b. Jarrah advanced with the troops pouring into Makka in front of the Holy Prophet. Some people, as Sa'd b. Ubada thought, that day was meant for killing the infidels. But the Holy Prophet had issued strict orders to the commanders not to use their arms except in self-defence.

On the other hand, Safwan b. Ummaya, Ikrima b. Abu Jahl and Suhayl b. Amr had collected some men in Khandama to invade upon the Muslims. They had been supplied with the ammunition by Himas b. Qays. A skirmish followed and as a result Kurz b. Jabir, Salama b. Mayla, Khunays b. Khalid and Habeesh b. Usher were martyred. The Syrian horsemen of Khalid's detachment had taken a road of their own apart from Khalid and were killed together. Thirteen polytheists lost their lives. It was just a token struggle.

A general amnesty was declared except some outlaws to be killed wherever found even beneath the curtains of the Ka'ba.[79] Some of them escaped from Makka and after some time embraced Islam. This treatment with them was not out of enmity or revenge but this order was only for those whom even justice condemned. They were all guilty of specific crimes. They were :

Abdullah b. Abi Sarh :

He had been a Muslim and acted as Muhammad's amanuensis. Later on he apostatized and claimed that he had distorted the Holy Quran. The Holy Prophet ordered to kill him. He took refuge with his foster-brother, Usman b. Affan who prayed for his immunity. The Holy Prophet remained silent for some time and then pardoned him. Abdullah re-embraced Islam. He was entrusted with some important State responsibilities during the reigns of Umar and Usman.

Abdullah b. Khatal :

He belonged to Tamim b. Ghalib. He had embraced Islam. He was sent to collect *sadaqah* in the company of a freed slave. When they halted at a place, he ordered his slave to slaughter a goat for him and prepare some food. Meanwhile he went to sleep. When he woke up the man had done nothing so he gave him a beating from which he died. Subsequently he apostatized and made for Makka alongwith the animals of poor tax. On the day of the conquest of Makka he hid himself beneath the curtain of the Ka'ba but was killed by Said b. Hurayth al-Makhzumi and Abu Barza al-Aslami.

Safwan b. Umayya :

He was a number-one enemy of Islam. He went out to Jedda, with Ikrima, to take ship to Yemen. He was to embark when Ummi-Hakim appeared on the scene who told them the good news of their immunity. Umayr b. Wahb prayed for their immunity. The Holy Prophet took off his turban and sent it to Safwan through Umayr as an emblem of security and pardon.

Ikrima b. Abu Jahl :

He was also a top ranking enemy of Islam. He invaded the detachment of Khalid on the day of the conquest of Makka. After the conquest he fled to Yemen. Umm-i-Hakim, his wife and niece of Abu Jahl, prayed for his immunity which was granted. She went in search of Ikrima and escorted him to Makka. When the Holy Prophet saw him he got up, emotionally, to receive him that his sheet rolled down from his shoulders saying, "Welcome O rider to migrate."[80]

Huwayrith b. Nuqadh :

He was a poet and wrote satirical songs about the Holy Prophet besides giving him tortures. When Abbas was escorting Fatima and Umm-i-Kulthum, the daughters of the Holy Prophet, to Medina he goaded the beast so that it threw them to the ground. Ali killed him.

Hibar b. Aswad :

He had goaded the beast carrying Zainab daughter of the Holy Prophet so that it ran away. He drove the end of his lance against Zainab who was far advanced in pregnancy. She fell upon the ground causing the abortion. Now he fled away and hid himself. After some time he came to the Holy Prophet and confessed that he had embraced Islam. Although his crime was atrocious yet pardon was unconditionally granted.

Miqyas b. Dubabah :

He had been a Muslim but later on he apostatized. He was killed by Numayla b. Abdullah who belonged to his own nation.

Harith b. Tulalah :

He was killed by Ali.

Ka'b b. Zuhair :

He came to the Holy Prophet in 9 A.H. with his brother. He recited some verses in his praise. The Holy Prophet was much pleased to hear these verses. He not only pardoned him but also gave him a sheet.

Wahshi :

He came to the Holy Prophet and embraced Islam. The Holy Prophet asked him to narrate the events of the martyrdom of Hamza which he did. He was asked not to come to him in future lest he should be overcome by his feelings. Despite embracing Islam Wahshi used to drink. Umar used to say: "I know that God would not leave the slayer of Hamza unpunished."

Abdullah b. Zabaar :

He was also a poet. After some time he came to the Holy Prophet who pardoned him.

Hind d. Utba :

She was also a top-ranking enemy of Islam. She tried to swallow the liver of Hamza. She had mutilated his dead body, chopped off his nose and ears and strewn into a thread and wore like a necklace. Anyhow the Holy Prophet pardoned her.

Tariba Batsaghir :

She was a freed-woman of Khatal. She was a singer and sang satirical songs about the Holy Prophet. She was executed.

Fartana :

She was, also, a freed-woman of Khatal. She also, sang satirical songs about the Holy Prophet. She ran away but later on embraced Islam. During the reign of Umar she was crushed by a horse and consequently she expired.

Uzbat :

She was, also, a freed-woman of Khatal. She was executed.

Umm-i-Sa'd :

'She was also executed.

Before these culprits were put to death, the Holy Prophet went to the Ka'ba and made seven circuits on his camel touching the black stone with a stick which he had in his hand. Then he summoned Usman b. Talha and took the key of the Ka'ba from him. He entered the Ka'ba where he saw pigeons made of wood. He broke and threw them away. Then he stood by the door of the Ka'ba and delivered the following address :

> "There is no God but Allah alone; He has no associate. He has made good His promise and helped His servant. He has put to flight the confederates alone. Hear! Every claim of privilege or blood or property is abolished by me except the custody of the Ka'ba and the watering of the pilgrims. The intentionally slain in a quasi-intentional way by club or whip, from him the bloodwit is most severe; a hundred camels, forty of them to be pregnant.
>
> O Quraish! God has taken from you the haughtiness of paganism and its veneration of ancestors. Listen! Man springs from Adam and Adam sprang from dust.[81]
>
> After this God sent down the following verse:[82]

> "O mankind! We created you from a single (pair) of a male and a female, and made you into nations and tribes, that ye may know each other (not that ye may despise each other). Verily the most honoured of you in the sight of God is (he who is) the most righteous of you."

Then the Holy Prophet asked the Quraish, "Descendants of the Quraish, how do you think I should act towards you?" (His old persecutors, relentless and ruthless, were now completely at his mercy.) Curiosity and fear mingled their feelings because they were fully aware of the treatment they meted out over a period of thirteen years. Anyhow trembling in their shoes they replied, "We hope for kindness and pity because you are a gracious brother and nephew."

Upon this Muhammad (P.B.U.H.) asked them, "Go your way for you are the freed ones." At this tears trickled down from the eyes of the Holy Prophet. He continued to say, "I shall speak to you as Joseph spake unto his brothers. I shall not reproach you today. God will forgive. He is the Most Merciful and Compassionate."[83] He forgave those who threw thorns and filth on his door particularly when he returned late in the darkness of the night. During his prayers they placed heavy stones or abdomens of the immolated animals on his back or the head. But now he did not gratify his ambition, satiate his lust or glut his revenge.

Now he returned the key of the Ka'ba to Othman b. Talha. Hadrat Ali requested him the grant of Saqaya[84] and the Hijaba,[85] but he was given the Saqaya only because it was a job which demanded labour.

On the day of the conquest of Makka the Holy Prophet saw the images of the angels and Abraham. He ordered to efface the figurative frescoes.[86] He was riding on a she-camel. He pointed at them with his stick and the idols were unrelentingly stuck down. At this time he said, "Truth has (now) arrived, and Falsehood perished : for Falsehood is (by its nature) bound to perish."[87] It was at this time that he abolished the nude processions[88] and the other abuses of its worship.

When the prayer-time came Bilal ascended on the roof of the Ka'ba and called the people to prayer. Although the pride of the Quraish had been crushed yet there were still signs of that. Upon hearing the Adhan (call to prayer) Attib b. Asid, one of the pagan chiefs, uttered spontaneously, "God has honoured my father in not letting him hear this for it would have enraged him."[89] But Muhammad *(P.B.U.H.)* was merciful even to the enemies that he not only forgave Attib but appointed him the governor of Makka.90

On the next day of the conquest of Makka Banu Khuza'a murdered a polytheist as a result of their old enemity. When the Holy Prophet came to know about it he addressed the people in these words :

"O people! God made Makka holy the day He created heaven and earth and it will be the holiest place till the Day of Resurrection. It is not lawful for anyone, who believes in God and the Last Day, to shed blood nor to cut down trees therein. It was not lawful to anyone before me and it will not be lawful to anyone after me. Indeed, it is not lawful for me except at this time because of (God's) anger against its people. Now it has regained its former holiness.

Let those who are present here tell those who are not present here. If anyone should say the Apostle killed even in Makka, say God permitted His Apostle to do so but He does not permit you. Refrain from killing, you men of Khuza'a for there has been too much killing even if there were profit in it. Since you have killed a man I will pay his bloodwit. If anyone is killed after my sojourn here his people have a choice, they can have his killer's life or the blood-money."[91]

After delivering his speech he asked Banu Ka'b to pay one hundred she-camels as bloodwit of Junaydib b. Akwa.[92]

In his address Muhammad (P.B.U.H.) made the following announcements, the echoes of which were heard during the French Revolution of 1852 :

1. Declaration Of Peace :

Mecca is a place of peace and God had made it *Haram* even before the creation of the universe. On this occasion the following revelation was sent by God.[93] No one is allowed to shed blood there keeping in view its holiness. Even it is prohibited to cut the trees there On certain occasions its holiness was set aside temporarily as at the time of the murder of Ibn Khatal and his companions. No one from among the Companions of the Holy Prophet or their successors doubted in its status of being *Haram*. Even it is narrated that Umar said, "If I see the murderer of my father Khattab here, I will ignore him so that he may slip from here." Similarly Abdullah b. Umar said on one occasion, "If I see the murderer of Umar here I will spare him." Even Ibn Abbas is said to have remarked, "If I see the murderer of my father in the *Haram*, I will say nothing to him unless he leaves the *Haram*."[94]

2. Declaration Of Independence :

Muhammad (P.B.U.H.) let the Makkans to carry on their business as they wished. Now they were free despite of the fact that they had persecuted and tortured the Muslims ruthlessly. He forgave the 'cruel scorn they had inflicted on him.' The Holy Prophet and the Muslims had received innumerable physical tortures and proprietary damages at the hands of the Quraish. They had tried their utmost to eliminate Islam. The Muslims were not safe at their hands. They sang satirical songs for the Holy Prophet. Among them were included those who even made the Muslims to lie on the burning coals. Still Muhammad (P.B.U.H.) treated them with kindness.

3. Sacredness Of Human Life :

The Arabs were accustomed to take revenge even generation after generation. It was their family duty. It was a matter of pride for them. The Holy Prophet told them that Islam did not believe in these petty things and he himself had crushed these customs under his feet. He proved, practically, that his mission was meant for reformation and reconstruction and not for devastation or destruction. His message was for the protection of human grandeur and not for bloodshed. We should compare it with the Crusaders who in 1099 A.C. put to death some seventy thousand Muslims when they conquered Jerusalem.

4. Declaration Of Human Equality

Muhammad (P.B.U.H.) established the equality on the

basis of world. He said : "All men are the descendants of Adam who sprang from dust. Whosoever is proud of his racial superiority has no concern with us. There is only one cause of superiority and that is the obedience of Islam and mercy upon the mankind." Theerefore we will not be proud of selfishness, vengeance and racial superiority.

After making circuits round the Ka'ba and clearing it from the idols, the Holy Prophet sat on Safa. Hosts upon hosts came to him. He took an oath from them :

1. "Rehman is Allah and He has no associate;
2. Muhammad is His messenger."
3. "We will not commit larceny, adultery and infanticide.
4. We will obey the Holy Prophet in the right path."

This clause granted the people complete freedom of conscience so that they might practise upon the right path in accordance with the above-mentioned principle and leave the wrong ones.

5. From the women he took the oath not to commit adultery, theft, level false allegations and kill girls. Furthermore, they were asked not to scratch their faces as part of mourning nor beat their faces. Nor they will wear black clothes, rend their clothes, derange their hair or sit over the grave to mark any occasion of mourning under any circumstances."[96]

The Holy Prophet stayed for fifteen days in Makka.

There is difference of opinions among the jurists about the nature of the conquest of Makka. The Shafiites are of the opinion that Makka was handed over peacefully while the Malikites and Hanafites think that it was conquered by force. The Holy Prophet kept in view the principle of indirect approach. This principle carries great importance in war strategy in the contemporary world. The opposing sentiments are crushed and the intention of resistance is weakened through propaganda in the enemy land under this principle. The enemy is segregated from its allies. Restlessness is created in the land and the enemy is discouraged by starting war of nerves. In this campaign the Holy Prophet got such a grand victory without shedding any blood due to his warfare talents, which is considered a strange model of war tactics in the world history.

Besides, the Muslim forces reached Makka swiftly through most difficult mountainous paths. All movements were kept secret and when the Muslim force appeared suddenly before Makka, the Quraish could do nothing. The forces moved in regular formation. From one side Khalid and from the other Zubair b. Awwam entered Makka with their forces. The Holy Prophet declared? "Whosoever seeks refuge in the house of Abu Sufiyan or shuts the doors of his house or enters the Ka'ba or puts down his weapons is safe." Had Makka been conquered merely by truce, the Holy Prophet would not have done so. Because truce is the guarantee of general peace.

Although Makka was conquered yet its lands were not distributed among the conquerors as is done in the case of spoils. Even the houses of the emigrants were not returned to them. Makka is a place of sacrifices, worship and Qibla of the followers, of Islam. So they all are shareholders of it collectively. Consequently the lands of Makka cannot be the property of anybody. Furthermore, the whole land of Makka is *Haram,* therefore, it cannot be the property of a particular man. The jurists like Mujahid, Atta, Imam Malik, Abu Hanifa, Sufiyan Thauri, Imam Ahmad and Ishaque b. Rahaway are agreed upon this point. This is the reason that *Kharaj* was not levied upon the agricultural lands of Mecca like other conquered lands. *Kharaj* is actually the *Jizya* of the land. As *Haram* is a venerated and respected place therefore *Kharaj* cannot be levied upon it.

The conquest of Makka put an end to the conflict between the two city states of Makka and Medina. Makka used to be the commercial, spiritual and political centre of the Arabs. And when it was conquered, the other Arab tribes thought it to be on the safer side by embracing Islam. Umra b. Salma is narrated to have said, "The Arabs waited for the time when the Quraish embraced Islam. They used to say that Muhammad should be let for the Quraish. If he overcomes them then no doubt he is a true prophet. Consequently when Makka was conquered every tribe advanced towards it."[97]

So far the delay in the propagation of Islam was mainly due to the national and family opposition. Now when the hinderance of Falsehood was removed the Arabs, who were leading a tribal life, became a nation which was to conquer the whole world in the near future. Now the preachers of Islam had no danger in preaching Islam. 'The capture of Makka was therefore not an end in itself.' 'Makka had long since been chosen as the geographical focus of Islam, and it was therefore necessary that the Muslims should have complete freedom of access to it. The orders to migrate were abrogated after the conquest of Makka. "The result of this diplomacy was two-fold –– the gradual addition in the reserve volunteers for the Muslim army and the depth of Islam among the converts."[98]

The conquest of Makka is an open proof of this thing that the battles of Muhammad (P.B.U.H.) were fought only for Islam. His conduct as a conqueror was so generous that no prejudices could resist. His battles were bloodless whence the worldly battles are best known for their characteristic ferocity. Had he wished he could have beheaded his vanquished foes who had spared no ingenuity to inflict tortures on the Muslims. 'Through all the annals of conquest, there is no triumphal entry like this.' Prof. Gibb writes about the causes of the bloodless occupation of Mecca in these words :[99]

"At Medina he set astride Makka's vital trade route to the north. All his expeditions against the Bedouin tribes seem to be part of a master plan, elaborated with great skill and insight, to take advantage of this position and to blockade Makka into surrendering. That this would provoke an armed conflict must have been foreseen, but the three major battles of Badr, Uhud, and the Trench fought in the second, third, and fifth years of the Hijra, have little more than episodic value, large as they may loom in Muslim tradition. It was essential for Muhammad's purposes that Makka should come in eventually of its own violation, and his outstanding political genius is shown by the way in which Makka was finally incorporated after seven years of struggle, not as a beaten and resentful enemy, but as a willing, if not enthusiastic partner. And when, two years later, Islam had to face its first great crisis on the death of Muhammad (p.b.u.h) Makka was in fact foremost in lending its support to the re-establishment of the Islamic supremacy in Arabia."

(2) Ghazwas And Expeditions Against The Jews :

By the Pact of Medina it was binding upon the Jews to share the joys and sorrows of the Muslims. But they took lead in its violations. Before the introduction of Islam in Medina the Jews had a prominent position in the city. There were three prominent Jewish tribes –– Qaynuqa'a, Nadir and Qurayzah. But there were about a dozen clans in addition to them –– such as B. Hadl and Tha'labah. Being Scriptuaries they enjoyed a respect among the inhabitants. They awaited for a prophet according to the predictions of Torah and Bible. They hoped to regain their lost power and subjugate whole of Arabia and inflict vengeance upon their enemies. Thus they could re-possess their synagogues. Aus and Khazraj had yielded at first some sort of obedience to the Jews as they were over-awed by their claims. The Arabs were weaker than the Jews –– thirteen Arab strongholds (*atam*) to fifty-nine Jewish ones is one figure.

Such were the political conditions of Yathrib when Muhammad (P.B.U.H.) made his appearance on the scene. When six individuals of Aus and Khazraj met the Holy Prophet in Aqba and he invited them to embrace Islam, they saw one another and said, "By God! He is the same prophet about whom the Jews predict. This is a golden chance for us lest the Jews steal the priority." In a quick exchange of opinions, they found themselves unanimous and immediately they embraced Islam.

This ancient firm Jewish belief that a Messiah would

come who would emancipate them from degradation contributed a lot in the propagation of Islam. This was the same belief which helped in the propagation of Christianity in Palestine. Many a people exploited this belief in Early and Middle Ages and claimed to be the personification of prophets. They presented some new teachings and announced that they were awaiting for a Messiah.

The prediction of coming of a great prophet (Muhammad) is mentioned in the Jewish scriptures and the Jews are still awaiting for a promised Messiah. The same was the condition of the Jews of Yathrib and many men, anxious as to their own fate, longed to find a guide. But it is strange that the people who claimed to be the promised Messiah were strongly refuted by the Jews. If Muhammad (P.B.U.H.) were not the Messiah, the Jews thought that he might at least be their tool to subdue their pagan rivals. It shows that this belief is mere a farce because their minds are not ready to accept this prediction.

After the migration of the Holy Prophet the Jews thought it better to remain silent instead of open opposition because there was a deadly conflict among their own ranks for years. In the battle of Bu'ath, Bani Nadir and Bani Qurayzah stood on the side of Aus against Khazraj. Their third tribe Bani Qaynuqa'a participated on the side of Khazraj. So it was not easy to formulate a common policy in these matters. In the beginning the Jews thought that this new movement and force would strengthen their cause. At first they were inclined to look with some favour on the preachings of the Holy Prophet, as they thought that Islam constituted a return to the uncontaminated religion of Abraham. But soon they came to know that this force which enlightened the hearts of the young Arabs was of no use to them. So they openly and knowingly infringed the terms of the Medina Charter.

The Jews had attached great hopes with the Holy Prophet because Islam recognizes Moses as a great prophet. They thought Islam a republication of Judaism. The Holy Quran mentions Moses and the other Jewish prophets frequently. They thought that judaism would absorb Islam.

Consequently it would add to their economic resources besides an increase in their population.

On the contrary, the Holy Prophet established friendly relations with the Jews through the Charter of Medina. It is just possible that he might have thought that they would embrace Islam as they had read his appearance in their religious books. Besides he had ordered the Muslims to keep fast in certain days during which the Jews used to keep fast. Similarly he had allowed the Muslims to marry the Jewish girls if they wished so. A verse of the Holy Quran goes :[1]

> This day are (all) things good and pure made lawful unto you. The food of the People of the Book is lawful unto you and yours is lawful unto them. (Lawful unto you is marriage) are (not only) chaste women who are believers, but chaste women among the People of the Book, revealed before your time, –– when ye give them their due dowers, and desire chastity, not lewdness, nor secret intrigues.

But despite the sincerest efforts of the Holy Prophet the conflict between Judaism and Islam could not be checked. Soon the Jews started their subversive activities. Their pin pricks had started. 'They showed hostility to the Holy Prophet in envy, hatred and malice, because God has chosen His Apostle from the Arabs.' They tried to sow disaffection among the Muslims. They opposed the Holy Prophet in every respect jealously and relentlessly. 'They broadcast adverse criticism of Muhammad's claims to be a prophet.' Anyhow he was ready to give them every possible concession except his beliefs. 'As a prophet, he could afford to ignore the jibes of the Jews, though they maddened him to fury; but as the chief of the city, the general in a time of almost continual warfare, when Medina was kept in a state of military defence and under a sort of military discipline, he could not overlook treachery.'[2] The Jews began to act with poison and treachery. "No kindness or generosity, however, on the part of the Prophet would satisfy the Jews; nothing could conciliate the bitter feelings with which they were animated. Enraged that they could not use him as their instrument for the conversion of Arabia to Judaism; and that his belief was so much simpler than their Talmudic legends, they soon broke off, and ranged themselves on the side of the enemies of the new Faith."[3] They tried to introduce confusion by asking different kinds of questions from the Holy Prophet. They planned to ask hard questions about the shrewdest aspects of life and religion so that he should keep silent in future or not invite them to Islam. First of all the Jewish rabbis concealed such religious matters which were included in Torah. Such an incident was faced by Mu'adh b. Jabal, Sa'd b. Mu'adh and Kha'arja b. Zaid. Upon this God sent down the following verse :[4]

> "Those who conceal the clear (Signs) We have sent down and the Guidance after We have made it clear for the People in the Book -- -- on them shall be God's curse and the curse of those entitled to curse."

When the Holy Prophet invited the Jews to embrace Islam Rafi' b. Kharja and Malik b. Auf said, "O Muhammad! We will not admit what you say rather we will follow the path of our forefathers because they were better than us and knew more than us."[5] It was on this occasion that God sent down the following verse :[6]

> "When it is said to them: Follow that God hath revealed". They say: "Nay! We shall follow the ways of our fathers." What! even though their fathers were void of wisdom and guidance?"

First of all the Jewish rabbis began to demand from the Holy Prophet some miracle as a proof of his prophethood. They used to say, "We have pledged with God not to embrace the faith of any apostle unless he shows us sacrifices consumed by fire." The Holy Quran mentions this incident in these words,[7] "They (also) said : 'God took our promise not to believe in an apostle unless he showed us a sacrifice consumed by fire (from heaven)." Say : "There came to you Apostles before me, with Clear Signs and even with what ye ask for : why then did ye slay them, if ye speak the truth?"

At another place the Holy Quran says :[8] "The People of the Book ask thee to cause a book to descend to them from heaven."

Once Raafi' b. Haritha, Sallam b. Mishkam, Malik b. Sayf and Rafi' b.Harmala came to the Holy Prophet and said, "O Muhammad! Don't you claim that you follow the *din* and *millat* of Abraham. You also believe in our Torah and stand witness that it has, actually, been sent down by God." But when they were not satisfied with the reply of the Holy Prophet they said, "Then we will go on following the same which we have. And we will be on the right path. Neither we will bring faith in you nor follow you."[9]

Once the Holy Prophet went to a Jewish school and invited the Jews present there to embrace Islam. Numan b. Amr and Harith b. Zaid asked him,"O Muhammad! What is your religion?" The Holy Prophet replied, "The religion of Abraham." They said, "But Abraham was a Jew." Now the Holy Prophet asked them, "Then let the Torah judge between us." But they refused. It was on this occasion that God sent the following verses:

1. "Hast thou not turned the vision to those who have been given a portion of the Book? They are invited to the Book of God, to settle their dispute, but a party of them turn back and decline (the arbitration). This because they say: "The Fire shall not touch us but for a few numbered days". For their forgeries deceive them as to their own religion."[10]
2. "Abraham was not a Jew nor yet a Christian; but he was true in Faith, and bowed his will to God's (which is Islam), and he joined not gods with God."[11]

Once two Jews named Miskeen and Adiy b. Zaid said to the Holy Prophet: "O Muhammad! We don't know that God sent down anything on a human being after Moses."[12] Then another Jewish party came to him to whom he said: "Listen to me! By God you do know that He has sent me to you." They replied, "We don't know neither we bear witness to it."[13]

Three prominent Jews named Abdullah b. Sayf, Adiy b. Zaid and Harith b. Auf said to one another, "Come! We should bring faith on Muhammad in the morning and refute it in the evening. It will create doubts in his religion. Thus his followers will be confused and they will also repudiate Islam."[14]

Similarly a rabbi Abu Raa'fi al-Qurazi said to the Holy Prophet, "Do you want us, Muhammad, to worship you as the Christians worship Jesus, Son of Mary?"

The Holy Prophet replied, "God forbid that I should worship anyone but God or order that any but He should be worshipped. God did not send me and order me to do that."[15]

Before the introduction of Islam in Medina Aus and Khazraj were at daggers drawn but after embracing Islam they were united. An old Jew Shas b. Qays, who was a bitter enemy of the Muslims, passed by a company of the Muslims. He was filled with rage to see the unity of the Aus and Khazraj. He persuaded a Jewish youth to recite to them some of the poetry composed by each side about the battle of Bu'ath.[16] And when he did so, they began to quarrel and were bent upon to fight. When the Holy Prophet was informed about it, he went out with some emigrants and said to them:[17]

"Will you act as pagans while I am with you after God has guided you to Islam and honoured you thereby and made a clean break with paganism, delivered you thereby from unbelief, made you friends thereby?"

After this people realized the Jewish trick so they embraced one another.

One day Abu Bakr went to a Jewish school. He saw several people had gathered around Finhas (of Qaynuqa) who was a great rabbi. Abu Bakr said to him, "Alas! Finhas! Be afraid of God and embrace Islam because by God you know very well that Muhammad is certainly the Apostle of Allah. He has been sent by Him with the Truth mentioned in the Torah and Bible." Finhas replied, "By God! O Abu Bakr! We don't need Allah but it is He Who needs us. We don't pray to him in the manner as He prays to us. We are independent of Him while He needs us. Were He independent of us He would not have asked us to lend Him our money as your friend pretends. God prohibits us not to take interest but He Himself takes it. Had He been independent of us He would not have given us interest.[18] (He was referring to this Quranic verse:[19] Who is he that will loan to God a beautiful loan, which God will double unto his credit and multiply many times?). Instead of understanding the true sense of this verse they began to say that God had become poor. At this God sent down the following verse:[20]

"Then if they reject thee, so were rejected apostles before thee, who came with Clear Signs, Books of dark prophecies, and the Book of Enlightenment."

Abu Bakr was enraged at this and consequently he hit hard in his face saying, "Were it not for the treaty between us I would have cut off your head." Finhas went to the Holy Prophet and complained to him about Abu Bakr's behaviour deleting his own point of view. Then God explained to the Holy Prophet the whole situation.[21]

Some Jews came to the Holy Prophet. Prominent among them were Abu Yasser b. Akhtab, Nafi' b. Abu Nafi' Azar b. Abu Azar, Khalid, Zaid and Ashja'. They asked the Holy Prophet, "From among the apostles on whom do you believe?"

The Holy Prophet replied, "We believe in God and what He has sent down to us and what was sent down to Abraham and Ishmael and Isaac and Jacob and the tribes and what was given to Moses and Jesus and what was given to the Prophets from their Lord; we make no difference between any one of them. And we submit unto Him."

When the Holy Prophet mentioned Christ they denied that he was a prophet and said that they did not believe in him or in anyone who believed in him.[22]

Abdullah b. Sallam was a learned rabbi of Medina. He embraced Islam alongwith his family. At the time of his conversion to Islam he asked the Holy Prophet, "Be kind enough for asking the Jews about me before exposing my embracing Islam." And when the Holy Prophet did so, a band of the Jews spoke unanimously, "He is our chief, and the son of our chief; our rabbi, and our learned man." But when he publicly proclaimed his conversion, Huyayy b. Akhtab, Ka'ab b. Asad, Abu Nafi' Ashih and Shamwil b. Zaid said to him, "There is no prophethood in Arabia and your friend is a king."[23] But when their efforts proved futile in making him a Jew again they accused him openly.

After the conversion of Abdullah b. Sallam to Islam a band of Jews came to the Holy Prophet and asked about Dhu'l-Qarnayn.[24] He told them what God had sent him about him from what he had already narrated to the Quraish. The Jews had asked the Quraish to ask such a question. It is remarkable that Nadr b. Harith and Uqba b. Abu Mu'ayt had come to the Jewish rabbis for this purpose.[25]

Kardam b. Qais, Usama b. Habib, Nafi' b. Abu Nabi, Bahri b. Amr, Huyayy b. Akhtab and Rifa'a b. Zaid used to go to some of the *Ansar* advising them not to contribute to the public expenses, 'for we fear that you will come to poverty. Don't be in a hurry to contribute for you do not know the outcome.[26]

The Jews were opposed to Islam to this much extent that they refused the truthfulness of Torah. They declared that they preferred idolatry, with all its attendant evils to Islam. They tried to conceal those articles which testified the message of the Holy Prophet.[27] Deuternomy (XVIII: 15-18) speaks very clearly of the rising of a prophet. The passage in question reads:

"The Lord thy God will raise up unto thee a prophet from the midst of thee, of thy brethren, like unto me; unto him ye shall hearken. According to all that thou desirest of the Lord thy God in Horeb in the day of assembly, saying, Let me not hear again the voice of the Lord my God, neither let me see this great fire any more, that I die not. And the Lord said unto me. They have well said that which they have spoken. I will raise them up a prophet from among their brethren, like unto thee, and I will put my words in his mouth; and he shall command unto them all that I shall command him."[28]

In these circumstances Muhammad (p.b.u.h.) had but one course open to him - - - to say they had suppressed or purposely corrupted their books.

A band of the Jews came to him and said, "O Muhammad Allah created creation but who created Allah?" On this occasion, God sent down the following Sura:[29]

"Say: He is God, The One and Only; God, the Eternal, Absolute; He begetteth not; and there is none like unto Him."

In reply they said, "O Muhammad! Tell us His characteristics. How is His hand? How is His arm?"[30] The Holy Prophet replied, " Not just estimate have they made of God, such as is due to Him: on the Day of Judgement the whole of the earth will be but His handful, and the heavens will be rolled up in His right hand: glory to Him! High is He above the Partners they attribute to him!"[31]

When Abdullah b. Sallam, Tha'laba b. Sa'ya, Usayd b. Sa'ya, Asad b. Ubayd and several other Jews embraced Islam, the Jewish rabbis said to the Holy Prophet, " It was only the bad Jews who believed in Muhammad and favoured him. Had they been good men they would not have forsaken the religion of their forefathers and adopted another."[32] Ka'b b. Asad, Ibn Saluba, Abdullah b. Suriya and Sha's b. Qais planned among themselves and said, "Let us go to Muhammad to see if we can seduce him from his religion, for he is only a mortal." Then they came to him and said, "O Muhammad! You know that we the rabbis hold a great status among the Jews. If we follow you, all the Jews will follow you and will not oppose us. But we have a quarrel outstanding with some of our people. If we appoint you arbitrator between us and you give your award in our favour, we will embrace Islam and endorse you."

But the Holy Prophet refused to do so.[33] Then God sent down two verses.[34]

Once Jabal b. Abu Qasheer and Shamwil b. Zaid asked the Holy Prophet, "Tell us when the Hour will be if you are a prophet as you say." So God sent down the following verse:[35]

"They ask thee about the (final) Hour - - when will be its appointed time? Say: "The knowledge thereof is with my Lord (alone): none but He can reveal as to when it will occur. Heavy were its burden through the heavens and the earth. Only, all of a sudden will it come to you." They ask thee as if thou were eager in search thereof. Say: "The knowledge thereof is with God (alone), but most men know not."

Again a learned Jew put three questions to the Holy Prophet. He said, "Where will the people remain when on the Resurrection Day the neaven and the earth will be changed." He said: "In the darkness behind the Bridge". He asked again: "Who will be the first to receive permission to enter into the Paradise?" He replied, "Those sojourners who are expelled from home, and rendered homeless in the way of truth." He said: "I will ask you now such a question as can be answered by nobody on earth except a prophet. Tell me as to why sometimes a male and sometimes a female are born." He replied, "The semen of a male is white and of a female is yellow. When these are united, if the semen of male is preponderent, then a male child is born with the permission of Allah. But when the semen of the female becomes predominant, then a female child is born." At this the Jew exclaimed, "You are truly a Prophet."

Once Finhas, Abdullah b. Suriya, Ibn Saluba, Kinana b. al-Rabi, Ashya, Ka'ab b. Asad, Shamwil b. Zaid, Jabal b. Amr, Mahmood b. Sayhan, Numan b. Adi , Uzayr b. Abu Uzair and Sallam b. Mishkam came to the Holy Prophet and said, "O Muhammad! Is it true that whatever you are presenting has been sent by God? We see it as organized as is Torah."

The Holy Prophet replied, "Listen! By God, you very well know that it has been sent by God. There is mention in your Books and if the Jinn and men (all) try together to present one like it, they will never succeed." Upon this they said, "O Muhammad! Does any man or jinn teach you?" He answered, "You know well that it is from God and that I am His Apostle. You will find it written in the Torah you have." They said, "When God sends an apostle He does for him what he wishes, so bring down a book to us from heaven that we may read it and know what it is, otherwise we will produce one like the one you bring."[36] So God sent down the following verse:[37] "Say: 'If the whole of mankind and jinns were to gather together to produce the like of this Quran, they could not produce the like thereof, even if they backed up each other with help and support."

Once the Holy Prophet tried to persuade some prominent rabbis. Among them were Abdullah b. Suriya and Ka'ab b. Asad. He said to them, "O Jews! fear Allah and embrace Islam because you, by God, do know that whatever has been sent down upon me is true." They answered, "O Muhammad! We don't know this."[38]

Rifa'a was a notable Jew. Whenever he spoke to the Holy Prophet he twisted his tongue and mispronounced the Quranic words so as to give them an offensive meaning. Thus these words became meaningless, absurd or blasphemous. He said, "O Muhammad! Give us your attention so that we can make you understand." Then he began to criticise Islam and revile it.[39]

It was a routine of the Jews that they greeted the Holy Prophet with the words *Assamu alaykum* which means 'Death on you' - - - instead of *Assalamu alaykum* (may peace be on you).

It was after the migration of the Holy Prophet to Medina that one day the Jewish rabbis assembled in their religious school. Under a plan a married man committed adultery with a married woman. They sent them to the Holy Prophet to ask what the law said about them. They said, "If he prescribes *tajbih* (which is scourging with a rope of palm fibre smeared with pitch, the blackening of their faces, mounting on two donkeys with their faces to the animal's tail) then follow him, for he is a king and believe him. If he prescribes stoning for them, he is a prophet so beware lest he deprives you of what you hold."

Accordingly the pair went to the Holy Prophet and sought his award after explaining the whole story. He went to their school and met their rabbis including Abdullah b. Suriya, Abu Yasser b. Akhtab and Wahab b. Yahudah. To judge their calibre he put them some questions. Then he concluded that Abdullah b. Suriya was the most learned man among them. He talked to him in solitude and consequently he said, "By God, Abu'l-Qasim, they know right well that you are a prophet sent by God but they envy you."

Then the Holy Prophet gave the award that the two should be stoned and, consequently, they were stoned at the door of the mosque.

One day some prominent Jews like Al-Nahham b. Zaid, Qardam b. Ka'ab and Bahri b. Amr came to the Holy Prophet and said, "O Muhammad! Do you not know that there is another god with God?" In reply he said, "There is no god except Allah and I have been sent by Him and I call you to that."

One of the shrewdest aspects of Jewish attitude was their skilful exploitation of racial prestige. They claimed that they were the chosen nation of God and Paradise was only for them.[40] But as Paradise can be had only after death therefore only those people are eligible for it who desire to die. On the contrary, the Jews consider this world the most dearest thing so how can they be the heir of Paradise? Furthermore, they are seditious and unruly.

Before reaching Medina after his migration the Holy Prophet was sitting in the mosque of Qaba. Some of the Jews were also present there. The Holy Prophet advised them not to boast of their race because only piety makes one nearer to God. How Jews could be pleased with this and on the same day they determined to oppose him. So they started his opposition with rumour. And the first rumour which was on the air by the Jews that all the Muslim women would become sterile. Similarly if any other woman embraces Islam would become sterile.

It is said in the Holy Quran:[41] (They are fond of) listening to falsehood, of devouring anything forbidden. If they do come to thee, either judge between them, or decline to interfere. If thou decline, they cannot hurt thee in the least If thou judge, judge in equality between them. For God loveth those who judge in equality."

These verses were sent down about blood-money between Bani Nadir and Bani Qurayza. The blood-money of the murdered men of Bani Nadir was paid in full because they had a superiority over the Bani Qurayza who were paid half blood-money. And when they sought judgement from the Holy Prophet, God sent down the above-mentioned verses. The Holy Prophet told them that they were on the right path and fixed equal blood-money for them.[42]

In the beginning Jerusalem was the Qibla of the Muslims.

But it was the desire of the Holy Prophet that it should be changed, because it was, also, the Qibla of the Jews.[43] One day while engaged in the worship in the quarter of B. Salimah the Divine Order was revealed to Muhammad (P.B.U.H.) to the following effect:[44]

> "We see the turning of thy face (for guidance) to the heavens: now shall We turn thee to a Qibla that shall please thee. Turn then thy face in the direction of the sacred Mosque wherever ye are, turn your faces in that direction. The people of the Book know well that that is the truth from their Lord. Nor is God unmindful of what they do."

This incident took place two months before the battle of Badr and after sixteen months after the Hijrat.[45] At this the Jews made different utterances. Then Rif'a'a b. Qays, Qardam b. Amr, Rafi' b. Abu Rafi' Ka'ab b. Ashraf, Hajaj b. Amr, Rabi b. Al-Rabi and Kinana b. Rabi came to the Holy Prophet and said, "O Muhammad! Why have you turned your back on *Qibla* you used to face when you alleged that you followed the religion of Abraham. If you return to the former Qibla we will follow you and declare you to be true."[46] On this occasion he received the following revelation:[47]

> "The Fools among the people will say: "What hath turned them from the *Qibla* to which they were used? Say: to God belong both East and West. He guideth whom He will to a Way that is straight. Thus have We made of you an Ummat justly balanced, that ye might be witnesses over the nations, and the Apostle a witness over yourselves; and We appointed the *Qibla* to which thou wast used, only to test those who followed the Apostle from those who would turn on their heels (from the Faith)."

The change of *Qibla* exposed the secrets of the Jews because the Muslims said, "We believe and owe allegiance. It is our faith that everything is from God." The polytheists said, "As Muhammad has changed his *Qibla* to our *Qibla*, it is possible that he may return to our religion. "The fact was that the Holy Prophet had changed his *Qibla* in accordance with the orders of God. It disappointed the Jews because their intention was to seduce him from his religion. Thus hypocrites said, "We don't understand to which direction Muhammad wants to have his *Qibla?* If the former position was correct why did he relinquish it? And if the latter position is correct then he was at wrong before this."

The reality is that the change of the *Qibla* was a matter of secret. The former *Ummas* deviated from it. As the Muslims are a superior *Umma* therefore a superior *Qibla* was a necessity for them. According to a tradition the Holy Prophet said that the Sacred Mosque (the Ka'ba) was the first mosque built in the world. He took the following plea for the change of the *Qibla* :[48]

> In it are Signs Manifest; (for example), the Station of Abraham; whoever enters it attains security; pilgrimage thereto is a duty men owe to God - - - those who can afford the journey; but if any deny faith, God stands not in need of any of His creatures. Say: "O People of the Book! Why reject ye the Signs of God, when God is Himself witness to all ye do?"

Thus Islam and Judaism were disconnected from each other. Mecca became the centre of Islam. The Jews were dismissed from the ruling scene of the world. This incident proved that Islam would be a permanent and complete religion. So they started their shameful activities.

After the Ghazwa of Badr the Holy Prophet visited the Jews in the market of Bani Qaynuqa'a and called on them to Islam before God should treat them as he had treated the Quraish. The Jews answered arrogantly, "O Muhammad! Don't deceive yourself. Do not be elated with the victory over the Quraish. You have killed a number of inexperienced Quraish who did not know how to fight. But if you fight us you will learn that we are men and that you have met your equal."[49]

It was a common practice among the Jews that they either beheaded the prisoners of war or made them slaves. Thus they led a life worst than the death. Muhammad (P.B.U.H.) introduced a law by which they were released on the payment of ransom. He said, "Manage the release of the prisoners."[50] He strictly opposed the beheading of a prisoner or making him a slave. The Holy Quran has even recommended gratuitous release.[51] The Jews did not like this attitude because they often enslaved persons even on non-payment of loans.

When Adhan was started in 2 A.H. it seemed strange to the Jews from their bell rung in their synagogues. They started twisting their tongues and mispronounced the Adhan in their meetings. Similarly when the first regular prayer was offered in the mosque of Qaba it was Friday. The Holy Prophet fixed Friday as the day of worship.This decision was not liked by the Jews who hoped that Muhammad (P.B.U.H.) would fix Saturday as the day of worship because it was their day of worship.

The Holy Quran has prohibited interest and gambling. The whole Jewish business was run on interest therefore the Jews considered it a severe blow to their economy.

To Islam every child is sin-free when he comes in this world. On the contrary, Judaism considers that woman is the spring of every vice and prefers to nip the evil in the bud. According to it woman is a source of enjoyment for man. On the contrary, Islam considers her the mistress of the household. Islam gives her equal rights with the man. Even in marriage she has equal rights with the man and he is responsible for her clothing and food. 'Before Islam the right of divorce was exclusively reserved for the benefit of the stronger sex; the wife was under no circumstances entitled to claim a divorce.' Under Judaism, women were not allowed to demand a divorce from their husbands for any reason whatsoever.[52] But Islam gives her the right for separation and man has been made bound to meet her expenses. Above all Islam gives her entitlement to share in the inheritance of her parents along with her brothers. She was devoid of such rights under Judaism. In Jewish law, daughters were excluded by the sons and mothers inherited nothing from their children. The Jewish poets and poetesses reviled Muslim women and thus outraged all decency by lampooning in obscene verses.

The Jews told the Muslims that:

1) Mary was not pious; and
2) Christ was crucified by them and thus defiled.

But Islam's point of view was quite different from it. The Holy Quran condemned them in the following verses:

1) "And when there came to them an Apostle from God, confirming what was with them, a party of the People of the Book threw away the Book of God behind their backs, as if (it had been something) they did not know!"[53]
2) "And when there comes to them a Book from God, confirming what is with them, - - - although from of old they had prayed for victory against those without Faith - - - when there comes to them that which they (should) have recognized, they refuse to believe in it but the curse of God is on those without Faith."[54]

Thus the gulf of enmity between the Jews and the Muslims was widened. The great majority of the Jews not merely did not accept Muhammad(P.B.U.H.), but became increasingly hostile. Both Muslims and Jews took a point and made it debatable till God prohibited the Muslims from debating any point: "Already has He sent you word in the Book, that when ye hear the Signs of God held in defiance and ridicule, ye are not to sit with them unless they turn to a different theme."[55]

Despite the change of *Qibla* and blasphemous talks of the Jews,God did not order the Holy Prophet to abrogate the Pact of Medina. Rather the Muslims were asked to be patient. After the Ghazwa of Badr, the Quraish wrote to the Jews, "You have war munition and strong forts. Why then you don't annihilate the Muslims. If you don't take such a step then nothing will hinder us in advancing to your women." Under these circumstances, energetic measures were often necessary to sustain the existence of the Muslim Commonwealth. When persuasion failed, pressure was required.[56] 'The illusion was over; the Jews would have nothing to say to Islam: they set themselves instead to oppose it, ridicule it, and vex its Preacher in every way that their notorious ingenuity could devise.'

Expedition Of Salim b. Umayr: (Shawwal, 2 A.H.)
(Shawwal, 2 A.H.)

Abu Afak was a poet and used to sing satirical songs about Muhammad (p.b.u.h.). He belonged to Banu Amr b. Auf which was a branch of Banu Ubaid. He used to instigate the people for allowing an outsider to control their affairs. When the Holy Prophet heard about these songs he asked the Muslims, "Who will deal with this rasçal for me?" Salim b. Umayr went forth and killed Abu Afak.[57]

Ghazwa Of Bani-Qaynuqa'a
(Shawwal, 2.A.H. February, 624 A.C.)

After the splendid victory of the Muslims in the Ghazwa of Badr the attitude of the Jews towards the Muslims became hostile. They did not participate in the Ghazwa of Badr probably they were not bound for helping the Muslims in the battles fought outside the city of Medina. It is why that the Holy Prophet did not demand from them such an assistance. At the same time he hoped that, at last, they would embrace Islam. Therefore he went on inviting them continuously to embrace Islam. One day he asked them to assemble in the market of Bani Qaynuqa'a and said, "O Jews, beware lest God bring upon you the vengeance that He brought upon the Quraish so become Muslims."

But the Jews were proud of their strength, they gave defiant answer, "O Muhammad! You seem to think that we are your people. Do not deceive yourself because you encountered a people with no knowledge of war and got the better of them; for by God if we fight you, you will find that we are real men."[58]

Thus Bani Qaynuqa'a deviated from the Charter of Medina. The Muslims had no choice but to fight with them otherwise the victory at Badr was futile. These Jews conducted a market and practised crafts such as that of the goldsmith. They were for the most part artisans employed in handicraft of all kinds.[59] They were also noted for the extreme laxity of their morals. Like their counterparts of Alexandria they were rebel-minded. In due course of time a

Muslim lady went to a Jew goldsmith for the purchase of jewellery. The goldsmith and some of his young scoundrel companions contrived to fasten her skirt in such a way that when she stood up a considerable portion of her person was revealed. A Muslim passer-by regarded this act as an insult and in the fray which ensued the Jew was killed. As the market was owned by the Jews so they were more in number. They pounced upon the Muslim and martyred him.

This incident caused a riot. When the Holy Prophet called the Jews for inquiry into the matter, they returned the papers of the agreement and pretended to go at war. The Holy Prophet gave Medina in charge of Abu Lubaba b. Abdul-Mundhir[60] and invaded Bani Qaynuqa'a on Saturday in the middle of Shawwal, 2 A.H. with a force. Hamza was the flag-bearer of this force. They shut themselves up in their fortified forts called *atam*. Siege was accordingly laid to their stronghold and all supplies were cut off. The siege continued for fifteen days.[61] At last they surrendered.

Now Abdullah b. Ubbay requested the Holy Prophet for a kind deal with them. But the Holy Prophet put him off. Whereupon he thrust his hand into the collar of the Apostle's robe and persisted his request. His plea was, "Four hundred men without mail and three hundred mailed protected me from all mine enemies." ('It is noteworthy that Qaynuqa'a were confederates of Abdullah b. Ubbay, who had fought by his side on several occasions before the Hijrah.'). His persistency softened the anger of the Holy Prophet. It is remarkable that Ubada b. Samit, who was one of the Bani Auf, who had the same alliance with them as Abdullah, went to the Holy Prophet and renounced all responsibility for them in favour of God and His Apostle.

When Abdullah b. Ubbayi stepped forward to request the Holy Prophet not to announce the banishment for the Bani Qaynuqa'a, one of the Muslims stepped forward to stop him. In this conflict Abdullah b. Ubbay was wounded. Seeing this the Jews said, "We cannot reside in a city where Abdullah, our ally, is wounded and we cannot take his side."[62]

Thus they left Medina and migrated to Wadi-i-Qura and later on proceeded to 'Adhra'at in Syria. It is notable that the Holy Prophet ordered the culprit clans - - - not all the Qaynuqa'a - - - to quit Medina.[63] In doing so they had in their mind the Promised land where every Jew wishes to shift in every age. Among them were six hundred warriors who were the bravest of all the Jews of Medina. But their banishment exposed their bravery. 'It was necessary to put an end to these disorders otherwise Medina would have turned into an amphitheatre.' They knowingly infringed the stipulations of Charter of Medina. When the Holy Prophet ordered their expulsion they said: But we have debts to recollect whose date of payment has not yet arrived. The Holy Prophet suggested: Capitalize them at a discount.[64] So far as the joke with a Muslim lady and as a result the two murders are concerned, the Holy Prophet could have taken a severe action as David had put the Ammonites in the kiln. But the Holy Prophet's action was far more softer than David.

Expedition Of Muhammad b. Maslama:
(Rabi'ul Awwal, 3 A.H./ September, 624 A.C.)

Ka'b b. Ashraf came of Bani Nadir. Naturally he was the supporter of the Charter of Medina. 'He used to instigate the Jewish tribes by outraging all common decency by lampooning in obscene verse the Muslim women.' He, also, inveighed against the Holy Prophet.[65] When the Muslims got victory in the Ghazwa of Badr, he was shocked. He cried out, "By God! If Muhammad actually has defeated the Quraish then the belly of earth is better than its back for us."[66]

Then he proceeded to Makka and excited the Makkans by his elegies. He used to say, "As long as I live I shall weep and remember the merits of people whose glory is in Makka's houses." His verses helped to rouse the Makkans to grief and anger and the desire for revenge. All his activities were against the spirit of the Charter of Medina. Then he plotted to assassinate the Holy Prophet by inviting him to his residence. For this purpose he managed a band of his coadjutors. The following verse of the Holy Quran refers to his malintentions:

"When certain men formed the design to stretch out their hands against you, but (God) held back their hands from you."67

Now the Holy Prophet sent Muhammad b. Maslama with five men to kill Ka'b. Muhammad b. Maslama was his foster-brother. Subsequently Ka'b was killed.

Ghazwa of Bani Nadir:
(Rabi'ul Awwal, 4 A.H.[68] August,
or early September, 625 A.C.).

It was incumbent upon the Jews to participate in the battle of Uhud as per stipulations of the Charter of Medina. But they did not as it was the day of Sabbath. Furthermore, they excused that they were not bound to fight outside Medina. Only one Jew, Mukhayriq, participuted in the battle. His parting testimony to his people was: "If I am killed today my property is to go to Muhammad to be used as God shows him.'[69] The Holy Prophet appreciated his role.

Some of the orientalists say that the Holy Prophet waged Jihad against the Bani Nadir due to their non-participation in the battle of Uhud. But it is merely a charge. There is no doubt that the Bani Nadir played a contrary role to the Charter of Medina but in this promise-breaking act Bani Qurayza were also included and he waged Jihad only against the Bani Nadir. Bani Nadir, always, prepared sinister designs against the Muslims. Musa b. Uqba has written, "Bani Nadir plotted with the Quraish, instigated them for a fight with the Holy Prophet and conveyed secrets to them."[70]

After their defeat at Badr the Quraish wrote to the Jews of Medina, "You are the owners of properties and forts. Fight against Muhammad otherwise we will treat you badly. We will put off the foot ornaments of your women."

This letter cemented the ill-intentions of the Jews therefore all their sympathies remained with the Quraish. After the Ghazwa of Uhud the Holy Prophet asked them to renew the Charter of Medina, Bani Qurayza accepted the offer but Bani Nadir refused to do so. They were very proud of their fortified cantons. Moreover, they depended much on Abdullah b. Ubbay, Suwayd, Malik b. Abu Qauqal, Da's and Wad'a. They tapped them and assured them all possible help. They told them that they would even prefer banishment with them but would not leave them alone.[71] God sent down the following verse in this connection:[72]

"Hast thou not observed the Hypocrites say to their misbelieving brethren among the People of the Book? 'If ye are expelled, we too will go out with you, and we will never hearken to any one in your affair; and if ye are attacked (in fight) we will help you."

This was the beginning of the sheer mischiefs of Bani Nadir. They tried several times to kill the Holy Prophet. Once they sent for him alongwith his three companions to have discussions with their scholars. And if he proved his truthfulness they would embrace Islam. The Holy Prophet accepted their offer but before his departure he was informed that the Jews had a plan to assassinate him so he dropped the idea of going there.

One of the companions of the Holy Prophet, Amr b. Umayya al-Damri, killed two men of Banu Amir unintentionally. The Holy Prophet had an alliance with Banu Amir. On the other hand there was a mutual alliance between Banu Nadir and Banu Amir. He sent the bloodwit of the two to their heirs. According to the treaty Bani Nadir had also to pay bloodwit. Muhammad (P.B.U.H.) asked them to comply with the stipulations of the Charter of Medina to contribute towards the payment of the blood-money. He proceeded to their settlement in the company of some disciples prominent among them were Abu Bakr, Umar and Ali. Apparently Bani Nadir were cordial with him but they hatched upon a secret plan to assassinate him. They deputed Amr b. Jahash to roll a heavy stone onto his head from the roof of a nearby house. Through intuition Muhammad (p.b.u.h.) got warning against the danger so he got up and returned to Medina.[73]

This was the climax of the treacheries of the Jews. They could go to any extent. In due course one of the Companions of the Holy Prophet died. He asked his dependants not to inform the Holy Prophet about his death at the time of night lest the Jews harm him in darkness.[74]

Now it was the high time to punish the Bani Nadir. The Holy Prophet despatched Muhammad b. Maslama, a chief of Aus, with an ultimatum to Bani Nadir. It was: 'Leave Medina within ten days otherwise I will be forced to fight against you." Watt opines that it was further said that they would still be regarded as owners of their palm-trees and receive part of the produce.[75] But Bani Nadir replied, "We will not leave our homeland. Go and do whatever you can."[76]

The Holy Prophet tried his utmost to give them chance to leave Medina. He adopted the maximum flexibility which he could in contrast to the breach of the treaty.[77] Thus it was they who started the fight. The Holy Prophet left Medina in charge of Umm Maktum[78] and besieged the Bani Nadir with a force. Ali was the standard-bearer of this force. Neither Abdullah b. Ubbay nor Banu Quraiza gave the Bani Nadir any assistance.

The siege continued for fifteen days.[79] At last the palm-trees of the oasis were cut down around their forts to put a blow to their economy. These groves served as their refuge. These trees included *Lina* - - - palms neither fruitful nor bearing good dates. At this the Jews taunted the Muslims that was it not the wanton destruction?[80] To warn them God sent down this verse:[81] "Whether ye cut down (O ye Muslims!) the tender palm-trees, or ye left them standing on their roots, it was by leave of God, and in order that He might cover with shame the rebellious transgressors."

Anyhow it cast terror in their hearts. Psychologically they were already overcome by awe by the murder of Ka'b b. Ashraf. They themselves sued for terms that they would evacuate Medina so their lives should be spared. They were allowed to take away their movable property (except swords, cuirasses and helmets) which they could carry on camels.[82] In order to prevent the Muslims from occupying their dwellings, they destroyed them down to the lintel of the door before their deportation.[83] They evacuated, proudly, Medina with six hundred loaded camels under the leadership of Huyyay b. Akhtab. Other prominents were Sallam b. Abu'l Huqayq and Kinana b. Rabi. Their women and slaves carried with them tambourines and pipes playing behind them.[84] The people of Khyber welcomed them wholeheartedly. Some of them settled in Khyber while others went to 'Adhraat in Syria. Only two of the Bani Nadir - - - Abu Sa'd b. Wahb and Yamin b. Umayr Abu Ka'b embraced Islam in order to retain their property and occupied it after their conversion.[85] When the Holy Prophet ordered their expulsion they said: "But different people owe us debts whose date of payment has not yet arrived." The Holy Prophet suggested: "Capitalize them at a discount."[86]

Bani Nadir were chiefly agriculturists and had some of the richest lands in the oasis. The Muslims got godowns full of grain. Besides their gardens and lands, 50 armours, 50 helmets and 340 swords were got. As these things did not fall in the category of booty therefore the Holy Prophet distributed them among the first emigrants (except one piece of land allotted for the paupers and destitutes) with the cordial approval of the *Ansar* keeping in view their poor means of subsistence. Anyhow Abu Dujana and Sahl b. Hunayf, both from the *Ansar*, were given equal share with the emigrants because they were extremely poor.[87]

Bani Nadir were the cause of all unrest. They were always busy in intrigues against the Muslims. Their banishment was necessary because they always acted as fifth columnists during an invasion upon Medina. Credit goes to Muhammad (P.B.U.H.) in establishing the balance of terror of the Muslims. Their deportation proved the beginning of peace and integrity in Medina. Now the Holy Prophet had no fear of the hypocrites. Similarly the financial position of the emigrants became a bit stable.

There was a Jew scribe of the Holy Prophet who wrote letters for him in Hebrew. He, also, migrated with the Bani Nadir. Now the Holy Prophet ordered Zaid b. Thabit to learn Hebrew for the interest of Islam. He learnt it within fifteen days.

Bani Nadir spreaded a network of intrigues and plots against Islam after their banishment. After two years they invaded Medina with a force of 24,000 men and forgot the benevolent behaviour of the Holy Prophet. He was, at that time, in a position to annihilate them completely. But he was above such revengeful steps. Their banishment was a preamble of the Ghazwa of Khyber.

Expedition Of Abdullah b. Atik: (Zilhij, 4 A.H;
(Zilhij, 4 A.H. May, 626 A.C.)

Abu Rafi'Sallam b. Abu'l Huqayq known as Abu Rafi' a member of Bani Nadir, had made great struggle to instigate different tribes such as Sulaim and the Ghatafan against the Muslims during the Ghazwa of Ahzab.He had inhabited, with a fraction of his tribe, in the territories of Khyber. Now he was re-managing to attack the Muslims. The Holy Prophet sent Abdullah b. Atik with five men to kill him because the security of the State was at stake. A prompt execution of such a traitor was the need of the time. Moreover, the punishment given to him could frighten the Jews. Consequently he was killed while he was sleeping. After his death a great hurdle in the propagation of Islam was removed.

Ghazwa of Bani Qurayza:
(5 A.H. April/May, 627 A.C.).

During the Ghazwa of Ahzab, Bani Qurayza joined hands with the enemy and did not regard the stipulations of the Charter of Medina. The Muslims had signed two treaties with them - - - one was Charter of Medina and the other signed at the time of the battle with Bani Nadir. Muhammad (P.B.U.H.) tried to make them neutral but did not succeed notwithstanding the fact that they were bound by the Charter of Medina to assist the Muslims against every assailant. At this time Huyyay b. Akhtab came to Bani Qurayza and tried to win them over. He mentioned that he had the co-operation of the Quraish and Ghatafan and expressed his hope that the annihilation of Muhammad was the easiest job at that time. Ka'b b. Asad, the chief of Bani Qurayza, replied, "You have brought such a cloud to me which has shed its water and has only lightning and thunder."[88] After long discussions Bani Qurayza yielded to the wishes of Huyyay b. Akhtab.

As soon as the Holy Prophet heard of their deflection he sent Sa'd b. Mua'dh (chief of Aus), Sa'd b. Ubada (chief of Khazraj), Khawas b. Jubayr and Abdullah b. Rawaha to appraise of the situation and entreat them to return to their duty. Bani Qurayza agreed to assist the Muslims on the condition of the re-settlement of Bani Nadir. Sa'd b. Mua'dh had his personal contacts with Bani Qurayza. Keeping in view he asked them to re-consider their decision lest they also meet the same end like Bani Nadir. The reply was defiant and sullen: "Who is the Apostle of God? Say Muhammad there is no bond or compact betwixt us and him."

Now the Muslims became alert lest any foreign power should attack upon Medina having plotted with the Bani Qurayza. On the same day the Holy Prophet left Medina in charge of Abdullah b. Umm Maktum[89] and marched with three thousand men (including 36 horsemen). Ali was sent in forward with a banner who heard Huyyay b. Akhtab and other Jews using abusive language against the Holy Prophet. He returned to meet the Apostle on the road and told him that he should not go there. The Holy Prophet understood that they must have spoken ill of him so he said, "When they see me they will not talk in that fashion." So he continued to march forward until he reached near them. He said loudly, "You brothers of monkeys, has God not disgraced you and brought His vengeance upon you?"

In reply they said, "O Abul Qasim! You are not unaware."[90]

Bani Qurayza possessed several fortresses at a short distance towards the south-east of Medina. They were besieged because such a 'sitting on the fence' could not be tolerated. The siege lasted for 25 days.[91] During this time they stoned at the Muslims twice or thrice while the Muslims shot arrows. But the Bani Qurayza did not dare to come out for an open combat. When they were sore pressed, Ka'b b. Asad, their chief, offered them three alternatives:[92]

Firstly: "Follow Muhammad and accept him as true. He is a prophet who has been sent and that it is he that you find mentioned in your Scripture." The Jews replied: "We will never abandon the laws of the Torah and never change it for another."

Secondly: "Let us kill our wives and children and send men with their swords drawn to Muhammad leaving no encumbrances behind us, until God decides between us and Muhammad. If we are perished, we shall not leave children behind us to cause us anxiety. If we conquer, we can acquire our wives and children."
The Jews replied, "Should we kill these poor creatures? What would be the good of life when they are dead?"

Thirdly: Tonight is the eve of Sabbath. It will well be that Muhammad will feel secure from us then, so come down, perhaps we can take Muhammad and his companions by surprise."
The Jews replied, "To spoil the holiness of Saturday is tantamount to invite destruction."

Now Ka'b b. Asad said, "Not a single man among you from the day of your birth has ever passed a night resolved to do what he knows ought to be done." Actually they were fed up from the length of the siege. At last they sent a message to the Holy Prophet saying, "Send Abu Lubaba b. Abdu'l Mundhir, we want to negotiate through him." Abu Lubaba came of the tribe of Aus and had personal relations with Bani Qurayza. So he was sent to them. The women and children went up to him weeping in his face and he felt sorry for them. It is reported that he tried to persuade them to abandon Huyyay, who had been mainly responsible for the resistance to Muhammad (P.B.U.H.) The Jews asked him, "What is your opinion? Should we submit to Muhammad?" Abu Lubaba replied in affirmation and pointed with his hand to his throat signifying slaughter. Abu Lubaba was ashamed of what had he done. Instead of going back to the Holy Prophet he went straight to the mosque and bound himself to one of the pillars. He determined not to leave the place until God forgave him for what he had done.

On the other side, Muhammad (P.B.U.H.) waited for Abu Lubaba but he did not come. When he was informed about him he said, "If he had come to me I would have asked forgiveness for him." Abu Lubaba remained tied to a stump for six nights. His wife used to come at every time of prayer and untie him for prayer. Then he would return and tie himself to the stump. At last God forgave him. When the people rushed out to set him free, he refused to be freed but only by the Holy Prophet, who set him free at the time of morning prayer.

Now the Bani Qurayza requested for arbitration. The request was accepted. Keeping in view the old alliance they nominated Sa'd b. Mua'dh their arbiter. They thought that he would take their side as Abdullah b. Ubbay had secured refuge for Bani Qaynuqa'a. A farsighted man like Sa'd, who was a fierce soldier too, had been wounded in the battle of the Trench. When the Holy Prophet sent for him the whole of the tribe of Aus asked him for a kind deal with Bani Qurayza. He kept silent but when the people persisted he said, "The time has come for Sa'd in the cause of God, not to care for any man's censure."[93] Thus people guessed that Bani Qurayza would be murdered.

Sa'd came to the Holy Prophet mounting on a donkey. He was told that he had been appointed arbiter. Sa'd, first of all, said to his people, "Do you covenant by Allah that you accept the judgement I pronounce on them?" They replied in affirmation. The Holy Prophet was also included among them in replying. Now Sa'd pronounced his judgement that :[94]

1. Fighting men should be put to death;
2. Women and children should be taken as captives; and
3. Their properties be divided.

Upon this the Holy Prophet said to Sa'd, "You have

given the judgement of Allah above the seven heavens."[95] Now it was the time of carrying the sentence into execution. Before it four persons embraced Islam. Umar b. Sa'd fled and thus escaped.[96] The Bani Qurayza were ordered to come out of the fortresses. They were confined in the quarter of Kaisa d. Harith, [97] a lady of B. Najjar. Then trenches were dug in the middle of the bazar. The criminals were brought in batches where their heads were struck off and buried in the trenches. Their number was 600 to 700.[98] Among them was, also, a woman who had killed Khallad b. Suwayd by throwing a millstone on him which inflicted a shattering wound.[99]

Their property, women and children were divided among the Muslims. The Holy Prophet fixed the shares of the horse and men, and took out the fifth. A horseman got three shares, two for the horse and one for his rider. A man without a horse got one share. On that day there were thirty six horses.[100] Then he sent Sa'd. b. Zaid to Najad with some of the captives who sold them for horses and weapons.

In the light of the end of the Bani Qurayza the Orientalists have sought a ground for attack on the Holy Prophet. They have tried to prove him a bloody Nero. Prominent among them are William Muir, Sprenger, Weil and Osborn. While the reality is that the punishment inflicted on the Bani Qurayza was very light in comparison to their crimes. Stanley Lane-Poole has so beautifully remarked that I cannot resist quoting him: "It was a harsh, bloody sentence worthy of the episcopal generals of the army against the Albiogenses, or of the deeds of the Augustan age of Puritanism; but it must be remembered that the crime of these men was high treason against the state during a time of siege; and those who have read how Wellington's march could be traced by the bodies of deserters and pillagers hanging from the trees, need not be surprised at the summary execution of a traitorous clan."[101] Some Muslims might naturally be inclined to say, with the Christian moralist Arnold: "It is better that the wicked should be destroyed a hundred times over than that they should tempt those who are yet innocent to join their company."[102]

The end met by the Bani Qurayza should be analysed in the light of the following events :

Muhammad (P.B.U.H.) had signed a Charter after his migration to Medina by which the Bani Qurayza were given the freedom of religion and conscience. They were promised the security of their life and property but they themselves caused the breach of the Charter. "When the Quraish and their allies were besieging Medina, and had well-nigh stormed the defences, this Jewish tribe entered into negotiations with the enemy, which were only circumvented by the diplomacy of the Prophet."[103] They proved themselves traitors in spite of their sworn alliance. So long as they abided it, the Holy Prophet did not wage Jihad against them.

The social status of the Bani Qurayza was far lesser than the Bani Nadir. If any of them killed a member of Bani Qurayza, he had to pay half blood-money. On the contrary, Bani Qurayza had to pay full blood-money. The Holy Prophet established parity between the two tribes.

After the deportation of the Bani Nadir the Holy Prophet renewed the treaty with Bani Qurayza notwithstanding their past treachery, open hostility and defection from the Compact. But they again broke the treaty and joined hands with the Confederates against the Muslims. 'They could assist the besiegers by showing them the weak points of the city' and thus they were a perpetual danger to the security of Medina. In the beginning of the battle of the Ditch, they remained neutral but when the siege was prolonged they, also, began the preparations to invade the forts where the Muslim ladies and children had taken refuge. It was the time when the national security of the Muslims was in danger. They were facing a strong army of the enemy and, on the other hand, the fifth columnists could turn turtle the situation. Under these circumstances, the Bani Qurayza broke with the Muslims and swore the extirpation of Islam.

Huyyay b. Akhtab had already been deported from Medina. He instigated the whole Arabia and created a war-confederation against the Muslims. Bani Qurayza joined hands with them. Their simple banishment could not serve the purpose because the Holy Prophet had gone through this experiment in the case of Bani Nadir who had played an important role in instigating the Quraish and other tribes of Arabia. To leave them alive was tantamount to the death of the Muslims themselves. Even Wensinck, who is otherwise very hostile to the Holy Prophet, admits that the leniency shown previously to the Jews of Bani Nadir had produced the contrary of the desired effect, and no statesman could possibly commit the same mistake of leniency again.[104] Still on capitulation Muhammad (P.B.U.H.) showed leniency, and asked them to select their own arbitrator, whose decision would be final. Had they appointed the Holy Prophet their arbitrator, he would have certainly be more lenient than Sa'd. At the most he might have deported them like Bani Nadir. Even after the arbitral award he exempted some persons from the execution of the decision, for example, Zubair and his family members were set free. Similarly he liberated Rifa'a b. Shamaw'al.

Bani Qurayza themselves chose arbitration for them and the Holy Prophet only honoured the award. It is a recognized law of the world about arbitration that when the parties choose an arbitrator, his decision is final. Furthermore, this decision was quite in accordance with the prevalent canons of war : "a strict application of admitted customs of war in those days."[105] Bani Qurayza never murmured at the award of Sa'd. They knew that had they been victorious they would have massacred their enemy. 'This arbitral award was in conformity with the Jewish personal law.' "When thou comest nigh unto a city to fight against it, then proclaim peace unto it. And it shall be, if it make thee answer of peace, and open unto thee, then it shall be, that all the people that be found therein shall be tributaries unto thee, and they shall serve thee. And if it will make no peace with thee, but will make war against thee, then thou shalt besiege it : And when the Lord thy God hath delivered it unto thine hands, thou shalt smite every male thereof with the edge of the sword : But the women and the little ones, and the cattle, and all that is in the city, even all the spoil thereof, shalt thou take unto thyself; and thou shalt eat the spoil of thine enemies, which the Lord thy God hath given thee." People judge the massacres of King David, according to the "Lights of his time."[107] "The conquered Ammonites he treated with even greater ferocity, tearing and hewing some of them in pieces with harrows, axes, and saws; and roasting others in brick-kilns."[108] On the contrary, only adult men of the Bani Qurayza were killed and the Muslims shouldered the responsibility of their women and children.

The battle with the Bani Qurayza was not fought in the battlefield. Rather it was a battle of the nerves. The Jews could not dare to break the siege of the Muslims notwithstanding the fact that they had abundant food, water and invincible forts. Actually their morale had fallen. After their defeat the Muslims succeeded in creating their awe and no one dared to march towards them in future. It is noteworthy that there were still Jews in Medina, prominent among them were of Banu 'Uraid. They were treated generously so long as they remained peaceful. They enjoyed full religious and economic autonomy.

Expedition Of Abdullah b Rawaha:
(Shawwal, 6. A.H./
February/March (628 A.C.).

In Shawwal, 6 A.H. the Holy Prophet was informed that Usayr b. Razim, a Jew, was collecting the men of Ghatafan in Khyber against the Muslims. So he sent Abdullah b. Rawaha with a detachment of thirty horsemen. Abdullah b. Unays was also among them. When the Muslims got near him they persuaded him that if he would come to the Apostle he would give him an appointment and honour him. Each of his companions mounted with one Muslim on his camel. Usayr mounted the camel of Abdullah b. Unays. When they were at Qarqara, six miles from Khyber, Usayr changed his mind about going to Medina. As he was preparing to draw his sword, Abdullah b. Unays perceived his intention. He rushed at him and struck him with his sword cutting off his leg. Yusayr had a stick of Shauhat wood in his hand.

He hit Abdullah b. Unays with it and wounded his head.[109] Subsequently each Muslim fell upon his co-Jew-rider and murdered him. Anyhow one Jew succeeded to escape.[110]

Expedition Of Kurz b. Jabir
(Shawwal, 6. A.H.)

The Holy Prophet had captured a slave called Yusar in the Ghazwa of Muharib and Banu Th'alaba. He put him in charge of his milch-camels to shepherd them in the neighbourhood of al-Jamma'. In due course of time some persons, from Kubba-a branch of Bajila, came to the Holy Prophet. They were suffering from an epidemic and enlarged spleens. The Holy Prophet told them that if they drank the milk of milch-camels, they would recover. They did the same and when recovered, they fell upon Yusar and killed him. They were so cruel that they struck thorns in his eyes. Then they drove away the milch-camels.

Now the Holy Prophet sent Kurz b. Jabir with 20 horsemen in their pursuit. They were caught and brought to Medina. The Holy Prophet had just returned from the expedition of Dhu Qarad. Subsequently they were killed.

Ghazwa Of Khyber:
(Muharram, 7 A.H./May/June, 628 A.C.)

Khyber is a word signifying a fortified place. It was a stronghold of the Jews situated at a distance of 200 miles in the north of Medina. After his migration to Medina the Holy Prophet concluded a treaty with all the tribes. The people of Khyber often violated the treaty and continued to intrigue assiduously against Medina. They assisted the enemies of Islam during the battle of the Trench. When the Truce of Hudaiybia was concluded, the Jews of Khyber had guessed that now a war was inevitable between them and the Muslims. So they began tremendous war preparations. They stored abundant food stuff in their eight forts and their twenty thousand soldiers, equipped with complete war weapons, were ready to fight. Before the conclusion of the Treaty of Hudaiybia the Jews of Khyber were the allies of the Makkans, so it was difficult for the Muslims to invade them. But this Treaty neutralized Makka. God had promised the Muslims great victories and spoils in future in reward of the patience and tolerance which they had shown at the time of the concluding of the Treaty of Hudaibiya. As is mentioned in the Holy Quran :[111]. "For He knew what ye knew not, and He granted, besides this, a speedy victory. It is He Who has sent His Apostle with Guidance and the religion of Truth, to proclaim it over all religions: and enough is God for a Witness."

On his return from Makka, the Holy Prophet stayed for twenty days in Medina and then set out for Khyber to punish the Jews for their constant treacheries. In his force were fourteen hundred soldiers besides twenty ladies for nursing service. He left Medina in charge of Numayla b. Abdullah.[112] Ali was the standard-bearer and its colour was white. The Muslims spent night in the vicinity of Khyber. After their morning prayer the Muslims saw the workers of Khyber coming out in the fields with their spades and baskets. When they saw the Muslim force, they turned tail and fled. When the Holy Prophet saw this he exclaimed out, "Allah-o-Akbar! Khyber is destroyed. When we arrive in a people's square it is a bad morning for those who have been warned." Now the Muslims encamped in the valley of Raji' situated between Khyber and Ghatafan. The purpose was to prevent the latter from reinforcing Khyber for they were on their side against the Muslims. When the Ghatafan came to know about the Muslims advance, they marched out to help the Jews. But they retreated after a day's journey on hearing a rumour about their property and families. They thought that they had been attacked during their absence.

The Jews were strongly garrisoned in vulnerable forts. The Holy Prophet conquered, first of all, the fort of Na'm. This was the same fort where the Jews had killed Mahmood b. Maslama throwing on him a millstone from it. Then Ali completed the conquest of formidable castles of al-Qamus. Then the castle of al-Watih and al-Sulalim were conquered after a ten days' siege. The war-cry of the Muslims was 'O victorious one, slay slay!' Here it is appropriate to mention the story of Kinana that he was tortured for the sake of disclosing the concealed treasure. This is a concocted story. It is said that Kinana b.Rabi' 113 had the custody of the treasure of Bani Nadir. He was asked about it. He replied, "That has been consumed by wars and daily necessities." The Holy Prophet said, "The period is near and the money was abundant." Then he handed him over to Zubair b. Awwam who tortured him. Finally he disclosed that he had seen Huyyay b. Akhtab roaming about such and such ruins. Subsequently Zubair excavated the ruins and succeeded in getting the treasure.

Now the Jews sued for forgiveness which was accorded. Various factors contributed to the Muslim success. The Jews were over-confident of their strongholds, many built on the tops of hills and virtually impregnable. They fell short of water supplies during the siege. They lacked unity among their ranks. They had made lavish use of their wealth to induce the Arabs of the neighbouring tribes against Medina. But their allies could not help them in need. The Holy Prophet told the Jews explicitly, "I will let you stay so long as God will let you stay."[114] Abu Dawud is more clear on this point, "If we wish to expel you we will expel you."[115] Buladhari is of the opinion that the Holy Prophet had the intention of expelling the Jews from Khyber but consented to their request that, "Let us remain here. We will work here and make reforms for it."[116]

The Holy Prophet treated the Jews of Khyber quite differently from Bani Qainuqua'a and bani Nadir.

After the conquest of Khyber the Jews were crushed as a power. Islam got predominance over all the religions of Arabia. After this conquest the whole earth was regarded the property of God. As the number of gardens, oases and land was abundant therefore its supervision and acquisition of its produce was quite a problem. Its distribution was made as under:

a) Some portion of the land was distributed among the soldiers;
b) Rest was let remained with the inhabitants.

It was decided that both would share the produce,

viz; half produce for the government and half for the cultivators. As God was declared the sole owner of the land therefore the government got the full powers to expel them at any time. Even the share given to the soldiers was not exempted from law and tax, rather the whole land was kept under the management and supervision of the government.

The Muslims of Medina were mainly agriculturists. But their personal lands could not be inhabited without their own shifting from Medina to Khyber. And this was not possible. Moreover they were the backbone of the defence of Medina and their settlement in Khyber was tantamount to weaken the defence of Medina. It was more than satisfaction for the Jews to cultivate the lands as their "prestige" had been buried. They had lost their forts like Shaqq, Nata, Mitaqa and Katiba. Only two forts - - - Watih and Sallam - - - had been left with them therefore they requested for peace. The Holy Prophet distributed the produce of Khyber over 36 shares further fixing 100 shares in each of them. Then half, viz; 18 shares were separated from that for the expenses for deputations and other national necessities. The remaining 18 shares were distributed.117 The conquered portion of Khyber was distributed but the portion subjugated through peace was left for the general betterment of the Muslims. Even the ladies were allowed a small portion of the booty but it was not a definite share.118 Muhammad (P.B.U.H.) conceded to the Jews even judicial autonomy where the parties were of the same community. But they were told that their quarter would be forfeited if they hid their property.[119] Safiya, daughter of Huyyay b. Akhtab, who was the wife of Kinana b. al-Huqaiq, fell in booty. Muhammad (P.B.U.H.) elevated her to the position of his wife at her request.

In this Ghazwa the Holy Prophet prohibited the Muslims from committing the following:120

1) Carnal intercourse with pregnant women who were captured;
2) Meat of domestic donkeys;
3) Eating any carnivorous animal; and
4) Selling booty before it had been duly allotted.

After the conquest Zaynab d. Harith (wife of Sallam b. Mishkam), a Jewess, invited the Holy Prophet and some of his Companions to a feast at her home. She served them a poisoned roast lamb. He chewed a morsel of it but he did not swallow it. So he forbade his Companions from eating it. When the hostess was called for, she confessed putting forth the plea, "I said to myself, if he is a king I shall ease myself of him and if he is a prophet he will be informed (of what I have done)." The Holy Prophet let her off. 121 But when his Companion, Bishr b. al-Bara died after he had taken a few mouthfuls, she was executed.

In this Ghazwa the following Muslims met martyrdom:[122]

1.	Rabi'a b. Aqtham	Took part in Badr, Uhud, Trench, Hudaibiya. Age: 34
2.	Abdullah b. Hubayb	Took part in Badr.
3.	Mas'ud b. Sa'd	Took part in Badr.
4.	Mahmood b. Maslama	Took part in Uhud and Trench The Jews threw a millstone on him when he was standing below a castle. After three days he died.
5.	Thaqif b. Amr	
6.	Rifa'a b. Masruh	
7.	Abu Dayyah b. Thabit	
8.	Harith b. Hatib	Took part in the battle of Trench and Hudaibiya. Killed by an arrow shot from a castle of Khyber.
9.	Urwa b. Murrah	
10.	Aus b. Aiz	
11.	Unayf b. Habib	
12.	Thabit b. Athla	
13.	Talha	
14.	Umara b. Uqba	
15.	Amir b. Akwa'	
16.	Aswad Rahi	Negro slave of a Jew of Khyber. Died on the same

day when he embraced Islam.

17. Mas'ud b. Rafi'a
18. Aus b. Qatada

On the other hand, 93 Jews were killed.

The Holy Prophet used to send Abdullah b.Rawaha every year to Khyber. He acted as an assessor for the Muslims and the Jews. If the Jews would say, "You have made wrong with us." In reply he would say, "If you wish it is yours and if you like it is ours."[123] Once they collected the ornaments of their women and tried to bribe him so that he might lessen their levies. He said, "O Jews! You are the worst of creatures in my eyes.[124] Still I don't want to make you oppressed. Whatever you bribe me is unlawful and we Muslims don't accept it." Upon hearing this the Jews said, "On this (foundation) heavens and earth stand."[125] After the martyrdom of Abdullah b. Rawaha in the battle of Mu'ta, the Holy Prophet appointed Abdullah b. Sahl the assessor in his place. The Jews killed him, during the reign of the Holy Prophet, and threw his dead body by the bank of a canal.[126]

Politically the Ghazwa of Khyber bears great importance because, for the first time, the non-Muslims were included in the Islamic State as citizens. The real purpose of Islam is preaching and if any nation does not obstruct it, it has neither war with it nor needs to subjugate it. Only a truce is enough. In this connection there are numerous examples in the Islamic history. But when a nation is determined to oppose it and wants to annihilate it, then the Muslims have to defend themselves. According to this principle Khayber was the first conquered land in Islam.

Apparently Khyber enjoyed full internal autonomy because no Muslim governor was appointed there. The real danger to Islam was from the polytheists and the Jews because the Christians were not active in Arabia. There was an alliance between the polytheists and the Jews on political grounds despite their religious differences. After the conquest of Khyber the power of the Jews was given a severe blow and an arm of the polytheists was broken.[127] Consequently the Muslims got a full opportunity to propagate Islam.

Ghazwa of Wadiu'l Qura:
(Muharram, 7 A.H. 128)

Wadiu'l Qura was situated between Khyber and Taima.It had been inhabited by A'ad and Thamud but after their annihilation the Jews settled here. There they made their colonies.

After the conquest of Khyber the Holy Prophet went to Wadiu'l Qura with 382 Companions. A band of the polytheists joined hands with the Jews.[129] His aim was to propagate Islam but the Jews were bent upon mischief. They, immediately, began shooting arrows. A slave of the Holy Prophet was shot dead by an arrow. Actually the Muslims were not ready to face the sudden onslaught. Now the Holy Prophet gave banners to Sa'd b. Ubada, Khabab b. Mundhir, Sahl b. Hanif and Ubada b. Bashar.[130] After this he invited the Jews to embrace Islam and assured them the security of their property and lives. But they rejected the offer and sent a Jew for combat. Zubair b. Awwam fought with him and killed him. Similarly another Jew was sent, whom again Zubair killed. Another single combat was between another Jew and Ali whom the latter killed. Now the Jews were invited to embrace Islam.[131] Meanwhile the sun was set and during the night the Holy Prophet had occupied the whole land. In this fight eleven Jews were killed.[132]

After the conquest Muhammad (P.B.U.H.) treated them like that of Khyber. The booty was divided among the Companions. The land and the oases were left with the Jews on the condition of half produce. Amr b. Saeed was appointed the governor of Wadiu'l Qura.[133] When the people of Taima heard of the fall of Wadiu'l Qura they made peace with the Holy Prophet on the same conditions. After staying for four days, he returned to Medina.

(3) Ghazwas And Expeditions Against Bani Hawazin

Expedition Of Dhatul-Araq:
(Rabi'u'l Awwal, 8 A.H.)

Bani Hawazin had extended assistance to the enemies of Islam several times. Now they had provided a force which assembled at the distance of 5 miles from Medina. In order to impress them the Holy Prophet sent Shujah b. Wahab Asadi with 25 men. No fighting took place but the Muslims got some camels of the enemy.

Expedition Of Omar:
December, 628 A.C.)

Umar Farooq was sent at the head of thirty riders towards Hawazin. When they got news they ran away. When the Muslims reached there, the enemy had gone so the Muslims returned. The guide of the detachment asked Umar, "Will you like to have a combat with Banu Jusham who are coming to this side?" But he declined as he was not instructed to do so by the Holy Prophet.

Ghazwa Of Hawazin:
(Shawwal, 8 A.H./30 January, 630 A.C.)

This Ghazwa is also known as Hunain or Autas, Hunain was a deep and narrow defile about ten miles to the north-east of Makka. When the Bani Hawazin heard of the fall of Makka, its chief Malik b. Auf al-Nasri began to collect a strong force against the Muslims. He thought it to be a threat to his tribe. Moreover, 'when he heard that he was marching on Mecca, he may have expected a bloody and indecisive battle and may have hoped to have an easy victory over one or both of the exhausted combatants.' Bani Thaqif, first of all, assembled to him. Then the tribes of Nasr, Jusham, Sa'd b. Bakr, Hilal and Qays 'Aylan declared to assist him and as a token sent some volunteers. They formed a league. Anyhow the important branches of Hawazin like Ka'b and Kilab kept away. Durayd b. Simma, the chief of Banu Jusham was a very old man. He was carried in a howdah. He participated in the war due to his long knowledge of war. Qarib b. Aswad was appointed the commander of the Ahlaf. Two chiefs were appointed for Banu Malik - - - one was Dhul-Khimar Subay b. Harith and the other was his brother Ahmar. The general command was in the hands of Malik b. Auf. He ordered to take the cattle, wives and children with them so as to make them fight to death in their defence. After this formation this force halted at Autas.

The Holy Prophet was still in Makka after its conquest when he received the news of the march of this force. He left Mecca on 27 January, 630 A.C. with twelve thousand soldiers to meet the Hawazin. Makka was left in the charge of 'Attab b. Asid.[1] Due to the shortage of weapons one hundred coats of mail with sufficient arms were borrowed from Banu Safwan.[2] The Muslims approached in the wadi of Hunain in the twilight of morning. Enemy had already got there and hidden themselves in bypaths, side tracks and narrow places of the valley. From there thousands of archers of the enemy took the Muslims by storm who fled in all directions. Most of the fleeing soldiers were the newly-converts. Volleys of arrows continued to be thrown at Muhammad's august person. He was surrounded by a compact wall of enemies. He was literally left alone in the chaos of retreat. In the midst of such a catastrophe, he withdrew to the right in this grim situation and shouted at the top of his voice, "Where are you going men? I am God's Apostle. Rally round me. I am Muhammad, the son of Abdullah."

The situation was so grim that camels bumped one into the other. People were running to and fro except a number of *Muhajirin, Ansar* and men of his family. Prominent among them were Abu Bakr, Umar, Ali, Abbas, Abu Sufiyan, Fazal b. Abbas, Rabia b. Harith, Usama b. Zaid and Ayman b. Ubayd.[3]

One man of Hawazin was riding on a red camel holding a black flag fastened at the end of a long spear. He was leading the Hawazin. Whenever he overtook a man he thrust him with his spear. When people moved out of his reach he lifted his spear to those behind him and they went after them.

The Holy Prophet asked Abbas b. Abdul Muttalib to cry loudly, "O comrades of the acacia tree" and they answered, "Here we are." Now everyone of them tried to turn his beast he could not do it. He would take his mail and throw it on its neck, and take his sword and shield and get off his mount and let it go its way and make for the voice until he came to the Holy Prophet. Thus almost one hundred men gathered around him. They fought steadfastly. It was on this occasion that the Holy Prophet said,"Now the oven is hot."[4] Now God sent angels for the help of the Muslims and at last the hosts were completely routed. The sign of the angels was their red turbans.[5] Almost seventy men of the Hawazin were killed including Malik b. Auf. The following Muslims were martyred:

1.	Ayman b. Ubayd	Remained steadfast throughout the battle.
2.	Yazid b. Zamaʿa	A horse of his called al-Jinah, threw him and killed him.
3;	Suraqa b. Harith	
4.	Abu ʿAmir al-Ashʿari	
5.	Juraith b. Abd	Known as Abi al-Laham because he used not to eat meat without being slaughtered even before embracing Islam.
6.	Murrah b. Suraqa	

Hunain was the major encounter during the lifetime of the Holy Prophet between the Muslims and the nomadic tribes. The victory over Hawazin was a mass-movement towards Islam. The captives and spoils of Hunain included six thousand women and children, twenty-four thousand camels, more than forty thousand cattle and four thousand *auqia* silver.[6] All these things were kept at al-Ji'rana under the charge of Masood b. Amr Ghifari. The Holy Prophet liberated all the captives without ransom and gave them even clothes. He allowed compensation from the public treasury to all those who were not willing to part with their booty of slaves.[7] Among the captives was, also, his foster-sister Shima. He paid a great reverence for her and gave her a slave named Makhul and a freedwoman. Shima arranged their marriage after liberating them.

Ghazwa Of Tayef: (Shawwal 8 A.H.)

After the Ghazwa of Hunain the fugitives of Banu Thaqif

managed to retreat safely to Tayef[9] where they took refuge in their fort. The tribe of Thaqif consisted of two sections known as Banu Malik and the Ahlaf. They stored daily necessities in abundance which could meet their needs even for one year.[10] Now they started preparations for war. When the Holy Prophet was informed about their activities he set forth to Tayef with twelve thousand soldiers and besieged them. Thus his vigilance disappointed them. The Banu Thaqif began to throw stones and shoot arrows from the fort thus killing some of the Muslims.[12] The Holy Prophet adopted the following techniques to conquer Tayef:

1. He used testudo, catapult and other instruments. But the people of Tayef had probably experience of defence therefore these techniques proved futile. Thaqif let loose on them scraps of hot iron so they came out from under it and Thaqif shot them with arrows and killed some of them.
2. Thorns were spread out around the walls of the fort to create hurdles in the movement of the enemy.
3. It was announced to affect psychologically that if any slave came fleeing from the fort and embraced Islam, he would be treated as free. This announcement made positive effects.
4. To exert economic pressure they were warned that the vineyards might be cut down. (It is remarkable that this was merely a threat).

Urwa b. Masud and Ghabdan b. Salma had learnt the art of using testudo and catapult from Jursh. So the Muslims had an upper hand. The two sides exchanged arrows for a long time till battle was fought at Shudkha --- a place near the walls of Tayef. Some Muslim soldiers went under a testudo and advanced up to the walls to make gap in it. Thaqif let loose on them scraps of hot iron so they came out from under it and some of them were shot dead. The people asked the Holy Prophet to invite the Thaqif to Islam which he did. It was announced that whosoever would get down from the fort would be liberated. Upon this ten persons came to him and they were liberated.[13] But this did not affect the Thaqif. Now the Holy Prophet asked Naufal b. Muawiya about the future course of action. He said, "The fox has entered into its den. If it is tried to catch it, it will be caught. And if it is ignored, it will not harm." So the Holy Prophet asked Umar to tell people to raise the siege. But the people were not prepared for it without the victory. The Holy Prophet asked them to fight the next day. The next morning the Muslims changed their mind and thus the siege was raised after fifteen days.[14] "If he allowed the siege to drag on, his men would become restive, blood would be shed and a final reconciliation with Thaqif would be rendered more difficult; in the course of a long siege, too much of the prestige gained at Hunain would be dissipated."[15] The following were the reasons for raising the siege:

1. The forts of Thaqif were strong and they were brave too. They had abundant food stores. All these factors were responsible for their invincibility.
2. More than one month had lapsed that the Muslims were out of Medina before the beginning of the siege of Tayef. And almost two months had lapsed from the battle with Thaqif and Hawazin to the end of the siege. During these months the converts had felt boredom and some of them had already asked permission to go back to their homes. Furthermore, it was necessary for the Holy Prophet to strengthen his victories and preach Islam.
3. The month of Dhi Qaʿda was approaching and due to its sacredness fighting could not be continued.
4. The people of Thaqif had begun to embrace Islam and it was necessary that they should stick to Islam. Time was a great factor for it.

After some time the people of Tayef embraced Islam themselves. Following Muslims were martyred in this battle:

1. Saeed b. Saeed
2. Urfuta b. Jannab

3. Abdullah b. Abu Umayya
4. Amir b. Rabi'a
5. Sa'b b. Harith
6. Abdullah b. Harith
7. Julayha b. Abdullah
8. Thabit b. Judha
9. Harith b. Sahl
10. Ruqaym b. Thabit
11. Abd b. Qawwal

(4) Ghazwas And Expeditions Against The Christians

Ghazwa Of Dumatu'l-Jandal:
(Rabi'u'l Awwal, 5 A.H./August/September, 626 A.C.)

Dumatu'l-Jandal was a place some 500 miles from Medina and seven days' journey to the south of Damascus. The Holy Prophet came to know that the Christian Arabs of Dumatu'l-Jandal had stopped the Medinite traffic with Syria and even threatened to invade Medina. So the Holy Prophet set out from Medina with one thousand men leaving it in the charge of Saba'a b. Urfata. He returned home, not having reached the place, without fighting as these marauders fled on the approach of the Muslims. On his way home, the Holy Prophet concluded a treaty with Uyayna b. Hisn.

Expedition Of Dumatu'l-Jandal:
(Sha'aban, 6 A.H./627 A.C.)

It is known as the expedition of Abdur Rahman who was ordered by the Holy Prophet to make preparations for the expedition. He set out from Medina with 700 men. He was instructed to "fight everyone in the way of God and kill those who disbelieve Him. Do not be deceitful with the spoils; do not be treacherous, nor mutilate, nor kill children. This is God's ordinance and the practice of His Prophet among you."1

The prince of Dumatu'l - Jandal made a treaty of alliance with Medina and gave his daughter Tumadir in marriage to Abdur Rehman. Furthermore, Subh b. Amr Kalbi, the chief of the tribe, alongwith many others embraced Islam.

Expedition Of Mu'tah :
(8 A.H./September, 629 A.C.)

After his return from the Fulfilled Pilgrimage the Holy Prophet remained in Medina for some months. Then he sent a force to Mu'tah, a village not far from Balqa in Syria, because many a mercenary Arab tribes had assembled there under the Greek banner to fight against the Muslims. These tribes were inhabited near the borders of Syria. In addition, the Holy Prophet wanted to get information about the economy, strength, produce and the physical effects of that land. Above all, some of them had betrayed the Muslim preachers and it was necessary to punish the culprits. They had killed all the preachers except one, Ka'b b. Umayr al-Ghifari, who had been sent to Dhat Atlah. Total number was fifteen. Secondly, the Holy Prophet had sent a letter to the ruler of Busra. Shurahbil b. Amr and the ambassador, Harith b. Umayr,. was assassinated ignoring all the canons of International Law. Medina had demanded reparations but the demand was turned down. Prof. Joseph Hell is wrong when he says, "But the real reasons are unascertained to this day. Probably there were economic reasons outside the scope of the Prophet's plan; for it is strange that he did not accompany this campaign; in fact, he predicted its defeat."[2] I think that Watt had accurately visualized the situation. He writes, "Poor health (perhaps the result of an attempt to poison him at Khyber) or pressure of affairs kept Muhammad at home."[3]

The Muslim force consisted of 3,000 men. It was sent by land and some reinforcements by sea. After putting Zaid b. Haritha in command the Holy Prophet said, "If Zaid is martyred then Ja'far is to take command and if he is killed then Abdullah b. Rawaha should perform these duties."[4] Zarqani has further written, "And if he is also killed then the Muslims should appoint anyone amongst them as their commander."[5] At the time of the departure of the army the Holy Prophet advised the soldiers, "First of all call the infidels to Islam. If they accept it then there is no need to fight. To show sympathy do visit the place where Harith b. Umayr had been killed while performing his duty."[6] Now the force made its way north. When it reached at Ma'an in the Balqa it heard about an overwhelming force of 100,000 Greeks led by Heraclius. It was joined by men from Lakham, Judham, al-Qaym, Bahra and Bali commanded by a man of Bali of Irasha called Malik b. Zafila.

Now the Muslims pondered over the situation. They were in favour of writing to the Holy Prophet telling him the whole state of affairs. If he sent reinforcements well and good otherwise they would wait for his next orders. Abdullah b. Rawaha encouraged the Muslims saying, "O Muslims! By God! What you dislike is for which you have come out in search of, viz; martyrdom. We are not fighting with numbers of strength or multitude, but we are confronting with this religion with which God has honoured us. So come on! Both prospects are fine : victory or martyrdom.[7] Now the Muslims supported his point of view and started their march forward till they reached near the border of Balqa. The enemy forces were encamped on Masherif. The Muslim force withdrew to a place called Mu'tah having Qutba b. Qatada on the right and Ubaya b. Malik on the left. Fighting started. Zaid b. Harith fought bravely and was killed. Now Ja'far took the flag and fought till his right arm was cut. He took the standard in his left hand till it was also cut. Then he got off his sorrel and hamstrung her and fought until he was killed. He was only 33. Now Abdullah b. Rawaha took the standard and fought until he was also killed. Then Thabit b. Arqam took the standard and called on the Muslims to rally round one man. They replied, "We rally to you." He refused as he thought he could not perform such a duty. Subsequently Khalid b. Walid was elected as their commander.[8]

When the fighting was in its full swing Qutaiba b.Qutada

attacked upon Malik b. Zafila and killed him. The new commander, Khalid b. Walid, inflicted heavy losses on the enemy. Simultaneously, he tried to keep the enemy off. He asked the army to retreat. It was the best he could do in these circumstances. 'It was a contest of so few against so many, of so little against so much.'

When this army got near Medina, the Holy Prophet received it outside Medina. Boys, also, came running. He asked, "Take the boys and carry them and give me Ja'far's son." When the people saw the army they began to throw dirt at it saying, "You are runaways. You fled from the way of God!" But the Holy Prophet said, "They are not runaways but come again if God wills."[9] Actually people greeted them with derision because they had retired without taking revenge of the assassinated ambassador.

No doubt the battle of Mu'tah was indecisive yet it increased respect for the Muslim power. The Bedouin tribes who were thinking to throw the yoke of Islam refrained from it. Credit goes to the Muslims for gallantry as they fought against an overwhelming force. It over-awed the Quraish. The Muslims came to know about warfare methods of the Byzantines and it helped them in the future. The size and consequent importance of the expedition to Mu'tah is an indication that Muhammad's strategic aim by 629 A.C./8A.H. was the unification of the Arabs under himself and their expansion northward.[10]

Following were the casualties on the Muslim side :

1.	Jafar b. Abi Talib	
2.	Zaid b. Harith	
3.	Masud b. Aswad	
4.	Wahb b. Sa'd	
5.	Abdullah b. Rawaha	
6	Abbada b. Qays	Present at Badr, Uhud, Trench, Khyber and Hudaibiya.
7.	Harith b. Nu'man	
8.	Suraqa b. Amr	Present at Badr, Uhud, Trench, Khyber and the Fulfilled Pilgrimage.
9.	Jabar b. Abi Sa'asa'a	

10.	Abu Kalab b. Abi Sa'asa'a	
11.	Abbad b. Qays	Present at Badr.
12.	Masud b. Al-Aswad	Present at Hudaibiya.
13.	Suwaid b. Amr	
14.	Huwaija b. Bahair	

Expedition Of Abdullah b. Hudhafa :
(Rabi'u'l Awwal, 9 A.H.)

In Rabi'ul Awwal 9 A.H. the Holy Prophet sent Abdullah b. Hudhafa with three hundred men to disperse those pirates who had assembled on the coast of Jedda. They intended to invade Makka. Consequently they ran away.

Expedition Of Tayyi :
(9 A.H. July/August 630 A.C.)

It is also known as the expedition of Ali b. Abi Talib. It was sent to the tribe of Tayyi. He led one hundred and fifty men of the *Ansar* who had one hundred camels and fifty horses. They had two standards –– one white and the other black. The aim was to reduce the tribe to obedience and to destroy their idol –– al-Fulus or al-Fils. The Muslims destroyed it and captured cattle, goats and captives. Sufana, sister of Adi b. famous Hatim, 'whose generosity and munificence have been sung by poets and minstrels throughout the Eastern world' was also among them. Adi, the chief of the tribe, himself fled to Syria. Three swords and three coats of mail were got from their home. Abu Qatada took the charge of the captives and Abdullah b. Attik of the cattle and slaves. Some of the spoils were distributed. When Sufana came before the Holy Prophet, she addressed him in the following words: "Apostle of God, my father is dead; my brother, my only relation, fled into the mountains on the approach of the Muslims. I cannot ransom myself; it is thy generosity which I implore for my deliverance. My father was an illustrious man, the prince of his tribe, a man who ransomed prisoners, protected the honour of women, nourished the poor, consoled the afflicted, never rejected any demand. I am Sufana, daughter of Hatim." "Thy father," answered Muhammad, "had the virtues of a Musulman; if it were permitted to me to invoke the mercy of God on any one whose life was passed in idolatry, I would pray to God for mercy for the soul of Hatim." Then addressing the Muslims around him, he said, "The daughter of Hatim is free, her father was a generous and humane man; God loves and rewards the merciful." So all the captives were set at liberty. Muhammad (P.B.U.H) bestowed on her many valuable gifts and sent her home with respect.

Ghazwa Of Tabuk :
(Rajab, 9 A.H./January, 631 A.C.)

The Holy Prophet was informed that Heraclius intended to invade Medina with a strong army. These news caused some consternation among the Muslims. It was necessary to repulse the gathering of these forces. It was a time when the Muslims were hard-pressed. There was intensity of heat. A severe drought had lately afflicted the State. The date crops had been ruined and the beasts of burden had died in large numbers. Majority of the people demurred to marching because it was harvest time. Generally the Holy Prophet nearly always referred allusively to the destination of a raid and announced that he was making for a place other than that which he actually intended. This was the sole exception, for he said plainly that he was making for the Byzantines because the journey was long, season difficult, the enemy in great strength, so that the men could make suitable preparations.[11] *Munafiqin* spared no endeavours to fan discontent into the unwillingness of the lukewarms. But they could not succeed. 'Your harvest, it lasts for a day, said the Holy Prophet, "what will come of your harvest through all eternity?" When they complained of the burning sun, "Hell is hotter", he replied. It is said that water was so scarce in this expedition that the fainting troops were obliged to kill the camels and drink the water out of their stomachs. The Holy Prophet set out from Medina with thirty thousand men. He left Medina in charge of Muhammad b. Maslama. When the Muslim army reached Thaniat-ul-Wada' (the Mount of Farewell) Abdullah b. Ubbay separated from the Muslim army and returned to Medina. Anyhow the Muslims marched forward reaching the border area. They, though outmatched, stroke so much terror in the hearts of the enemies that they took to their heels. They retraced their steps after a stay of ten days in Tabuk to evade defeat. When this army reached near Medina it was received by men, women and children outside the city. The children were reciting these verses:[12]

> The full-moon has arisen on us
> From the Thaniyatu'l-Wada.
> Thanksgiving is incumbent on us
> So long as an invoker may invoke God.
> O thou Divinely sent among us,
> Thou hast brought a commandment that shall be
> Obeyed!

The Ghazwa of Tabuk was entirely defensive in its nature. From strategic point of view its importance is :

1. When the Holy Prophet announced his march for Tabuk, it put positive effects on the enemy. He could not believe therefore he did not make suitable preparations. During this Ghazwa, treaties were concluded with Azrah and other tribes.
2. Not a single drop of blood was shed but all the advantages of victory were gained.
3. The Muslim force was trained in the best way. In the contemporary world the forces have to undergo different sorts of exercises to make them tough. The soldiers are asked to pass through narrow passages, ascend high peaks, traverse long distances, march in different difficult circumstances, and even they are deprived of food stuffs.
4. The morale of the Muslims became high. Before this Ghazwa everybody was frightened by the Byzantines. The Muslims established contacts with the people of different areas of Syria. Before this they were under the influence of the Byzantines.
5. The non-Muslim tribes came under the influence of the Muslims. After this Ghazwa several deputations visited Medina and embraced Islam.

In reality the Ghazwa of Tabuk was a tough exercise for the Muslims. Muhammad (P.B.U.H) desired that the Muslims should be ready to go for the propagation of Islam even outside the Arabian Peninsula.

Expedition Of Dumatul-Jandal:
(Ramadan, 9 A.H./630 A.C.)

Ukaider, a local chieftain, was molesting the caravans coming from the north to Medina.[13] So Khalid b. Walid was sent with four hundred men to take him to task. Ukaider was arrested while his brother was killed. Ukaider was set at liberty by the Holy Prophet. Several treaties were concluded with the other Christian governments.

Expedition Of Usama b. Zaid :
(26 Safar, 11 A.H.)

Usama was the son of Haritha who was the Holy Prophet's freed slave and adopted son. He was put over as the commander of a Muslim army to exact the long-delayed reparation for the murder of the envoy in Syria. He was directed to take spies with him. Usama was only 20 at that time therefore some people criticised his leadership as many prominent Companions of the Holy Prophet were included in this great army. When Muhammad (P.B.U.H.) came to know about this development he was displeased. At this time his head was splitting. He came in the mosque and addressed the people, "O men, dispatch Usama's force, for though you criticise his leadership as you criticised the leadership of his father before him, he is just as worthy of the command as his father was."[14]

After this address people made haste to fasten their bag and baggage. They went out as far as al-Jurf, about a stage from Medina and encamped there. Meanwhile the pain of the Holy Prophet became severe. Therefore the Muslim army stayed there. Usama returned to Medina. The Holy Prophet was unconscious at that time. Usama, again, visited him on the morning of Monday when he was feeling relief. He prayed for him and bade him farewell.

Now Usama returned to his force and ordered to march. But the preparations were still underway that a messenger from Umm Ayman came and told that the Holy Prophet was near dying. Usama, Umar and Abu Ubayda rushed to Medina. On the same day the Holy Prophet died.

This force was sent to Syria by the first Caliph, Abu Bakr Siddique, after his assuming this post.

(5) Ghazwas And Expeditions Against The Banu Ghatafan And Juhayna

Ghazwa Of Dhu Amarr :
(Rabi‘u'l Awwal, 2 A.H. September, 624 A.C.)

After his return from the Ghazwa of Sawiq, Muhammad (P.B.U.H.) stayed the remaining days of Dhu'l Hijja in Medina. Then he mustered four hundred and fifty men and set out from Medina leaving it in the charge of Othman b. Affan. He stayed almost for the whole month in Najd. No fighting took place because Banu Tha‘lba and Banu Muharib, who had assembled to invade Medina, had dispersed.

But this march had some positive results. The pagan nomads in the neighbourhood of Medina were much readier to profess Islam. The whole tribe of Muharib embraced Islam under their chief, Du'thur b. al-Harith.

Ghazwa Of Qarqarat'ul-Kurd :
(Muharram, 3 A.H.)

This is also known as the Ghazwa of Banu Sulaym. In Muharram, 3 A.H. the Holy Prophet was informed that the enemy intended to invade upon Medina. So he set out from Medina with two hundred men leaving Medina in the charge of Saba‘a b. Urfta Ghifari or Ibn Maktum.[1] He went on marching till he reached on the watering-place called al-Kudr. Yaqut opines that this place was situated at the distance of nearly ninety-six miles from Medina.[2] He stayed there for three days. No fighting took place as the enemy had fled. Anyhow one slave named Yusar was arrested. The Holy Prophet set him at liberty.

After some time the Holy Prophet sent Ghalib b. Abdullah al-Laythi as the enemy had again assembled. Some men of the enemy were killed while the remaining fled.

Ghazwa of Banu Mustaliq
(3 Sha'aban, 5 A.H./3 November/ December, 627 A.C.)

This Ghazwa is also known as Ghazwa of Muraysi'. It is a place near Red Sea. After the deportation of Bani Nadir from Medina, the Mustaliq succumbed to the temptations of becoming mercenaries of these Jews, and wanted also to participate in the siege of the Trench. This tribe up to this time had been on friendly terms with the Muslims. But recently they had thrown off their alliance. Their chief Harith b. Dirar had joined hands with the enemies of Islam to crush the infant Commonwealth. The Holy Prophet sent Bureeda b. Haseeb Al-Aslami to bring news. He went and talked with Harith b. Dirar. Then he came back and told the Holy Prophet the whole situation. He thought of a forward policy to scatter the enemies before they unite. Consequently he set out from Medina on Monday. A group of hypocrites also accompanied him notwithstanding the fact that they had not participated in any Ghazwa before this.[4] Medina was left in charge of Zaid b. Harith.[5]

The Muslim force stopped at a watering-place of Banu Mustaliq called al-Muraysi'. It was situated in the vicinity of Qudayd towards the seashore. There the Holy Prophet straightened the ranks of the Muslims. There were two standards —— one held by Abu Bakr for the *Muhajirin* and the other by Sa'd b. Muadh for the *Ansar*. For sometime arrows were exchanged from both sides. Then the Holy Prophet ordered the Muslims to attack the enemy unexpectedly with overwhelming force. Some men of Banu Mustaliq were killed. Their women and children were taken captives besides a large number of cattle and goats. In this Ghazwa one Muslim, Ibn Hubaba, was killed in error by an Ansari who thought he was an enemy.[6] Juwairiya, daughter of al-Harith, was also among the captives. The Holy Prophet took her in marriage. As soon as the soldiers heard of this alliance they hastened to release the prisoners of war they held because they had become the relatives of the Holy Prophet.[7]

This expedition is an indication of how Muhammad's sway was encroaching on the sphere where Makka recently had been supreme.[8]

Ghazwa Of Dhu Qarad :
(Rabi'u'l Akhar, 6 A.H.)

This Ghazwa is known as the Ghazwa of Ghaba. Dhu Qarad was a watering-place at the distance of a day's journey from Medina. Here the camels of the Muslims used to graze. Uyayna b. Hisn raided those camels with the help of the cavalry of Ghatafan in Ghaba (a place in the north of Medina). Dharr b. Abu Dharral-Ghifari was in charge of those camels and used to live there alongwith his wife. Uyayna carried off his wife, Laila, and drove off a large herd of camels. Salama b. Amr al-Akva'al-Aslami was the first man to know about this mishap. That morning he was making for al-Ghaba armed with bow and arrows. He hurried off after the raiding party like a lion. When he shot an arrow he exclaimed, "Take that, al-Akva's son am I. Today, mean crowd, you die!" He ordered the alarm to be sounded in Medina. The Holy Prophet gave the slogan, "Danger, Danger." Upon this the cavalry rallied to him. Miqdad b. Amr was the first to reach. The Holy Prophet left Medina in the charge of Sa'd b. Zaid and asked the Muslims, "Go in pursuit of the band until I myself overtake them with the army."[9] The Muslims were immediately on their track. They were five hundred in total. The Holy Prophet left Medina in charge of Ibn Maktum.[10] The Muslims recovered their animals and Laila. They killed Habib b. Uyayana b. Hisn. Three Muslims were martyred in this Ghazwa :

1. Dharr b. Abu Dharr Ghifari.
2. Muhriz b. Nadla. — Present at Badr, Uhud and Trench.
3. Waqas b. Muhriz.

Every hundred Muslims got one camel out of booty. The Holy Prophet returned to Medina after one day and one night.[11]

Expedition Of Wadi'l-Qara : (Rajib, 6 A.H.)
(Rajab, 6 A.H.)

Zaid b. Harith had gone on an expedition with twelve men that the inhabitants of Wadi'l Qara invaded them. Nine Muslims were martyred and one wounded. Zaid himself was carried wounded from the field. After his recovery the Holy Prophet sent him against them with a force. He fought with them in Wadi'ul Qara and killed some of them.

Expedition Of Munqa'ah :
(Ramadan, 7 A.H.)

The people of Munqa'ah were allies of the people of Khyber. Ghalib b. Abdullah al-Laythi went there. Only skirmishes took place.

Expedition Of Harqah
(Ramadan, 7 A.H.)

1. Usama b. Zaid was passing through the land of Banu Murra in the company of Ghalib b. Abdullah al-Laythi. On their way they saw a man, Nahik b. Mirdas, descending from a mountain. They attacked him with their weapons but he pronounced the *Shahada.* But they did not believe this pronouncement and killed him. When they narrated this event to the Holy Prophet he said, "Who will absolve you, Usama, from ignoring the confession of faith?" Usama replied, "O Apostle of God! He pronounced *Shahada* merely to escape death." But the Holy Prophet repeated his question and continued to do so until Usama repented, and pledged that he would not murder anybody in future in this way.[12]
2. This expedition was sent against Juhayna. When the army reached there, the commander sent spies to get information. On getting information he ordered to march forward until the army reached near the enemy at night. Then the commander stood up and praised God and then said, "I advise you that you should fear God Who has no associate. Obey me becaue,who is not obeyed his opinion carries no weight." Then he straigh-

tened their ranks making their pairs. Then he said, "God is Great." After this they attacked the enemy with an united force and got victory.

The war-cry of the Muslims was, "Kill, Kill."[13]

Ghazwa Of Dhatu'l-Riqa:
(Muharram, 7 A.H.)

Banu Ghatafan had made alliances with the Banu Muharib, Banu Tha'laba and Banu Anmar with the intention of attacking the Muslims. When the Holy Prophet came to know about this he set out from Medina with four hundred men leaving it in the charge of Othman b. Affan and to some Abu Dharr Ghifari.[15] Then he encamped at Nakhl.

There is conflict of traditions for saying this Ghazwa as Dhatu'l Riqa. Some say that there was a tree in this locality known by this name. Another narration is that a mountain was known as such. And some say that there were patches in the standards of the Muslims.[16] The Muslims had scarcity of camels, viz; six and one. They mounted on it by turn. At last their feet were wounded and they wore rags on them.[17]

No fighting took place as the enemy avoided confrontation.

Expedition Of Muharib :
(Sha'ban, 8 A.H.)

Banu Ghatafan, who had attacked several times, were again assembling at a place Khazra. The Holy Prophet sent Abu Qatada with fifteen men towards Idam. Among them was also Muhallim b. Jathama. Amar b. Adbat Ashja'i passed by them on a camel with a supply of provisions and a skin of laban. They saluted him as a Muslim but he did not reply. Muhallim stepped forward and killed him because quarrel they had had.[18]

When this party returned to Medina the Holy Prophet was informed about the incident. He asked, "Why did you kill a man when he had professed Islam?" In the year 7 A.H. Uyayna b. Badr came to the Holy Prophet and demanded vengeance for the blood of Amr b. Adbat. He was offered fifty camels at present and fifty camels later on as blood-money but he insisted on taking more. At last after a long debate he agreed.[19]

Expedition Of Qutba b. Aamir:
(Safar, 9 A.H.)

Qutba b. Aamir was sent with twenty men towards the tribe of Khutham because they were plotting against the Muslims. They went on ten camels; two men riding on one camel. They caught hold of a man and tried to know something from him. He beat about the bush and then started crying loudly in order to inform the inhabitants of the locality. Upon this the Muslims killed him and stayed there themselves until the inhabitants of the locality slept. During the night they invaded them. A severe battle was fought and men from both sides were wounded.

The Muslims returned to Medina with their women, cattle and goats.[20] The enemy followed them but God sent a flood which created hindrance between them and thus the Muslims succeeded to escape.

Expedition Of Tarya :

Tarya was a place at two days distance from Makka. The people of Tarya were the allies of Banu Ghatafan. Umar was sent with thirty men against them. The enemy dispersed.

Expedition Of Ali
(Rabi'u'l Awwal, 10 A.H.)

This expedition was sent to Yemen under the leadership of Ali with 500 horsemen. Then another force was sent under the command of Khalid b. Walid and he was asked that if they came across, Ali would lead the command. Ali began to preach Islam to the tribe of Muzhaj but they gave him reply with brickbats, stones and arrows. The Muslims in self-defence responded to them by counter-attack. As a result, they left twenty of their men dead in the field and fled away. Sometimes after, the chiefs approached Ali and embraced Islam of their own accord.

(6) Expeditions Against Banu Sulaym :

Incident Of Bi'r-Ma'unah :
(Safar, 4 A.H./July, 625 A.C.)

Banu Sulaym sometimes joined with Hawazin against Ghatafan. Two clans of Sulaym were certainly responsible for the massacre of Bi'r-Ma'unah and seven hundred men of Sulaym are said to have joined in besieging Medina as a result of Jewish bribes and intrigues. Three of the grand mothers – from fourth to sixth generation –– of the Holy Prophet, bearing all the name of 'Aatika, were Sulaymite.

In Safar 4 A.H. Abu Bara' Aamir b. Malik came to the Holy Prophet. He was known as 'player with the spears.' He was invited to embrace Islam. He neither admitted nor refused but said, "O Muhammad! If you were to send some of your Companions to the people of Najd and they invited them to your affair I have good hopes that they would give you favourable answer."[1] He also promised to stand by these missionaries.[2]

Subsequently, the Holy Prophet sent seventy missionaries under the headship of Mundhir b. Amr to Bi'r-Ma'unah. They were choice reciters and scholars' of Islam. This place was situated between the land of Bani Aamir and the *harra* of Banu Sulaym. When this band of missionaries reached Bi'r-Ma'unah, Haram b. Milhan was sent with a letter of the Holy Prophet to Aamir b. Tufayl. He went near to their houses and said loudiy, "O people of Bi'r-Ma'unah! listen to me! I am a messenger to the Apostle of God. I stand witness that only God is worth worship and Muhammad (P.B.U.H.) is His Servant and Apostle." Upon hearing it Aamir b, Tufayl thrust his spear from his back side and its point came out of his chest. He exclaimed out spontaneously. "By the Lord of the Ka'ba I have reached my ambition."

After this Amir b. Tufayl asked Banu Aamir to kill the rest of missionaries but they refused to do so due to Abu Bara'. Then he went to Banu Sulaym and instigated them. Three men –– Usayya, Ri'l and Dhakwan –– showed their inclination to do so. They surrounded the missionaries as they were with their camels. They were treacherously murdered near a brook called Bi'r-Ma'unah except Ka'b

b. Zaid.[3] Enemy left him while breath was in him. He was martyred in the Ghazwa Trench.

On the other side, Amr b. Umayya Damri and Mundhir b. Uqba did know nothing about their companions until they saw vultures circling round the camp. They went forward and came to know the sad state of affairs. Mundhir's eyes flashed fire. He fought but was killed. Amr was caught hold of. When the enemy came to know that he was of Mudar, Amir b. Tufayl let him go after cutting his fore-lock because of an oath taken by his mother.[4]

Amr came back and stopped at Qarqara on the bank of a canal. Meanwhile two men of Banu Amir came there and lied down to take rest. Soon they slept. Amir killed them thinking that he had taken vengeance on them for the killing of the missionaries. He narrated this incident to the Holy Prophet on his return to Medina who was deeply grieved to hear it. He said, "You have killed two men, I will pay blood-money for them."[5]

Following are the names of some of the martyrs of Bi'r-Ma'unah:

1.	Mundhir b. Amr	Present at Uqba, Badr, Title : 'The Quick to seek death.'
2.	Hakam b. Kian	
3.	Haram b. Milhan	Present at Badr, Uhud.
4.	Salam b. Milhan	
5.	Harith b. al-Simma	Present at Badr, Uhud. He was killed with several arrows.
6.	Thabit b. Khalid	Present at Badr, Uhud.
7.	Amir b. Fuhayra	Freedman of Abu Bakr. He was 60. His murderer, Amir b. Tufayl says that when he thrust his spear into his body, a light came out of it. He was raised between the heavens and the earth rather above the heavens.[6] Seeing this Amir b. Tufayl embraced Islam. His dead body disappeared from the scene.

8.	Urwa b. Suma	Belonged to Banu Sulaym. As the murderer also belonged to this tribe, he offered *aman* (asylum) but Urwa refused to accept it.
9.	Aaid b. Mais	Present at Badr.
10.	Mu'adh b. Ma'as	Present at Badr, Uhud.
11.	Masud b. Qays	
12.	Sufyan b. Thabit	
13.	Malik b. Thabit	
14.	Sufyan b. Hatib	
15.	Sahl b. Amir	
16.	Sa'd b. Amr	
17.	Tufayl b. Sa'd	
18.	Sahl b. Amr	
19.	Qutba b. Abd	
20.	Mundhir b. Muhammad	Present at Badr, Uhud.
21.	Nafai' b. Budayl	
22.	Anas b. Mu'awiya	
23.	Ubbay b. Thabit	
24.	Ubbay b. Mu'adh	Present at Badr.
25.	Masud b. Khulda	Present at Badr, Uhud. Some people think that he was martyred at Khyber.

The Holy Quran says about them that the martyrs of Bi'r-Ma'unah were completely contented. They wished a message to be delivered to the Muslims, "We have our Lord. He is happy with us and we are happy with Him." The Holy Prophet said about them, "Their souls are in the green birds. The chandeliers of the Heaven are for them. They are allowed to fly throughout the Heaven, graze and peck, and take rest in these chandeliers. Once God asked them, "Do you want something?" They replied, "O God! We have been given everything in Heaven and don't need anything further." God repeated His question twice and then thrice. Then they said,"O God! We wish to be alive again and wage Jihad for You and then be martryed." Now God was happy that they were contented.[7]

'There was certainly considerable loss of life for the Muslims, and some encouragement for other enemies to take similar measures.'

Expedition Of Jamum : (Rabi'u'l Akhar, 6 A.H.)

A woman named Halima supplied false reports against Banu Sulaym. Zaid b. Harith was sent and as a result some men were arrested while one was killed. The Holy Prophet set them at liberty. Among them was also her husband.

Expedition Of Ibn Abi'l-Awja'
(Dhil Hijja, 7 A.H.)

This expedition was sent to demonstrate on the border of Banu Sulaym because they were making preparations to invade Medina. Ibn Abi'l'Awja', himself a Sulaymi. led fifty men and went there on foot. He, alongwith his companions, were killed in the fighting.[8] Watt is wrong in writing that this was an old quarrel within the tribe which was being prosecuted by one party in the name of Islam.[9] In plea he says that there is no mention of revenge being taken.

Expedition Of Qadid :
(Safar, 7 A.H.)

Ghalib b. Abdullah al-Kalbi was sent with sixty riders for a night raid on Bani Mulawwah because they had killed a Muslim named Bashir b. Suwaid. When they reached Qadid, they met Harith b. Malik whom they took as captive. He said that he was a Muslim and was going to the Apostle.

Ghalib b. Abdullah told him that if he was a Muslim it would not hurt him to be tied up for a night, and if he were not they should make sure of him. So they bound him tightly and left him in charge of a companion and told him to cut off his head if he tried to attack him. Then he went on until they came to Qadid at sunset where they went to sleep. Towards dawn they attacked B. Mulawwah and killed some of them and drove off the cattle.[10] Then they came to Harith and his captor and took them. On the other hand, B. Mulawwah followed them and when they were quite near them God sent a flood in the valley. It is to be noted that there were neither clouds nor rain. None could resist it and cross it. So the Muslims succeeded to escape.

(7) Expeditions Against Banu Kilab And Banu Murra :

Expedition Of Amr b. Umayya al-Darmi :

Amr b. Umayya was the only survivor of the seventy missionaries sent to Bi'r-Ma'unah. When he was on his way to Medina, he found two men sleeping. They belonged to Banu Kilab. Amr misunderstood that they were from among the murderers and killed them. Both of them belonged to a friendly tribe. When the Holy Prophet came to know, he paid their blood-money.

Expedition Of Muhammad b. Maslama : (5 A.H.)

After the Ghazwa of Banu Qurayza the Holy Prophet sent a cavalry of thirty men under the headship of Muhammad b. Maslama against the unruly elements of Najd. Thumama b. Uthal, chief of Bani Hanifa, was taken prisoner. He was brought to Medina where he was tied up with a pillar of the Mosque.[1] When Muhammad (P.B.U.H.) passed from there he urged Thumama to accept Islam. He replied, "O Muhammad! If you kill me you kill one whose blood must be paid for. If you want a ransom ask what you like." He went forward but when he passed from there for the second time, he repeated the same question. Thumama's reply was the same. Now when the Holy Prophet passed from there for the third time, he said, "Release him." So he was released. Thumama went outside to take bath and after purifying himself he came back and embraced Islam. Then he asked permission to perform *Umra.*

While in Makka the Quraish asked him, "O Thumama! Have you changed your religion?" He replied, "No, but I follow the best religion, the religion of Muhammad, and by God not a grain of corn will reach you from Yamama until the Apostle gives permission. So he stopped the transport of provisions to Makka. This stoppage by Thumama reduced the Makkans to the direct straits. Failing to move the Hanafites, they at last addressed themselves to Muhammad, and besought him to intercede for them.[2] They Holy Prophet's heart was touched with pity and he asked the Hanafites to let the carriage of food go on. The Apostle sent them 500 gold coins to be distributed among the poor of Makka.4

This was the time when the Quraish were bitter enemy of the Holy Prophet. The above-mentioned incident proves that he let a man on liberty who considered himself worth to be executed. His pious manners deeply exerted their influence on a man who hated Islam, Medina and the Holy Prophet from the core of his heart. But after three days he embraced Islam of his own accord. It was all due to his piety, kind-heartedness and goodness that he did not like to stop the supply of food provisions even to the Quraish who wanted to annihilate him.

Expedition Of Banu Kilab :

This tribe was an ally of Banu Muharib and Banu Anmar and was making preparations to invade upon the Muslims. Abu Bakr was sent with a force against them. The Muslims got victory and the enemy ran away. Some of them were killed and some taken prisoners.

Expedition Of Bani Murra :
(Shawwal, 7 A.H.)

Bani Murra were the allies of the people of Khyber. Bashir b. Sa'd was sent with thirty men to them. While on their way they came across shepherds. The Muslims drove their cattle and goats to Medina. The shepherds followed them and when they approached near them at night they shot arrows on them. When the arrows of the Muslims were hausted they fought with hands. Bashir was wounded and stayed with the Jews till his recovery.

Expedition Of Dihak b. Sufyan Kilabi :
(Rabiul Awwal, 9 A.H.)

This expedition was sent against Kilab under the headship of Dihak b. Sufyan. Umayya b. Salma was also with this force. His father had embraced Islam but, later on, apostatized. After a light fighting Umayya killed him.

(8) Expedition Against Banu 'Adal And Banu Qarah :

Expedition Of al-Raji' :
(4 A.H./July, 625 A.C.)

It was during the month of Safar that a band of Banu Adal and Banu Qarah came to the Holy Prophet and requested that some missionaries be sent with them to instruct them in religion. He sent the following six men with them :[1]

1. Marthad b. Abu Marthad al-Ghanawi
2. Khalid b. Bukayr al-Laythi
3. Asim b. Thabit
4. Khubayb b. Adiy
5. Zaid b. al-Dathinna
6. Abdullah b. Tariq

Marthad was put in command. When these missionaries reached a watering-place of Raji' in a district of the Hijaz, the infidels betrayed them and attacked them. The Muslims fought well but their number was too less to be victorious. Three were killed and Khubayb, Zaid and Abdullah were taken prisoners.

Banu 'Adal and Banu al-Qara summoned Hudhayl against them who wanted to take Asim's head and sell it to Sulafa d. Sa'd She had sworn a vow that if she could get possession of his head she would drink in his skull. So when the Hudhayl intended to do so, the bees came between. Thus the infidels could not fulfill their purpose and then a flood ripped through the valley and carried Asim away. It is narrated that he had made a covenant with God that no polytheist should touch him nor would he ever touch a polytheist for fear of contamination.[2]

The Hudhaylis bound the three prisoners to take them to Makka to be sold there. When they reached al-Zahran, Abdullah broke loose from his bonds and drew his sword. The infidels drew back from him and stoned at him. He was so severely wounded that he died. Khubayb and Zaid were sold to the Quraish. Both of them had killed many chiefs of the Quraish in the Ghazwa of Badr. Khubayb was purchased by Hujayr b. Abu Ihab so that he could kill him in revenge of his father. Safwan b. Umayya purchased Zaid for the revenge of his father, Umayya b. Khalaf. The Quraish took them to al-Tan'im — a place outside Makka. Zaid was put to the gallows on the appointed day. Abu Sufyan asked him, "I adjure you by God, Zaid, don't you wish that Muhammad were with us now in your place so that we might cut off his head, and you were with your family?"

Zaid replied boldly, "By God! I don't wish that Muhammad were in the place I occupy now and that a thorn could hurt him, and that I were sitting with my family.

Now Abu Sufyan said, "I have never seen a man who was so loved as Muhammad's companions love him."[3]

After this conversation Nistas, slave of Safwan b. Umayya killed Zaid.

On the other hand, Khubayb was imprisoned in the house of Mawiya, a freedwoman of Hujayr b. Abu Ihab. When the time of his execution came, he asked Mawiya to bring a razor for him with which he wanted to cleanse himself before he died. Mawiya sent her boy with a razor but afterwards she thought lest Khubayb take revenge by killing the boy. Khubayb said to the boy, "Was not your mother afraid of my treachery when she sent you to me with this razor?" It is greatness on the part of Khubayb that he did not even hurt the boy.[4]

Khubayb was brought in Tan'im and when he was to be crucified he asked to give him time to make a prostration. He was allowed to do so. After his prayer he said to them, "Were it not that you would think that I only delayed out of fear of death I would have prolonged my prayer." On crucification he said, "O God! I have delivered the message of your Apostle; so tell tomorrow what has been done to me." Then he recited this prayer, "O God! reckon them by number and kill them one by one, let none of them escape."

After this the Quraish killed him and lances were pierced through every part of his body.

Abu Sufyan threw himself to the ground out of fear of Khubayb's curse. It was their belief that if a man was cursed and was thrown to one side the curse would pass over him. At the time of Khubayb's martyrdom Ikrima b. Abu Jahl, Saeed b. Abdullah, Akhnas b. al-Thaqfi, Ubayda b. Hakim and Umayya b. Abu Utba were present there.

(9) Expedition Of Banu Tha'lba :

Expedition Of Dhu'l-Qissa
(Rabi'u'l Akhar, 6 A.H.)

Dhu'l Qissa was the name of a place. The Holy Prophet had sent ten missionaries to instruct the precepts of Islam, on the request of Banu Tha'lba. But they were killed by the host tribe while they were asleep. Thus nine of them were martyred while Muhammad b. Maslama was wounded.

Now Abu Ubayda b. Jarah was sent with forty men to teach them a lesson. One man of the enemy was wounded and the rest of them fled. The Muslims took possession of their rotten goods.

Expedition Of Tarf :
(Jamadiu'l Akhar, 6 A.H.)

This expedition is also known as the expedition of Tarq. It was sent to punish the criminals of Dhu'l Qi'ssa. It was led by Zaid b. Harith. Fifteen men were in his company. The enemy fled and the Muslims took possession of twenty camels.

Expedition Of Hasmi :
(Jamadiu'l Akhar, 7 A.H.)

Dihya b. Khalifa al-Kalbi had been sent as an envoy to the Caesar. On his way home he took merchandise with him but Humayd b. 'Us and his son 'Us seized everything he had with him in the valley of Shanar. News of this mishap reached some of al-Dubayb of the kin of Rifa'a b. Zaid who had embraced Islam and they went after Humayd and his son. Among them was Nu'man b. Abu Ji'al (of Banu Dubayb). They recovered what Humayd and his son had taken and restored it to Dihya. On his return Dihya told the Holy Prophet what had happened and asked him to let him kill the culprits. Subsequently he sent a force consisting of five hundred men under Zaid b. Harith.

This force came up from the direction of Aulaj and attacked Maqis from the *harra*. Two men of Banu Ahnaf were killed besides Humayd and his son. The Muslims rounded up the cattle and one hundred men as prisoners.1

It is appropriate to mention that letter which the Holy Prophet had given to Rifa'a b. Zaid for his nation. In this letter there was an invitation for them to embrace Islam. They embraced Islam. After a short period of time the incident of Dihya occurred. When Zaid's force was in the jungle of Madan, Hassan b. Milla, Unayf b. Milla and Abu Zaid b. Amr came across it. The Muslims caught hold of them. Hassan told them that they were Muslims. They were brought before Zaid who asked them to recite first *Sura, Al-Fatiha* proving themselves Muslims. Hassan recited it. Zaid ordered that it should be proclaimed throughout the army that God had declared their land sacrosanct except as regards those who had broken their covenant.

Among the captives was, also, the sister of Hassan who was the wife of Abu Wabr b. Adiy. She clasped him by the waist. So Zaid ordered to release her. Upon this Ummu'l Fizr of Dulay said, "Are you taking your daughters and leaving your mothers?" One of Banu Kasib said, "She is of Banu Dubayb and their tongue utters spells all the day long."

These remarks were overheard by a man who conveyed to Zaid. He ordered that the hands of Hassan's sister be loosed from his waist and told her to sit with other prisoner women until God should decide what should be done with them.

So they went back.

Now Abu Zayd b. Amr, Abu Shammas b. Amr, Suwayd b. Zaid, Ba'ja b. Zaid, Bardha b. Zaid, Tha'laba b. Zaid, Mukharrib b. Adiy, Unayf b. Malik and Hassan b. Milla went to Rifa'a b. Zaid. Hassan b. Milla said to Rifa'a, "Here you sit milking goats while the women of Judham are dragged as prisoners. The letter which you brought has deceived them."

Then these men came to the Holy Prophet. When Rifa'a started conversation, one man said, "O Apostle of God! These men are sorcerers." He repeated this sentence twice. At this Rifa'a said, "God be gracious to him who treats us well today." Then Rifa'a handed over the Apostle his letter and said, "Take it, O Apostle; it was written long since but its violation is recent." The Holy Prophet asked him to read it openly. Then Rifa'a read it. The Holy Prophet asked what had happened, and they told him the whole story. The Holy Prophet said three times, "What am I to do about the slain." Rifa'a answered, "You know best, O Apostle. We do not regard as wrong what you think is right or the converse."

Abu Zaid b. Amr said, "O Apostle! Give us back those who are alive and those who are dead I disregard." Now the Holy Prophet ordered to set their prisoners at liberty and return goods.[2]

(10) Expedition Against Banu Tamim :

Expedition Of Uyayna b. Hisn :
(Muharram, 9 A.H.)

This tribe instigated the tribes under its influence not to pay *Kharaj* to Medina. The Holy Prophet sent fifty riders under Uyayna b. Hisn against them. Among them was neither any Ansar nor Muhajir.[1] They journeyed at night. At last they suddenly attacked the enemy who fled away. Anyhow 11 men, 2 women and 30 children were taken prisoners.[2] Thus this rebellion came to and end.

The prisoners were kept in the house of Ramlah d. Harith. For their recovery a deputation of Banu Tamim visited Medina. It consisted of its prominent chiefs like Atard b. Hajib, Rabi'a b. Rufay, Qays b. Asim, Zibarqan b. Badr,

Aqra b. Habis, Firas b. Habis, Malik b. Amr, Wardan b. Muhriz, Sabara b. Amr, Naeem b. Sa'd, Qa'qa' b. Ma'bad and Ribah b. Harith.

When they came to the Mosque it was noon prayer time. After performing his prayer the Holy Prophet sat with the members of the deputation in the courtyard of the Mosque. Atrad b. Hajib started negotiations. Thabit b. Qays served as spokesman of the Holy Prophet and pleaded the case well. Then the Holy Prophet liberated some of the prisoners gratuitously and some on the payment of ransom.[3]

(11) Ghazwas And Expeditions Against Banu Lihyan :

Expedition Of Abdullah b. Unays
(5 Muharram, 4 A.H.)

The Holy Prophet came to know that Ibn Sufyan Hudhali was collecting a force against the Muslims in Nakhla or Urana. He sent Abdullah b. Unays to get correct information. Abdullah asked him how to recognize him. He told him, "If you see him he will remind you of Satan. A sure sign is that when you see him he will feel a shudder."[1]

When Abdullah got near him he saw him with a number of women in a howdah seeking a halting place for them. It was the time for afternoon prayer and he was feeling a shudder. He asked Abdullah, "Who are you?" Abdullah replied, "I am an Arab and have heard that you are gathering a force against the Apostle. I have come with the same intention."

Ibn Sufyan replied, "Very good. I am also working for the achievement of the same purpose."

Then Abdullah walked a short distance with him and wnen got chance he struck him with his sword and killed him. He cut off his head, brought it with him and put it before the Holy Prophet[2] who gave him a stick. Abdullah said, "O Apostle of God! It is a sign between you and me on the Day of Resurrection." When he was about to die he ordered that it should be put in his winding sheet and it was buried with him.

Abdullah remained eighteen nights in the journey.

Ghazwa Of Bani Lihyan :
(Rabi'u'l Awwal, 6 A.H./April, 628 A.C.)

The aim of this Ghazwa was to avenge the killing of missionaries at al-Raji . There were 200 riders in this force. The Holy Prophet showed as if he had an intention to go to Syria because he wanted to keep it confidential.[3] He left Medina in charge of Ibn Umm Maktum. He went past Ghurab, a mountain near Medina on the road to Syria, then by Mahis, then by al-Batra, then he turned off and came out by Bin, then by Sukhayratu'l-Yamam, then the track went by the Makkan highroad. He quickened the pace until he came down to Ghuran, the haunts of Bani Lihyan. There he encamped. He came to know that Bani Lihyan had fled into the mountains. Now he expressed his desire and said, "Were we to come down to 'Usfan the Makkans would think that we intend to come to Makka."

So he went to 'Usfan and from there he sent two riders to see Bani Lihyan as far as Kurau'l-Ghamim. But when nobody came to fight then the Holy Prophet returned.[4]

Second aim of this Ghazwa was to put a severe blow on the morale of the Quraish and the other adjacent tribes. The Quraish could not dare to come out and fight with the Muslims.

Actually it was a march of power demonstration by which the Quraish were over-awed.

(12) Expedition Against Jusham b. Mu'awiya

Expedition Of Abu Hadrad Aslami :

Abu Hadrad Aslami was sent on an expedition by the Holy Prophet because Qays b. Rifa'a of Jusham b. Mu'awiya had come with great numbers. He was a man of high reputation among Jusham. When the Holy Prophet heard about it he summoned Abu Hadrad and two other Muslims and asked to bring news of him. They went to his locality and reached there in the evening as the sun was setting. They hid in different directions. They told one another that when they heard one's cry 'Allah o Akbar'' they were to do the same. When much of the night had passed, not a single shepherd of the locality came. Their chief, Rifa'a, insisted on going alone in their search. Some of his companions begged him not to do alone. When he passed by Abu Hadrad, he shot him in the heart with an arrow. Abu Hadrad cut off his head and then he shouted out 'Allah o Akbar.' Both of his companions did likewise. Enemy was so much frightened that they fled with their women, children and light goods. The Muslims drove off a large number of camels and sheep and brought them to Medina. Abu Hadrad took Rifa'a head with him. The Holy Prophet gave him thirteen of the camels.1

(13) Expedition Against Bani Jadhimah:

Expedition Of Khalid b. Walid:
(Shawwal, 8 A.H.)

This expedition is also known as the expedition of Ghamit which was the name of a well of Bani Jadhimah. After his return from the annihilation of al-Uzza, Khalid b. Walid was sent forth as a missionary to Bani Jadhima during his stay at Makka. Khalid went with three hundred and fifty men of *Muhajirin* and *Ansar.* Bani Sulaym were also with him. When he reached there, he asked them that who were they?

They replied, "We are Muslims. We have endorsed Muhammad and constructed mosques in our territory where Adhan is delivered."

Khalid asked them, "Then why are you carrying weapons?"

They replied, "We have enemity with an Arab nation. We mistook you for the hostile nation."

Another narration is that they were puzzled and they could not say that they were Muslims.

After this conversation they laid down their arms. Then Khalid ordered their hands to be tied behind their backs and then they were distributed among their companions. At dawn Khalid ordered that every captor should execute his captive. Bani Sulaym did so. But the *Ansar* and the *Muhajirin* released their captives. Ninety-five men were killed in total.

When the Holy Prophet came to know about it he was shocked at this wanton bloodshed. He cried raising his hands towards heaven, "O Lord! I am innocent what Khalid has done." Then he recalled Khalid and sent Ali to make every possible reparation to Bani Jadhimah. Every loss was made good even for a dog's bowl. Ali made careful inquiries so that none should be left without payment. When he was told that none had been left, he distributed the remainder of the money.[1] 'Blood-money was paid for every life; and even dogs killed were compensated. A considerable amount of money was added for unknown damage that may have been done.'[2]

(14) Expeditions Against Banu Asad And Banu Quza'ah

Expedition Of Qatan:
(1 Muharram, 4 A.H./June, 625 A.C.)

This expedition is, also, known as expedition of Abu Salmah Makhzumi. After the Ghazwa of Uhud the Holy Prophet was informed that the two sons of Khuwaylid - - - Talha and Salma were instigating against the Muslims and had joined hands with Bani Asad b. Khazimah. Their aim was to loot and make destruction. The Holy Prophet sent forth Abu Salamah Makhzumi with one hundred men of Ansar and Muhajirin to break their alliance up. Among them were included Abu Ubayda and Sa'd b. Abi Waqqas. They were instructed to travel by night and leave the general track; and then invade Banu Asad suddenly and forcefully The Muslims went up to Qatan, a watering place near the border of Najd. The culprits ran away. The Muslims got one camel and one goat.[1]

Expedition Of Ukkashah:
(Rabi'u'l Akhar, 6 A.H.)

This expedition is, also, known as Ghamar Mazrooq. Banu Asad had provided men to invade Medina. So the Holy Prophet sent forth forty men under Ukkashah b. Mehz al-Asadi against them. The enemy dispersed but the Muslims got two hundred camels.

Expedition Of Dhatul Salasil:
(Jamadiu'l Akhar, 8 A.H.)

The purpose of sending this expedition was to take vengeance of the martyrs of Mu'tah from the tribes which had been on the side of the Byzantines. They were: Lakhm, Judham, Ba'l-Qayn, Bahra, Bali, Tayyi, and Udhrah. Now they were reported to be preparing a further concentration of men at Medina. So Amr b. al-'As was sent forth with three hundred riders. They were carrying a white flag. They had thirty horses. It is worth mentioning that the grand-mother of Amr belonged to the tribe of Bali. The Holy Prophet ordered that the people of Bali, Udhra and Ba'l-Qayn, when they meet on their way, should be convoked to war on Syria. The Muslims travelled only by night. Then they reached a watering-place of Judham, called Salasil from which the expedition took its name.

When they reached near the enemy, they came to know their large number. Now Amr b. al-'As sent Rafi'a b. Makees Jahni to Medina for reinforcement. Consequently Abu Ubayda b. Jarrah was sent with two hundred first Muhajirin. Abu Bakr and Umar were, also, among them. They were, also, supplied with a flag. Abu Ubayda was advised not to quarrel with Amr b. al-'As and consequently he acknowledged his leadership.

Now the Muslims marched forward until they reached the last quarter of Qazah. Here they had a skirmish with a force but the enemy ran away to the cities. The news of the victory was sent to Medina through 'Auf b. MalikAshj'ai

(15) Expeditions Against Bani Fizarah, Udhrah, Quza'ah

Expedition Of Umm Qurfah,
(Ramadan, 6 A.H.)

Some part of Bani Fizarah was sometimes included in Wadi'l-Qura on the usual road to Syria. They had looted a trade caravan of Zayd b. Harith on the instigation of Umm Qurfah. The Holy Prophet sent a detachment under Abu Bakr on their track. Salamah b. al-Akwaʿ was also with this detachment. Enemy was defeated. Umm Qurfah and her daughter were taken prisoners. Their companions fled away. Umm Qurfah was executed.

Expedition Of Fidak:
(Safar, 7 A.H.)

Ghalib b. Abdullah al-Laythi was sent against the people of Fidak. Some men of the enemy were killed.

Expedition Of Bashir b. Sa'd Ansari:
(Shawwal, 7 A.H.)

Husayl b. Nawira, the Apostle's informant, reported that there was a large concentration of enemy between Yemen and Ghatfan. The Holy Prophet sent him to Uyaynah with the message that either his men should come to this side or the Muslims proceed to him. He invited the Muslims to his side.

The Holy Prophet consulted with Abu Bakr and Umar who were of the view that Bashir b. Sa'd should lead the expedition. So he was sent with three hundred men[1] with Husayl as a guide. He was ordered to travel by night and hide in the day light. When they reached in the lower territory of Khyber, they got near the enemy. There they attacked their cattle. When the enemy came to know, they fled away. When Bashir went to their settlement there was none. The Muslims drove the cattle with them. Afterwards Uyaynah killed one of their informants and two men were taken prisoners who were brought to Medina. Later on, they embraced Islam.

Expedition Of Dhat Atlah:
(Rabiʿu'l Awwal, 8 A.H.)

This expedition was sent to Dhat Atlah (Banu Qazaʿah) because people of that place wanted to invade the Muslims with a great force. Therefore a detachement was sent to make them afraid. Its head was Ka'b b. Umayr al-

Ansari and there were five men in it. The number of the enemy was far more than them and consequently all the Muslims were killed.

(16) Expedition Against Banu Umayya b. Zaid

Expedition Of Umayya b. Adiy al-Khatmi:
(Ramadan, 2 A.H.)

This expedition was sent to kill 'Asma d. Marwan who came of Banu Umayya b. Zaid. When Abu 'Afak had been killed she displayed disaffection. She was the wife of Yazid b. Zaid of Banu Khatmah. She was very charming and she sang in her sweet voice. She composed verses taunting and insulting the Holy Prophet. She said:[1]

I despise B. Malik and al-Nabit
And 'Auf and B. al-Khazraj.
You obey a stranger who is none of yours,
One not of Mudar or Madhhij.[2]
Do you expect good from him after the killing of your chiefs.
Like a hungry man waiting for a cook's broth?
Is there no man of pride who would attack him by surprise.
And cut off the hopes of those who expect aught from him?

When the Holy Prophet came to know about her thoughts he asked,"Who will rid me of Marwan's daughter?" When Umayr b. Adiy heard it, he went to her home by night and killed her. She was his sister in relation. Next morning he informed the Holy Prophet who said, "You have helped God and His Apostle."[3]

Umayr was so daring that he went to 'Asma's five sons and told them about her murder. No one dared take vengeance on Umayr. That was the first day that Islam became powerful among B. Khatma and many of her clan now professed Islam openly.

(17) Expedition Against Banu Sa'd b. Bakr:

Expedition Of Fidak:
(Sha'a ban, 6 A.H.)

It was informed that Banu Bakr were instigating those Jews, against the Holy Prophet, who had been deported from Medina. They had promised their assistance to them. Consequently Ali was sent forth with two hundred men against them. The enemy fled away leaving behind one .hundred camels and two thousand goats for the Muslims.

(18) Expedition Against Banu Kinanah.

Al-Uzza was aphrodite of Banu Kinanah. It was in Nakhla. It was a temple venerated by the Quraish, Kinanah and Mudar. Its guardians were B. Shayban and B. Sulaym, both allies of B. Hashim. Khalid b. Walid was sent to destroy it. When the Sulaymi guardian heard of Khalid's coming he hung his sword on her, climbed the mountain on which she stood and prayed to her for Khalid's destruction. But it was in vain as Khalid broke it into pieces.

(19) Expedition Against Banu Hudhayl:

Expedition Of Amr b. al-'Aus :
(Ramadan, 8 A.H.)

This expedition was sent to destroy Suwa'a, the idol-place of Banu Hudhayl. So Amr b. al-'Aas destroyed it.

(20) Expedition Against Aus And Khazraj:

Expedition Of Sa'd Ashhali :
(Ramadan, 8 A.H.)

Manat was the idol of Aus and Khazraj. Sa'd b. Zaid Al-Ashali of Ansar was sent to destroy it which he did.

5

Islam And Sword

Islam found its way into the hearts of millions of people so rapidly that it is an unique chapter in world chronology. There is not the least aggression in its spread. But the controversialists and the Orientalists have stigmatized the glories of Islam. Its remarkable success and marvellous effect upon their minds have given rise to the charge that Islam is a religion of scymitar.

It is unfortunate indeed that mythologies of fertile brains, exaggerations and interpolations have misconceived the Islamic injunctions on Jihad. Most of the Western writers, while interpreting the meaning of 'Jihad' have, in their bigotry, presented it as a holy war waged by the Muslims against the non-Muslims with a view either to winning them over to Islam or to exterminating them in case they refused to embrace Islam.[1]

If we have a computerized analysis of the causes of the Muslims' battles, we conclude that it were the non-Muslims who always started them. Muslims did not take sword except in their defence. Islam is a religion of peace and love. It strictly believes in 'Live and let live.' It guarantees the safety of humanity and peaceful co-existence. It has contributed to mitigate the horrors of war and made it more humane. "Islam," says an able writer, "offered its religion, but never enforced it; and the acceptance of that religion conferred co-equal rights with the conquering body, and emancipated the vanquished States from the conditions which every conqueror, since the world existed up to the period of Muhammad, had invariably imposed." Islam does not believe in any such war which is fought for personal or national benefits, e.g. imperialist or aggressive in nature, possession of means or enslavement of non-Muslims. The central idea in Islam is peace and war is lawful only in extraordinary and exceptional circumstances. Islam "grasped the sword" in self-defence; Christianity grasped it in order to stifle freedom of thought and belief.2

By temperament the Arabs are men of firm determination. Prof. Dozy considers that they are not religious by nature. And from this point of view there is a vast difference between them and the other races. Burkharat, a tourist who knew the Arab Bedouins, stood witness to the fact that they were the most tolerant nation of Asia and their tolerance was ancient. Because a nation which guarded its liberty in such a way could not make others oppressed, even in the sphere of religion.

Marthad, a king of Yemen of fourth century, used to say, "I reign over men's bodies, not over their minds. I require of my subjects that they should obey my government; of their opinion God alone will judge."

Whatever the historians opine about Marthad is also true about the Holy Prophet who did not try to win over his Companions by sword. Because the sword may make silence, it cannot convice; it may enforce hypocrisy, it can never force belief. Rather it was the sword of faith that he and his Companions went under the tortures at the hands of the Quraish for thirteen years. Bilal was made to lie down on the scorching sand at full noon time. But he used to reply with determination that "God is one." After this some of his Companions migrated to Abyssinia. Then he himself migrated to Medina. Was it coercion or altogether force of faith?

Muhammad (P.B.U.H.) was allowed to fight only on 12 Safar, 2 A.H. with the condition to fight only with those who fought with him. And he had recourse to arms for self-defence. After the permission of Jihad the infidels were divided into three categories: people with whom the treaties were made, belligerents and Dhimmis. The Muslims were ordered not to wage Jihad against the people with whom the treaties had been made so far as they fulfilled the pledge.

Treaties were temporary and permanent. After the revelation of Sura Al-Bara'at it was allowed to fulfill the treaty, which was for a fixed time, for the rest of the period. So far as the permanent treaties were concerned infidels were given four months. But Islam did not allow to fight against the Dhimmis and it was the duty of the Muslims to protect them as they protected themselves.

The purpose of Jihad is the safeguard of human rights and the annihilation of oppression and coercion. The meanings of Jihad are self-explanatory and enough to put an end to the misconception. It is under God's name to instal God's justice in the world. It is to be waged solely for the purpose that the "Word of God shall alone prevail."[3] Jihad is of four kinds, viz. by heart, by tongue, by hands and by sword.[4] In other words it is based on three pillars, namely, intensification of Islam in oneselves and eradication of evil, extension of God's injunctions throughout the world by wisdom and persuasion and military preparedness to repel aggression.

The term Jihad is derived from the verb Jahada (abstract noun, Juhd) meaning ability, exertion or power. It also signifies war, hostility and fighting. Literally it means 'an effort attracted towards a determined objective either against a visible enemy, against the devil, or against oneself - - - *Nafs.*' 'In its broader sense it does not necessarily mean war or fighting, since exertion in Allah's path may be achieved by peaceful as well as violent means. It may be regarded as a form of religious propaganda that can be carried on by persuasion or by the sword.

Shaikh Abdul Wahaab al-Khallaf observes, "The verses concerning war in a number of Makkan and Medinite Suras of the Quran generally explain Jihad's 'raison d'etre,' which boils down to one of two things, either to defend against attack, or to rout *fitnah* (persecution inspired by religious prejudices); in other words to protect the mission of Islam. Jihad is therefore far from being synonymous with war, while the meaning of 'war undertaken for the propagation of Islam' which is supposed by European writers to be the significance of Jihad, is unknown equally to the Arabic language and the teachings of the Holy Quran. Muslim history is full of such numerous incidents which depict means adopted for persuasion, propaganda and debates for good. Proselytism by the sword was wholly contrary to the instincts of the Holy Prophet." The episode of Abu Jandal, at the time of Truce of Hudaibiya, should dispel all prejudices against the notion that Islam was spread by force. The reality is that it was Islam which was the most persecuted, in the very land of its birth. Sword fell on the faith of Islam from all sides, but instead of destroying it helped as it were to spread it.

The Ghazwas and Expeditions of the Holy Prophet's life-time were purely defensive in nature. A clear proof is that the pagans imposed wars on the Muslims during the months when the Muslims considered unlawful to fight. When this was the case of the Muslims, how could the Holy Prophet ignore the sacredness of these months? But is it wisdom not to use the right of self-preservation?

'Islam regards war as an abnormal and destructive activity to which recourse should be had only as the last resort. 'God ordered the Muslims to be patient and tolerant so far as the integrity of Islam was not endangered. But beyond it God says:5

> "Fight in the cause of God those who fight you, but do not transgress limits; for God loveth not transgressors. And slay them whenever ye catch them, and turn them out from where they have turned you out; for tumult and oppression are worse than slaughter; but fight them not at the Sacred Mosque, unless they (first) fight you there; but if they fight you, slay them. Such is the reward of those who suppress faith. But if they cease, God is Oft-Forgiving, Most Merciful. And fight them on until there is no more tumult or oppression, and there prevail justice and faith in God; but if they cease, let there be no hostility except to those who practise oppression.
>
> The prohibited month for the prohibited month, - - - and so for all things prohibited, - - - there is the law of equality. If then any one transgresses the prohibition against you, transgress ye likewise against him. But

fear God, and know that God is with those who restrain themselves."

Keeping in view the above-mentioned injunctions of the Holy Quran it becomes the duty of the Muslims to set aside all their worldly affairs and fight with the enemy. This is the difference between war and Jihad. War is a curse but Jihad is the religious obligation. Another war is inevitable after a war is over while Jihad helps to establish an environment of peace and safety. The Holy Prophet is reported to have said: "I am the prophet of mercy, I am the prophet of battle."[6] And: "Both I smile and I fight."[7] And again: "Every prophet had some profession (for livelihood) and my profession is Jihad; and in fact my means of subsistence are placed under the shadows of my spear."[8] He fought to subjugate the people peacefully to the religion of "submission to the Will of God." He taught that to kill a man without reason is to kill the whole world: "If any one slew a person - - - unless it be for murder or for spreading mischief in the land- - - it would be as if he slew the whole people."[9]

And again:

> "Wherewith God guideth all who seek His good pleasure to ways of peace and safety."[10]

And then again:

> "And let not the hatred of others to you make you swerve to wrong and depart from justice."[11]

Coercion and force were not a part of the policy of the Holy Prophet because there is no compulsion in religion.[12]

The purpose of war in Islam is not the propagation of Islam but the safeguard of the liberty of propagation. The Muslims fought only in that case when their religious freedom was in danger or they were attacked upon. There were two pre-requisites for the Jihad. Firstly that it should be for the sake of God and it should be against those who attacked them. No other kind of war is known in the life of the Holy Prophet. No doubt that military success had been a forceful element in the completion of the fate of Islam. Sword represented the militant spirit in the Arabian Peninsula. A country where iron was not produced, it was the most precious metal; and that is why that it was a ruling incentive of the life of the Arabs. With the passage of time, which was the dearest asset of the Arabs, a mysterious importance was labelled with the sword which, later on, took a religious role. The Muslims adopted these theories but this emotion was not due to mere strength. Because before Islam they were free from all sorts of the prohibitions of discipline. But after embracing Islam they subjugated three grand empires of the then known world in less than a century. Islam adopted that way of argumentation which was embossed on the hearts.

Referring to the exaggerated and inflammable versions of Jihad given by some biased Western Orientalists, Toynbee writes: "In the first place we can discount the tendency --- which has been popular in Christendom --- to over-estimate the extent of force in the propagation of Islam... In the conquered provinces of the Roman and Sasanian Empires the alternatives offered were not 'Islam or death' but 'Islam or a super-tax,'- - - a policy traditionally praised for its enlightenment when pursued long afterwards in England by a Laodicean Queen Elizabeth."[13]

There is only one slogan in the development of Islamic culture and civilization, viz. slogan of peace. The use of sword has especially been limited in Islam not altogether refuted. Sword cannot take the place of logic or justice but sometimes it has to be ousted from their domains. The cause of the Islamic wars is the progress of *Hizb Allah*. War has been permitted in the following circumstances:

From the point of logic and law it is lawful to wage war for self-defence. If the attack is not repulsed the safety of the nations is endangered and civilization and culture are ruined. When attack is launched death begins to dance before eyes, it is foolishness to advise peace as it is contrary to human psychology and the principles of survival of life. To break the falsehood it is necessary to put an end to the miscreants and give a severe blow to their force. To help the oppressed is an holy human sentiment. Unless the blood of the murderers is shed, the blood of the murdered does not stop. It is why God says:[14]

"In the Law of Equality there is (saving of) life to

you, O ye men of understanding; that ye may restrain yourselves."

In this connection it is appropriate to refer to the half-dozen marked Jews which is generally called assassination because a Muslim was sent secretly to kill each of the criminals. "The reason almost too obvious to need explanation. There were no police or law-courts or even courts-martial at Medina; some one of the followers of Muhammad must therefore be the executor of the sentence of death, and it was better it should be done quietly, as the executing of a man openly before his clan would have caused a brawl and more bloodshed and retaliation, till the whole city became mixed up in the quarrel. In secret assassination is the word for such deeds, secret assassination was a necessary part of the internal government of Medina."[15]

It was a custom among the Arabs not to distinguish between the murderer and non-murderer. They killed in vengeance whosoever was caught by them. Thus innumerable lives were lost. This is why that the concept of life for life was enforced by Islam. It had a positive result and the innocent lives were saved in future. The sole purpose of Jihad is the assistance and patronization of the oppressed men and nations. Islam permits to support the Truth and defeat the Falsehood. The Holy Prophet fought only for the uplift of this cause. From here the notion of Jihad has been the victim of misrepresentation by its enemies. God says[16] about the annihilation of oppression:

> "To those against whom war is made, permission is given (to fight), because they are wronged; and verily, God is Most Powerful for their aid. (They are) those who have been expelled from their homes in defiance of right, (for no cause) except that they say, 'Our Lord is God.' "
>
> That is:
>
> When the Muslims are deprived of their lawful rights; they are ousted from their homeland; they are made powerless and oppressed for their faith then it is lawful for them to fight with them. It is in this connection that God says:[17]

"Had not God checked one set of people by means of another, monasteries, churches, synagogues, and mosques, would have been surely pulled down in which the name of God is commemorated in abundant measure. God will certainly aid those who aid His (cause)."

The Muslims have been ordered to wage Jihad against those infidels and hypocrites who want to create disruption and disorder in the Muslim State:

"O Prophet! strive hard against the Unbelievers and the Hypocrites, and be firm against them."[18]

Simiiarly the Muslims have been asked to punish those who break their pledges:[19]

"But if they violate their oaths after their covenant, and taunt you for your Faith, - - fight ye the chiefs of Unfaith."

Although Islam has permitted to fight but there is not a single verse of the Holy Quran which may give the indication to make an infidel a Muslim by compulsion. Neither there is a single instance of this sort throughout the life of the Holy Prophet. Rather it has been ordered:[20] "A (declaration) of immunity from God and His Apostle, to those of the Pagans with whom ye have contracted mutual alliances."

The reality is that Islam allows the use of sword only when it becomes inevitable. Generally the result of a decisive battle is good for the victor, and evil for the vanquished. But the victorious Muslim is required to offer peace, not the annihilation of the enemy. Islam cools down the war: "Everytime they kindle the fire of war, God doth extinguish it; but they (ever) strive to do mischief on earth. And God loveth not those who do mischief."[21]

The notion of "conquest by fire and the sword" does not conform to reality . . . Even the "pagan" population of the conquered territories were not put to the sword.[22] All the wars of the Holy Prophet were either defensive or purely cultural expeditions from spiritual point of view. Several orientalists have either misunderstood this point or they do it intentionally. They attach the element of power with the development of Islam and distort the concept of

Jihad altogether. It may be stated categorically that the wars of Muhammad (P.B.U.H.) were defensive in nature. Had they not been waged, the Muslims would have been perished - - - with what dire results for the future of civilization one can only imagine.[23]

The human history is full of wars. They were fought for power lust, selfishness and mischievousness. In the contemporary world declaration of war is considered a blunder as Man is after establishing colonies and his national aggrandizement. Since the Second World War it has become outdated. In recent Arab-Israeli wars no declaration was ever made. In Vietnam war had been fought without any declaration for seven years.

The Arabs were accustomed to invade their enemy at night. But the Holy Prophet prohibited this thing. Anas b. Malik quotes that whenever he approached an enemy he did not attack till morning. Although war has the physical position of the relation between the Muslims and the non-Muslims. But to make truce with the enemy is not contrary to the real motives of Islam. Even the Holy Quran itself has permitted to make treaties with the non-Muslims:

> "How can there be a league, before God and His Apostle, with the Pagans, except those with whom ye made a treaty near the Sacred Mosque? As long as these stand true to you, stand ye true to them."

And again:[25]

> "But if the enemy incline towards peace, do thou (also) towards peace, and trust in God."

It was also a custom among the Arabs that they made much noise whenever they went out for war. They teased everyone who came across them. Abu Musa Ash'ari narrates: "We were with the Holy Prophet and whenever we reached a valley, we raised slogans of *takbir* and *tahleel* loudly. Upon this the Holy Prophet asked them, 'O people! go gracefully. Whom you are calling for is neither deaf nor absent. He is with you. He hears everything and is very near to you.' "

The belligerents are divided into two kinds: combatants and non-combatants. The first are those who take part in the fighting physically. The people included in the second category do not fight or usually do not take part in fighting, e.g. women, children, disabled and sick, etc. Islam permits to fight only with the combatants and has disliked to fight with the other kind unless they give their advices against the Muslims. Muhammad (P.B.U.H.) prohibited the Muslims not to inflict injuries in vengeance of their injuries. They should not molest the harmless inmates of domestic seclusion. He advised to spare the weakness of the female sex. He saw a corpse of a woman in a battle and remarked, "When she was not included among the fighters then why has she been killed?" Then he sent a directive to Khalid b. Walid ordering him not to kill women and infants at the breast. Then he issued orders in general of the same nature.[27] It was his habit that whenever he sent troops he directed them not to kill them who were sick, monks or hermits. Islam orders not to demolish the dwellings of the unresisting inhabitants; destroy the means of their subsistence, nor their fruit trees and touch the palm trees. He prohibited to torture enemy before killing. Abu Ayub Ansari narrates: "I have heard the Apostle saying 'Don't fasten your enemy with the intention of killing. By God! Had it been a hen I would have not fastened it to kill."[28] When Abdul Rehman b. Khalid came to know it he set four slaves at liberty as he ordered to kill four men of enemy after fastening.

Similarly Muhammad (P.B.U.H.) prohibited mutilation. Whenever he sent a force to any quarter he enjoined upon it, "Do not cheat and break trust. Do not mutilate."

Before Islam several nations used to throw their enemy alive into fire. Islam strictly prohibited it and regarded it uncivilized and barbarous. The Holy Prophet said, "To give torture with fire is not fit for anyone except the Creator of fire."[29]

Compare these teachings with the commands of the Israelite Prophet: "Thus said the Lord of Hosts . . . Now go and smite Amalek, and utterly destroy all that they have, and spare not; but slay both men and women, infant and suckling, ox and sheep, camel and ass."[30] And again, "Slay utterly old and young, both maids and little children and women."[31]

It is about these people that the Holy Quran says, "When he turns his back, his aim everywhere is to spread mischief through the earth and destroy crops and cattle. But God loveth not mischief."[32]

Certain orientalists try to prove in vain that Islam permits devastation and destruction by projecting the example of cutting of palm trees during the Ghazwa of Bani Nadir. The reality is that they were *Lina* which were neither fruitful nor bore good dates. Bani Nadir used only *Ujwa* and *Barni.* Anyhow *Lina* served as their refuge. Now it has been proved that Muhammad (P.B.U.H.) did not order to cut down the trees but the army had cut down some trees as it was necessary due to the requisites of the siege. Later on, God maintained that their action was correct as their intention was not mischief.[33]

Once some soldiers looted some goats, during the journey of a Jihad, in order to cook. When the Holy Prophet heard of it he turned down the pots and said, "The goods got by loot are not better than dead body.[34] "He gave the Muslims a war code which is unique in the history of warfare. He, even, did not allow to milk the cattle during the journey without the permission of their masters. In dire necessity he permitted to do so calling out thrice their masters and if nobody turned up then they could drink it.[35]

Islam taught its followers to treat the prisoners of war with kindness so that they were induced to embrace it. It liked to release them gratuitously. But it told them the other way, too : to accept ransom or exchange prisoners. On the occasion of the conquest of Makka the Holy Prophet forgave his enemies who had inflicted every type of torture upon him. He forbade to attack the runaways and kill the prisoners. It was announced that whosoever shuts his doors was safe.[36] General amnesty was proclaimed for the Makkans and only seven persons were executed. Islam prohibited the slavery of the innocent and plunder of the household.

On the contrary, millions of men were killed during the wars of Ramayan and Mahabharata. Rama and Krishna, the two deities of Hindu India, are notorious for their heroic bloodshed in the cause of righteousness. The Mosaic law is admittedly very severe in retaliation. The gentle teacher of Nazareth the very personification of love and tenderness, also at a certain time in his life advised his disciples to purchase swords by selling their clothes; and openly avowed that he had come to send "fire and sword" into the world.[37]

In 782 A.C. some 4,500 Sexan prisoners were brutally slained in Wordon. From 1480 A.C. to the Second World War 278 wars were fought. Out of them 135 were of world, 65 of imperialist and 78 of civil nature.[38] After the invasion of Vikings in the ninth century thirty years war brought unparallel devastation, havoc and oppression. Continuous devastations gave birth to drought and epidemic diseases. Cannibalism became a daily routine. Generally these were the dead bodies of the executed criminals which were eaten up. In Alsak prisoners were killed for food purposes. It was the savage boast of Attila, the genius of destruction, the 'scourge of God,' that the grass never grew where his horse had once trodden. And in the Albigensian war, the Papal Legate had quieted the scruples of too conscientious general, 'Kill all, God will know His own.' In the capture by the Crusaders, the brains of young children were dashed out against the walls; infants were pitched over the battlements; men were roasted at fires; some were ripped up, to see if they had swallowed gold; the Jews were driven into their synagogue, and there burnt; a massacre of 70,000 persons[39] took place; and the Pope's legate was seen partaking in the triumph.[40] For a long period of time the historians had been thinking that three-fourth persons were killed and according to the later estimates 70 lakh men were killed.[41] Sufferings caused by World War I conservative estimate of losses is 10,000,000 dead and 20,000,000 wounded.[42] Some 338,000,000,000 dollars were spent on this war.[43] The losses of the World War II were much more than this. Some 2 crore 20 lakh men were killed and 1,117,000,000,000 dollars were spent on it.[44]

From Adam to Muhammad (P.B.U.H.) great kings had appeared on the stage of the world. They subjugated vast territories and established peace in bazars and streets but they could not establish peace in the domains of hearts. Muhammad (P.B.U.H.) succeeded to establish a stable government in unruly Arabia only during a short period of ten years. He took in only 19 Ghazwas.[45] If we consider Ghazwas[46] and Expeditions[47] together then the total losses of the Muslims and their opponents were as under :

Number of the total killed was 1,018 and 6,564 were taken prisoners including 6,000 prisoners of the Ghazwa of Hunain. It means the average number of prisoners of war of the rest battles is only seven.[48] All the "wars" of the Holy Prophet were humane and bloodless; not even 300 enemy people were killed to conquer three million square kilometers of territory. It is an unique example of his diplomacy that the Arabs started, for the first time, international relations and "the record of breadth and depth of conquests established by them has not so far been broken by any other nation."[49] It was the dynamic nature of his conquests and his liberal treatment of the enemy that it proved extremely congenial for the growth, popularity and permanence of Islamic civilization and culture.

Some writers are of the view that if he was a prophet he should not have participated in the battles. It is a wrong notion. Because this maxim was not included in his teachings that "My kingdom is not of this world."[50]

REFERENCES

Preamble

1. Watt, Montgomery; *Muhammad At Medina,* PP. 81-82.

Chapter 1

1. *Politics,* bk. I, Ch. 7.
2. Cited by Lawrence; *Principles Of International Law,* P. 15 (6th ed.)
3. Hell, Joseph; *The Arab Civilization,* P.15
4. Khaldun, Ibn; *History,* P. 126.
5. *Al-Quran* 16:59
6. Ali, Syed Amir; *The Spirit Of Islam,* P. Lxvi.
7. Nicholson, Reynold A; *A Literary History Of The Arabs,* p. 34.
8. *Ibid,* P. 136.
9. Poole, Stanley Lane - -; *Studies In Mosque,* PP. 1-2.
10. Hell, Joseph; op. cit; P. 8.
11. Nicholson, Reynold A; op. cit; P. 28.
12. Hell, Joseph; op. cit; P. 9.
13. Nicholson, Reynold A; op. cit; PP. 38-39.
14. *Bible, I, Samuel XV, 1-3.*
15. Ali, Syed Amir; op. cit; P. xviii.
16. Muir, William; *Life Of Mahomet,* P. xcv.
17. *cf. St. Matthew 10:6 Al-Quran 3:48-49.*
18. Smith, R. Bosworth; *Muhammad And Muhammadanism,* P.3.
19. Hamidullah, Dr. Muhammad; *Rasul-i-Akram Ki Siyasi Zindgi,* P. 417.
20. Al-Quran 30:22
21. Hanbal, Ibn; *Musnad*
22. Al-Quran 32:7-8.
23. Al-Quran 49:10.
24. Al-Quran 49:13.
25. *Mustadrak Hakim,* vol. 2, P. 93.
26. Al-Quran 3:63.
27. Al-Quran 2:256.
28. Al-Quran 109:6.
29. *Sunan Abi Dawood,* vol. iv, pp. 112-114; *Nasai',* vol. ii, pp. 64-65
30. Krehl, *Mohamed,* P. 140.
31. Al-Quran 18-29.
32. Al-Quran 5:92.
33. Smith, R. Bosworth; op. cit; P. 152 Footnote.
34. Sa'd, Ibn; *Tabqat,* II, P. 94.
35. Qayyim, Hafiz Ibn; *Zadul Ma'ad;* II, P. 162.

36. Iqbal, Afzal; *Diplomacy In Islam*, PP. 131-132.
37. *Encyclopaedia Britannica*, vol. 23; PP. 94-95.
38. Sarkhasy, *Mabsut*, X, P. 92; *Zadul Ma'ad, II, P. 163.*
39. Gibb, H.A.R; *Muhammadanism*, P.4.

Chapter 2(A)

1. Matthew 15:24.
2. Al-Quran 34:28.
3. Al-Quran 21:107.
4. Al-Quran 61:9.
5. Al-Quran 7:158.
6. Ibn Athir; *Tarikh ul Kamil*, II, P. 22.
7. *Miskhat*, P. 512.
8. *Bukhari & Muslim* cited by Ibn Kathir in connection with the verse 28:34.
9. Al-Quran 8:12.
10. Hamidullah, Dr. Muhammad; *Ahd-i-Nabawi Mein Nizam-i-Hukamrani, 1,* P. 219.
11. Ibid.
12. Mansoorpuri, Qazi Muhammad Sulaiman; *Rahmatul-lil-Alameen,* I, P. 148.
13. Al-Quran 3:63.
14. *Muslim*, V, P. 50.
15. Cited by *Asahus Siyar*, P. 428.
16. Ibid. It is narrated that a son of the Negus also embraced Islam, and later on settled in Medina, as client of the family of the Holy Prophet.
17. Ibn Sa'd, II, P. 34.
18. Ibid, P. 35.
19. Cited by Khadduri, Majid; P. 348.
20. *Sunan Nasa'i;* Explanation by Siyuti with notes by Abul Hassan,II, p. 65, Footnotes.
21. *Sunan Abu Dawood*, IV, PP. 112-114; *Nasa'i*, II, PP. 64-65.
22. *Futuhul Buldan*, P.-128.
23. Hamidullah, Dr. Muhammad; Cited in *Rasool-i-Akram Ki Siyasi Zindagi*, P. 350.
24. *Futuhul Buldan*, P. 130.
25. Hamidullah, Dr. Muhammad; *Rasool-i-Akram Ki Siyasi Zindagi*, P. 350.
26. *Futuhul Buldan*, P. 124.
27. Ibn Sa'd, II, P. 39.
28. *Futuhul Buldan*, P. 124.
29. Hamidullah, Dr. Muhammad; *Rasool-i-Akram Ki Siyasi Zindagi*, P. 447.
30. *Futuhul Buldan*, PP. 124-125.
31. *The ambassador of Muhammad (P.B.U.H.)*.
32. Basra was a city of Huran situated between Hijaz and Syria. It was known for its forts.
33. *Muslim, V, Ch. Bk. The Prophet.*
34. Ibn Sa'd, II, P. 35.
35. Ibn Ishaque, P. 654.
36. Ibid; *Bukhari, Bk. Al-Jihad.*

37. Ibid, P. 653.
38. Ibn Sa'd, II, P.35.
39. Ibn Ishaque, P. 656; Ibn Sa'd, II, P. 36; ***Tajreed ul Bukhari,*** P. 14.
40. Hanbal, Imam Ahmad bin; ***Musnad,*** Cited in ***Asahus Siyar*** P. 435.
41. Mansoorpuri, Op. Cited; P. 155.
42. It was a white mule known as *Duldul* which was given to Ali. This mule remained alive till the reign of Muawiyah I. Muqauqis sent two maid-servants whose names were Maria and her sister Shirin, Both embraced Islam. Muhammad (p.b.u.h.) married with Maria. She gave birth to Ibrahim who died in his childhood. Shirin was married with Hassan bin Thabit.
43. Ibn Sa'd, II, P. 37.
    Anyhow the bond of friendship was for ever cemented between Egypt and Hijaz.
44. They included one thousand *mithqal* gold, twenty Coptic clothes, one eunuch slave named Mabore (it is said that he was a cousin of Maria, one horse named Alzaz, one glass bowl and honey.
45. ***Futuhul Buldan,*** P. 139.
46. Ibid.
47. Ibn Sa'd, II, P.39.
48. Ibid, P. 38.
49. One Mithqal was equivalent to 4½ Mashas.
50. Numani, Shibli. ***Seerat un Nabi,*** I, P. 470.
51. Mansoorpuri, Op. Cited; P. 158.
52. Ibid.
53. Ibn Sa'd, II, P. 36.
54. Ibn Ishaque, P.659.
55. Ibn Sa'd, II, P. 38.
56. Ibn Ishaque, P. 644.
57. Ibn Sa'd, II, P. 157.
58. Ali, Syed Amir; ***The Spirit Of Islam,*** P. 91.
59. Thumama Haran bin Habib commonly known as Musailima, the Liar.
60. Ibn Ishaque, P. 637.
61. Ibn Hisham, II, P.737.
62. ***Zadul Ma'ad.*** II, P. 163.
63. Ibn Hisham, II, P. 737.
64. "For the earth is God's to give as a heritage to such of His servants as He pleaseth; and the end is (best) for the righteous." ***Al-Quran*** 7:128.
65. Ibn Hisham, II, P. 737.
66. Ibid I. P. 475. Habib was the son of Nusayba who pledged at the Second Pledge of Aqba. She went to al-Yamama with the Muslims and participated in the war in person until God slew Musailima. She returned having suffered twelve wounds from spear or sword.
67. These were the names of the chiefs of Humair. See Tabari, I. P, 455; Ibn Sa'd, II, P. 158; *Futuhul Buldan,* P. 117.This very thing is clear from the letter of the Holy Prophet. But Ibn Khaldun is of the view that the letter of the king of Humair was sent to Muhammad (P.B.U.H.) through Harith bin Abd Kala, Naeem bin Abd Kulal and No'aman. See History of Ibn Khaldun, I, P. 187. But this view is baseless. Ibn Hisham is also of the view that these

people informed about their embracing Islam through Malik bin Marwah Ahadi. See: Ibn Hisham, II, P. 723.

68. Only Ibn Sa'd mentioned this part of the letter.
69. *Tabari,* I, P. 456; Ibn Hisham, II, PP. 723-725; Ibn Ishaque, PP. 43-44.
70. *Futuhul Buldan,* PP. 117-118.
71. Ibn Sa'd, II, P. 157.
72. Ibid.
73. Bahrayn was not the modern island of this name, but the modern Alhasa province on the eastern coast of Saudi Arabia.
74. Ibn Sa'd, P. 55.
75. Ibid, PP. 56-57.
76. Ibn Ishaque, P. 656; Tabrari, I. PP. 351-352.
77. Ibn Sa'd, II. P. 58.
78. Ibid, P. 60.
79. Ibid, P. 59.
80. Ibid, P. 61.
81. Ibid, P. 63.
82. Ibid.
83. Ibid, P. 66.
84. *Futuhul Buldan,* P. 129.
85. Ibid, P. 131.
86. *Zadul Ma'ad,* III, PP. 122-123.

Chapter 2(B)

1. Watt, W. Montgomery; *Muhammad At Medina.* P. 80.
2. Maqriziy; *Imta'a*, I, P. 509.
3. Bukhari, 56:176; Kattaniy, I, P. 451.
4. Tabari, *History*, 1, P. 1574; Kattaniy, 1, P. 390.
5. Ibn Sa'd, II, P. 75.
6. Numani, Shibli; *Seerat un Nabi,* II, P. 36.
7. Qayyim, Hafiz.Ibn; Op. cit; III, P. 114.
8. Numani, Shibli; Op. cit; II, P. 39.
9. Ibn Ishaque; Op. cit; P. 635; Ibn Hisham, II, P. 705; Ibn Qayyim, III, P. 134.
10. Ibn Hisham, II, P. 705; Ibn Qayyim, III, P. 134.
11. Ibn Sa'd, II, P. 86.
12. Ibid, P. 94.
13. Ibid.
14. Ibid, P. 125.
15. Qayyim, Hafiz Ibn, Op. cit; III, P. 106.
16. Ibn Sa'd; II, P. 149.
17. Qayyim, Hafiz Ibn; III, P. 107.
18. Ibid,P.115.
19. Ibid,P.117.
20. Ibid.
21. Ibn Sa'd; II, P. 155; Ibn Qayyim, III, P. 117.
22. Ibid.

23. Ibid, P. 157.
24. Ibid, P. 130.
25. Ibid.
26. Ibid.
27. Ibid, P.95.
28. Ibid,P.121.
29. Qayyim, Hafiz Ibn; Op. cit; III, P. 160.
30. Ibid, P. 159.
31. Ibn Sa'd; II, P. 122.
32. Nawawi, Imam; *Sharah Muslim,* 1, P. 91. But Ibn Sa'd mentions their number twenty, Ibn Sa'd, II, P. 105.
33. Ibn Hisham, II, P. 707.
34. Ibn Sa'd, II, P. 105. Qazi Ayaz agrees with him. (cited by ***Asahus Siyar,*** P. 456.). Hafiz Ibn Qayyim is of the view that the apostle advised them to act upon only four injunctions. So the deputation came in 9 A.H. and the Haj had not been enforced yet. Ibn Khaldun thinks that the deputation came in 10 A.H. Ibn Khaldun, ***History,*** I, P. 196.
35. Nawawi, Imam; Op. cit; I, P. 92.
36. Ashjah's name was Mandhar b. Ayaz. He had a wound on his forehead so the Holy Prophet called him Ashjah. See: *Sharah Muslim,* I, P. 92. But according to Ibn Sa'd his name was Abdullah b. Al-Asjah. See; Ibn Sa'd II, P. 106.
37. Ibn Sa'd, II, P. 106.
38. Ibn Khaldun, ***History,*** I, P. 196.
39. Ibn Sa'd, II, P. 96.
40. Ibid, P. 97.
41. Qayyim, Hafiz Ibn; Op. cit; II, P. 325.
42. Ibn Hisham, II, P. 589; Ibn Ishaque, P. 592.
43. Ibid, Ibn Khaldun, ***History,*** I, P. 172.
44. Ibid, P. 590; Ibid, Ibn Ishaque, P. 593.
45. Ibid, Ibn Ishaque, P. 593.
46. Ibn Ishaque, P. 493.
47. Al-Quran 49:6.
48. It seems that the deputations of Thumala and Al-Haddan came at one and the same time.
49. According to the Sa'd eleven women were included in the deputation. See; Ibn Sa'd, II, P. 79. But Hafiz Ibn Qayyim does not agree with him and tells that their number was twenty one. See; Ibn Qayyim, II, P. 348.
50. Ibn Sa'd, II, P. 79.
51. Ibn Hisham, II, P. 686.
52. Ibid, PP. 686-687; Ibn Ishaque, P. 629.
53. Ibid, P. 695; Ibn Ishaque, P. 631.
54. Al-Quran 49:4.
55. Ibn Hisham, II, P. 696; Ibn Ishaque, P. 631; Ibn Sa'd, II, P. 80.
56. Ibn Sa'd, II, P. 128.
57. Ibid, P. 126; Ibn Qayyim, III, P. 150.
58. Ibn Qayyim, Op. cit; III, P. 113.
59. Cited by ***Asahus Siyar,*** P. 466.

60. Qayyim, Hafiz Ibn; Op. cit; P. 112.
61. Ibn Hisham, II, P. 464; Ibn Ishaque, P. 614; Ibn Sa'd, II, P. 102.
62. Ibn Sa'd, II, P. 103. But Ibn Ishaque and Ibn Hisham are of the view that the deputation consisted of six members including Abdu Yalil. See; Ibn Ishaque, P. 615; Ibn Hisham, II, P. 648.
63. Ibn Hisham, II, P. 649.
64. Ibid.
65. Ibid; Ibn Ishaque, P. 615.
66. Hamidullah, Dr. Muhammad; ***Muhammad Rasoolulah,*** P. 93.
67. Ibn'ul Athir, II, P. 217.
68. Tabari, III, PP, 161-163.
69. Ibn Hisham, II, P. 653; Ibn Ishaque, P. 617.
70. Al-Quran 49:17.
71. Ibn Sa'd. II, P. 77.
72. Qayyim, Hafiz Ibn; III, P.145.
73. Ibn Sa'd,II, P. 83.
74. Qayyim, Hafiz Ibn; III, P. 145.
75. Ibn Sa'd; II, P. 90.
76. Ibid.
77. Abd Amr Al-Bakkai was also with them who was deaf. See: Ibn Sa'd, II, P. 91.
78. Ibid, P. 92.
79. Ibid.
80. It is a dish prepared in ghee or fat after mixing dates and dried flour.
81. Qayyim, Hafiz Ibn; Op. cit; III, P. 147.
82. Ibn Khaldun, ***History,*** I,P. 187.
83. Ibn Sa'd, II, P. 127; Ibn Qayyim, III, P. 147.
84. Zaydu'l Khayr was a poet, orator and warrior. His both sons Maknaf and Hureth were the Companions of the Holy Prophet. See: Ibn Hisham, II, P. 710.
85. Ibn Ishaque, P. 637; Ibn Sa'd, II, P. 115.
86. Ibid; Ibid. But Hafiz Ibn Qayyim, has stated with reference to Ibn Abdu'l Bar that Zayd died in the last days of the caliphate of Umar. See: Ibn Qayyim, III, P. 103. But the first statement seems weighty. Ibn Khaldun is also of the same view. See: Ibn Khaldun, ***History,*** I, P. 200.
87. Ibn Ishaque, P. 637; Ibn Hisham, II, P. 711; Ibn Sa'd, II, P. 115.
88. Ibn Sa'd, II, P. 115.
89. Ibn Hisham II, P. 714.
90. Ibn Sa'd, II, P. 117.
91. Ibid.
92. Ibid, P. 118.
93. Ibid.
94. Ibid.
95. ***Ashus Siyar,*** P. 480.
96. Ibn Sa'd,II, P. 137. But Hafiz Ibn Qayyim is of the view that the deputation visited Medina in Rabi'ul Akhar or Jamadi'ul Awwal 10.A.H. See: ***Zadul Ma'ad,*** III, P. 110. Maulana Shibli Numani thinks that the year was 9 A.H.

See: *Seerat un Nabi,* II, P. 41.

97. Ibn Sa'd, II, P. 137; Ibn Qayyim, III, P. 110.
98. Ibn Hisham, II, P. 729.
99. Ibn Hisham writes his name Amr b. Dibabi. See: Ibn Hisham, II, P. 729.
100. Ibn Ishaque, P. 646; *Zadul Ma'ad,* III, P. III.
101. Ibn Sa'd, II, P. 138.
102. Ibid.
103. *Mishkat,* Ch. حرم المدينة حرسها الله تعالى
104. Ibn Sa'd, II, P. 118; *Zadul Ma'ad,* III, P. 154.
105. Ibid, P. 119.
106. Ibid. *Zadul Ma'ad,* III, P. 156.
107. *Zadul Ma'ad,* III, P. 155.
108. Ibn Khaldun, *History,* I, P. 194.
109. Qayyim, Hafiz Ibn; Op. cit; III, P. 166; Ibn Sa'd, II, P. 146.
110. Ibid, P. 161; Ibn Khaldun, *History,* I,P. 194. But Ibn Sa'd is of the view that their number was thirteen. See: Ibn Sa'd, II, P. 137. It is astonishing that Ibn Sa'd also tells their number as three in his descriptions. Ibid.
111. Ibn Sa'd, II, P. 137; Ibn Qayyim, III,P. 161.
112. Ibid, P. 129; Ibid, P. 162.
113. Qayyim, Hafiz Ibn, III, PP. 162-163.
114. Ibid.
115. Ibn Sa'd, II, P. 136.
116. Ibid.
117. Qayyim, Hafiz Ibn; Op. cit; III. 167-168.
118. Ibid, P. 168.
119. Ibn Sa'd, II, P. 136.
120. Ibid, P. 124. But Ibn Khaldun tells that their number was ten. See: Ibn Khaldun, History, I, P. 196. Ibn Hisham, with reference to Zuhri b. shihab, writes their number as eighty. See: Ibn Hisham, II, P. 720.
121. Ibn Sa'd, II, P. 124.
122. Ibn Ishaque, P. 641; Ibn Hisham, II, P. 720.
123. Ibn Sa'd, II, P. 124.
124. Ibid, P. 149. But Ibn Khaldun writes that the Kinanah deputation had accompanied the Hadramut deputation. See: Ibn Khaldun, *History,* I,P. 197.
125. To Ibn Khaldun his name was Jamad. See: Ibn Khaldun, *History,* I, P. 197. But Ibn Sa'd writes his name as Hamadah. See: Ibn Sa'd, II, P. 149.
126. Ibn Sa'd, II, P. 150.
127. Makhus had said something proudly to Muawiyah which God did not like.
128. Ibn Khaldun says that his name was Salman b. Hanzala. See: Ibn Khaldun, *History,* I,P. 196. But Ibn Sa'd writes it Salama b. Hanzala. See: Ibn Sa'd, II, P. 107.
129. Ibn Sa'd, II, P. 108.
130. Ibid.
131. Ibid.
132. This was the same Wahshi who had killed Hamza, an uncle of the Holy Prophet, in the battle of Uhad.
133. Qayyim, Hafiz Ibn; Op. cit; III, P. 123.

134. This valley was so wide that a swift rider could cross it in one day. About seventy three villages were located in it and one lac warriors lived there. See: *Zadul Ma'ad, III,* P. 124.

135. Ibid.

136. Ibid.

137. Ibid.

138. Al-Quran 3:58-60.

139. Its definition is that a Muslim and his adversary curse upon the liar in an open field outside the inhabited area.

140. Qayyim, Hafiz Ibn; Op. cit; III, P. 125.

141. Ibid; Ibn Sa'd, II, P. 160; Ibn Khaldun, *History,* I,P. 198.

142. Ibid, P. 120; Ibn Khaldun, *History,* I,P. 198.

143. He was a bishop, scholar and religious leader. He controlled their religious schools. King of Constantionople had a great respect for him.

144. He was known as *Sayyid.* He was their administrator and judge. He was responsible for transport and general arrangements.

145. He was known as *'Aaqib,* a man of affairs. He was their chief adviser whose opinion governed their general policy.

146. Qayyim, Hafiz Ibn; Op. cit; III,P. 120. Ibn Ishaque tells that their number was fourteen. Ibn Ishaque, P. 271.

147. Ibid.

148. Al-Quran 3:64-67.

149. Ibn Sa'd, II, P. 123.

150. Ibid.

151. Ibid, P. 150.

152. Ibid, P. 99; Ibn Khaldun, *History,* I,P.199. But others write his name Arbd b. Qays, See: Ibn Ishaque, P. 631; Ibn Hisham, II, P. 696, *Zadul Ma'ad,* III, P. 94.

153. Ibn Ishaque and Ibn Hisham think that the third person was Jabbar b. Salama. See: Ibn Ishaque, P. 631; Ibn Hisham, II, P. 696.

154. Ibn Ishaque, P. 631; Ibn Hisham, II, P. 697; *Zadul Ma'ad,* III, P. 94.

155. Qayyim, Hafiz Ibn; Op. cit; III, P. 94; Ibn Sa'd, II, P. 100; Ibn Khaldun, *History,* I,P. 199.

156. Watt, W. Montgomery; Op. cit; P. 99.

157. Ibn Sa'd, II, P. 88.

158. Ibid.

159. It was a plot of land in which there were springs and gardens of dates.

160. Ibn Sa'd, II, P. 90.

161. Ibid, P. 98.

162. Ibid, P. 119.

163. Ibid, P. 120.

164. Ibid.

165. Ibid, P. 121.

166. Qayyim, Hafiz Ibn; Op. cit; III, P. 169.

167. Ibid, P. 172.

168. Qayyim, Hafiz Ibn; Op. cit; III, P. 138.

169. Ibid, P. 139.

170. Ibn Sa'd, II, P. 112.
171. Ibid, P. 114.
172. Ibn Khaldun writes it the deputation of Muluk-i-Kinda (Kings of Kinda). See: Ibn Khaldun, ***History, I,*** P. 195.
173. Ibn Sa'd, II, P.123.
174. Ibid; Ibn Hisham, II, P. 717.
175. Ibid, P. 124; But Ibn Khaldun tells that their number was ten. See: Ibn Khaldun, ***History, I,*** P. 198.
176. Ibn Sa'd, II, P. 135.
177. Ibid, P. 142.
178. Ibid, P. 156.
179. Ibid, P. 147. But it is strange that he writes their number two hundred on Page. 148.
180. Ibn Khaldun, ***History,*** I,P. 197. But Ibn Sa'd writes its name as Al-Rahdeyeen. See: Tabqat Ibn Sa'd, II, P. 143.
181. Ibn Sa'd, II, P. 144.
182. Ibid, P. 152.
183. Qayyim, Hafiz Ibn; Op. cit; III, P.176.

Chapter 3(A)

1. Al-Quran 5:8.
2. Ibid 4:135.
3. (i) "He hath only forbidden you dead meat, and blood, and the flesh swine, and that on which any name hath been invoked besides that of God." 2:173.
   (ii) "Eschew all sin, open or secret: those who earn sin will get due recompense for their 'earnings'. 6:120.
4. Ibn Hanbal, V, P. 371.
5. **Sarakhsi, *Sharh As-Siyar Al-Kabir,* IV, PP. 4-5; Tabariy, P. 1474.**
6. Al-Quran 5:51.
   "O ye who believe! take not the Jews and the Christians for your friends and protectors: they are but friends and protectors to each other. And he amongst you that turns to them (for friendship) is of them."
7. Al-Quran 8:61.
   "But if the enemy incline towards peace, do thou (also) incline towards peace, and trust in God."
8. Al-Quran.
   (i) 5:51.
   (ii) "Your (real) friends are (no less than) God, His Apostle, and the (Fellowship of) Believers – those who establish regular prayers and regular charity, and they bow down humbly (in worship). 5:55.
   (iii) "O ye who believe! take not for friends and protectors those who take your religion for a mockery or sport, – whether among those who received the Scripture before you, or among those who reject Faith." 5:57
9. Al-Quran. 9:23

10. Al-Quran. 9:1-2
"A (declaration) of immunity from God and His Apostle, to those of the Pagans with whom ye have contracted mutual alliances. Go ye, then, for four months, backwards and forwards (as ye will), throughout the land, but know ye that ye cannot frustrate God (by your falsehood).
11. Hamidullah, Dr. Muhammad; ***The Muslim Conduct of State,*** **P. 272.**
12. Al-Quran. 2:282
"O ye who believe! When ye deal with each other, in transactions involving future obligations in a fixed period of time reduce them to writing."
13. Khadduri, Majid; ***War And Peace in the Law of Islam,*** **P. 204.**
14. Tabari, PP. 1724-1725.
15. Ibid, P. 1474; Sarakhsi, *Sharh As-Siyar Al-Kabir,* IV, P. 5.
16. Al-Quran. 16:92
17. Al-Quran. 16:94
18. Sarakhsi, Op. cit; IV, P. 64.
19. Ibid, P. 80.
20. Ibid, P. 7.
21. Ibn Hisham, II, P. 654.
22. Ibid, P. 658.
23. Al-Quran 6:165
24. Al-Quran. 17:15
25. Al-Quran. 35:18
26. Al-Quran. 39:7
27. Al-Quran 53:38
28. Al-Quran. 5:1
29. Al-Quran. 8:55-58
30. Al-Quran. 9:1-2
31. Al-Quran. 8:4
32. Al-Quran. 17:34
33. Al-Quran. 23:1-8
34. Al-Quran. 9:4
35. Al-Quran. 9:5
36. Al-Quran 9:7-8
37. Al-Quran. 9:10-14
38. Bukhari, ***ch. Al-Jizya***
39. Mishkat, Ch. *Al-Kabayir & Signs of Hypocrisy.*
40. Ibid, ch. ***Ma-Ala ul Walat Minat Tasir.***
41. Ibid, ch. ***Al-Aman.***
42. Ibid, ch. ***As-Sulah.***
43. Al-Quran 8:58
44. Al-Quran 9:2
45. Al-Quran. 9:12-13
46. Al-Quran. 9:4
47. Khadduri, Majid, Op. cit; P. 254.
48. ***Zadul Ma'ad,*** **I, ch**. Jizya.
49. Ibid.
50. Bukhari, Muslim, Abu Daud. Topic: Khybar.

51. Abu Daud, ch. *Akhdhul Jizya.*
52. Ibid.
53. Al-Quran. 2:256
54. Al-Quran. 2:256
55. Al-Quran. 109:6
56. Mishkat, ch. *As-Sulah.*

Chapter 3(B)

1. Ibn Sa'd, I, P. 315.
2. It lies between Tayef and Nakhla. At this place a great annual fair was held in the sacred month of Dhi Qa'da. It was a great national affair. It lasted for twenty days. It presented a gay scene of pleasure and excitement. What Ukaz said to-day all Arabia would repeat that tomorrow. "The old Arabs made a sort of wine from dates, honey, wheat and barley. To their own native wines the Jews and the Christians added wines made of grapes. These wines they brought to the annual market; and there, in the wine booths, sat the sons of the desert, sipping wines out of cups and glasses, and listening to the merry tunes of the singing girls provided for the enhancement of their joy."

   The Arab Civilization, P. 13. Joseph Hell.
3. Here also a fair was held. It was near Marr uz-Zuhran, not far from Makkah.
4. It was at the foot of Mount Arafat. A fair was held here.
5. Ibn Sa'd, 1, p. 316.
6. Al-Quran. 14:37
7. Its original name was Yathrib. To Banu Najjar, a Medinite tribe, the Holy Prophet was related from his grandfather's mother side. The grave of his father, Abdullah, was in Medina. His mother, Amina, used to visit her husband's grave every year. She died at Abwa, near Medina and was buried there.
8. *Zadul Ma'ad,* II, P. 110.
9. There was a hill named Sal'a in Yathrib. The environs of that city were inhabited by the Amalekites. The Jews had come from Syria. Two brothers of the tribe Azd b. Ghaus Qahatani were the settlers of Yathrib and had come from Yemen. Aus and Khazraj were their descendants. The mother of Abd al-Muttalib (Muhammad's grandfather) hailed from the Khazraj.
10. A place situated between Al-Hara and Mana. Literally it means an elevated hilly passage. In ancient times it was thought that the Satan and evil spirits passed from there.
11. Ibn Khaldun, *History,* I.P. 65.
12. Ibid; Ibn Hisham, I, P. 442.
13. Ibid; Ibid, P. 553.
14. Ibid; Ibid; *Zadul Ma'ad,* II, P. 110; Ibn Sa'ad I, P. 318.
15. Ibid; Ibid, P. 444; Ibn Sa'd, I. 319.
16. With reference to *Asahus Siyar,* P. 103.
17. It is also known as 'Pledge of Women' as no fighting was involved, cf. Al-Quran. 60:12
18. Ibn Hisham, I, P. 444; Ibn Sa'd, I, P. 319; Ibn Khaldun, *History,* I, P. 56;

Zadul Ma'ad, II, P. 111.

19. Ibn Khaldun, *History*, I. PP. 56-57.
20. He remained in Makkah and afterwards migrated to Medina. Therefore he was known as Muhajir-Ansari.
21. This branch was known as Qwaqal because whenever a person took refuge with them, they gave him an arrow and said, "Take this arrow and go where-ever you like in Yathrib."/Qwaqala is also a sort of speed.
See: Ibn Hisham, I, P. 444.
22. Ibn Hisham, I, P. 445; Ibn Sa'd, I, PP. 319-320; Ibn Khaldun, *History*, I, P. 57.
23. Ibid; Ibid, 320.
24. Ibn Sa'd, I. P. 320.
25. Ibn Hisham, I, P. 446.
26. Ibn Sa'd, I, P. 320. But Ibn Hisham, Hafiz Ibn Qayyim and Ibn Khaldun opine that Mus'ab b. Umayr was sent after the First Pledge of Aqba.
See: Ibn Hisham, I, P. 446; *Zadul Ma'ad*, II, P. 112; Ibn Khaldun, *History*, I, P. 57. Hafiz Ibn Qaiyyim and Ibn Khaldun have mentioned another companion of the Holy Prophet named Amr b. Umm-i-Maktum, father of Ibn Maktum and maternal-uncle of Hazrat Khadija, who had accompanied Mus'ab to Yathrib and taught Holy Quran there.
See: *Zadul Ma'ad*, II, P. 112; Ibn Khaldun, I, *History*, P. 57.
27. Mus'ab hailed from an affluent family and was one of those who embraced Islam at the earliest stage. Whenever he rode, several slaves accompanied him. He wore very precious dress but he relinquished all sorts of luxurious life. When he was in Medina his dress was only a small piece of blanket stuck with thorns of acai - a tree. He was the standard bearer in the battle of Badr. He was also known as the Muhajir of Abyssinia.
28. Ibn Hisham, I, P. 446.
29. Sa'd b. Mua'dh and Asad b. Dhurarah were conscious.
30. Ibn Sa'd, I, P. 318; Ibn Khaldun, *History*, I. P. 56.
31. Ibid, P. 320; Ibid, P. 59.
32. Ibn Hisham, I, P. 451; Ibid.
33. Ibn Sa'd, I. P. 320.
34. It is the period of three days which follow immediately the celebration of the rites of pilgrimage, i.e. 11th, 12th and 13th of Zilhajja.
35. Ibn Sa'd, I, P. 321.
36. Ibn Hisham, I, P. 468; *Zadul Ma'ad*, II, P. 113. But Ibn Sa'd writes that their number was seventy. See: Tabqat Ibn Sa'd, I, P. 321.
37. Ibn Hisham, I, PP. 468-475.
38. A prominent leader. He was not present at Badr.
39. He was present at Badr.
40. His name was Malik. He was present at Badr.
41. His name was Hani b. Niyar. He was present at Badr.
42. A prominent leader. He was present at Badr. He was martyred when he was in the company of the Holy Prophet.
43. A prominent leader. He was present at Badr. He was martyred at Uhad.
44. He was present at Badr. Martyred at Uhad. He was commanding the archers

for the apostle.

45. He was present in all the battles fought during the life of the apostle. He was martyred in the battle of Yamama in the reign of the first Caliph.
46. He was also present in all the battles fought during the life of the apostle. He died in the land of Rome while praying in the reign of Muawiyah.
47. He was present in Badr, Uhad, the Trench and all the other battles fought during the life of the Holy Prophet.
48. He was martyred in Badr.
49. He was martyred in Badr. He killed Abu Jahl, Mu'adh, Auf and Maoudh were all three brothers.
50. He took part in all the battles fought during the life of the apostle. He was martyred in the battle of Yamama.
51. A prominent leader. He died before the Badr took place.
52. He was present at Badr.
53. He was present at Badr.
54. His name was Zayd b. Sahl. He was present at Badr.
55. These were called the B. Budayla.
56. He was present at Badr where the apostle put him in command of the rearguard.
57. A prominent leader. He took part in Badr. He was martyred in Uhad.
58. He was present at Badr and was martyred in Uhad.
59. A prominent leader. He was present at Badr, Uhad, the Trench, and the battles fought later on. The apostle appointed him a commander in the battle of Mauta in which he died.
60. He was present at Badr.
61. He was shown how to call to prayer and was ordered by the apostle to perform it.
62. He was present at Badr, Uhad and the Trench He was martyred on the day of Qurayza when a mill stone was thrown on him from one of the forts of the Qurayza which crushed his skull. The apostle said, "He will have the reward of two martyrs."
63. His *Kunya* was Abu Mas'ud. He was the youngest of the persons who took pledge. He was not present at Badr. He died in the reign of Muawiyah.
64. He was present at Badr.
65. He was present at Badr.
66. He was present at Badr.
67. A prominent leader.
68. He is known as Muhajir Ansari. He was present at Badr and was martyred at Uhad.
69. He was present at Badr.
70. He was present at Badr.
71. A prominent leader, First of all he took pledge. He died before the apostle migrated to Yathrib.
72. He was son of Bara. He was present at Badr, Uhad and the Trench. He died in Khyber as he ate the poisonous mutton in a feast.
73. He was present at Badr. He was martyred in the battle of Trench
74. He was present at Badr. He, also, was martyred in the battle of Trench

75. He was present at Badr.
76. He was brother of Ma'qil. He was present at Badr.
77. He was present at Badr.
78. He was present at Badr.
79. He was present at Badr.
80. He was present at Badr.
81. He was present at Badr.
82. He was brother of Qutba. His *Kunya* was Abu Mundhir. He was present at Badr.
83. His name was Ka'b b. Amr and was present at Badr.
84. He was present at Badr and was martyred in the battle of the Trench.
85. He was present at Badr.
86. A prominent leader. He was present at Badr and was martyred at Uhad.
87. He was son of Abdullah b. Amr.
88. He was present at Badr.
89. He was martyred in Tayef.
90. He was present at Badr.
91. He took part in all the battles fought during the life of the Holy Prophet. He died in the reign of the Second Caliph in Amwas.
92. A prominent leader. He took part in all the battles fought in the life of the apostle.
93. He is known as Ansari-Muhajir. He was martyred at Uhad.
94. He was known as Qwaqil.
95. He was present at Badr. His *Kunya* was Abul Walid.
96. He was present at Badr. He was known as Muhajir-Ansari.
97. They were known as Bani al-Hubla. As Saleem or Satan's belly was very large so was known as Al-Hubli.
98. A prominent leader.
99. A prominent leader. Present at Badr. The Holy Prophet appointed him commander in Bir'-Ma'una. He was martyred. It was said of him, 'He hastened to death.
100. Her *Kunya* was Umm 'Amara.
101. The Arabs used the term to cover both Khazraj and Aus.
102. Ibn Hisham, I, P. 454; Ibn Sa'd, I. P. 321.
103. Ibid; Ibid.
104. Ibid, PP. 454-455.
105. Ibid, P. 455.
106. Ibid.
107. Ibid, P. 459; Ibn Ishaque, P. 204. But Allama Shibli Nu'mani writes that his name was Sa'd b. Dhurara. See: *Seerat un Nabi,* I, P. 266.
108. Ibn Hisham, I, P. 459.
109. Ibn Sa'd, I, P. 459.
110. Ibn Hisham, I, P. 475.
111. Ibid, P. 455. But Ibn Khaldun opines that they were selected by the apostle himself. See: Ibn Khaldun, I, P. 60.
112. Some writers are of the view that he was Abu'l Haytham b. al-Tayyiham. See: Ibn Hisham, I, P. 456; *Zadul Ma'ad,* II, P. 113; Ibn Khaldun, I, P. 60.

113. Ibn Hisham, I, P. 461; Ibn Sa'd, I, P. 322.
114. Ibid; Ibid, P. 323.
115. Muir, Sir William. *Life Of Mahomet,* II, P. 228.
116. It was the title of both the Aus and the Khazraj. Originally they were one and the same.
117. Ibn Sa'd, I, P. 287.
118. Hamidullah, Dr. Muhammad, *Rasool-i-Akram Ki Siyasi Zindgi,* P. 106.
119. Ibn Khaldun, I, P. 167.
120. A simple formula determines roughly the correspondence of the Muslim with Christian year. If H is the year of the Hijra and G the Gregorian year, we have:

$$\left(H - \frac{3H}{100}\right) + 622 = G.$$

Source: Muslim Institutions, P. 184.

121. i. Al-Quran. 3:195
ii. Al-Quran. 4:97-98
iii. Al-Quran 4:100
iv. Al-Quran. 8:74
v. Al-Quran 9:20
vi. Al-Quran. 16:41
vii. Al-Quran. 22:58
122. Poole, Stanley Lane-; *Studies In a Mosque,* P. 151.
123. Hell, Joseph; *The Arab Civilization,* P. 23.
124. Ibn Sa'd, I, P. 233.
125. Bukhari, 79:20
126. Hamidullah, Dr. Muhammad; *'Ahd-i-Nabwi Mein Nizam-i-Hukamrani,* P. 82.
127. Ibn Sa'd, I, P. 318; Ibn Khaldun, I, P. 56.
128. Austin, R.W.J; *'The Prophet of Islam',* Article published in: *The Challenge of Islam.* P. 77.
129. Ibn Hisham, I, PP. 517-524; Abu Ubaid, *Amwal,* P. 517; Ibn Kathir, *Bidayah,* III, PP. 224-26.
130. Hamidullah, Dr. Muhammad; *Ahd-i-Nabwi Mein Nizam-i-Hukamrani,* P. 76.
131. Ibid, P. 87.
132. Ibid, P. 98.
133. Ibid, P. 91.
134. Ali, Syed Amir; *Spirit Of Islam,* P. 59.
135. Hell, Joseph; *Arab Civilization,* P. 25.
136. Nicholson, *A Literary History Of The Arabs,* P. 173.
137. Watt, Montgomery; *Muhammad At Medina,* P. I.
138. Hamidullah, Dr. Muhammad; *Ahd-i-Nabwi Mein Nizam-i-Hukamrani,* I, P. 91.
139. Ibid, P. 98.
140. Ibid, PP. 95-96.
141. Ibid, P. 99. Actually balance of power alliances were made by Muhammad (P.B.U.H.).

142. Mansoorpuri, Qazi Muhammad Sulaiman; *Rahmatul-lil-'Alameen,* I, P. 83.

143. Hamidullah, Dr. Muhammad; *Ahad-i-Nabwi Mein Nizam-i-Hukamrani,* I, P. 83.

144. Ali, Syed Amir; *Spirit Of Islam,* P. 58.

145. Ansari, Maulana Hamid; *Islam Ka Nizam-i-Hukumat,* P. 362.

146. Ibn Sa'd, I, P. 344.

147. Aa'is, Rabah and Kharar were situated near the coast in the south-west of Medina. The trade caravans of the Quraish used to go to Syria and Egypt from this route.

148. Ibn Sa'd, I, P. 344.

149. Ibid, II, PP. 49-51.

150. Hamidullah, Dr. Muhammad; *Rasool-i-Akram Ki Siyasi Zindgi,* PP. 364-365.

151. There was certainly a period falling between the first and the second treaty because the state of Medina was not extended far and wide at the time of concluding the first treaty. Therefore question of granting of feoffs does not arise. Certainly it relates to a later stage.

152. The Quraish caravans passed also through this place. This was a difficult hilly passage and a best ambuscade. When Abu Basir could not migrate to Medina due to the Truce of Hudaibiya, he took refuge in this passage and there formed a party. Then the importance of Dhi Al-Merwah emerged.

153. Ibn Sa'd, II, P. 54.

154. Ibid, I, P. 347; Tabari, I, P. 406.

155. Ibn Sa'd, II, P. 53.

156. Ibid, P. 53.

157. Tabari, I, P. 277; Ibn Sa'd, I, P. 406.

158. Tabari, I, P. 284. But Ibn Sa'd adds that he also asked them to disunite the attacking forces. See: Ibn Sa'd, I, P. 417.

159. Tabari, I, P. 285.

160. Ibn Sa'd, I, P. 417.

161. Ibid, II, P. 53.

162. Ibn Hisham, I, P. 580; Ibn Khaldun, I, P. 81. But Tabari is of the view that the change of Qibla took place in the middle of the month of Sha'ban after one year and six months of the *hijrat.* See: Tabari, I, P. 158.

163. Bukhari, *Ch. Muqadam un Nabi & Ashab-i-Medina.*

164. Al-Quran 48:27.

"Truly did God fulfil the vision for His Apostle: ye shall enter the Sacred Mosque, if God wills, with minds secure, heads shaved, hair cut short, and without fear. For He knew what ye knew not, and He granted besides this, a speedy victory."

165. Ibn Hisham, II, P. 353; Tabari, I, P. 325; Ibn Athir, II, P. 152. But Ibn Khaldun mentions that people who accompanied him were between thirteen and fifteen hundred. See: Ibn Khaldun, History, I, P. 134.

166. Ibn Hisham, II, P. 353.

167. Ibid; Tabari, I, P. 325; Ibn Khaldun, I, P. 134.

168. Gibbon, Edward; *The Decline And Fall Of the Roman Empire,* V, P. 263.

169. Ibn Hisham, II, P. 355.

170. He belonged to Tahama and was apostle's confident internally.

See: Tabari, I, P. 355. Ibn Hisham has written with reference to Zuhri that Khuza'ah were his special confidants including Muslims and pagans. They did not hide whatever happened in Makkah.

See: Ibn Hisham, II, P. 357

171. Ibn Hisham, II, P. 356.
172. Ibid, P. 357; Ibn Ishaque, P. 501.
173. On this point Ibn Hisham and Tabari differ. Ibn Hisham is of the view that Urwa b. Mas'ud came after Miqraz and Hulays. But Tabari, first of all mentions Urwa and then Hulays and Miqraz.
174. Ibn Hisham, II, P. 357; Ibn Ishaque, P. 501; Tabari, I, P. 332.
175. There is a mountain near Makkah called Habash or black. The people living there were known as Ahabeesh or Black. Their chief was hulays or Ibn Zamman who was at that time chief of the black troops.
176. Ibn Hisham, II, P. 357; Tabari, I, P331.
177. Ibid, P. 358; Ibid, P. 332.
178. After a few years he embraced Islam and went to his people to preach Islam. While preaching one day, he was mortally wounded by an arrow and immediately succumbed to the injuries.
179. Tabari, I, P. 330; *Zadul Ma'ad,* II, P. 219.
180. Ibn Hisham, II, P. 358; Ibn Ishaque, P. 502.
181. Ibid, P. 359; Ibid, P. 503; Tabari, I. P. 331; Ibn Athir, II, P. 154; Abul Fida, P. 61.
182. Ibid, P. 360; Ibid; Ibid, P. 334.
183. Ibid; Ibn Ishaque, P. 503; Tabari, I, P. 334.
184. Tabari, I, P. 333.
185. Ibid, P. 334; Ibn Hisham, II, P. 360; Ibn Ishaque, P. 503.
186. Ibid; Ibid, P. 361; Ibid.
187. Ibid; Ibid; Ibid.
188. Tabari, P. 335.
189. Ibn Hisham, II, P. 362; Tabari, I, P. 335.
190. Tabari, I, P. 335.
191. Ibid; Ibn Hisham, II, P. 361.
192. Ibn Hisham, II, P. 362.
193. Al-Quran 48:18

"God's Good Pleasure was on the Believers when they swore Fealty to thee under the Tree."

This is called the Pledge of Ridwan (The Agreeable Pledge) and Pledge of the Tree (Bai'at ush-Shajra). It is also called the Pledge of War as the Holy Prophet took undertaking on death. But Nafah told Ibn Umar that he took fealty on patience.

See: *Tajreed ul Bukhari.* Ch. *As-Sulah.*

Jabir b. Abdullah says that they undertook not to escape in any case. See: Ibn Hisham, II, P. 361.

194. He embraced Islam after a few years and became a great preacher of Islam.
195. Ibn Hisham, II, P. 362.
196. Ibid, PP. 362-363.

Ibn Hisham has written with reference to Zuhri that Umar was repentent throughout his life over his utterances made at that moment. He gave alms, kept fasts and freed slaves.

See: Ibn Hisham, II, P. 363.

197. Ibn Hisham, Tabari and Ibn Ishaque are of the view that the treaty was written by Ali.

See: Ibn Hisham, II, P. 373; Tabari, I, P. 336; Ibn Ishaque, P. 504. But Imam Nawavi has written with reference to Qazi Ayaz that some people think that the Holy Prophet wrote this treaty himself. Although he was illiterate yet it was his miracle..

See: *Sharah Muslim,* V, Ch. *Jihad.*

198. Ibn Khaldun, I, P. 135.

199. Ibn Hisham has mentioned the clauses 1,2,6,7, and 8. Fifth clause has been mentioned by Abu Ubaid in his book *Amwal* andBuladhri in *Futuhul Buldan.* Ibn Khaldun has mentioned the second and third clauses with some amendment: "Go back this year after making sacrifices." Dr. Muhammad Hamidullah has elaborated the fourth clause.

200. Narrated by Abu Ubaid Iraq or Syria.

201. There is no mention of the properties of the Muslims in these stipulations which they had left in Makka at the time of the *Hijrat.* The Holy Quran says: "(Some part is due) to the indigent *Muhajirs,* those who were expelled from their houses and their property." 59:8

Dr. Muhammad Hamidullah writes in the same context:

"And tacitly the Muslims accepted the status quo regarding the validity of the enemy occupation." Op. cit; P. 282.

202. Ibn Hisham, II, P. 366; Tabari, I, P. 338; Ibn Athir, II, P. 156; *Mishkat,* Bk. XVII, Ch. 10, Pt. I. Dr. Muhammad Hamidullah adds one witness in the list of the Muslims, i.e. Abu Ubaida b. Jarrah. See: *Rasool-i-Akram Ki Siyasi Zindgi,* P. 128. Similarly the same writer opines that the Apostle and Suhail both sealed the treaty.

203. Hamidullah, Dr. Muhammad; Op. cit; P. 505.

206. Ibid, P. 339; Ibid; Ibn Hisham, II, P. 366; Ibn Khaldun, *History,* I, P. 136.

207. Al-Quran 48:27

"Truly did God fulfill the vision for His Apostle."

208. *Zadul Ma'ad,* II, P. 229.

209. Al-Quran. 48:15

210. Khadduri, Majid; *War And Peace In The Law Of Islam,* P. 294.

211. They were so ignorant that they did not want to hear to the Truth. Allah says about them: "God hath set a seal on their hearts and on their hearing, and on their eyes is a veil." Al-Quran 2:7.

212. Iqbal, Afzal; *Diplomacy In Islam,* P. 41.

213. Sarakhsi, *Mabsut,* X, P. 86; *Sharah as Siyar al-Kabir,* I, P, 201.

214. Hamidullah, Dr. Muhammad; *Rasool-i-Akram Ki Siyasi Zindgi,* PP. 119-120.

215. Sarakhsi, *Mabsut,* X, PP. 91-92; *Sharah as Siyar al-Kabir,* I, P. 69.

216. Ibn Hisham, II, P. 371.

217. Al-Quran 48:I

218. Al-Quran 48:3

219. Watt, Montgomery; ***Muhammad At Medina,*** **P. 49.**
220. Ibn Hisham, II, P. 377.
221. ***Zadul Ma'ad,*** **II, P. 228.**
222. Ibn Hisham, II, P. 372; Tabari, I, P. 340; Ibn Khaldun, ***History, I,*** P. 136.
223. Ibid; Ibn Ishaque, P. 507.
224. Ibid; Ibid, P. 508.
225. Ibid, P. 373; Tabari, I, P. 341.
226. Al-Quran 60:10-11.
227. Ibn Hisham, II, PP. 376-377; Tabari, I, P. 341.
228. Hamidullah, Dr. Muhammad; *'Ahd -i-Nabwi Mein Nizam-i-Hukamrani,* I, PP. 249-250.
229. Al-Quran 59:8
230. Hamidullah, Dr. Muhammad; ***Muslim Conduct Of State,*** **P. 277.**
231. Ibn Hisham, II, P. 364; Ibn Ishaque, P. 504; Tabari, I, P. 337.
232. Hamidullah, Dr. Muhammad; *Rasool-i-Akram Ki Siyasi Zindgi,* P. 373.
233. Ibn Hisham, II, P. 389; Tabari, I, P. 363.
234. Ibid; Ibid.
235. *Futuhul Buldan,* P. 49.
236. Ibn Hisham, II, P. 389.
237. Ibid; *Futuhul Buldan,* P. 48
238. Ibid, P. 390; Ibid.
239. Ali, Syed Amir; Op. cit; P. 93.
240. **Muatta, Ch.** ***Ma Ja'a Fil Masaqat.***
241. ***Futuhul Buldan,*** **P. 50.**
242. Ibid, P. 56. But Ibn Hisham is of the view that the conquest of *Khyber* had created awe in the hearts of the people of Fidak and they themselves had requested for a truce.
    See: Ibn Hisham, II, P. 406.
243. Ibn Khaldun, History, I, P. 151.
244. Ibn Hisham, II, P. 390; *Futuhul Buldan,* P. 56.
245. Ibid.
246. *Futuhul Buldan,* P. 62.
247. Ibid P. 63.
248. Ibid.
249. Ibn Sa'd cited by Dr. Muhammad Hamidullah in *Rasool-i-Akram Ki Siyasi Zindgi,* P. 346.
250. Ibn Hisham, II, PP. 447-448; Ibn Khaldun, *History,* **I, P. 157.**
251. According to Ibn Hisham every person of Banu Bakr was not under his command. See: Ibn Hisham, II, P. 448; Tabari, I, P. 387. But Ibn Khaldun writes that almost seventy per cent of his tribesmen accompanied him in this raid.
    See: Ibn Khaldun, ***History***, I, P. 157.
252. Ibn Hisham, II, P. 448; Tabari, I, P. 387.
253. Tabari, I, P. 387.
254. Ibid; Ibn Hisham, II, P. 448.
255. **For complete poetical statement see: Ibn Hisham, II, P. 453; Tabari, I, P.**
256. Ibn Hisham, II, P. 457; Tabari, I, P. 391.

257. See: For first three stipulations Ibn Hisham, II, P. 468; for the fourth Ibid, P. 474; for the fifth Tabari, I, P. 397.
258. Hamidullah, Dr. Muhammad; *Rasool-i-Akram Ki Siyasi Zindgi,* P. 393.
259. Futuhul *Buldan,* P. 99.
260. Ibn Hisham, II, P, 723; Tabari, I, PP. 466-467.
261. Daibly cited in *Rasool-i-Akram Ki Siyasi Zindgi,* PP. 393-394.
262. *Futuhul Buldan,* P. 99.
263. Cited in *Rasool-i-Akram Ki Siyasi Zindgi,* PP. 374-375.
264. Ibid, P. 375.
265. Ibid.
266. Ibid, P. 376.
267. Ubaid, Abu: *Kitab ul Amwal,* P. 506. Cited in *Rasool-i-Akram Ki Siyasi Zindgi,* PP. 388-391.

    Ibn Hisham and Ibn Ishaque have quoted the writ in these words:

    "In the name of Allah, Most Merciful and Beneficent. From Muhammad, the Apostle of Allah, to the believers. The acacia trees of Wajj and its game are not to be harmed. Anyone found doing this will be scourged and his garments confiscated. If he repeats the offence he will be seized and brought to the Prophet Muhammad. This is the order of the Prophet Muhammad, the Apostle of Allah."

    See: Ibn Hisham, II, P. 653; Ibn Ishaque, P. 617.
268. According to the narration of Ibn Abd'ul Bar and Lissan ul Arab it was written: „Then the principal may be paid and the interest will be charged at the time of Ukāz and not after it."
269. Daumat ul Jandal was a meeting place of trading caravans and had a great politico-economic importance.
270. Ibn Hisham, II, P. 631; Ibn Ishaque, P. 607; Tabari, *History,* I, P. 443; Ibn Khaldun, *History,* I, P. 179.
271. *Futuhul Buldan,* PP. 103-104. Ibn Sa'ad is of the view that the Holy Prophet did not seal it but made a mark with his nails. Ukaider belonged to the Babylonian soil where it was the custom that the treaty maker used to make crescent on the treaty with the nail of his thumb. Probably the Holy Prophet did so to gain his heart and his insistence for it.
272. Ibn Hisham, II, P. 630; Tabari, I, P. 443; *Zadul Ma'ad,* III, P. 43; Ibn Khaldun, I, PP. 178-179.
273. Khadduri, Majid; *War And Peace In The Law Of Islam,* P. 252.
274. Ibid.
275. Ibn Hisham, II, PP. 630-631; *Zadul Ma'ad,* III, P. 43.
276. *Futuhul Buldan,* P. 100.
277. Ibn Sa'd of *Rasool-i-Akram Ki Siyasi Zindgi,* P. 345.
278. Ibn Hisham, II, P. 630; *Futuhul Buldan,* P. 100; Tabari, I, P. 443.
279. *Futuhul Buldan,* P. 100.
280. Ibn Hisham, II, P. 630; *Futuhul Buldan,* P. 100; Tabari, I, P. 443.
281. *Futuhul Buldan,* PP. 101-102.
282. Only Ibn Sa'd and Buladhri have mentioned this treaty while Yaqut, Ibn Kathir and Ibn Qayyim have denied to admit its validity. Credit goes to Ibn Qayyim for refuting this treaty after discussing deliberately its pros and

cons. Buladhri and Ibn Sa'd both were contemporaries. According to Buladhri he was provided a copy of this treaty by a person who had seen it there himself. Buladhri has added many a things in the text of Ibn Sa'd, for example, remission of past murders, the chief of Maqna would be from amongst the people of Maqna or the family of the Holy Prophet, and they would hand over their weapons, slaves, animals and clothes to the Muslims. In the end there is the name of the writer.

The people of Maqna never fought with the Holy Prophet. Ali did not participate in th Ghazwa of Tabuk because he was left behind in Medina. Moreover, Muhammad bin Ahmad bin Asaakar says that the use of the word 'Ali bin Abu Talib' is wrong analytically. Ali was the inventor of the science of analysis so how could he commit such an analytical blunder. The inclusion of the year in the treaty is also contrary to the historical facts. The Hijra calendar was introduced by Umar, the second Caliph, in 16 A.H. and before this the Muslims used to write only month in any document.

Actually this document was prepared by the Jews during the Abbaside reign. The Mu'tazilites declared that the Holy Quran was a creature and Mamun al-Rashid patronized them. He adopted a secular policy during the last four years of his reign but immediately after his death a strong reaction was launched against the Mu'tazilite movement. The Mu'tazilites were severely oppressed by Caliph Al-Mutwakkil (232-247 A.H.) who is known as Nero of the Arabs. The non-Muslims were also the target of this reaction. And they prepared that document in order to save their skin from these violences. This was copied by Buladhri and Ibn Sa'd in their books as an authentic document. They incorporated some hypothetical facilities bestowed upon them by the Holy Prophet.

Besides Buladhari and Ibn Sa'd the Egyptian Jews of the Fatimide period, also, prepared a prolix document. This document is in Hebrew and was obtained from a Jewish ginza of Egypt. The Arabic paragraphs have been written in Hebrew calligraphy. Maqna was, at that time, included in the Fatimide empire. When Al-Hakam Bai-Amarillah(386-411 A.H.) aggravated the Jews then they prepared a document under the caption 'Treaty of Maqna' in which they mentioned the so-called facilities granted to them by the Holy Prophet. Following additions were made in it which were different from those of Ibn Sa'd and Buladhari

This treaty has concern with both the peoples of Maqna and Khyber and their descendants for ever. The reason of giving these facilities to the Jews was the marriage of the Holy Prophet with Safiya who was a Jewess, before embracing Islam, and belonged to Khyber. The Jews were not deprived of their slaves, weapons and property. They were allowed to ride a horse and wear nice clothes. They were exempted from *Russam,* i.e.; official tax. If any Muslim was killed by a Jew, he would be treated as if he had been a Muslim murder. The people of Maqna and Khyber would be preferentially treated than the other Dhimmis. They were allowed to enter the mosques. They could take their funeral processions through the general roads of the city. In case they embrace Islam their status would be those of the members of the Holy Prophet and entitled to get stipend as such.

It is said that Ali was the writer of this treaty. Witnesses included Ammar b. Yasir, , Salman Farsi, and Abu Dharr Ghafari. The treaty was concluded on

3 Ramadan, 5 A.H.

This treaty has been reproduced as an authentic document by three Jewish writers, i.e.; Hershfield in his German book "Jewish Arabia"; Yashnki in his essay published in the British Journal "Jewish Quarterly Review" 1903, PP.173-174; Rashprier in his essay published in the German Journal Ms, Os 1916, PP. 48-51. Thus they have tried to prove this false document to be true but in vain because:

1. This false treaty was prepared by the Jews in order to save themselves from Al-Hakam Bai-Amarillah who made them the object of his oppressions. Thus they tried to claim that they had had been enjoying the rights during the time of the Holy Prophet but now had been deprived of them.
2. 3 Ramadan 5 A.H. has been mentioned in the treaty as the date of writing this treaty. Moreover, it has been mentioned that the treaty was meant both for the peoples of Khyber and Maqna. It is notable that Khyber was conquered in 7 A.H. and Maqna in 9 A.H.
3. The name of the writer has been told Ali b. Abu Talib which is analytically erroneous. Furthermore, it is remarkable that Ali did not participate in the Ghazwa of Tabuk.
4. In the treaty the names of those companions of the Holy Prophet, as witnesses, have been mentioned who are respectable to the Shi'ites. It is just to instigate the Fatimide tendencies.
5. As there had been no fight with the people of Maqna, therefore, the nature of the treaty should have been on the same lines as the treaties concluded with the peoples of Jurba and Uzra.
6. "The treaty" exempts the Jews from Jizya while the Holy Quran ordered the receipt of Jizya from the Dhimmis in 9 A.H. to set aside the same order only for the Jews of Maqna seems curious and how could the Muslims repudiate those orders. Furthermore, it is remarkable that the Jizya was demanded from the people of the conquered lands during the Ghazwa of Tabuk.
7. So far as the permission of riding the horses and wearing nice dress, instead of wearing distinctive dress, e.g; ghiyar, patched yellow sacred thread, tall coloured cap or turban, is concerned there was no such restriction upon them in the time of the Holy Prophet. All such orders were issued by the Abbasides. It will be appropriate to mention the prescribed dress of the Dhimmis of the Second Caliph, Umar's time. This prescribed dress was the dress of the Persians. If there was any declaration for the Dhimmis not to wear such and such dress, it was also mentioned that "We will wear the same dress which we have been wearing till now."
8. The mosques did not exist in their lands at the time of concluding the treaty.
9. The Muslims could have no objection if the Dhimmis carried their funeral processions through the public roads.
10. The exemption of the people of Maqna from the forced labour is not without interest. The curse like the forced labour did not exist during the time of the Holy Prophet. How could the people of Maqna be related with it? This inhuman act existed during the Byzantine period. Islam considers all

the men alike and has prohibited the violation of others' rights.

11. The mentioning of making over the weapons, slaves, cattle and clothes in the texts of Ibn Sa'd and Buladhari does not come true in the case of the people of Maqna, because this condition was imposed upon only those tribes who were subjugated only after war. This condition was imposed upon the Jews of Khyber in 7 A.H.

12. It is ridiculous to consider the people of the Apostle of Allah to be the people of the family of the Apostle of Allàh.

In the last, we refer to the opinion of Dr. Muhammad Hamidullah who writes:

"The condition of making over their (people of Maqna) weapons and clothes was actually imposed upon the Jews of Khyber in 7 A.H. at the time of its conquest and Ali participated in this battle. No wonder that he might have written this treaty. During the time of Umar these Jews, whom the Islamic Government was authorised to banish in accordance with the treaty, were ordered to settle in Syria. We presume on account of this that when these Jews from Khyber reached Syria and Palestine, they took the treaty concluded with them by the Holy Prophet. Thus the local Jews, including the people of Maqna, came to know about this. In the following years in the time of Ibn Sa'd and Buladhari or some time before it, i.e., during the Shi'ite or Abbaside movement, the people of Maqna concocted a new document keeping in view both their original treaty and the treaty of Khyber. They inserted in it the sentences or paragraphs of both the original treaties according to their needs. Similarly some new things were added in it and as a writer of the treaty of Khyber (or keeping in view the timely importance) the name of Ali was added in the last. Later on, when the non-Muslim were made the object of torture severely during the Fatimide regime, particularly in the time of Al-Hakam Bai-Amarilla, then the Egyptian Jews prepared a new document. They omitted, added and changed a lot in it according to the needs of time. The procurement of this document from Egypt, the presence of the Shi'ite element in such an abundance and the relation of Fatimides-all these matters support our doubt." (*Rasool Akràm Ki Siyasi Zindgi,* PP. 277-278).

283. *Futuhul Buldan,* PP. 108-109; *Zadul Ma'ad,* III, PP. 126-127; Abu Yusuf, *Kitab Al-Khiraj,* PP. 72-73.

284. Buladhari's statement goes like this, "Whosoever from amongst you has received interest before this."

Futuhul Buldan, P. 109.

But this statement carries no weight because the preceding statement records that "No one, from amongst you, will be called to account for any crime or murder committed during the days of Ignorance." Hafiz Ibn Qayyim and Yaqubi, etc; have stated the same "afterwards."

See: *Zadul Ma'ad,* III, P. 127; Yaqubi, II, P. 62.

285. Ali, Syed Amir; *Spirit of Islam,* P. 272.

286. *Futuhul Buldan;* P. 99.

287. *Rasool Akram Ki Siyasi Zindgi,* P. 366.

Chapter 4(1)

1. Ibn Hisham, I,P.645; Tabari, I, P. 149, *Zadul Ma'ad,* II, P. 174.
2. Tabari, I, P. 149; *Zadul Ma'ad,* II, P. 174. Ibn Hisham has not mentioned the exact number but is contented to write the number sixty or eighty. Ibn Hisham, I, P. 640.
3. Ibid.
4. Tabari, I, P, 150; *Zadul Ma'ad,* II, P. 174.
5. Ibn Hisham, I, P. 640; Tabari, I, P. 150; *Zadul Ma'ad,* II, P. 174. It is remarkable that Tabari has also quoted Mikraz b. Hafs using an unknown reference.
6. Ibn Hisham opines that their number was eight. Ibn Hisham, I, P. 652. But Tabari differs and writes that Sa'd b. Abi Waqqas himself had gone on this expedition with twenty or twenty one persons on foot. Tabari, I, P. 150.
7. Ibn Hisham, I, P. 650. But according to Tabari and Ibn Khaldun it was Rabiul Thani. Tabari, I, P. 151; *History,* I, Ibn Khaldun, P. 76. At one place Tabari has, also, written Rabiul Awwal. See: P. 153.
8. Ibn Hisham, I, P. 650; Ibn Khaldun, I. P. 76. But according to Tabari Sa'd b. Mu'adh was appointed as deputy. See: Tabari, I, P. 153.
9. Tabari, I, P. 153; Ibn Khaldun, I, P. 76.
10. Ibn Hisham, II, P. 3.
11. Ibid, I, P. 653. Hafiz Ibn Qayyim has stated that they were twelve but has not mentioned their names. See: *Zadul Ma'ad,* II, P. 174. Understandable figure is twelve. See: *Rahmatul-lil-'Alameen,* II, P. 181, Mansurpuri.
12. *Zadul Ma'ad,* II, PP. 174-175.
13. Ibn Hisham, I, P. 653.
14. Ibid, PP. 653-654; *Zadul Ma'ad,* II, P. 176.
15. This was before God had appointed a fifth of the booty for the Holy Prophet. It was the first *Khumus,* first murder and the first prisoner in Islam.
16. Ibn Hisham, I, P. 657.
17. Ali, Syed Amir, *Spirit of Islam,* P. 61.
18. *Zadul Ma'ad,* II, P. 176. Ibn Hisham has cited the number ranging between thirty and forty. See: Ibn Hisham, I, P. 659.
19. Hafiz Ibn Qayyim has mentioned the number as 314 (83 emigrants, 61 Ausites and 170 Khazrajites). According to Ibn Sa'd's reckoning there were 238 of the Ansar and 86 Emigrants. See: Tabari, III, 2; iii.i. But the exact number was 313.
20. Ibn Hisham, I, P. 665.
21. The caravan or the army.
22. Ibn Hisham, I, P. 669.
23. Ibid, P. 672.
24. Ibid.
25. Ibid, P. 675.
26. Ibid, P. 677; *Zadul Ma'ad,* II, P. 180.
27. In Greek it is called Fallens. This drawing up flanks is twisted in accordance with the circumstances making different forms such as triangle, square or circles. The faces of all the soldiers of this triangle, square or circle are towards the enemy while their backs are towards the inner side of this triangle,

square or circle. Consequently, the enemy could not invade upon from the rear as it has to face the combatants from all the sides.

The Holy Prophet adopted these war tactics in the Arabian Peninsula for the first time as the Arabs did not know them.

28. Ibn ul-Athir, II, P. 97.
29. Ibn Ishaque, P. 303.
30. Al-Quran 8:9
31. Al-Quran. 44:10-16
32. Al-Quran. 8:5
33. Al-Quran. 8:7
34. Muir, William; *Life Of Mahomet,* III, P. 122.
35. Al-Quran 21:107
36. Ali, Syed Amir; *Spirit of Islam,* P. 65.
37. Ibn Ishaque, P. 303.
38. Ibn Hisham, I, P. 676.
39. Nicholson, *A Literary History Of The Arabs,* P. 175.
40. Watt, Montgomery; *Muhammad At Medina,* P. 20.
41. Ibn Hisham, II, P. 2.
42. Watt, Montgomery; Op. Cit; P. 20
43. Nicholson, Op. Cit; P. 60.
44. Ibn Hisham, II, P. 27.
45. *Zadul Ma'ad,* II, P. 192
46. Ibn ul-Athir, II, P. 118.
47. Ibn Hisham, II, P. 62.
48. Ibid, PP. 99-103.
49. Some writers think that it was Dhi Qa'da. But Ibn Hisham thinks that it was Sha'ban. See: Ibn Hisham, II, P. 226.
50. Ibid. But according to Hafiz Ibn Qayyim he was Abdullah b. Rawaha. See: *Zadul Ma'ad,* II, P. 204.
51. Ibn Hisham, II, P. 206.
52. Ibid, P. 239; Ibn Sa'd, II, P. 47; *Fath ul Bari,* VII, P. 301.
53. Ibid, P. 234.
54. Ibn Sa'd, II, P. 47.
55. Ibn Hisham, II, P. 243; *Zadul Ma'ad,* II, P. 210.
56. Ibid, P. 234.
57. Ibid, P. 239.
58. Ibid, P. 243.
59. Ibid, P. 249.
60. Al-Quran 44:9

    "O ye who believe! remember the Grace of God, (bestowed) on you, when there came down on you hosts (to overwhelm you): but we sent against them a hurricane and forces that ye saw not: but God sees (clearly) all that ye do."
61. Hell, Prof. Joseph; *The Arab Civilization,* P. 32.
62. Watt, Montgomery; *Muhammad At Medina,* P. 38.
63. Ibid, P. 37.
64. Hell, Prof. Joseph; Op. Cit; P. 32.

65. Ibn Hisham, II, P. 273.
66. Ibid.
67. Ibid, P. 776.
68. Ibid, P. 420.
69. Ibid, P 421.
70. Ibid.
71. Ibid, P. 422.
72. Muir, William; Op. Cit; III, P. 402.
73. **Ali, Syed Amir; *Spirit of Islam,* P. 94.**
74. Ibn Hisham, II, P. 460.
75. Ibid, P. 468; Sarkhasy, *Mabsut, X, P. 39;* Mas'udy, *Tanbih,* P. 267, Abu Yusuf, *Kharaj,* P. 131.
76. This army was called so because its weapons looked greenish-black. Ibn Hisham, II, P. 469.
77. Ibid.
78. Ibid.
79. Ibid, P. 474.
80. *Mishkat, Kitab ul Adab.*
81. Ibn Hisham, II, P. 478.
82. Al-Quran 49:13
83. Al-Quran 12:31; Ibn Hisham, II, P. 478; Tabari, II, P. 134.
84. Distribution of water amongst the pilgrims.
85. Keeper of the keys of the Ka'ba.
86. According to the historians, on the conquest of the town, the Prophet had ordered to wash away frescos; but traces were still visible for more than half a century, until Abdullah b. Zubair demolished the building to reconstruct it.
    See: *Muhammad,* P. 16, Dr. Muhammad Hamidullah.
87. Al-Quran 17:81
88. Al-Quran 7:27 sq.
89. **Ibn Hisham, II, P. 480; *Bukhari, Ch. Conquest Of Mecca, The Prophet At Mecca.***
90. *Futuhul Buldan,* P. 71.
91. Ibn Hisham, II, P. 483
92. Ibid.
93. "O ye who believe! Truly the Pagans are unclean; so let them not, after this year of theirs, approach the Sacred Mosque. And if ye fear poverty, soon will God enrich you, if He wills, out of His bounty." Al-Quran 9:28
94. *Zadu Ma'ad,*. II, PP. 308-309.
95. "The Believers are but a single Brotherhood." Al-Quran 49:10.
96. "O Prophet! When believing women come to thee to take the oath of fealty to thee, that they will not associate in worship any other thing whatever with God, that they will not steal, that they will not commit adultery (or fornication), that they will not kill their children, that they will not utter slander, intentionally forging falsehood, and that they will not disobey thee in any just matter, — then do thou receive their fealty, and pray to God for the forgiveness (of their sins): for God is Oft-Forgiving, Most Merciful. O ye

who believe! turn not (for friendship) to people on whom is the Wrath of God. Of the Here-after they are already in despair, just as the Unbelievers are in despair about those (buried) in graves. Al-Quran 60:12-13.

97. *Bukhari, Ch. Conquest Of Mecca.*
98. Hamidulah, Dr. Muhammad; *Ahd-i-Nabwi Mein Nizam-i-Hukamrani,* P. 264.
99. Gibb, Prof. H.A.R; *Muhammadanism,* P. 29.

Chapter 4(2)

1. Al-Quran. 5:5
2. Poole, Stanley Lane-; *Studies In Mosque,* P. 68.
3. Ali, Syed Amir; *Spirit of Islam,* PP. 59-60.
4. Al-Quran 2:159
5. Ibn Hisham, I, P. 538.
6. Al-Quran. 2:170
7. Al-Quran. 3:183
8. Al-Quran. 4:153
9. Ibn Hisham, I, PP. 606-607.
10. Al-Quran. 3:23-24
11. Al-Quran. 3:66
12. Ibn Hisham, I, P. 598.
13. Ibid, P. 599.
14. Ibid, P. 586.
15. Ibid, P. 587.
16. In this battle Aus and Khazraj fought against one another. Victory went to Khazraj. The chiefs of Aus and Khazraj Abu Usayd b. Hudayr b. Simak al-Ashli and Amr b. Nu'man al-Bayadi were killed.
17. Ibn Hisham, I, P. 590.
18. Ibid, P. 593.
19. Al-Quran. 2:246
20. Al-Quran. 3:181
21. Al-Quran. 5:184
22. Ibn Hisham, I, P. 606.
23. Ibid, P. 611.
24. Dhu'l-Qurnayn in its primitive sense means "the lord of two horns."
25. Ibn Hisham, I, P. 611.
26. Ibid, P. 595.
27. As to the prediction of a prophet like Moses, it is contained in the following terms:
    "I will raise them up a Prophet from among their brethren like unto thee (O Moses), and will put My words in his mouth; and he shall speak unto them all that I shall command him." Deuteronomy 18:18.
28. Deuteronomy 18:15-18
29. Al-Quran. 112-1-4
30. Ibn Hisham, I, P. 612.

31. Al-Quran 39-67
32. Ibn Hisham, I, P. 591.
33. Ibid, P. 605.
34. Al-Quran. 5:49-50
35. Al-Quran. 7:187
36. Ibn Hisham, I, PP. 610-611.
37. Al-Quran. 17:88
38. Ibn Hisham, I, PP. 596-597
39. Ibid, P. 596.
40. Al-Quran 2:94; 62: 6-7
41. Al-Quran 4:42
42. Ibn Hisham, I, PP. 604-605.
43. *Zadul Ma'ad,* II, P. 126.
44. Al-Quran 2:144
45. *Muatta, Bk. Prayer; Zadul Ma'ad,* II, P. 126. But Ibn Hisham is of the view that it was Rajab 2 A.H. Ibn Hisham, I, P. 580.
46. Ibn Hisham, I, P. 581.
47. Al-Quran 2:142-143
48. Al-Quran 3:96-97
49. Ibn Hisham, I, P. 584.
50. Bukhari, 50: 171.
51. Al-Quran of 47:4
52. Ex.21:2; Deutronomy 21:14, 21:i.
53. Al-Quran. 2:101
54. Al-Quran. 2:89
55. Al-Quran 4:140
56. Ali, Syed Amir; *Spirit of Islam,* P. 209.
57. Ibn Hisham, II, P. 779.
58. Ibid, P. 4.
59. Tabari, II, P. 8.
60. His name was Bashir b. Abdul Mundhir. Hafiz Ibn Qayyim has written that his name was Abu Lubaba b. Abdullah. See: *Zadul Ma'ad,* II, P. 155. But the correct name is Abdul Mundhir as written by Ibn Hisham, See: Ibn Hisham, II, P. 5.
61. Ibn Hisham, II, P. 5.
62. Watt, Montgomery; *Muhammad At Medina,* P. 182.
63. Hamidullah, Dr. Muhammad; *Muhammad Rasulullah,* P. 94.
64. Sarakhsy, *Sharah As-Siyar ul-Kabir,* II, P. 180.
65. Ibn Athir, II, P. 53; *Fath ul Bari,* VII, P. 236.
66. Maudoodi, Syed Abu'l Ala'; *Al-Jihad Fil Islam,* P. 258.
67. Al-Quran. 5:11
68. Tabari says it was the month of Safar. Tabari, III, P. 55.
69. *Futuhul Buldan,* P. 41.
70. *Fath ul Bari,* VII, P. 233.
71. Ibn Hisham, II, P. 200.
72. Al-Quran 59:11
73. *Fath ul Bari,* VII, P. 253; *Zadul Ma'ad,* II, P. 156.

74. *Asad ul Ghaba,* III, P. 57
75. Watt, Montgomery; ***Muhammad At Medina,*** **P. 211.**
76. Tabari, III, P. 38; *Fath ul Bari,* VII, P. 233.
77. Maudoodi, Syed Abu'l Ala'; *Al-Jihad Fil Islam,* P. 253.
78. Ibn Hisham, II, P. 199.
79. *Futuhul Buldan,* P. 40. But Tabari says that it lasted for eleven days. Tabari, III, P. 54.
80. Ibn Hisham, II, P. 199.
81. Al-Quran 59:5
82. Ibn Hisham, II, P. 200; *Futuhul Buldan,* PP. 40-41; *Fath ul Bari,* VII, P. 232; Abul Fida, P. 49.
83. Al-Quran 59:5; Ibn Hisham, II, P. 200.
84. Ibn Hisham, II, P. 200.
85. Ibid, P. 201.
86. **Sarakhsy,** ***Sharah As-Siyar ul Kabir,*** **III, P. 180.**
87. Ibn Athir, II, P. 133; Tabari, III, P. 54.
88. Ibn Hisham, II, P. 240; *Zadul Ma'ad,* II, P. 157.
89. Ibid, P. 254.
90. Ibid, P. 255. But Ibn Ishaque says that they replied, 'O Abu'l Qasim! You are not a barbarous person.' P. 461.
91. Ibid.
92. Ibid, P. 256.
93. Ibid. P. 260; Al-Quran 26:33 (Commentary Ibn Kathir).
94. Ibid, P. 261; Ibn Athir, II, P. 141.
95. Ibid; *Zadul Ma'ad,* II, P. 160.
96. *Zadul Ma'ad,* II, P. 166.
97. Ibn Hisham, II, P. 261.
98. Ibid, P. 262.
99. Ibid, P. 263.
100. Ibid, P. 265.
101. Poole, Stanley Lane-; *Studies In Mosque,* P. 70.
102. Arnold's Sermons, 4th Sermon, "*Wars Of The Israelites.* PP. 35-36.
103. Poole, Stanley Lane-; *Studies In Mosque,* P. 70.
104. Cf. *Der Islam,* II, P. 289. Cited in *The Muslim Conduct Of State,* P. 241.
105. *An Observation of Grote, History Of Greece,* VI, P. 499.
106. Deuteronomy 20:10-14
107. Sam 8:2
108. Sam 31:12;
Maitland, *Jewish Literature And Modern Education,* P. 21.
109. Ibn Hisham, II, P. 759. But Hafiz Ibn Qayyim has written that he hit his eye which was wounded. But the eye was saved. *Zadul Ma'ad,* II, P. 255.
110. Ibn Hisham, II, P. 759; *Zadul Ma'ad,* II, P. 255.
111. Al-Quran 48: 27-28
112. Ibn Hisham, II, P. 377. But Hafiz Ibn Qayyim opines that Saba'a b. Urfitah was appointed the chief of Medina. See: *Zadul Ma'ad,* II, P. 230.
113. Ibid, P. 388. He was the uncle of Huyyay b. Akhtab. Hafiz Ibn Qayyim has written that his name was Saeed. See: *Zadul Ma'ad.* II. P. 165. Buladhri

says that he was Sa'ata b. Amr. See: *Futuhul Buldan,* P. 49.

114. Bukhari; Bk. *As-Shroot.*
115. Abu Dawood, Ch. *Ma ja'a Fi Hikam Ard Khyber.*
116. *Futuhul Buldan,* P. 49; *Zadul Ma'ad,* II, P. 166.
117. Abu Dawood, Ch. *Ma Ja'a Fi Hikam Ard Khyber.*
118. Ibn Hisham, II, P. 394.
119. Sarakhsi, I, PP. 185-187.
120. Ibn Hisham, II, P. 381.
121. Ibid, P. 390; Ibn Athir, II, P. 170; Tabari, III, P. 104; *Sunan Darmi,* Ch. *Conquest of Khayber.*
122. Ibid, PP. 394-395.
123. Ibid, P. 407.
124. Because they killed their prophets and blamed Him.
125. Muatta, Ch. *Ma Ja'a Fil Masafat.*
126. *Asad ul Ghaba,* III, P. 179 cited in *Al-Jihad Fil Islam,* P. 262.
127. After the death of the Holy Prophet, Abu Bakr continued the same arrangement until his death. During the early years of his reign Umar, also, practised the same arrangement. But gradually the Jews began to rise against the State and a time came when the property and lives of the Muslims did not remain safe. Once Abdullah b. Umar went to Khyber. In the darkness of night he was attacked as he was asleep on his bed and his arms were dislocated at the elbows. (Ibn Hisham, II, P. 780; *Futuhul Buldan,* P. 31). To check their increasing mischiefs Umar consulted the Companions of the Holy Prophet. Then he himself said, "The Holy Prophet had let them stay on the condition that they worked the land for half the date crop. We will allow you to do so on that condition so long as we wish.' Now Abdullah had gone there but was attacked at night and his arms were dislocated. Now there is no enemy on the spot except them. Therefore in my opinion they should be expelled from Khyber." (Bukhari, Bk. *As-Sharoot. Ch. Iza-Shatarat Fil Mazarah*).

    Umar was told that the Holy Prophet laid down three things in his last indisposition, viz; that the Rahawiyun, Dariyun, Sabai'yun and Ash'ariyun should keep land which produced a hundred loads. Two different religions should not be allowed to remain in the Arabian Peninsula. Umar verified it from different sources and in the last he decided to expel them. He told the Jews, "God has given permission for you to emigrate. If anyone has an agreement with the Apostle let him bring it to me and I will carry it out; he who has no such an agreement let him get ready to emigrate." As the Jews had no agreement with them so expulsion was imposed upon them. He transported them alongwith other undesirable elements from Arabia to Mesopotamia. They were fully compensated whatever they left behind them. They were provided camels for transportation and even ropes to fasten their paraphernalia. (Bukhari, Bk, As-Sharoot).

128. Buladhari is of the view that this Ghazwa was fought in Jamadi'ul Akhar, 7 A.H. *(Futuhul Buldan,* P. 63)
129. *Zadul Ma'ad,* II, P. 250.

130. Ibid.
131. Ibid, P. 251.
132. Ibid, P. 250.
133. *Futuhul Buldan,* P. 63.

Chapter 4(3)

1. Ibn Hisham, II, P. 520.
2. Ibid.
3. Ibid, P. 524; *Zadul Ma'ad,* II, P. 319. Ibn Ishaque and Hafiz Ibn Qayyim have written this name as Ayman b. Umm Ayman. See: Ibn Ishaque, P. 569.
4. He had never uttered such a sentence before this.
5. Ibn Ishaque, P. 303.
6. *Zadul Ma'ad,* II, P. 332.
7. Tabari, History, PP. 1675-79.
8. Ibn Hisham, II, P. 542.
9. It was the only Arabian city which had a wall around it. It was constructed on the orders of an Emperor of Persia in recognition of the services of an inhabitant of Tayef. It was completed under the supervision of a Persian engineer and masons. In ancient times it was known as Wajj.
10. *Zadul Ma'ad,* II, P. 338.
11. Ibn Hisham, II, P. 575.
12. Ibid, P. 581.
13. *Zadul Ma'ad,* II, P. 339.
14. *Futuhul Buldan,* P. 93.
15. Watt, Montgomery; Muhammad At Medina, P. 73.

Chapter 4(4)

1. Ibn Hisham, II, P. 775.
   Compare these injunctions with the commands of the Israelite Prophet; "Thus saith the Lord of Hosts . . .Now go and smite Amalek, and utterly destroy all that they have, and spare them not; but slay both man and woman, infant and suckling, ox and sheep, camel and ass."
   (I. Sam. XV. 3)
   (b) "Slay utterly old and young, both maids, and little children, and women."
   (Ezek, IX. 6)
2. Hell, Prof. Joseph; Op. Cit. P. 33.
3. Watt, Montgomery; Muhammad at Medina, P. 54.
4. Ibn Hisham, II, P. 425.
5. Cited by ibid.
6. Numani, Shibli; *Seerat un Nabi,* I, P. 506.
7. Ibn Hisham, II, P. 428.
8. Ibid, P. 433.
9. Ibid, P. 437.
10. Watt, Montgomery; ***Muhammad At Medina,*** P. 65.
11. Ibn Hisham, II, P. 619. But Hafiz Ibn Qayyim differs from it. He says that

complete secrecy was maintained in this Ghazwa due to the tough conditions and long distance.
See: *Zadul Ma'ad,* III, P. 33.

12. Some people are of the view that these verses were recited at the time of the Hijrat. But it is not sound reasoning because the hills of Wada are situated towards Syria. And no one coming from Mecca to Medina can see them.
13. **Masudi, *Tanbih,* P. 248.**
14. Ibn Hisham, II, PP. 796-797.

Chapter 4(5)

1. Ibn Hisham, II, P. I.
2. With reference to the above.
3. Ibn Ishaque says that it was in Sha'ban 6 A.H. See; Ibn Ishaque, P. 490.
4. *Zadul Ma'ad,* II, P. 205.
5. Ibid. But Ibn Hisham says that Abu Dhar Ghifari took the charge of Medina. See: Ibn Hisham, II, P. 32'. Another narration is that Medina was left in the charge of Numaila b. Abdullah al-Laythi. See: *Zadul Ma'ad,* II, P. 205; Ibn Hisham, II, P. 328.
6. Ibn Hisham, II, P. 329.
7. Ibid, P. 335.
8. Watt, Montgomery; *Muhammad At Medina,* P. 35.
9. Ibn Hisham, II, P. 319.
10. Ibid, P. 321.
11. Ibid.
12. Ibid, P. 764; *Zadul Ma'ad,* II, P. 256.
13. *Zadul Ma'ad,* II, P. 255.
14. According to Ibn Ishaque this Ghazwa was fought after the deportation of Bani Nadir. See: Ibn Ishaque, P. 445.
15. Ibn Hisham, II, P. 219; *Zadul Ma'ad,* II, P. 203.
16. Ibid.
17. Muslim, *Ch. Ghazwa of Dhatu'l-Riqa.*
18. Ibn Hisham, II, P. 768; *Zadul Ma'ad,* II, P. 259.
19. *Zadul Ma'ad,* II, P. 260.
20. Ibid, P. 350.

Chapter 4(6)

1. Ibn Hisham, II, P. 192.
2. Ibid.
3. Ibid, P. 193; *Zadul Ma'ad,* II, P. 201.
4. Ibid.
5. Ibid, P. 194; *Zadul Ma'ad,* II, P. 202.
6. Ibid.
7. Ibn Kathir. He has written this in the commentary of the verses 3:169-175.
8. Ibid, II, P. 751.

9. Watt, Montgomery; *Muhammad At Medina,* P. 52.
10. Ibn Hisham, II, P. 749; *Zadul Ma'ad,* II, P. 257.
11. Ibid, P. 750; Ibid.

Chapter 4(7)

1. *Zadul Ma'ad,* II, P. 213.
2. Ali, Syed Amir; Spirit of Islam, P. 85.
3. *Zadul Ma'ad,* II, P. 214.
4. Hamidullah, Dr. Muhammad; *Muhammad Rasulullah,* P. 71.

Chapter 4(8)

1. Ibn Hisham, II, PP. 172-173. Ibn Ishaque also thinks that they were six in number. See: Ibn Ishaque, P. 426. But Imam Bukhari opines that thei number was ten. See: Bukhari, *Ch. Incident Of The Day Of al-Raji.*
2. Ibn Hisham, II, P. 175.
3. Ibid, P. 176.
4. Ibid, P. 177.

Chapter 4(9)

1. Ibn Hisham, II, P. 752.
2. Ibid, P. 755.

Chapter 4(10)

1. *Zadul Ma'ad,* II, P. 348.
2. Ibid.
3. Ibn Hisham, II, P. 762.

Chapter 4(11)

1. Ibn Hisham, II, P. 760.
2. *Zadul Ma'ad,* II, P. 199.
3. Ibn Hisham, II, P. 316.
4. Tabari, III, P. 72; Ibn Athir, II, P. 143.

Chapter 4(12)

1. Zadul Ma'ad, II, pp. 258-59

Chapter 4(13)

1. Ibn Hisham, II, P. 506.
2. Numani, Shibli; *Seerat un Nabi,* II, P. 22.

Chapter 4(14)

1. *Zadul Ma'ad,* II, P. 199.
2. Ibid, P. 274.
3. Ibn Hisham, II, P. 765; *Zadul Ma'ad,* II, P. 274.

Chapter 4(15)

Zadul Ma'ad, II, P. 258.

Chapter 4(16)

1. Ibn Ishaque, PP. 675-676.
2. Two tribes of Yemeni origin.
3. Ibn Hisham, II, P. 782.

Chapter 5

1. Andre, Servier; *Islam And The Psychology Of The Musulman,* P. 10.
2. Ali, Syed Amir; *The Spirit of Islam,* P. 221.
3. *Bukhari* 3:45:55:10;57:8;98:28.
   Muslim 33:149,151.
   Tirmidhiy 20:16.
   Nasa'y 25:21.
   Ibn Majah 24:13.
4. Khadduri, Majid; *War And Peace in The Law Of Islam,* PP. 55-56.
5. Al-Quran 2:190-194.
6. Ibn Taimiyah, *As-Siyasat ul Shariya,* P. 8; Tabari, *History,* I, P. 1788; Mawardi, *Al-Ahkam us Sultania,* Ch. IV: *"Ba'asata Marghamata Wa Marhamata."*
7. Ibn Taimiyah, Ibid.
8. Sarakhsi; *Al-Muheet,* I, fol. 567 a, b. (MS. Waliuddin, Istanbul, No 1356). Cited In *The Muslim Conduct Of State,* P. 13.
9. Al-Quran 5:32
10. Al-Quran 5:16
11. Al-Quran 5:8
12. Al-Quran 2:256
13. Toynbee, Arnold J; *A Study Of History,* P. 488.
14. Al-Quran 2:179.
15. Poole, Stanley Lane- - -; *Studies In Mosque,* P. 69.
16. Al-Quran 22:40
17. Al-Quran 22:40.
18. Al-Quran 9:73
19. Al-Quran 9:12
20. Al-Quran 9:1
21. Al-Quran 5:64

22. Lichtenstadter; *Islam And The Modern Age,* PP. 94-95.
23. Gulick, Robert; *Muhammad, The Educator,* P. 53.
24. Al-Quran 9:7
25. Al-Quran 8:61
26. Cited in *Al-Jihad Fil Islam,* P. 192.
27. *Muatta,* Bk. Jihad.
28. *Al-Jihad Fil Islam,* PP. 184-185.
29. Ibid, P. 184.
30. I. Sam. XV. 3.
31. Ezek. IX. 6.
32. Al-Quran 2:205
33. *Al-Jihad Fil Islam,* P. 188.
34. Ibid, P. 185.
35. Ibid, P. 186.
36. Buladhari, *Futuhul Buldan,* P. 47.
37. Luke 12:49; Matthew 10:34
38. Wright, Q; *A Study of War,* P. 641 ff.
39. They were all Muslims. 10,000 of them were killed in the Mosque of Umar only.
40. Draper, *History Of The Intellectual Development Of Europe,* II, P. 22.
41. *Encyclopaedia Britannica,* Vol. 23, P. 331.
42. *The Columbia-Viking Desk Encyclopaedia,* P. 1076.
43. *Encyclopaedia Britannica,* Vol. 23, P. 333.
44. Ibid, P. 334.
45. Bukhari, Ch. *Illness Of The Prophet;* Muslim, V. Bk. *Al-Jihad.*
46. The movement of the Holy Prophet is called *'Ghazwa.'*
47. The movement of any Muslim individual or group is called *'Saryya'* (expedition). It was for patrolling purposes on the high ways that connected Makkah and Medina for purely security measures.
48. Mansoorpuri, Qazi Muhammad Sulaiman; *Rahmatul-lil-Alameen,* II, P. 188.
49. Hamidullah, Dr. Muhammad; *Rasool-i-Akram Ki Siyasi Zindgi,* P. 18.
50. Arnold, T.W; *Preaching of Islam,* P. 48.

EXCURSUS[1]

Different Tribes Confronting Medina

(a) Tribes To The West Of Medina And Makkah :

Khuza'ah - - - - - - - - -
Aslam ; Ka'b b. 'Amr; al-Mustaliq
Kinanah - - - - - - - -
Bakr b. 'Abd Manat- -
Damrah (with Ghifar); Layth; ad-Du'il; Mudlij
al-Harith b. 'Abd Manat (part of Ahabish)
Muztainah
Juhaynah
Azd Shanu'ah (with Daus).

(b) Tribes To The East Of Medina And Makkah :

Khuzaymah (b. Mudrikah; Kinanah belonged to Khuzaymah) -
Asad b. Khuzaymah; (Adal, al-Qarah)
Tayyi' (with Nabhan)
Hudhayl (b. Mudrikah) - -
Lihyan
Muharib (b. Khsafah)
Ghatafan- - - -
Ashja' ; Fazarah; Murrah; Tha'labah (with Anmar, 'Uwal)
Sulaym (with Ri'l, Shayban)
Hawazin - - - -
'Amir b. Sa'sa'ah- -
al-Bakka' ; Hilal; Kilab (with al-Qurta, 'Uraynah); Rabi'ah
Jusham; Nasr; Sa'd b. Bakr; Thumalah
Thaqif (B. Malik, Ahlaf)
(Bahilah).

(c) Tribes To The North:

Sa'd Hudhaym; 'Udhrah

Judham
Quda'ah (with Jarm, al-Qayn, Salaman)
Bali
Bahra
Lakhm with (Dar)
Ghassan

(d) Tribes South Of Makka:

Khath'am (and near it Azd Shanu'ah)
Madh'hij- - - -
'Aus; Ju'fi; Khawlan; an-Nakha'; Ruha'; Sa'd al-Ashirah (with Zubayd); Suda'
Bajilan
Hamdan
al-Harith b. Ka'b (with Nahd)
Murad
Kindah (with Tujib)
Himyar (and the Yemen)] perhaps not strictly tribal names
Hadramawt
'Akk and Ash'ar.

(e) Tribes In The Rest Of Arabia:

Mahrah
Azd 'Uman; 'Abd al-Qays (in al-Bahrayn)
Hanifah
Tamim
Wa'il- -
Bakr (with Shayban); Taghlib.

BIBILOGRAPHY

(a) Translations Or Works in Urdu :

1. Ansari, Maulana Hamid al-; *Islam Ka Nizam-i-Hukumat,* Delhi, 1956.
2. Azad, Maulana Abul Kalam; *Rasool-i-Rehmat,* Lahore, 1970.
3. Bukhari, Abu Abdullah Imam; *Bukhari,* I, II, III; Karachi, 1952.
4. Baladhri, Ahmad b. Yahya b. Jabir Al-Shaeer; *Futuhul Buldan.* Tr. Abul Khair Maudoodi; Karachi, 1962.
5. Darmi, Abu Huhammad Ubaidullah; *Sunan Darmi,* Lahore
6. Din, Dr. Atta Mohyud; *Arabi Paighmbar – Un Kai Paighamat Aur usool,* Lahore, 1955.
7. Hamidullah, Dr. Muhammad; *Rasool-i-Akram Ki Siyasi Zindagi:* Lahore.
8. Hamidullah, Dr. Muhammad; *'Ahd-i-Nabwi Mein Nizam-i-Hukamrani,* Hyderabad.
9. Haykal, Dr. Muhammad Hussain; *Hayat-i-Muhammad,* Lahore, 1955.
10. Ibn Hisham, *Seerat un Nabi,* I, II.
    Tr. Maulana Abdul Jalil & Maulana Ghulam Rasool Mahar, Lahore, 1962.
11. Ibn Kathir, Imaduddin Ismail; *Tafsir Ibn Kathir,* Lahore.
12. Ibn Khaldun, *Tarikh,*
    Tr. Hakim Muhammad Hussain Usmani, Karachi, 1966.
13. Ibn Qayyim, Allama Hafiz; *Zadul Ma'ad,* I, II.
    Tr. Raees Ahmad Jafari, Karachi, 1962.
14. Jurejo, Constaine Weirzail; *Muhammad – Paighambar-i-Islam,*
    Tr. Mushtaq Hussain Mir, Gujrat.
15. Khan, General Muhammad Akbar, *Hadith-i-Difa'* Lahore, 1958.
16. Khan, General Muhammad Akbar; *Islami Tareeq-i-Jang;* Lahore, 1959.
17. Malik, Imam; Mutta, Karachi, 1954.
18. Maudoodi, Syed Abul Ala'; *Al-Jihad Fil Islam,* Lahore, 1948.
19. Maudoodi, Syed Abul Ala'; *Tafhimul Quran,* Lahore.
20. Muhammad, Imam Abu Isa; *Tirmidhi,* I, Karachi.
21. Muslim, Abul Hussain; *Muslim,* I, II, III, IV, V, VI, Karachi.
22. Nasar, Umar Abun; *Nabi-i-Ummi,* Lahore, 1957.
23. Numani, Maulana Shibi & Maulana Syed Sulaiman Nadvi *Seerat un Nabi,* I, II, III, IV, V, VI, Azam Garh, 1951.
24. Rauf, Maulana Abdul; *Asahus Siyar,* Karachi, 1957.
25. Rizwi, Syed Wajid; *Rasool ullah Maidan Jang Mein,* Lahore, 1958.
26. Sa'd, Muhammad b; *Tabqat,* I, II,
    Tr. Allama Abdullah Al-'Imadi, Karachi.

27. Shait, Mahmood Khattab; *Aan Hazrat Bahaseeyat Sipah Salar,* Lahore.
28. Tabari, Abi Jafar Muhammad b. Jurair; *Tarikh,* Tr. Syed Muhammad Ibrahim, Karachi.
29. Taimiya, Imam Ibn; *Siyasat-i-Ilahiya,* Lahore.
30. Taqi, Maulana Muhammad; *Islam Ka Zara'i Nizam,* Azam Garh.
31. Zubairi, Allama Hussain b. Mubarik; *Tajreed ul Bukhari,* Lahore.

(b) Works in English:

32. Ali, Abdullah Yousaf; *Commentary On The Quran,* Lahore.
33. Ali, Syed Amir; *A History of Saracens,* New York, 1955.
34. Ali, Syed Amir; *Spirit of Islam,* London, 1922.
35. Andre, Servier; *Islam And The Psychology of The Musulman,* 1924.
36. Andre, T; *Muhammad, The Man And His Faith,* London, 1936.
37. Arnold, T.W: *The Preaching of Islam,* London, 1961.
38. Bakhsh, Khuda; *Politics In Islam,* Lahore, 1954.
39. Besant, Annie; *The Life And Teachings Of Muhammad,* Madras, 1932.
40. Carrie, Rene Albrecht; *A Diplomatic History Of Europe Since The Congress Of Vienna,* London, 1961.
41. Demombynes, Maurice Gaudefroy –; *Muslim Institutions,* London, 1961.
42. Dozy, Prof; *Spanish Islam,* London.
43. *Encyclopaedia Britannica,* Vol. 23, London.
44. Foakes, F.J; *Biblical History Of The Hebrews,* Cambridge, 1921.
45. Frankel, Joseph; *International Politics Conflict And Harmony,* England, 1973.
46. Galwash, Ahmad A; *The Religion Of Islam,* London, 1961.
47. Gauba, K.L; *The Prophet Of The Desert,* Lahore, 1962.
48. Gibb, H.A.R; *Muhammadanism,* New York, 1955.
49. Gibbon, Edward; *The Decline And Fall Of The Roman Empire,* III, IV, V, London, 1966.
50. Guillaume, A; *The Life Of Muhammad* (A translation of Ibn Ishaque's Seerat Rasool Allah), London, 1955.
51. Gulick, Robert L; *Muhammad, The Educator,* Lahore, 1953.
52. Hamidullah, Dr. Muhammad; *The Muslim Conduct Of State,* Lahore, 1961.
53. Hamidullah, Dr. Muhammad; *Muhammad Rasulullah,* Karachi, 1979.
54. Hell, Joseph; *The Arab Civilization,* Lahore, 1943
55. Hitti, Philip K; *History Of The Arabs,* London.
56. Holland, Edith; *The Story Of Muhammad,* London.
57. Iqbal, Afzal; *Diplomacy In Islam,* Lahore, 1962.
58. Irving, Washington; *Life Of Mahomet,* London.
59. Khadduri, Majid; *War And Peace In The Law Of Islam,* Baltimore, 1955.
60. Levy, Reuben; *The Social Structure Of Islam,* Cambridge, 1957.
61. Lichtenstadier, Isle; *Islam And The Modern Age,* London.
62. Macdonald, D.G; *The Religious Attitude And Life In Islam,* Chicago.
63. Mansurpuri, Qazi Muhammad Sulaiman; *Rahmatul-lil-' Alameen,* I, I, III, Lahore.
64. Margoliouth, D.S; *Muhammad And The Rise Of Islam,* London, 1905.
65. Muir, Sir William; *Life Of Mahomet,* Edinburg.

66. Nicholson, Reynold A; *A Literary History Of The Arabs,* Cambridge, 1956.
67. Pickthall, Muhammad Marmaduke; *Islamic Culture,* Lahore.
68. Poole, Stanley Lane —; *Studies In Mosque,* Lahore.
69. Sprenger, *Life Of Muhammad,* Allahabad, 1851.
70. Smith, R. Bosworth; *Muhammad And Muhammadanism,* Lahore.
71. *The Columbia-Viking Desk Encyclopaedia,* New York, 1953.
72. Toynbee, Arnold J; *A Study Of History,* London, 1956.
73. Watt, W. Montgomery; *Muhammad At Medina,* Oxford, 1956.
74. Wellhausen, J; *Muhammad In Medina* (An abridged translation of Waqdi's work of Muhammad's Campaigns), Berlin, 1882.
75. Wright, A; *A Study Of War,* London, 1942.